Applied Ethics and Ethical Theory

ETHICS IN A CHANGING WORLD
is a series that responds to issues
dealing with the ethical implications
of developments in science and technology.
Publications in this series present technically reliable accounts
of such developments and an extended examination
of the ethical issues they raise.

ᵣ 38528

VOLUME 1 • ETHICS IN A CHANGING WORLD

BJ
1012
A 66
1988

Applied Ethics and Ethical Theory

edited by

David M. Rosenthal

and

Fadlou Shehadi

Foreword by
Margaret P. Battin and Leslie P. Francis

University of Utah Press
Salt Lake City
1988

Copyright © 1988 by the University of Utah Press
"Ethical Experts in a Democracy,"
Copyright © 1988 by Peter Singer
Printed in the United States of America
All rights reserved.

VOLUME 1

ETHICS IN A CHANGING WORLD

Margaret P. Battin and Leslie P. Francis, Editors

Permission to include the following essays in this volume is duly acknowledged:

"Can Ethics Provide Answers?" by James Rachels originally appeared in
the *Hastings Center Report*, X (June 1980): 32–40; reprinted in *Ethics and
Hard Times*, ed. Arthur L. Caplan and Daniel Callahan (New York:
Plenum Publishing Corp., 1981); permission granted by editors and publisher. "Theory and Reflective Practices," by Annette Baier reprinted with
permission of the University of Minnesota Press, Minneapolis, from *Postures of the Mind: Essays on Mind and Morals*, by Annette Baier. Copyright
1985 by the University of Minnesota. "Theoretical and Applied Ethics: A
Reply to the Skeptics," by Ruth Macklin was originally published in *The
Nature of Clinical Ethics*, Barry Hoffmaster, Benjamin Friedman, and Gwen
Fraser, eds. (Clifton, N.J.: The Humana Press, 1988). Reprinted by per-
mission of the publisher. "Why Do Applied Ethics?" by R. M. Hare origi-
nally appeared in *New Directions in Ethics*, J. de Marco and R. Fox, eds.
(London: Routledge & Kegan Paul, 1986, pp. 225–37); reprinted by per-
mission of the author. "How Can We Individuate Moral Problems?" by
Onora O'Neill appeared in *Social Policy and Conflict Resolution: Bowling Green
Studies in Applied Philosophy*, vol. VI (1984), pp. 104–19, Thomas Attig,
Donald Callen, and R. G. Frey, eds.; reprinted by permission of the au-
thor and editors. "Kant's Arguments in Support of the Maxim 'Do What
Is Right Though the World Should Perish' " by Sissela Bok also published
in *Argumentation*, Vol. II, no. 1 (February 1988). Copyright 1988 Sissela
Bok. Reprinted by permission of the author.

Library of Congress Cataloging-in-Publication Data

Applied ethics and ethical theory.

    (Ethics in a changing world ; v. 1)
    1. Ethics. 2. Social ethics. I. Rosenthal,
David M. II. Shehadi, Fadlou. III. Series.
BJ1012.A66 1988   170   88–14304
ISBN 0-87480-289-X

CONTENTS

Foreword

With this volume, we are pleased to introduce a new book series addressed to ethical issues posed by new developments in science and technology. This series is distinctive in bringing together significant scientific or technological research and philosophical reflection: each volume will present both a sustained, technically reliable account of the specific development in question and extended examination of the ethical issues raised by that development. Ethical problems are often empirically complex, and much of the applied-ethics discussion of specific developments in science and technology suffers from the fact that partisans in these discussions are often not very well informed. This series aims to alleviate this deficiency by bringing together, in single volumes, significant scientific research and probing philosophical reflection, that is, by presenting *both* the science and the philosophic discussion which sophisticated inquiry requires.

Each of the subsequent volumes in the series will treat a specific area of scientific or technological research. Each will include detailed, reliable accounts of the relevant scientific or technological background, with particular attention to those empirical facts or claims which are relevant to the ethical issues raised. Thus the scientific material will provide the focus for extended ethical analysis, but it will also provide that background which first makes responsible ethical analysis possible.

This introductory volume is presented as a prelude to the series, rather than as an item in it, for it focuses on background philosophical issues on which the enterprise of applied ethics rests. Applied ethics, of the sort which will be at work in the series volumes to come, rests of course on empirical issues, but it also rests on backgrounds in ethical theory. This introductory volume explores issues of the relationship between ethical theory and ethical judgment—that is, it explores how applied ethics is "applied" in specific, concrete cases. As the series explores applied-ethics issues concerning new developments in science and technology, these background issues will remain of continuing relevance. The next volumes to appear in the series will discuss, respectively, new reproductive technologies, testing in the AIDS epidemic, and the use of animal models in diabetes research; another twenty volumes are anticipated over the next several years. The intention of this series is to promote informed, responsible discussion of ethical issues raised by new developments in science and technology.

Margaret P. Battin and Leslie P. Francis

Introduction

This volume is about the relation of applied ethics to ethical theory. Most of the essays were written specially for this volume and appear here for the first time.

The last fifteen years have seen a dramatic rise of interest among philosophers in ethical questions about pressing everyday matters calling for decisions that often have far-reaching consequences. This focus on such practical moral questions has come to be known as *applied ethics*.

Traditional ethical theorists, in pursuing their primary goal of establishing general moral theories and principles, also dealt with specific moral questions. But these questions were addressed as examples or test cases for the theories under consideration. Because of this indirect interest in specific practical issues, the issues addressed by traditional ethical theories have a relatively abstract character, seemingly removed from the immediacy of everyday life. Examples are abstruse questions, such as whether to honor a promise one later learns would cause damage to an innocent third party, and uncontroversial claims about the wrongness of dishonesty, theft, and murder.

By contrast, work in applied ethics concentrates on many of the pressing issues of the day, and these often seem not to be resolvable in a clear-cut or an uncontroversial way. Examples are the problems of euthanasia, abortion, genetic research, nuclear armament, and nuclear war; whether and to what extent business corporations can be said to be morally responsible; how and how far morality should influence political activity; what ethical standards there are for professional conduct; how we should allocate scarce resources, especially in new areas made possible by technological developments; what our duties are toward animals, the environment, and future generations; racism, sexism, and reverse discrimination.

Moreover, unlike traditional ethical questions, which focused mainly on problems facing the individual, issues in applied ethics, as is evident from the examples given, often stem from a concern to bring morality to bear on social policy.

As interest in practical issues has grown, the gulf between that work and ethical theory, traditionally conceived, has widened. During the first half of the century, philosophical work in ethics focused on the methodology of ethical theory, and especially on the nature of ethical knowledge and the language of moral discourse. These discussions seldom said much about substantive ethical issues. Increasing interest in applied ethics has been felt to be a salutary corrective to this earlier concern with abstract theory. Since one set of interests was seen as displacing the other in general philosophical discussion, little attention has been directed to the connections between theory and application.

Traditional normative discussions have not helped much in bridging this gap. Traditional normative discussions focus on issues that bear most directly on the adequacy of ethical theory. On the other side, those who work in applied ethics are primarily interested in practical issues of vital importance. For these writers, the development of satisfactory philosophical theories has taken second place to resolving substantive moral questions. So it has remained unclear whether, and to what extent, ethical theory can help solve issues at the practical level, and whether those with philosophical training are, among all those concerned, in any way specially qualified to deal with these questions. Do philosophers, by virtue of their distinctive training, have anything special to contribute here, given that public policy analysts, members of the clergy, theologians, social scientists, and practitioners of the various professions themselves have long been addressing these issues?

These questions in their general form are the focus of the essays in Part One of this collection. In Part Two, each essay takes one particular moral problem as its point of departure and shows how the crucial features of that problem relate to ethical theory and, in most cases, to one or more of the known theories. These theories, or some of their assumptions, are then approached for criticism or for showing their irrelevance to some crucial feature of the problem at hand or for showing which specific form their application favors.

It is the nature of a volume such as this to arrive at few conclusions. But it is our hope that a collection devoted to the bearing ethical theory has on practical ethics and public decision will help bridge the gap that has come to separate the two kinds of ethical thinking, and thus enhance both discussions.

II

The possibility of theoretical normative ethics, as the systematic exposition and rational justification of the principles of morality, was called into question earlier in this century by positivist philosophers as well as by some social scientists. What James Rachels calls "the case against ethics" would score not only against theoretical ethics, but against applied ethics as well. It is the wider challenge to the place of rationality at any level of thinking about ethics.

Opening Part One of the present collection, Rachels discusses this case against ethics. To the sociologist and cultural anthropologist who point to the variety of standards among different societies, Rachels replies that diversity of belief on ethical matters does not as such show that there is no truth about these matters. To the psychologist who explains the individual's values as a function of the different and changing psychological conditions that caused them, his answer is that one must distinguish the question of what causes one to believe something from the question of whether that belief is true.

The positivists explained ethical utterances as just the expression of pro or con attitudes toward various things. A common criticism of this move is that it excludes the role of reason and thus reduces disputes in morals to attempts to change the attitudes of others when those attitudes differ from our own.

This view, according to Rachels, takes to be morally relevant any fact that can cause a change in the other's attitude. But it fails to account for the place of rationality in ethics; for arguments in support of moral judgments can be shown to be adequate or inadequate on any of a number of grounds—relative, for example, to how they represent the facts, their relevance, their consistency. In Rachels's view, one may determine the right course of action by formulating and assessing the arguments that can be given for or against it. "In any particular case, the right course of action is that which is backed by the best reasons." Rachels then proceeds to illustrate this by a brief discussion of such issues as euthanasia, abortion, and equality. He concludes with a thoughtful acknowledgment that there is a limit to what rational methods can achieve.

Annette Baier leads off the second section of Part One by challenging the assumption that there is such a thing as one true moral theory which can then be applied. The variety of existing theories and codes rooted in different intuitions look like arbitrary constructions. The multiplicity of theories added to the variety of traditional codes produce skepticism and fail to guide us in real life.

According to Baier, there is a mistaken assumption which is made by a number of ethical theorists who model morality on the legal system: the assumption that, to be useful, every moral precept must be able to be codified and made part of a hierarchical structure that has universal application. She believes that the norms we follow from our moral traditions can function effectively, often without codification and without the hierarchical structure of the legal model. This is especially true of the effectiveness of virtues as norms. Baier then develops a view of morality as the control of our natural responses. Reflectiveness guides and corrects our natural responses to situations which contain the promise of good and the risk of evil.

The business of applied ethics can no longer be the application of ethical theory. It becomes the attempt to analyze and understand several aspects of an actual situation, such as the roles of the relevant agents, how those roles have changed, what grievances are felt by whom, and the rights, powers, and responsibilities attached to those roles. Beyond this, one can show the place for the virtues such as honesty, integrity, humanity, and mercy.

Ruth Macklin is aware that there is no universally agreed-upon moral theory, but proceeds to argue that the usefulness of theory does not depend on there being one theory accepted as correct, to the exclusion of others. Referring to the regulations of the Department of Health and Human Services, she points out that there is a blend of utilitarianism (risk-benefit analysis, protection from undue harm) and Kantianism (the rights of the human subject in research). Both high-level theories, such as utilitarianism and Kantianism, and "small-scale" theories, for example, of paternalism or of privacy, can yield directives for resolving moral problems. The directives can then be supported by the best reasons one can give. A stronger concept of resolving is unrealistic, and a weaker concept is too modest. Those who attack the usefulness of ethical theory are seen by Macklin as attacking the usefulness of any rational approach to ethics, and they should have to show how we would be better off without theory.

The question of the special advantage that the philosopher has as an applied ethicist, to be discussed more fully in the second section of Part One, is taken up by Macklin. According to her, this advantage derives not so much from the philosopher's knowledge of ethical theory as from the philosopher's more general training as a philosopher. An ethical theory is more than just its normative content. There is also the "epistemological underpinnings," and theories are more likely to differ on these than on normative content. In the philosophical discussion of ethics there are few "purely" moral problems, "so philosophical analysis of a more general sort is what is usually called for in applied contexts," and the philosopher has the advantage here.

On the broader issue of whether ethical theory can be useful in resolving practical problems, R. M. Hare would share Macklin's conviction and contest Baier's skepticism. For Hare the task of applying ethical theory is enhanced by the possibility of reconciling the two major ethical theories; he refers to himself as a "Kantian utilitarian." Baier's skepticism can be at least partly avoided, and Macklin would not have to settle for some unresolved loyalty to two different theories if this reconciliation could be effected.

For Baier, the various ethical theories are nothing more than the articulation of systems of moral laws rooted in widely diverse intuitions. Hare is fully aware of the inadequacy of supporting theory by appeal to intuitions, be they diverse or not; so he takes theory through a different route. According to him, ethical theory starts with an account of the logic of moral concepts. This should yield rules of moral reasoning, which can yield answers when applied to practical moral problems. We would appeal to people's moral convictions not in order to test substantial moral truth, but rather to test a metaethical hypothesis about what moral terms mean and what rules of moral argument they generate. One can then see whether people's actual conclusions, when their reasoning is free from ignorance, muddle, and prejudice, "tally with what sound argument, in accordance with those rules, would justify."

Theory, according to Hare, can guide practice, but practice can also help theory. Practice can help one gain confidence in certain parts of the theory one has, and show the need for improvement in others.

Onora O'Neill takes the question of the usefulness of theory in a different direction from that of the "solution" of practical issues. She uses the term 'theory' in a sense broad enough to include low-level codes such as: personal devotion and serving one's country are good. This is assumed in Jean-Paul Sartre's supposedly theory-stumping example of the man torn between joining the Free French and staying home with his aging mother. Macklin also counts as theoretical what she calls "small-scale" theories on privacy, paternalism, autonomy.

Two uses of theory are proposed by O'Neill; in one, theory is indispensable, in the other, desirable. In reaction against the Wittgensteinian tradition of approaching morality by taking particular examples rather than theory, O'Neill argues that it would not even be possible to recognize a problem as being a moral problem at all without moral theory (at some level). Whenever we select some particular example, we assume some moral principle requisite for identifying as a moral problem the difficulty in the example. Moreover, one desirable use for moral theory is to help one locate moral problems that may lie outside any current repertoire and to help counter the tyranny of fashion about what will or will not be discussed in applied ethics.

III

In the third section of Part One the discussion continues about the usefulness of ethical theory. The emphasis here is on (1) whether the philosopher, as a philosopher, should be involved in doing applied ethics, and (2) whether in such involvement the philosopher qualifies as a moral expert. The four authors in this section all give affirmative answers to these two questions.

Jan Narveson and Dale Jamieson survey various kinds of criticisms that have been advanced, some that cut at once against theoretical and applied ethics, some directed at applied ethics alone. Both come to the defense of applied ethics. Jamieson, however, concedes to some of the critics that work in applied ethics to date has often paid insufficient attention to methodological concerns and to the social context in which moral problems arise. To that extent, Jamieson gives a qualified defense of work actually done thus far in applied ethics, holding that the jury is still out on its ultimate value.

There is a commonly used model for work in applied ethics, that in which the philosopher simply deduces the prescriptive implications for particular cases from general ethical principles. Narveson calls this *the deductive model*. Macklin and James W. Nickel refer to it as *strong applied ethics*. Others, like Frances Myrna Kamm, think of it as the method involving a mechanical application of theory. Narveson maintains that we may at some point end up with the deductive model, but we seldom start with it, since it is often far from clear which high-level premises to use, and it is not always easy to apply these premises to concrete situations. Jamieson is also wary of the simple view of "applying" theory, since the familiar examples of ethical theory are really a family of theories and are as complicated as the practical issues to which they are "applied."

Jamieson, Nickel, and Peter Singer take up the question of the special competence of the philosopher as an applied ethicist, resuming the discussion started earlier in this volume by Macklin and touched on more briefly by Narveson. Like Macklin, they hold that the philosopher has knowledge of ethical theories and general training in logic and critical conceptual analysis, and that these serve as unique qualifications for resolving issues in applied ethics. Jamieson adds the fact that the philosopher, unlike most others, has the actual time to devote to the task and, being relatively impartial, would follow the thinking wherever it leads. Not only does all this uniquely qualify the philosopher as a moral expert; for Jamieson, it also results in a duty for the philosopher to bring a special expertise to bear on the problems of real life. That expertise in itself becomes a reason why the philosopher should do applied ethics.

Nickel separates more explicitly the general skills in conceptual analysis which are part of the philosopher's qualifications from his knowledge of moral concepts and moral theories. Of course, this knowledge is characteristically shaped by the skills that are now directed at positive ethical construction. The philosopher has the ability to test "general moral claims or principles for inconsistencies, posing hard cases, or suggesting analogies from less problematic areas." Besides skills, this requires moral sensitivity and understanding. Moreover, the philosopher is in a special position to develop a critically examined moral perspective: "beliefs about values and moral norms that have been critically examined, tested for inconsistency, and systematized to some degree." Finally, the philosopher has the "ability to give persuasive formulations of widely held moral principles and to argue cogently from these to interesting results about policy." So the philosopher has a special place in the discussion of moral problems, although not an authoritative monopoly, in virtue of possessing both special skills and special knowledge. Moreover, distinguishing general philosophical skills from knowledge about moral theorizing allows Nickel to locate the philosopher's particular expertise with the knowledge, and not with the skills as such.

Whether the philosopher can now confidently offer prescriptive directives on moral problems (strong applied ethics) or merely "illuminate" those problems (weak applied ethics) depends, according to Nickel, on whether one assumes that there is some one true or well-founded ethical theory from which one can derive prescriptions for settling policy issues (Nickel places Hare in this camp) or, instead, one has less confidence about whether ethical theories are true, but is content to offer clarifications of issues and suggestions in the light of one or more theories. A position is represented midway between these two as possible, however, and it is represented in this volume by Rachels and Macklin. According to them, one can go beyond illumination to support of directives for action by the best reasons possible.

Peter Singer discusses the further question of whether the idea of a moral expert is elitist and inconsistent with the principles of democracy and the pluralist ideal. No inconsistency is found, since the philosopher as moral expert would advise, and not issue binding pronouncements. Moreover, pluralism is desirable, within limits. And more important than pluralism, as the ritualistic representation of different segments of the population—say, on an ethics commission—is the belief "that there are ways of reasoning about complex ethical issues, that this is an area in which clear thinking, dispassionate reflection, and careful argument can get us somewhere." This is where the philosopher as a moral expert has a special place.

In a general discussion of the goals, methods, and problems of applied ethics, which serves in this volume to close out Part One, Frances Kamm begins with the statement of a model of how applied ethics is usually practiced. According to this, the philosopher thinks about the moral aspect in the world and then solves the practical problems by applying general ethics and general philosophical concepts. The methods of application vary, depending on what is applied (a theory, a principle, a core concept) and on the mode of application: either applying a theory in almost mechanical fashion or first reaching a decision on a case and then making explicit the general principles, factors, concepts, or theories that lie behind the decision.

This model is subjected to analysis and criticism. Kamm insists that the scope of the philosopher's work here, as philosopher, should not be too narrow. "[W]e should have a broad view of what an ethical issue is, what ethical factors bear on action, and of the significance of discussion not related to action," for example, the character and motive of the agent.

More basic objections to the model are then critically evaluated, criticisms that challenge the usefulness and relevance of theory, but more specifically doubts about putting into practice what one has determined as ethically correct solutions.

Her final considerations concern the actual work, the application of applied ethics. Here, Kamm believes, there is need for perceptiveness in spotting relevant factors and investigating the ability to carry out what is thought to be correct, given certain resources and laws, and co-workers with a certain ability (or inability) to grasp crucial distinctions. Finally Kamm raises the problem of the ethically right way of telling others what to do without humiliating or castigating: the ethics of applying applied ethics.

IV

In a discussion of the relation between theoretical and applied ethics one can move from theory to practice. That is the direction of the questions in Part One. But one can also move from practice to theory. That is the approach of the selections in Part Two. One might start with specific applications and move to theoretical considerations because there are different questions to ask when moving in that direction. Or it may be that one has a view of the concrete issues as having a certain status or weight of their own, demanding to have a wider impact on theory than the role of waiting to appear as examples for some existing theory, or to submit to its application.

Nuclear Annihilation; Intimacy

Starting with the concrete level, one can use examples to test the adequacy or flexibility of an ethical theory; this is what Sissela Bok does in her essay on Kant and the maxim "Do what is right though the world should perish." Or one can use the concrete and test theories against it by asking whether those theories can give an adequate account of the moral significance of that concrete phenomenon. This is what Jeffrey Blustein does in his essay on intimacy.

The essay by Sissela Bok is as much a study of the moral aspects of nuclear annihilation as it is a work of Kantian exegesis. Given the contemporary possibility of total nuclear destruction, the danger and sheer madness of following the maxim Kant considers and seems to endorse are dramatically evident. This method of testing Kant's ethical theory is not unfamiliar to students of the history of ethics. What the possibility of nuclear annihilation adds is a dramatic magnification, in the manner of a microscope or a photographic enlargement. And it is precisely this magnitude of the destruction and pure horror along with the real possibility of its coming about that explodes before our intuitions. It is not clear what Kant had envisaged in the then hypothetical example of the world perishing.

After a careful analysis of Kant's views in different works, Bok proposes an interpretation according to which morality and prudence could coincide, so the world would not perish. The exegesis may save Kant from the charge of "moral fanaticism"; yet the sheer madness of doing what is right even if the result is nuclear annihilation might signal a limitation of Kantian moral absolutism.

In his essay on intimacy, Jeffrey Blustein joins Stephen Toulmin in contesting an assumption common to utilitarian and Kantian ethical theories: that impartiality is a necessary feature of the moral point of view. Insofar as these two theories are bound to that assumption, they cannot explain the moral significance of intimacy. According to Blustein, the other person in an intimate relationship is unique and irreplaceable, and it is that circumstance which governs our dealings with others as intimates. Utilitarianism provides a "sum-ranking decision procedure," and is "structurally indifferent to who experiences utility." By contrast, it is part of our understanding of intimate relations that we seek the good of the other just because that person is a unique individual. Furthermore, we do so not (just) because of the humanity of the other, as Kant insists, nor in accordance with some duty that enjoins "practical love" rather than "emotional love." We seek the good of our intimates because of our attachment to them as the irreplaceable individuals they are for us. Blustein argues in conclusion that intimate relations give one a stake in the world (my stake) without which there would be no good reason for one to bind oneself to the observance of impersonal morality.

Abortion and Theory

Roger Wertheimer uses the abortion issue as a way of showing how theorists can go wrong by "reliance upon substantive, methodological, and metaethical concepts and principles" that hinder discussion, rather than help it. The dilemma facing the theorist arises from acceptance of the commonly believed moral principle that something's being human is a good reason for refraining from harming it, together with the principle that biological properties are not in themselves morally relevant. This introduces an unnecessary separation between the cognitive and valuational sides of the term 'human being' and the belief that the truths of each side have to be established separately. On the cognitive side this has led to inconclusive debates over taxonomy and the dating of hominization and to the mistaken belief that the abortion issue can be solved by biological investigation. On the valuational side, the attempt to identify morally significant properties associated with the evolving development of the fetus has lacked compelling argument, as have

the claims about the independent and inherent value of the humanity of the fetus.

By contrast with the discussion of the theorists, the common-
sense debate shows that what matters are the moral and legal consequences that follow from classifying some being as human, not from
the reasons for that classification. And the task of classification here
should be viewed as adjudicatory, not taxonomical; for we, as rational humans with interests in the world, classify for a purpose
beyond dispassionate scientific curiosity. The notion of a human
being gives us identity, self-understanding. Here there is no separation between the correctness of our classifying and the correctness of
our interpretation of the moral principle. The crucial questions on
abortion become questions of justice, in the interpretation and application of the principle. Is it fair to exclude some being from the
protection-from-harm principle when others are included? Or is it
fair to include a being when it lacks morally significant features,
and heavily burden those who are certainly included?

According to Milton Fisk, treating the abortion issue as essentially a problem of when a fetus can be considered a person is
typical of "liberal theory." On the liberal moral and political model,
he holds, the individual is the focal point, and the state the neutral
arbitrator of squabbles among individuals about the rights and interests of each. But Fisk insists that this kind of theory is out of step
with the pattern of events.

If one switches to what Fisk calls the "group model," a woman
is seen as a member of a class, an oppressed class, in a patriarchal
society. The issue of abortion becomes the issue of the right of a
member of this class to choose, when her class is engaged in a
struggle against the patriarchal system which wants to decide for
her. In such a struggle and under the patriarchal system in which
childbearing enhances male dominance, it should be up to the
woman to decide. If she decides to conceive and give birth, her
decision should not be based upon the ideology that sees her chief
function as childbearing; and in that case society must have a major
responsibility for child care. On the other hand, she may decide to
abort, in the justified belief that the goal of liberation overrides the
right to life of the fetus.

If liberal theory prevents us from seeing the problem of abortion as part of the problem about a group that has the right to

organize in order to bring about social change, then this constitutes a basis for rejecting that theory.

Taxation; Wickedness

For any of a number of reasons, certain moral issues tend to be neglected by current or dominant moral theory and thus do not appear among the fashionable repertoire of issues. A philosopher has the right to widen this repertoire, and this has been happening in the last few years.

This may be done, as Onora O'Neill suggests, by putting the potential of a theory into wider use. Lawrence C. Becker here selects the "small-scale" theoretical principle of equity, to show that, on the basis of this principle, a specific form of taxation, the individual expenditure tax, is the form that ought to be adopted.

Philosophers who have talked about taxation heretofore have limited themselves to the more general question of the justifiability of taxation, neglecting such more specific topics as the forms and limits of taxation and leaving these to public-finance experts. Believing that "the best theory accommodates itself to the requirements of practice, and the best practice accommodates itself to the requirements of theory," Becker discusses the best form of taxation that the ("small-scale") theoretical principle of equity can justify. This turns out to be the individual expenditure tax, and not the sales, property, or income taxes.

The skepticism about moral theory that derived from the influence in philosophy of the logical empiricists resulted not only in a ban on the construction of normative ethical theory, but also in general strictures against making value judgments. One of the many casualties of that atmosphere "was the loss of the whole dimension of evil from the scene of official moral theory" and of the possibility of talking about human wickedness both in the explanation of evil acts and in assigning moral blame.

Social scientists in their turn denied that wickedness and aggression have an internal cause in human nature and made them instead the outcome of external conditioning. Moreover, the issue was thought to be simply empirical. Mary Midgley claims that the problem can be clarified by a philosophical analysis of the psychology of motives (fear, anger, aggression). From an analysis that reveals the complexities of motives and the varied ways in which a motive may express itself, some good, some bad, it becomes possible to accept wickedness as an inner principle without the fatalism implied by a mistaken and simplified model of how motives function. It also becomes possible to accept freedom—for one can direct the aggression or anger or fear in good or bad ways—and, hence, the moral evaluation of our acts.

Fadlou Shehadi and David M. Rosenthal

PART ONE
General Issues

To the Case Against Ethics

The Usefulness of Ethical Theory

The Feasibility of Applied Ethics: The Philosopher as Moral Expert

The Model in Practice

1
Can Ethics Provide Answers?*

James Rachels

Recently I saw a proposal written by a distinguished professor of business to add a course in "business ethics" to his school's curriculum. It was an enthusiastic proposal, detailing the virtues and benefits of such an offering. But it concluded with the remark that "Since there are no definite answers in ethics, the course should be offered on a pass-fail basis." I don't know why he thought that, lacking definite answers, it would be any easier to distinguish passing from failing work than B work from C work, but what was most striking was the casual, offhand manner of the remark—as though it were *obvious* that, no matter how important ethical questions might be, no "definite answers" are possible.

Can ethics provide answers? Philosophers have given a great deal of attention to this issue, but the result, unfortunately, has been a great deal of disagreement. There are generally two schools of thought. On one side there are those who believe that ethics is a subject, like history or physics or mathematics, with its own distinctive problems and its own methods of solving them. The fundamental questions of ethics are questions of conduct—what, in particular cases, should we do?—and the study of ethics provides the answers. On the other side are those who, like the professor of business, deny

---

*This is a revised version of an essay that originally appeared in the *Hastings Center Report,* x (June 1980): 32–40; reprinted in *Ethics in Hard Times,* Arthur L. Caplan and Daniel Callahan, eds. (New York: Plenum Publishing Corp., 1981).

that ethics is a proper subject at all. There are ethical questions, to be sure, and they are important; but since those questions have no definite answers, there cannot be a subject whose business it is to discover them.

In this essay I want to consider whether, in fact, ethics can provide answers. As a preliminary to that discussion, I will say something about the relation between ethics and the philosophical theory of ethics.

ETHICS AND ETHICAL THEORY

Ethics is the subject that attempts to provide directions for conduct: Should a manufacturer advertise a product as being better than it is? Should a lawyer suppress evidence that tends to show that his client is guilty? Should a physician help a dying patient who, because of constant misery, wishes to end his life sooner? And so on, endlessly.

Ethical theory, on the other hand, concerns itself with questions *about* ethics. These questions divide naturally into two categories. First, ethical theorists want to know about the relations between the various reasons and principles we use in justifying particular moral judgments. Can they be fitted together into a unified theory? Can these diverse principles be reduced to one ultimate principle, which underlies and explains all the rest? Much of modern moral philosophy has consisted in the elaboration of such theories: egoism, Kantianism, and utilitarianism, each purporting to have discovered *the* ultimate principle of ethics, are the most familiar.

Second, there are questions about the *status* of ethics. Are there any objective truths in ethics which our moral judgments may correctly or incorrectly represent? Or are our moral judgments nothing more than the expression of personal feelings, or perhaps the codes of the societies in which we live? Often it is helpful in dealing with such issues to analyze the meaning of moral concepts—to examine what is meant by such words as 'good', 'right', and 'ought'.

Twenty years ago the prevailing orthodoxy among English-speaking philosophers was that ethical theory, but not ethics itself, is the proper concern of philosophy. Philosophers, it was said, are theoreticians, not ministers or guidance counselors. The more radical philosophers even excluded what I have called the "first part" of ethical theory from their purview; they restricted their attention entirely to the analysis of moral language. The result was a body of literature which seemed, to those outside academic circles, curiously empty and sterile.

Today this attitude has been almost completely abandoned; the best writing by moral philosophers combines ethical theory with a concern for specific moral issues. Part of the reason for this change is that the traumas of the past two decades—especially the protest movements against racism, sexism, and the Vietnam war—forced philosophers to rethink their role in society. But there is a deeper reason, internal to philosophy itself. The rejection of ethics was the result of a preoccupation among philosophers during the first half of this century with understanding the different kinds of inquiry. Science, mathematics, religion, and ethics are very different from one another, and, as philosophers tried to sort out the differences, the idea took hold that philosophy's distinctive contribution is to analyze and clarify the concepts used in each area. It was an appealing idea, with ample historical precedent. After all, the patron saint of philosophy, Socrates, had conceived of his work mainly as an investigation into definitions; and the great figures such as Aristotle and Kant had appealed, at key points in their work, to linguistic considerations for support. Philosophers, then, were to study not ethics but only the language of ethics. That philosophers are not ethicists seemed as natural a conclusion as that philosophers are not scientists or mathematicians.

By the mid-1960s, however, it was becoming clear that the recognition of differences among kinds of inquiry does not require that they be pursued in isolation from one another. Indeed, separation may not be desirable or even possible. (One cannot do physics without mathematics.) Today philosophers generally do not recognize sharp boundaries between their own work and work in other areas. Thus W. V. Quine, whom many consider the most eminent living American philosopher, regards his work as continuous with that of theoretical science. Links between current philosophy and psychology, linguistics, and computer science are everywhere apparent. The reuniting of ethical theory with ethics, then, is merely a part of a larger movement within philosophy, to bring back into proper relation the disparate inquiries.

THE CASE AGAINST ETHICS

The professor of business whose statement I quoted is not unusual; a great many people, including many philosophers, believe that there are no "answers" in ethics. It is a remarkable situation: people make judgments every day about what should or should not be done; they feel strongly about those judgments, and sometimes they become angry and indignant with those who disagree. Yet, when they reflect on what they are doing, they profess that their opinions are no more "true" than the contrary opinions they reject so vehemently. The explanation of this puzzling situation goes deep into our history and into our understanding of the world and our place in it.

Throughout most of western history there was thought to be a close connection between ethics and religion. In Plato's *Euthyphro* Socrates offered powerful arguments for separating the two, but this point of view did not prevail. (Socrates, it will be remembered, was tried and convicted of impiety.) With the spread of Christianity, right and wrong came to be identified ever more closely with God's will, and human life was regarded as meaningful only because of its place in God's plan. The church was the guardian of the moral community and its main authority.

By the eighteenth century these ideas had begun to lose their grip on people's minds, largely because of changes that had taken place in the conception of the physical world. The physical sciences had successfully challenged the ancient belief that the earth is at the center of the cosmos; instead, it was recognized to be a relatively insignificant speck. The next step would be the realization that, from a cosmic point of view, human beings are themselves insignificant. In his great essay on suicide, published posthumously in 1783, David Hume took that step, declaring that "The life of a man is of no greater importance to the universe than that of an oyster."[1]

The aim of Hume's essay was to defend the permissibility of suicide; in doing that, he was particularly eager to separate religious from moral notions, and to dispel the idea that human life is a gift from God that can rightly be taken only by God. This belief he considered to be a compound of "superstition and false religion,"

---

[1]The essay on suicide is conveniently reprinted in *Hume's Ethical Writings,* Alasdair MacIntyre, ed. (New York: Collier, 1965).

and he held that the purpose of our thinking should be to replace superstition and false religion with reason and understanding. The truth, in his view, is that *we* care about human life, because we are human, and that is all there is to it.

Hume would no doubt have felt vindicated by the second great modern change in our conception of the world and our place in it, which from the biological sciences came after his death. The thought that we are the products of an evolutionary history much like that of all the other animals has further eroded confidence about any special place for humanity in the scheme of things, underscoring Hume's point.

In our own time, however, it has been the social sciences that have presented the greatest challenge to traditional ideas about human beings. In particular, the understanding of human nature derived from contemporary sociology and psychology has seemed to many people incompatible with a belief in the objectivity of ethics— that is, with a belief in objective standards of right and wrong.

Sociologists have impressed upon us that moral standards differ from culture to culture; what the "natural light of reason" reveals to one people may be radically different from what seems obvious to another. This, of course, has been known for a long time. Herodotus made the point very clearly in the fifth century B.C.:

> Darius, after he had got the kingdom, called into his presence certain Greeks who were at hand, and asked—"What he should pay them to eat the bodies of their fathers when they died?" To which they answered, that there was no sum that would tempt them to do such a thing. He then sent for certain Indians, of the race called Callatians, men who eat their fathers, and asked them, while the Greeks stood by, and knew by the help of an interpreter all that was said—"What he should give them to burn the bodies of their fathers at their decease?" The Indians exclaimed aloud, and bade him forbear such language. Such is men's wont herein; and Pindar was right, in my judgment, when he said, "Custom is the king o'er all."[2]

Today any educated person could list countless other examples of cultural variations in ethics: the Eskimos allow first-born daughters to die of exposure; the Moslems practice polygamy; the Jains will not eat meat. With the communications media providing constant contact with other parts of the world, it may now seem simply naive

---

[2]*The History of Herodotus,* George Rawlinson, trans., adapted by John Ladd in *Ethical Relativism* (Belmont, Calif.: Wadsworth, 1973), p. 12.

to think that our moral views are anything more than one particular cultural product.

Psychological studies tend to undermine confidence in ethics in a different way, by making us aware of the nonrational ways in which moral beliefs are formed in the individual. The general picture remains remarkably constant even when we consider radically different psychological theories. Sigmund Freud and B. F. Skinner, for example, tell much the same story. The child learns from an early age that certain types of behavior will be followed by pleasure, often in the form of parental approval, and that other actions produce unpleasant consequences, often parental disapproval. Thus he learns to behave in some ways and to avoid others; and when his vocabulary has become sufficiently rich he calls the former acts "right" and the latter "wrong." The 'super-ego' is the name Freud gives to the internal mechanism that takes over the parent's activity of approving and disapproving, rewarding and punishing.

Skinnerian psychology could hardly be more different from Freudian thought; nevertheless their fundamental ideas concerning moral development are similar. Where Freud speaks of pleasure and parental approval, Skinner speaks of "positive reinforcement." The individual is positively reinforced (rewarded) when he performs certain acts, and so tends to repeat that behavior; he is negatively reinforced (punished) for other acts, which he subsequently tends not to repeat. The concepts of good and evil become attached to the two kinds of behavior. Indeed, Skinner goes so far as to suggest that 'good' may be *defined* as "positively reinforcing." The point is that, on both theories, persons who had been raised differently would have different values. The obvious conclusion is that the belief that one's values are anything more than the result of this conditioning is, again, simply naive.

Thus, in many people's minds, sociology and psychology swallow up ethics. They do not simply explain ethics; they explain it *away*. Ethics can no longer exist as a subject having as its aim the discovery of what is right and what is wrong; for this supposes, naively, that there *is* a right and wrong independent of what people already happen to believe. And that is precisely what has been brought into doubt. Ethics as a subject matter must disappear, to be replaced, perhaps, by something like "values clarification." We can try to become clearer about what our values are and about the possible alternatives. But we can no longer ask questions about the truth of our convictions.

With such impressive intellectual forces behind it, it is not surprising that this way of thinking about ethics has been tremendously influential. However, most contemporary philosophers have, with good reason, taken a dim view of these arguments. In the first place, the fact that different societies have different moral codes proves nothing. There is also disagreement from society to society about scientific matters: in some cultures it is believed that the earth is flat and in others that disease is caused by evil spirits. We do not on that account conclude that there is no truth in geography or in medicine. Instead, we conclude that in some cultures people are better informed than in others. Similarly, disagreement in ethics might signal nothing more than that some people are less enlightened than others. At the very least, the fact of disagreement does not, by itself, *entail* that truth does not exist. Why should we assume that, if ethical truth exists, everyone must know it?

Moreover, it may be that some values are merely relative to culture, whereas others are not. Herodotus was probably right in thinking that the treatment of the dead—whether to eat or to burn them—is not a matter governed by objectively true standards. It may be simply a matter of convention that respect for the dead is shown in one way rather than another. If so, the Callatians and the Greeks were equally naive to be horrified by each other's customs. Alternative sexual customs—another favorite example of relativists—might also be equally acceptable. But this does not mean that there are *no* practices that are objectively wrong: torture, slavery, and dishonesty, for example, could still be wrong, independently of cultural standards, even if those other types of behavior are not. It is a mistake to think that, because some standards are relative to culture, all must be.

The psychological facts are equally irrelevant to the status of ethics as an autonomous subject. Psychology may tell us that beliefs are acquired in a certain way—perhaps as the result of positive and negative reinforcement—but nothing follows from this about the nature of those beliefs. After all, *every* belief is acquired through the operation of some psychological mechanism or other, including the simplest factual beliefs. A child may learn to respond "George Washington" when asked to name the first American president,

because she fears the disapproval of the teacher should she say anything else. And, we might add, if she were reinforced differently she
might grow up believing that someone else first held that office. Yet
it remains a matter of objective fact that Washington was the first
president. The same goes for one's moral beliefs: the manner of
their acquisition is logically independent of their status as objectively true or false.

Thus the outcome of the psychological account of ethics is remi-
niscent of the fate of nineteenth-century attempts to reduce mathematics to psychology. In the late 1900s there was considerable
interest in explaining mathematics by reference to psychological
theories of human thought—but that interest waned when it was
realized that little light was being shed on mathematics itself. Regardless of how it might be related to our thought processes, mathematics remained a subject with its own integrity—its own internal
rules, procedures, problems, and solutions—in short, its own standards of truth and falsity. The reason ethics resists explanation by
sociology or psychology is that, like mathematics, it is also a subject
with its own integrity.

EMOTIVISM AND THE REJECTION OF ETHICS

Although contemporary philosophers have not been impressed by
the social-scientific arguments concerning ethics, they have nevertheless found certain other arguments to be plausible. Those arguments go back to Hume, who maintained that belief in an
objectively correct ethical system is part of the old "superstition and
false religion." Stripped of false theology, Hume said, we should
come to see our morality as nothing more than the expression of
our feelings.

But Hume did not merely assert this; he attempted to prove it
by giving arguments. His most influential argument was based on
the idea that there is a necessary connection between moral belief
and conduct. The test of whether we sincerely believe that we ought
to do something is whether in fact we are motivated to do it; if I say
that I believe I ought to do such and such, but have not the slightest
inclination to do it, my statement is not to be believed. Thus, having a moral belief is at least in part a matter of being motivated to
act, or, as Hume put it, of having a sentiment. On the other hand,

a person's capacity to discern truth and falsehood—in Hume's terms, his reason—has no necessary connection with his conduct at all: "Morals move men to act; reason alone is utterly impotent in this particular." The point is that, if moral belief is conceived as the perception of truth or falsity, its connection with conduct remains mysterious; whereas if it is regarded as an expression of sentiment, this connection is made clear.

In our own time Hume's thoughts have been adapted to support a theory according to which moral judgments are not really judgments at all, but disguised imperatives. According to this theory, *emotivism,* when one makes a moral judgment "*X* is wrong" one is actually saying no more than "Don't do *X*!" Alternatively, it was sometimes said, one is doing nothing more in making these judgments than expressing one's attitude and urging others to adopt that attitude. Even though they may be sincere or insincere, imperatives and expressions of attitude are neither true nor false—and so moral judgments are neither true nor false.[3] By connecting their theory of ethics with the analysis of different kinds of language use, the emotivists gave ethical subjectivism a new and powerful formulation.

But, if *this* is what moral judgments are, then, once again, ethics has lost its status as a subject. There are no truths for it to investigate. It cannot even be a branch of psychology; for, although psychology is concerned with attitudes, it is concerned only with nonmoral truths *about* attitudes, which, unlike expressions *of* attitude, are true or false.

Among English-speaking philosophers, emotivism has been the most influential theory of ethics in the twentieth century. Earlier I remarked on some of the reasons that led philosophers to reject normative ethics as part of their subject. Clearly, the influence of emotivism was another important element in this rejection, and little was written by philosophers on concrete moral issues until fairly recently—the mid-1960s—when emotivist ideas had begun to lose their influence. Until then, the literature on moral issues was mainly the work of the theologians, who, standing firmly against

---

[3]The classic defense of emotivism is Charles L. Stevenson, *Ethics and Language* (New Haven: Yale, 1944). J. O. Urmson, *The Emotive Theory of Ethics* (London: Hutchinson, 1968), provides a critical assessment.

the trends of thought I have been describing, never lost confidence in the integrity of ethics as a subject.

There is now an extensive philosophical literature cataloguing the deficiencies of emotivism, but, as is usually the case with important theories, its failure is instructive. One of the main problems with emotivism was that it could not account for the place of reason in ethics. It is a point of logic that moral judgments, if they are to be acceptable, must be founded on good reasons: if I tell you that such-and-such an action is wrong, you are entitled to ask *why* it is wrong; and, if I have no adequate reply, you may reject my advice as unfounded. The emotivists were able to give only the most anemic account of the relation between moral judgments and the reasons that support them. Moral reasoning, on their view, turned out to be indistinguishable from propaganda. If moral judgments are merely expressions of attitude, then reasons are merely considerations that influence attitudes. It was a natural outcome of the theory that *any* fact that influences attitudes counts as a reason for the attitude produced; thus, if the thought that Goldbloom is Jewish causes you to distrust him, then "Goldbloom is a Jew" becomes a reason in support of your judgment that he is a shady character.

Obviously, something had gone wrong. Not just any fact can count as a reason in support of just any judgment. For one thing, the fact must be relevant to the judgment, and psychological influence does not necessarily bring relevance with it. But this is only the tip of an iceberg. Arguments in support of moral judgments can be criticized and found adequate or inadequate on any number of other grounds. Once this is realized, we have taken a big step away from emotivism and all the other trends of thought I have been describing, toward the recognition of ethics as an autonomous subject.

ETHICS AND RATIONALITY

Ultimately the case against ethics can be answered only by demonstrating how moral problems are solvable by rational methods. How does one go about establishing what is the right thing to do? If there are answers in ethics, how are they to be found? Considered abstractly, these may seem to be very difficult questions. But I believe they are not so hard as one might think.

The key idea may be expressed quite simply: In any particular case, the right course of action is the one that is backed by the best reasons. Solving moral problems is largely a matter of weighing up the reasons, or arguments, that can be given for or against the various alternatives. Consider, for example, euthanasia. Many people feel that mercy killing is wicked; the American Medical Association condemns it as "contrary to that for which the medical profession stands." Others feel that, in the right circumstances, there is nothing wrong with it. Who is right? We may determine whether euthanasia (or anything else, for that matter) is right or wrong by formulating and assessing the arguments that can be given for and against it. This is at bottom what is wrong with psychological and cultural relativism: if we can produce good reasons for thinking that this practice is wrong and show that the arguments in its support are unsound, then we have proved it wrong, regardless of what belief one has been conditioned to have or what one's cultural code might say. And emotivism runs afoul of the same fact: if a stronger case can be made for euthanasia than against it, then mercy killing *is* permissible, no matter what one's attitude might be.

But how are arguments to be tested? What distinguishes strong arguments from weak ones?

The first and most obvious way that a moral argument can go wrong is by misrepresenting the facts. A rational case for or against a course of conduct must rest on some understanding of the facts of the case—minimally, facts about the nature of the action, the circumstances in which it would be done, and its likely consequences. If the facts are misrepresented, the argument is no good. Even the most skeptical thinkers agree that reason has this role to play in moral judgment: reason establishes the facts.

Unfortunately, however, attaining a clear view of the facts is not always a simple matter. In the first place, we often need to know what the consequences of a course of action will be, and this may be impossible to determine with any precision or certainty. Opponents of euthanasia sometimes claim that, if mercy killing were legalized, it would lead to a diminished respect for life throughout the society and that we would end up caring less about the elderly, the physically handicapped, and the mentally retarded. Defenders of euthanasia, on the other hand, heatedly deny this. What separates the two camps here is a disagreement about "the facts," but we cannot settle the issue in the same easy way we could settle an argument about the melting point of lead. We seem to be stuck with different *estimates* of what would happen if euthanasia were legalized, which may be more or less reasonable, but which we cannot definitively adjudicate.

Moreover, it is often difficult to determine the facts because the facts are distressingly *complex*. Take, for example, the question of whether someone who requests euthanasia is "competent"—i.e., is rational and in full control of his (or her) faculties. I take this to be a question of fact, but it need not be a *simple* matter of fact. In order to decide the matter we must fit together into a pattern all sorts of other facts about the individual, his state of mind, his attitudes, the quality of his reasoning, the pressures influencing him, and so on. That he is, or is not, competent is a kind of conclusion resting on these other facts; it is a matter of what the simpler facts add up to.

Suppose, though, that we have a clear view of the relevant facts, and so our arguments cannot be faulted on that ground. Is there any other test of rationality which the arguments must pass? Hume's official view was that, at this point, reason has done all it can do, and the rest is up to our "sentiments." Reason sets out the facts; then sentiment takes over and the choice is made. This is a tempting idea, but it only illustrates a common trap into which people may fall. Philosophical theses may seduce with their beautiful simplicity; an idea may be accepted because of its appeal at a high level of generality, even though it does not conform to what we know to be the case at a lower level.

In fact, when Hume was considering concrete ethical issues, and not busy overemphasizing the role of sentiment, he knew very well that appeals to reason are often decisive in other ways. In the essay on suicide he produced a number of powerful arguments in support of his view that a person has the right to take his own life, for example, when he is suffering without hope from a painful illness. Hume specifically opposed the traditional religious view that, since life is a gift from God, only God may decide when it shall end. About this he made the simple but devastating observation that we "play God" as much when we save life as when we take it. Each time a doctor treats an illness and thereby prolongs a life, he decrees that this life shall not end *now*. Thus if we take seriously that only God may determine the length of a life, we have to renounce not only killing but saving life as well.

This point has force because of the general requirement that our arguments be consistent, and consistency, of course, is the prime requirement of rationality. Hume did *not* argue that the religious opponent of euthanasia has got his facts wrong—he did not insist that there is no God, or that God's will has been misunderstood. If Hume's objection were no more than that, there would be little reason for the religious person to be bothered by it. Hume's objection was much stronger; for he was pointing out that we may appeal to a general principle (such as "Only God has the right to decide when a life shall end") only if we are willing to accept *all* its consequences. If we accept some of them (the prohibition of suicide and euthanasia), but not others (the abandonment of medicine), then we are inconsistent. This point, which has fundamental importance, will be missed if we are entranced by overly simple doctrines like "Reason establishes the facts; sentiment makes the choice."

There are other ways in which an ethical view may fail to pass the test of consistency. A person may base his ethical position on his "intuitions"—his prereflective hunches about what is right or wrong in particular cases—and, on examination, these may turn out to be incompatible with one another. Consider the difference between killing someone and "merely" allowing someone to die. Many people feel intuitively that there is a big moral difference between these two. The thought of actively killing someone has a kind of visceral repulsiveness about it which is missing from the more passive (but still unpleasant) act of standing by and doing nothing while someone dies. Thus it may be held that, although euthanasia is wrong, since it involves direct killing, nevertheless it is sometimes permissible to allow death by refraining from life-prolonging treatment.

To be sure, if we do nothing more than consult our "intuitions," there seems to be an important difference here. However, it is easy to describe cases of killing and letting die in which there does *not* seem to be such a difference. Suppose a patient is brought into an emergency room and turned over to a doctor who recognizes him as a man against whom he has a grudge. A quick diagnosis reveals that the patient is about to die, but can be saved by a simple procedure—say, an appendectomy. The doctor, seeing his chance, deliberately stalls until it is too late to perform the life-saving procedure, and the patient dies. Now most of us would think, intuitively, that the doctor is no better than a murderer, and the fact that he did not directly kill the patient, but merely let him die, makes no difference whatever.

In the euthanasia case, the difference between killing and letting die seems important. In the grudge case, the difference seems unimportant. But what is the truth? Is the difference important, or isn't it? Such cases show that unexamined intuitions cannot be trusted. That is not surprising. Our intuitions may be nothing more than the product of prejudice, selfishness, or cultural conditioning; we have no guarantee that they are perceptions of the truth. And when they are not compatible with one another, we can be sure that one or the other of them is mistaken.

To make progress, we need arguments. We need to ask *why* the distinction does, or does not, make a difference. Can any reason be given to support the idea that killing is worse than letting die? It certainly does not matter, from the patient's point of view, whether he is killed or allowed to die; either way he ends up dead.[4] Perhaps the reason there *seems* to be a difference is that killings are so often accompanied by bad motives, whereas acts of letting die are usually done from acceptable motives. Perhaps it is the difference between the motives, and not the difference between the acts themselves, that is morally significant.

Recently there has been a lot of discussion of this distinction in the philosophical literature, and at first it was largely a matter of the different writers' citing their intuitions, with each one producing cases in which the favored intuition "seemed" correct. Now, however, the debate has reached a more profitable stage in which the emphasis is on investigating whatever reasons can be produced to support one view over the other.

Let me mention one other way in which the requirement of consistency can force a change in one's moral views. I have been emphasizing that a moral judgment, if it is to be acceptable, must be backed by reasons. Consistency requires, then, that, if there are exactly the *same* reasons in support of one course of conduct as there are in support of another, those actions are equally right, or equally

---

[4]In the euthanasia case, it may matter to the patient that he die sooner rather than later, because he is suffering—therefore, it may be preferable that he be killed, because it is quicker. But what governs choice here is an argument about suffering, not the importance of killing versus letting die *as such.*

wrong. We cannot say that X is right, but that Y is wrong, unless there is a relevant difference between them. This is a familiar principle in many contexts: it cannot be right for a teacher to give students different grades unless there is a relevant difference in the work they have done; it cannot be right to pay workers differently unless there is some relevant difference between the jobs they do; and so on. In general, it is this principle that underlies the social ideal of equality.

This principle has some surprising consequences. Its implications are much more radical than egalitarians have realized; for, if applied consistently, it would not only require us to treat our fellow humans better, it would require us to rethink our treatment of non-human animals as well. To take only one instance:

We routinely perform experiments on chimpanzees that we would never perform on humans—but what is the difference between the chimps and the humans that justifies this difference in treatment? It might be said that humans are far more intelligent and sensitive than chimpanzees; but this only invites a further query: suppose the humans are mentally retarded and so *less* intelligent and sensitive than the chimps? Would we be willing to experiment on retarded humans in the same way? And if not, why not? What is the difference between the individuals in question, which makes it all right to experiment on one but not the other? At this point the defender of the *status quo* may be reduced to asserting that, after all, the humans are *human,* and that is what makes the difference. This, however, is uncomfortably like asserting that, after all, women are *women,* or blacks are *black,* and that is why *they* may be treated differently. It is the announcement of a prejudice, and nothing more.[5]

This example brings us back to the point at which we started. We have adjusted in many ways to the idea that the earth is not the center of the universe and that we humans are but one race among others that have developed here. But, where ethics is concerned, we cling to the idea that humanity is still at the center of the cosmos. The idea that every human life is sacred has been replaced by its secular equivalent, that every human life has special value and dig-

---

[5]This argument is advanced very persuasively by Peter Singer in *Animal Liberation* (New York: New York Review Books, 1975).

nity just in virtue of being human. As a plea for equality among people, the idea has some merit; as a justification for our treatment of the nonhuman world, it won't do.

I have left until last a matter which many moral philosophers believe is at the heart of their subject. In many instances we cannot make progress in moral deliberation until we become clearer about the meaning of the concepts employed in our arguments—and the analysis of concepts has always been the philosopher's special concern. The most important concepts for ethics in general are the concepts of rightness, goodness, and obligation. We want first to be clear about what *they* mean, and this is not merely a matter of idle curiosity, but a necessity for making progress in our thinking. In the preceding discussion I have, without announcing the fact, made a number of points that depend on the analysis of these concepts: that the right thing to do is the course of action supported by the best reasons, and that, in the absence of relevant differences, it cannot be right to treat individuals differently, are, in my opinion, propositions that follow directly from the meaning of the moral concepts.

The importance of conceptual analysis may not be obvious, however, if we concentrate only on such general concepts. Where particular moral issues are concerned, the analysis of more specific concepts may be crucial. By now it seems obvious that the argument over whether fetuses are persons and so fall under the protection of the moral rules governing the treatment of persons, is not an argument over "the facts." We all know what sort of biological and psychological entity a fetus is, or we think we do, and yet disagreement persists about whether they are persons. People on both sides of the dispute look at the same fetus and agree about its other characteristics; then one says "It's a person" and the other says "No it isn't." What divides the parties is their differing understandings of what it means to be a person—the analysis of the concept.

Opponents of abortion like to show photographs of fetuses, to underscore the point that it is not merely a blob of tissue that is destroyed in abortion. What makes the photographs effective is that they seem to show *people*, albeit very tiny and helpless ones, just like you and me. Yet, the proabortionist might point out, what the pictures show is only that the fetus has the *physical* characteristics normally associated with persons. In addition, persons have psychological characteristics—beliefs, desires, hopes, and so forth—which define their lives as individuals. Since fetuses do not have this complex of psychological characteristics, the proabortionist can argue plausibly that they are not persons in any morally important sense. The whole argument hinges on what is meant by "person."

In one respect I believe the proabortionists are right. It is a person's psychological characteristics, and not the fact that he or she has a certain kind of body, that is important from a moral point of view. That is why, when someone has become irreversibly comatose, it is pointless to maintain him or her alive by artificial means. Without consciousness, with all that it involves, being alive does one no good. Indeed, many are tempted to say that such unfortunate people are already dead, in recognition of the fact that their biographical lives are over, even though biologically they are still alive.

The case of the fetus is, however, different, because, although the fetus may lack the psychological characteristics of a person, it nevertheless *will* have them if it is allowed a normal development. The major unresolved question about the morality of abortion is how much, if at all, this potentiality counts. People have differing intuitions, but I am not aware that anyone has produced a really convincing argument either way.

THE LIMITS OF RATIONALITY

The preceding discussion will not have dispelled all the nagging doubts about ethics. Rational methods can be used to expose factual error and inconsistency, in the ways I have described, but is that enough to save ethics from the charge that, at bottom, there is no "truth" in its domain? Couldn't two people who are equally rational—who have all the relevant facts, whose principles are consistent, etc.—still disagree? And if "reason" were inadequate to resolve the disagreement, wouldn't this show that, in the end, ethics really is only a matter of opinion? These questions will not go away.

There is a limit to what rational methods can achieve, which Hume described perfectly in the first appendix to his *Inquiry concerning the Principles of Morals,* published in 1752:

> Ask a man *why he uses exercise;* he will answer, *because he desires to keep his health.* If you then inquire *why he desires health,* he will readily reply, *Because sickness is painful.* If you push your inquiries further and desire a reason *why he hates pain,* it is impossible he can ever give any. This is an ultimate end, and is never referred to any other object.

Perhaps to your second question, *why he desires* health, he may also reply that *it is necessary for the exercise of his calling.* If you ask *why he is anxious on that head,* he will answer, *because he desires to get money.* If you demand, *Why? It is the instrument of pleasure,* says he. And beyond this, it is an absurdity to ask for a reason. It is impossible there can be a progress *in infinitum,* and that one thing can always be a reason why another is desired. Something must be desirable on its own account, and because of its immediate accord or agreement with human sentiment and affection (*Hume's Ethical Writings,* p. 131).

The impossibility of an infinite regress of reasons is not peculiar to ethics; the point applies in all areas. Mathematical reasoning eventually ends with axioms that are not themselves justified, and reasoning in science ultimately depends on assumptions that are not proved. It could not be otherwise. At some point reasoning must always come to an end, no matter what one is reasoning about.

But there is a difference between ethics and other subjects, and that difference is in the involvement of the emotions. As Hume observed, when we come to the last reason, we mention something we *care* about. Nothing can count as an ultimate reason for or against a course of conduct unless we care about that thing in some way. In the absence of any emotional involvement, there are no reasons for action. The fact that the building is on fire is a reason for me to leave only if I care about not being burned; the fact that children are starving is a reason for me to do something only if I care about their plight. (On this point the emotivists were right, whatever defects their overall theory might have had.) It is the possibility that people might care about different things and so accept different ultimate principles between which "reason" cannot adjudicate, which continues to undermine confidence in the subject itself.

I believe that this possibility cannot ever be ruled out entirely and that it will always be the source of a kind of nervousness about ethics. The nervousness cannot be eliminated; we have to live with it. There is, however, one further point that needs to be considered—a point which goes some way toward minimizing the worry.[6]

---

[6]Among contemporary moral philosophers W. D. Falk has made this point most forcefully; see, for example, his essay "Action-guiding Reasons," *Journal of Philosophy,* LX, 23 (Nov. 7, 1963): 702–18. I owe much of my understanding of these matters to Falk.

What people care about is itself sensitive to pressure from the deliberative process and can change as a result of thought. This applies as much to people's "ultimate" cares and desires as to their more passing fancies. Someone might not care very much about something before he thinks it through, but come to feel differently once he has thought it over. This fact has been considered extremely important by some of the major philosophers. Aristotle, Butler, and others emphasized that responsible moral judgment must be based on a full understanding of the facts; but, they added, after the facts are established a separate cognitive process is required for the agent to understand fully the import of what he or she knows. It is necessary not merely to know the facts, but to rehearse them carefully in one's mind, in an impartial, nonevasive way. *Then* one will have the kind of knowledge on which moral judgment may be based.[7]

Aristotle even suggested that there are two distinct species of knowledge: first, the sort of knowledge had by one who is able to recite facts, "like the drunkard reciting the verses of Empedocles," but without understanding their meaning; and, second, the sort of knowledge had when one has thought carefully about what one knows. An example might make this clearer. We all know, in an abstract sort of way, that many children in the world are starving; yet for most of us this makes little difference to our conduct. We will spend money on trivial things for ourselves, rather than spend it on food for them. How are we to explain this? The Aristotelian explanation is that we "know" the children are starving only in the sense in which the drunkard knows Empedocles's verses—we simply recite the fact (*Nicomachean Ethics,* 1147b). Suppose, though, that we thought carefully about what it must be *like* to be a starving orphan. Our attitudes, our conduct, and the moral judgments we are willing to make might be substantially altered.

A few years ago a wire-service photograph of two Vietnamese orphans appeared in American newspapers. They were sleeping on a Saigon street; the younger boy, who seemed to be about four, was

---

[7]John Dewey took the distinction between what one cares about before reflection and what one cares about after reflection to mark the difference between what is desired and what is desirable. For an account of Dewey's ethics which emphasizes the importance of this, see my "John Dewey and the Truth about Ethics," in Steven M. Cahn, ed., *New Studies in the Philosophy of John Dewey* (Hanover, N.H.: University Press of New England, 1977).

inside a tattered cardboard box, and his slightly older brother was curled up around the box. The explanation beneath the photograph said that while they begged for food during the day, the older boy would drag the box with them, because he didn't want his brother to have to sleep on the sidewalk at night.

After this photograph appeared, a large number of people wrote to relief agencies offering to help. What difference did the picture make? I don't believe it was a matter of people's being presented with new information—it wasn't as though they did not know that starving orphans have miserable lives. Rather, the picture brought home to them in a vivid way things they already knew. It is easy to think of starving children in an abstract, statistical way; the picture forced people to think of them concretely, and it made a difference to people's attitudes.

In moral discussion we often recognize that thinking through what one knows is a separate matter from merely knowing; and we exploit this in a certain strategy of argument. It is the strategy that begins "Think what it is like . . ."

—Those who favor voluntary euthanasia ask us to consider what it is like, from the point of view of the dying patient, to suffer horribly. If we would, they imply, we would feel more favorably disposed toward mercy killing.
—Albert Camus, in his essay on capital punishment, "Reflections on the Guillotine," argued that people tolerate the death penalty only because they think of it in euphemistic terms ("Pierre paid his debt to society") rather than attending to the sound of the head falling into the basket.[8] If we thought about it nonevasively, he says, we could not avoid detesting it.
—And, as I have already mentioned, opponents of abortion show us pictures of fetuses, to force us to pay attention to what it is that is killed. The assumption is that, if we did, we could not approve of killing it.

Often this method of argument is dismissed as nothing more than a demagogic appeal to emotion. Sometimes the charge is true. This type of argument may also serve, however, as an antidote for the

---

[8]*Resistance, Rebellion, and Death* (New York: Knopf, 1961), pp. 175–234.

self-deception that Bishop Butler saw as corrupting moral thought. When we do not *want* to reach a certain conclusion about what is to be done—perhaps we would rather spend money on ourselves than give it for famine relief—we may refuse to face up to what we know in a clear-minded way. Facts that would have the power to move us are put out of mind or are thought of only bloodlessly and abstractly. Rehearsing the facts in a vivid and imaginative way is a needed corrective.

Now let us return to the question of ethical disagreement. When disagreement occurs, two explanations are possible. First, we might disagree because there has been some failure of rationality on the part of one of us. Or, second, the people who disagree might simply be different kinds of people, who care about different things. In principle, either explanation may be correct. But, in practice, when important matters are at issue, we always proceed on the first hypothesis. We present arguments to those who disagree with us on the assumption (in the hope?) that they have missed something: they are ignorant of relevant facts, they have not thought through what they know, they are inconsistent, and so on. We do not, as a practical matter, credit the idea that they are simply and irreconcilably "different."

Is this assumption correct? Are we simply ignoring any real-life examples where the explanation of ethical disagreement is that the people who disagree, while being rational enough, care about different things? It is possible; but if such cases do exist, they are notoriously hard to find. The familiar examples of the cultural anthropologists turn out upon analysis to have other explanations. The Eskimos who allow their first-born daughters to die of exposure and who abandon feeble old people to a similar fate do not have less respect for life than other peoples who reject such practices. They live in different circumstances, under threat of starvation in a hostile environment, and the survival of the community requires policies which otherwise they would happily renounce.

Or, consider the Ik, an apparently crude and callous people of Africa who are indifferent even to the welfare of their own children. They will not share food with their children, and they laugh when others are sick. Surely, one might think, the Ik are radically different people. But not so: they took on those characteristics only after a prolonged period of near-starvation which virtually destroyed their tribal culture. Of course human behavior will be modified by calamity; but, before their calamity, the Ik were much too "normal" to attract attention.

There may be some disagreements that reflect cultural variables—Herodotus's Greeks and Callatians, for example—but, beyond that and barring the kind of disaster that reduced the Ik, it is plausible to think that people are enough alike to make ethical agreement possible, if only full rationality were possible.[9]

The fact that rationality has limits does not subvert the objectivity of ethics, but it does suggest a certain modesty in what can be claimed for it. Ethics provides answers about what we ought to do, given that we are the kinds of creatures we are, caring about the things we will care about when we are as reasonable as we can be, living in the sort of circumstances in which we live. This is not as much as we might want, but it is a lot. It is as much as we can hope for in a subject that must incorporate not only our beliefs but our ideals as well.

---

[9]The idea that people are basically alike in matters that affect morality is supported by recent developments in sociobiology. For example, sociobiology says that animals, including humans, can be expected to be altruistic toward their own kind, at least to a limited degree, because this has survival value from an evolutionary point of view. For an interesting exposition, see Singer, *The Expanding Circle: Ethics and Sociobiology* (New York: Farrar, Straus, & Giroux, 1981).

2
Theory and Reflective Practices*

Annette Baier

The usual assumption, when one speaks of "applied ethics," is that there is something called moral theory, and that such a theory can be applied to give guidance in concrete human situations, perhaps with the help of a body of professionals, heirs to the casuists, whose job it is to show how a given moral theory applies to a case. I want to challenge the value of that assumption, and, very sketchily, to suggest an alternative idea of how we can, by taking thought, act more wisely than we might otherwise have done.

The casuists who applied Christian moral teaching to concrete, sometimes to novel, human situations, were a bit like judges who, given an accepted body of statute law and precedents, applied these to the case before them to get a decision on what should be done. What they applied was not a theory but a set of commandments. Philosophers may try to turn such a set of laws into an "ethical theory" by supplying unifying principles or background assumptions, but those who gave the guidance did not see themselves as drawing out practical guidance from a theory.

In any case, whether what the casuists had was a body of law or a moral theory, they had only one such body or theory. The obvious trouble with our contemporary attempts to use moral theory to

*Read at Applied Ethics Conference at Rutgers, October 1980, organized by Fadlou Shehadi and David Rosenthal. *Postures of the Mind: Essays on Mind and Morals.* University of Minnesota Press, 1985.

guide action is the lack of agreement on which theory we are to apply. The standard undergraduate course in, say, medical ethics, or business ethics, acquaints the student with a variety of theories, and shows the difference in the guidance they give. We, in effect, give courses in comparative ethical theory, and like courses in comparative religion, their usual effect in the student is loss of faith in *any* of the alternatives presented. We produce relativists and moral skeptics, persons who have been convinced by our teaching that whatever they do in some difficult situation, some moral theory will condone it, another will condemn it. The usual, and the sensible, reaction to this confrontation with a variety of conflicting theories, all apparently having some plausibility and respectable credentials, is to turn to a guide that speaks more univocally, to turn from morality to self-interest, or mere convenience. In what conceivable way have we helped, say, hospital administrators make a difficult decision if we have given them, in their course on medical ethics, the awareness that a contractarian would do *x*, a believer in natural rights would do *y*, and a utilitarian would do *z*? What guidance is that?

Most of us do not aim to produce moral skeptics when we teach introductory ethics. But that is what we do, with most of our students, when we teach moral theories and their different applications to cases. What we aim to do is increase reflective awareness of what is at stake in difficult decisions, to produce more thoughtful, better informed, and presumably wiser people. The best reason to believe that there is something amiss with the whole procedure is that it is defeating its own ends. In attempting to increase moral reflectiveness we may be destroying what conscience there once was in those we teach.

Such moral convictions as people have before studying moral philosophy were not acquired by self-conscious acceptance of a theory. Most parents lack the intellectualist's compulsion to transform their moral beliefs into theories. What they pass on to their children may be a few slogans or principles or commandments, but mainly they impart moral constraints by example and by reaction to behavior, not by handing on explicit verbal codes of general rules, let alone moral theories. Now if philosophers choose to see implicit rules wherever there is a tradition and a teachable practice, and implicit systems or theories wherever there are general rules, that is their hang-up (and one that a reading of the *Brown Book* might cure). It is a mere Kantian dogma that behind every moral intuition lies a universal rule, behind every set of rules a single statable principle or system of principles.

In a pluralistic society like this one there is no escaping the fact that there are a plurality of moral traditions, that what people learn at their parents' knees varies from one ethnic or religious group to another. This substantive moral disagreement is a fact that no reforms in the teaching of introductory ethics will conjure away. Catholic hospitals will make different decisions from non-Catholic hospitals on many cases, whatever we philosophers do in our classes. What I am deploring is not the variety of moral traditions, and the disagreement that brings when these traditions co-exist in one nation. I am deploring the additional and unnecessary variety and conflict produced by insisting on turning every moral judgment into an instance of a law or principle that has its niche in a moral theory. The array of moral theories that philosophers have produced does not match the array of working moral traditions in this society, or in the world at large. It is not as if a rights theory fits the Catholic tradition, a contract theory the Protestant, intuition-ism the Moslems, utilitarianism the atheist residue. Cultural historians may discern some genetic linkages between ethical and metaethical theories and cultural moral forces, but the moral philosopher who is, say, a contractarian, does not see him or herself, when putting the theory to a class of students from all sorts of backgrounds, as either trying to convert some of them from Catholicism, or as saying "this view will suit those of you who come from a Protestant background." The result of the teaching of moral theories is that, in addition to the variety of cultural traditions initially there, we add a variety of theories. So we might expect to end up with Catholic utilitarians, Catholic contractarians, Catholic intuitionists; Protestant variants of all of these; atheist variants of all of these. In fact the alternatives tend to cancel one another out, leaving a moral vacuum.

All intelligent persons—aware that the tradition in which they have been reared is one of several, that it is the lottery of nature-cum-culture that has made one Catholic, another Muslin; made one believe that eating pork is unclean and wrong, the other believe only that eating pork on Fridays is wrong; one believe that adulterers should be stoned, the other that adultery is preferable to divorce—must entertain some doubts about the point and validity of the constraints they have been trained to observe. They come to us, into our introductory ethics classes, with some questions in their minds about the rationale for their moral beliefs. We offer them a variety of rationales, and a corresponding variety of decision procedures, no one of which may justify all their pre-philosophy-course moral beliefs. By then they are thoroughly confused. To the variety of cultural traditions we have added, crosscutting that, a variety of "rational" procedures, each backed by a theory. A better recipe for moral cynicism could scarcely be deliberately devised.

Before suggesting what we might do which would be less counterproductive, I want to raise some questions about the very idea of a moral theory. Even if we had no problem of choosing between theories, even if only one were available at a time, or if one were by common consent superior to its competitors (which is decidedly not the case at present), there would still be room for questioning the point in having a moral theory at all. A theory, in its traditional and oldest sense, is an outcome of contemplation of some world or independently existing reality, a way of representing what it is, how it works, how its various different parts are connected, how its different aspects hang together. The paradigm object of contemplation in traditional theory was God, and derivatively the world seen as the creation of God, an expression of the divine nature. In that nature different attributes flowed or emanated from a center, a point of unification. It is quite understandable that the idea of a scientific system, in which different laws hang together in interdependence, with less fundamental laws hierarchically dependent on higher laws, was the natural model for those who contemplated the universe as heirs or successors to those who saw it as the expression of its creator's nature, a world in which there was the maximum of order along with the greatest plenitude or variety of manifestations of that order. This theological paradigm of *theoria* has some plausibility where the task is to understand an already existent reality, a system of nature; to predict its new manifestations; to codify its features in a succinct, coherent way; to concentrate its essence into a basic formula or name, or secular version of Yahweh, that which is what it is. But normative moral "theory" does not describe an existent world; at best it guides the conduct of one species of living things within that world, a species a little prone to hubris and mega-lomania, to treating their own guidelines as world blueprints, to confusing the attempted articulation of their taboos with the description of a contemplated world.

Some moralists *have* sketched Utopias, written as if they have contemplated an ideal society which they then describe for us—its laws, its unifying structure, its unity in variety. But Plato's *Republic*, or More's *Utopia*, or Rawls' well-ordered, just society with full compliance, do not guide us in the actual world. The real moral guidance comes when we are told not how the law of an ideal community would apply to a concrete case in that ideal world, but when we are told what we should therefore do, in this nonideal world. The description or contemplation of an imagined utopia is an escape from, not a solution to, the problems of this world.

Actual moral traditions—the Christian, the Buddhist, or the Bantu ethos—for all their limitations, do address directly the question of what to do now, and do not retreat into accounts of what one should do in hypothetical conditions such as just institutions or full compliance by others to ideal moral constraints. Indeed Christian attempts to describe heaven, a world in which there are only conformist saints, typically yield very thin accounts, and do not get much beyond talk of singing in harmony. Full compliance by one's fellows may transform morality into music, rather than inform us what is basic to morality. Detailed advice for here and now may imply nothing about what a heaven would be like, and descriptions of ideal societies imply nothing about how to act in this society. Even if one derives the vague injunction to act so as to change the actual society in the direction of the ideal one, one is still left with all the hard questions concerning how one is to do it—by revolution, by gradual qualitative improvement, by making things so intolerable that everyone will opt for drastic change? Is one to sacrifice only oneself for one's cause, or drag others with one? Is one to lie, cheat, and kill so that there can be a society without liars, cheats, or killers? Knowing what sort of society a utilitarian or a contractarian would deem satisfactory tells us nothing about our or their duty now, in this society. Richard Brandt takes the brave but implausible Kantian line that "in a situation like the present in which the 'ideal' moral code is not accepted . . . a person is nevertheless morally obligated to do what would be required by the rules of a rationally supported code for his society."[1] But John Rawls, and most others, suppose that there is no simple step from knowing what would be right in some ideal world to knowing what should be done here and now. For Rawls one must know that one's society, although not perfect, is well ordered in its basic institutional structure before his principles of justice can guide behavior within it.[2] But although Rawls believes that this society is thus well ordered, many do not, and I wonder whether the most basic structure of our society, that governing relations between parents and between parents and children can be well ordered by principles of justice, when a theorist like Rawls can so uncritically suppose that a family has a "head"

---

[1]Richard B. Brandt, *A Theory of the Good and the Right*, (Oxford: Clarendon Press, 1979), p. 304. In the preceding discussion, Brandt had made clear how the constraints on the content of what one believes to be the moral code rule out *self-serving* private codes, and require that the code address real world conditions. One must believe that general obedience to it will be better than any alternative general policy. But these more or less Kantian constraints do not, as far as I can see, ensure any coordination between different private versions of what would be best for all. The road to chaos may be paved with conscientious obedience by different moral agents to their different versions of the best scheme of coordination.

[2]See John Rawls, *A Theory of Justice*, (Cambridge, Mass.: Harvard University Press, 1971), secs. 1, 39, 53, for his concept of a well-ordered society and for his distinction between ideal theory, assuming strict compliance, and nonideal and partial compliance theory. In his discussion of civil disobedience, as in many parts of his discussion of political and economic arrangements, Rawls assumes not only "that the context is one of a state of near justice, that is, one in which the basic structure of society is nearly just" (p. 351) but also assumes in effect that the contemporary United States provides such a context. In his Dewey lectures Rawls makes it even clearer that his theory is intended as "focused on the apparent conflict between freedom and equality in a democratic society. . . . We look to ourselves and our future and reflect upon our disputes since, let's say, the Declaration of Independence." (*Journal of Philosophy* 77, no. 9 [1980]: 518.) The conception of justice Rawls develops is intended to articulate a standard of criticism of institutions shared within this democratic tradition. The Dewey lectures also make clearer Rawls' conception of a well-ordered society (ibid., pp. 521–22). What does not become clear, to me at least, is what relation Rawls sees between the moral task of criticizing or evaluating institutions and the moral task of changing them. His principles are designed primarily to assist one in the evaluative task, but the discussion of civil disobedience suggests that he sees the same principles as capable of directing response to imperfect institutions.

who can articulate its interests.[3] I mention Rawls and Brandt at this point as typical moral theorists, although their approaches are very different, and I find much to admire and accept in Rawls' theory, especially in his account of the sense of justice, and of social union and the unity of good. My criticisms of Rawls concern mainly the first two parts of his *A Theory of Justice,* the codification of the principles of justice by working out the content of a hypothetical agreement between hypothetical beings in unreal circumstances.

My complaints about Brandt's theory are different—he has actual people in real conditions, and has them formulating moral codes that take account of the likelihood of compliance and the cost of having codes at all. Some of the criticisms of the codification business that I shall make do not apply to Brandt, since he keeps his eye on the real world in selecting his code. But the general criticism I am making, that philosophers' codifications of the moral law increase rather than decrease moral disagreement and conflict, does apply to Brandt. Although a moral code has as its supposed *point* the coordination and fair adjustment of different persons' concerns, Brandt advocates that each person form an ideal code for the real conditions and act on that, regardless of the lack of coordination and unpredictability and unreliability which would result. One may know the chosen moral codes of those closest to one, and so allow for their idiosyncracies in dealings with such persons, but I cannot possibly know where I am with the mailman, the shopkeeper, the bus driver, or my new employer, if each has her own operative code. To avoid the conflict of a state of nature, moral theorists in effect give us the basis for a recurrence of the war of all against all within

----

[3]Rawls, in assuming that every family has a head, in effect assumes that either patriarchy or matriarchy is just, or that there is some just procedure by which each monogamous family can appoint a head. See *A Theory of Justice,* p. 7, for inclusion of the monogamous family among the major institutions comprising the basic structure of society, and p. 128f. and p. 289f. for use of the concept of the head of a family. Rawls also speaks of parties in the original position as "representatives of family lines" (p. 128) and so one might generously interpret Rawls' "head of a family" as any representative of its interests, so that one monogamous family at one time might have several heads (namely all its currently adult members). There would still be a problem in making the arbiters of the justice of family relationships be representatives of the interests of families *qua* families.

society, when each person has her own version of the rules by which
the fight is conducted. A battle of rival umpires and adjudicators
replaces the Hobbesian state of nature. Even if the battle is now
more civilized, because within legal bounds, it is just as futile. With
or without hypothetical contracts and imagined full compliance,
such ideal codes, if produced by single persons or even single heads
of families, will decrease, not increase, coordination between persons. The search for an ideal fair mode of cooperation and coordination, if pursued by independent thinkers, can make cooperation
more difficult and unlikely, and can decrease the level of that minimal fairness which consists in having fair warning of what response
another will make. Brandt gives as an example of unilateral compliance to an ideal moral code, the keeping of a promise in circumstances of such difficulty that conventional morality would have
excused nonobservance.[4] But this is to cheat a bit. Suppose it went
the other way, as with a utilitarian it is more likely to—suppose that
the ideal code observer feels morally free to break promises in a
wider range of circumstances than do I, to whom the promise was
made. Must I ask each person to recite his particular moral code
before ever relying on him? It would be simpler never to accept a
promise or an agreement, but to insist on a contract, where the
small print and the law of contract ensure *standard* conditions of
validity. If everyone has his own moral code for dealings with others, soon no one will have any morality, all will rely entirely upon
the criminal law and the law of contract and torts. Private moral
codes, like private languages and private legal systems, fail the first
principle of practical reason, that she who wills the end should not
will the means that destroy that end.

Most moral theorists who outline and defend norms which are
valid in conditions of full compliance, which can be willed to be
universally followed in some system of moral nature, give some
recognition to the need for supplementary accounts of what norms
hold good in more realistic conditions, and give some promissory
notes about working back from the world they have presented in
their theory to the actual world. Maybe such promises can be kept,
but only when they have been kept will we know just how much
guidance the full-compliance world provided in the journey away
from it, back to the actual situation in which we act. Suppose we

---

[4]Brandt, *Theory of the Good and the Right,* p. 305.

imagine a simplified ideal world in which there is full compliance to the norm of not inflicting bodily injury on others, and so there is no question of compliance to norms concerning responses to injurers or their victims, since by hypothesis there are none. This world represents (by depicting ideal compliance to) one norm we might think is valid (with qualifications) in this world. But this world cannot *similarly* (that is, by full compliance) represent any norms concerning the punishment of offenders or aid to their victims, or other responses to noncompliance to this one norm. For that we must add additional worlds to the world of the noninjurers—the world of the perfect punishers, the world of the good Samaritans, or the world in which aggression and malice and other drives to injure others are "treated" in some way, in which there are norms for the rehabilitation or reforming of the injurers, or for seeing to it that the next generation has such drives diverted into harmless channels. Are we any closer to this world, or to representing all the injury-related norms valid in it? We have represented no norm telling us how to respond to the presence of bad punishers or bad Samaritans, or unsuccessful reformers of aggression, no norm telling us what to do in situations of imperfect compliance to what we could call the responsive norms. So we can imagine another world in which all the norms so far represented by perfect compliance in one of our earlier worlds are now imperfectly complied with, but this time we represent some norm concerning response to faulty *responsive* action, to the presence of corrupt police, unjust judges, brutal prison officials, bad Samaritans, ineffective psychiatrists, poor parents. This norm might be one demanding a corrective response to these evils, or one permitting conscientious disobedience to all bad authorities, or demanding acceptance and forgiveness. We add the Platonic world of perfect responders to imperfect responders to the worlds we already had. In principle, we could continue indefinitely. But would we by this procedure be representing norms accepted in this world? Do we have a moral norm specifically covering responses, individual or collective, to those who are, say, unforgiving to bad Samaritans? Do we have a moral norm dealing specifically with hypocritical conscientious disobedience? Our hierarchy of possible worlds quite quickly loses contact with the norms it was to represent. It might represent legal norms, which, because of their deliberate formulation and making, are likely to have a structure that "fits" the sort of structure which modal logicians, moral theorizers, and intellectuals generally find graspable and eminently representable. In the case of legal norms (leaving common law aside), representation and promulgation must accompany the demand for conformity, so human tastes in representation do dictate the structure of the law. A significant fact about moral conscience is that its deliverances need not come in verbal form, that it is often a difficult task to articulate what it is we are certain is wrong in an action, let alone what universal rule we think it breaks. In moral philosophy courses we insist that students make their moral intuitions articulate, that they represent them and "defend" them by subsuming them under some universal rule that coheres in some system, and we make them feel that they must have been muddled if their moral intuitions are inarticulate or resist tidy codifications. But it may be we the intellectualizers who are muddled, not those whose consciences we insist on tidying up. It is as if we are claiming that if you can't wear your heart on your sleeve then you haven't really got a heart (or perhaps that *all* you have is a heart, unaccompanied by a mind). In law it makes eminent sense to insist that, unless it is verbally represented and promulgated, it is no law. But it also makes good sense to have courts of equity to deal with grievances that cannot be represented as breaches of law. There is no reason to believe that actual moralities mimic legal systems in the way they control or regulate action, and it is only a dogma that we would improve actual moralities by making them mimic legal systems.

Moral theorizers usually appeal to clear moral intuitions as confirmers of their theory, which is presented as a systematization of and endorsement of such intuitions, and as a way of deciding cases in which no clear intuition was forthcoming, a way of inducing intuitions in a wider range of areas. I do not want to assert dogmatically that this cannot be done, merely to challenge the assumption that it must be possible, and that any person whose moral intuitions are not so systematized, and may not even be coherently stable in the theorist's preferred terminology, has an inferior moral capacity. That theorizers appeal to intuitions at all is a sign that they do recognize some pretheoretical faculty, call it conscience, as a touchstone for their theory, that with which it must maintain "reflective equilibrium," but such a conscience is expected to deliver its judgments in the right form of words, in some ready-made representation. If all moral training took a verbal form (as some, surely, must), it might be reasonable to expect that anyone who finds some action wrong must be able to say "It's a lie," "It's cheating," or "It's stealing," since in learning to avoid such behavior, that person learned to avoid precisely the behavior which would count as "lying," "cheating," "stealing." Some moral training is of this form, but surely some is not. A parent has not failed to give a child some sense of right and wrong simply because neither parent nor child can tell us what rules the child has been taught to obey, nor even which virtues the child has been encouraged to cultivate.

This lengthy insistence of mine on the dogmatic character of the assumption that a genuine morality must be codifiable, and in particular the assumption that it will, like a Kantian world or a legal system, be codifiable in terms of general rules, with hierarchies of the sort we can design and tidily represent, was prompted by my parody version of what happens when we try to represent moral demands by imagining worlds in which there is strict compliance to them. We can get an ordered series of worlds if norms are classifiable into different levels, with the higher levels containing norms for response to noncompliance to lower-level norms. The order we get, however, is not an order of approximation to this world, since here the likelihood of immoral officials seems if anything higher than the likelihood of immoral nonofficials. All these strict-compliance worlds are about equally far from this world, and it is dubious if the norms represented really are our moral norms. I suggested earlier that they might be expected to represent legal norms, but even there one would need to complicate the picture a lot to get the full variety of ways in which one law may be a response to some imperfection in another law's operation. We have laws not only for dealing with noncompliance, but for dealing with uncertainty, conflict, and immorality in laws, regulating our response to needless laws, to the need for some law in a new area, to faulty administrative machinery or procedures, to corrupt officials. In each of these dimensions of imperfection we can in principle go, as before, to higher and higher levels—responses to uncertain laws about the removal of uncertainties and other imperfections, responses to conflict in the laws concerning the settlement of conflict and concerning other imperfections, and so on. Whether we actually need to go to such higher levels to represent our own legal norms is not so clear. We may soon reach a ceiling, a supreme court or ombudsman whose job it is to respond to all imperfections, including imperfect supreme courts or complaints about the ombudsman. Actual rules don't exhibit as many levels as logicians' possibilities—because, as Hume said, the normal human mind soon loses track. We need a legal order in which at least some of us can understand our way around.

Do all these dimensions of imperfection diverge from one perfect world, that in which there is full compliance to needed, clear, nonconflicting, perfectly administered, morally acceptable rules, none of which need regulate our response to noncompliance, to uncertainty, to conflict of laws, to imperfect administrative machinery, to immoral or unnecessary laws? To say "yes" is, I believe, to express faith in the unity of justice. If that faith is reasonable, one might get insight into the structure of a legal order by contemplating a possible world, ideal in respect to compliance, definiteness, coherence, etc., and moving out from there in different directions to consider all possible deteriorations from this, in all the listed respects. One might even find a sketch of the actual world among those possibilities, so find a path from it to the "ideal" world. To call that world one with an ideal legal order, however, would be very strange, since it seems to have no legal order at all, if it has and needs no police, no courts, no appeal and adjudication procedures. To *add* idle police, judges, etc., to the perfect world is to destroy its perfection by adding wasteful public expense. If in that world there is no noncompliance, any norms specifying the duties of these needless officials will be unnecessary and so bad norms. The perfect world cannot contain them, any more than a perfect moral code contains rules whose inculcation is an unnecessary cost. Every accepted prohibition has its cost, either in frustration or in guilt, and in their unlovely offspring.

Here it might be objected that imagining full compliance to a contemplated norm is a preliminary test of the *fairness* of that norm, not the final test deciding its adoption. It will not matter, then, that we cannot imagine simultaneously full compliance to two fair norms, one forbidding assault, another specifying proper punishment of assaulters. But to imagine full compliance to any rule we must imagine *some* background conditions, or we have nothing dense enough to count as a world. Kant's test, which is a simultaneous test for fairness and for adoption, is "Can I will this as a universal law in a system of nature?" or "Can I will this as a member of a kingdom of ends?" I must, to use this test, fill in the other laws with which this one coheres, I must imagine a *system* of laws. What can be willed in isolation from the other things that are willed is not yet morally tested, for fairness or for any other virtue.

Whatever we say about imagining "perfect" worlds as a way of clarifying or representing the structure of a legal code, I think that this sort of hierarchy of possible worlds, even a complex hierarchy, cannot be used to represent the content of morality as understood by ordinary people. This is not simply for the reason already given, that in morality, unlike law, the representation of a norm may lag behind the recognition of its force. It is also because of a feature of moral demands once we do get them verbally formulated. This is that, in terms of the above notion of nonresponsive and responsive norms, all moral norms are responsive, yet they can be given no determinate place in a hierarchy of the sort sketched, since they refer back to no zero-level demands. I shall try to explain and substantiate this claim.

We do not in fact endorse a moral demand of the absolute form "Do not injure others," or "Do not kill." We accept killing and injuring of, for example, all animals when and if it suits our purposes, culinary, recreational, commercial, or whatever. So is it "Don't kill or injure other humans"? Not that either, since self-defense, war, judicial punishment, abortion, dumping nuclear wastes, making dangerous cars, allowing too many at too high speeds on the roads, and so on, are all accepted. We may need, as has often been suggested, to revise the formulation of these rules to "Do not kill or injure the innocent." But "innocence" is a norm-referring concept, and it may seem at this point that a norm like this one does indeed resolve itself into "Do not kill, unless x, y, z," where x, y, and z specify various ways in which the one we are licensed to kill has forfeited the right not to be killed—by being himself a killer, or being knowingly engaged in a high-death risk occupation, like war, or driving, or just living in an industrialized nation, or in an overpopulated world. We soon see that, in addition to specifying the forfeiters (not all of whom have broken this rule or any other we can cite), we must add some clause of the vague form "or unless you can't help killing them," where "can't help" never means literally can't help, but "can't help except at unreasonable cost." The "innocent" who are protected by this rule turn out to be a dwindling group, those whom we choose to save, just as "Don't eat people" can be accepted by cannibals, who protest that they eat only their enemies, who are not real people, not *fellow-persons*.

Is every rule about killing or eating of flesh then empty? Certainly the statute forbidding murder is not empty—in the law we make quite precise what the exception clauses are, and give unequivocal licenses to kill to certain classes of people (soldiers, executioners, hunters, sometimes doctors). They are licensed to kill only specific classes of living things, or of human living things. The legal rule against murder is a rule against unauthorized or unlicensed killing, but the constraints on the recognition or issuing of licenses are fairly weak.

When we wish to express moral outrage at the licenses tacitly given to, say, dumpers of poison in places whence it will get into human food, or into the air we breathe, we want to use words like *murder* to describe what the poisoners are doing, knowing quite well that it is not murder in the legal sense, since we know that the poisoners of our wells may have broken no law. We want a new law, revoking their license to kill or cause death. But what was their license? Only a tacit one, that they were merely going about their legitimate business. But now it looks as if all businesses, however predictably death-dealing, are licensed or legitimate unless explicitly forbidden, so we seem to come full legal circle. Can we both have a rule of the form "Don't kill unless authorized to do so" and another rule that says "Everything is authorized unless it is specifically prohibited"? If legal norms have this circular character, this provides further reason for claiming that the parody hierarchy of possible worlds sketched earlier does not represent *their* content any more than it does the content of morality. Neither morality nor the law are properly seen as comprised of straightforward zero-level directives, supplemented by fallback responses to noncompliance to these basic ones.

Whatever the complexity of the legal norm concerning murder, it does rule some action out, and *moral* attitudes to killing can take the form of a demand that more cases get counted as manslaughter or murder. What other form is taken by our moral attitudes to killing—do they take the form of definite prohibitions? When we morally condemn some actions of others as murderous, as showing a disregard for human life or for other animal life, we criticize the way such persons conduct themselves in a situation in which, given the press of human and other animal populations, and the strain on the resources, material and emotional, that living things need, the mere existence of another living thing is a sort of evil for every other—a threat to the size of my share of food, power, prestige, or other goods. Given the sometimes unavoidable competition for scarce resources, any response to another living thing is a response to what is, among its other aspects, a threat in this extended sense to oneself. Morality controls our responses in this situation of vulnerability and danger, staving off the outright barbarity of the unregulated way of all against all. Our moral feelings concerning when we may destroy other living things vary from one moral tradition to another, and are all controls of some sort on our response to the evil of a precarious life in conditions of scarcity.

Those who justify abortion by treating the human fetus as an attacker on the mother's resources, as an enemy within, could perhaps try treating the original offense as the offense of being alive at all. The zero-level rule would be "Don't come into existence," and all other rules could be treated as rules responding to offenders. Maybe the original sin is existence, and all morality is for sinners? This seems to me self-evidently absurd. The fact that overpopulation is a problem, and that even in conditions of underpopulation there may be competition and scarcity, does not make being alive something that is an initial count against one, an offense against others. For to cope with scarcity, vulnerability, and powerlessness, we need the cooperation and help of the very ones who also pose the threat. The good and hopeful aspects of our condition, as much as the evils, stem from the fact of interdependence. Moral feelings control by positively reinforcing our responses to the good of cooperation, trust, mutual aid, friendship, love, as well as regulating responses to the risk of evil.

"'Tis impossible to separate the good from the ill."[5] I think that this is as true of the conditions giving Hume's natural virtues their rationale as it is true of the conditions brought into existence by what he called the "artificial" virtues, namely conformity to the constitutive rules of well-functioning human institutions. A natural virtue like "gentleness" is a controlled response to conditions in which the good of cooperation and trust is inseparable from the evil of vulnerability and competition, since the ones we must work with

---

[5]David Hume, *A Treatise of Human Nature,* ed. L. A. Selby-Bigge and P. H. Nidditch (Oxford: Clarendon Press, 1978), p. 497.

are the ones who may, sometimes, through no fault of theirs, prove our enemies. We have to love our possible enemies, if we are to love anyone. The gentle person is, as Aristotle's analysis of virtues showed us, between two extremes. He is neither the coldhearted, self-defensive one, nor the willing slave, all loving service to others. Gentleness is a willingness to take a risk of exploitation and betrayal of trust, but not of course when it is more than a risk, but a certainty. It is a standing response to standing conditions of life in which the chance of good cannot be separated from the risk of evil. The gentle person is not gentle only to those known to be also gentle, or known to be trustworthy, but is gentle to all unless known to be violent. Some, such as Christians, may encourage us to behave to a person as if he were cooperating in the attempt to keep violence at bay, even when we are quite certain that he is guilty of, or intent upon, violence towards us, that is, to turn the other cheek and love our *declared* enemies. One question that a study of evolution, anthropology, and history as adjuncts to moral philosophy would force us to consider is that of what happens when a Christian community encounters one with less self-sacrificial norms, of what way of life succeeds in getting passed on to descendents when it competes with a more violent way of life. The study of history might tell us something about the survival value, for a community, of different sorts of norms. It isn't an *a priori* truth, indeed it seems not a truth at all, that the less violent go under, when we look at the moral community rather than at its individual members. Christianity made as great or greater advances when, in its early years, it was the way of life of a persecuted and apparently powerless group than when kings went to war for it, when it absorbed the martial virtues into its list, when it imitated its enemies. It may be, of course, that the way of living which keeps a community going in some conditions will not do so a century later, or that the only way of living which can continue is one we would, from within our own moral tradition, find abhorrent and immoral. But it is an important fact about any moral beliefs which anyone has acquired from parents that they have passed at least a minimal test for viability—they are two generations old. That is more than can be said for many philosophers' moral theories, which are entirely untested as respects their transferability to new members of a community at the age when such learning is still possible, the age of innocence, early childhood. Whatever else an acceptable morality must be, it must be in some sense "teachable" to young children, and understandable by nonintellectuals. Understanding is not the ability to verbalize, let alone to systematize, any more than acceptance of a morality is lip service to its slogans.

A moral virtue like gentleness seems to resist analysis into rules. We might try a rule of the form "Act towards others in a friendly and nonhurtful way, unless they are known offenders against this rule," or, for the Christian rule, "Act towards others in a friendly and nonhurtful way, even if they are known offenders against this rule." But what typifies the gentleperson is that they do not approach another intent first on getting clear whether they are or are not offenders against this or any other rule, insisting on seeing the other's moral credentials, even if willing to give them the benefit of any doubts. To frame a rule which explicitly either excludes or includes offenders seems to contradict the virtue which lies in acceptance of others as fellows, not in passing judgment on them. It is a response to others in conditions of risk, risk that the other may exploit that friendly response, but part of the friendly response is nonsuspiciousness, an avoidance of spelling out the risk, of seeing the other person as one who might return evil for good. The gentleperson acts as if there is no risk of return violence when there is such a risk. But that cannot be quite right either, if gentleness is a virtue, an *appropriate* response to others. Or is it that the appropriate response to those who do pose some risk to us, as everyone does, is to act as if they didn't? Are virtues ways of shutting one's eyes to danger, seeing the good not the bad prospects? Maybe they are. And certainly they seem to involve one another—a gentleperson whose gentleness is a virtue must also be patient and must have some courage and some pride, some sense of herself as a person the other would properly hesitate to insult or exploit.

I insisted earlier that we should not assume that moral norms can be easily represented in the forms of representation that have developed in the making and administering of written law, nor in the scientific description of a world assumed to be orderly and law-governed. Norms in the form of virtues may be very difficult to formulate, while being not so difficult to recognize and encourage. It is not part of my purpose here to attempt to formulate the content of any one virtue nor to show the virtues to be a system, on some possibly new paradigm of "system." I want merely to contrast some features we do seem to find with those more easily represented features to which normative theorists seem attracted. Norms in the form of virtues may be essentially imprecise in some crucial ways, may be mutually referential but not hierarchically orderable, may be essentially self-referential. But then again all these categories may be unhelpful ones to apply to such norms. I think we still need to learn how best to reflect on morality.

If we see morality essentially as control of our natural responses to the mixed risk of evil and chance of good inherent in our interdependent situation, we can see moral response, in the form of training, criticism, and so on, as a response to a natural response, and we can see the evils and goods which come from morally disapproved and approved action as themselves the offspring of those evils and goods, responses which morality controls. Suppose that what a child naturally fears includes withdrawal of trust and love from a person on whom he depends, for example, from a mother. Trust and love are natural goods, suspicion and hostility natural evils. Once moral training enters the picture, the child may be encouraged to become more confident of parental love in some conditions, more certain of a partial withdrawal of manifestations of love in others. The conditions will be determined by the parents' reactions to *other* fears and hopes the child has—his hope to take what he wants from his brothers, his fear that they will treat him similarly. The child's various natural hopes and fears are played off against one another, so that some become faint hopes, others confident expectations. The goods originally sought were love, food, and playthings. But the reaction to that search makes him also seek and hope for parental approval, and eventually he may have to choose between the approval of parents and the approval of his siblings and peers. Approval is not simply a means to more secure possession of love, food, and playthings, it becomes a good in its own right, and eventually he may be willing to risk his lower-level possessions to get it—he loses parental love and home comforts, for instance, by some daring exploit that gets him the approval of his gang. When any conflict develops within the group he now looks to for recognition, or when he confronts many rival sources of wanted approval, he may come to some choice among them, or possibly to renunciation of all of them, a response to the high risk of offending someone he would like to please, whatever he does. He develops loyalty to a cause, a party, a set of principles, a way of life. At this point he seeks a nonarbitrary way to either select among or reconcile the many possible claims on him, to make his choice seem nonarbitrary, as uniquely "selected" as the parents he initially looked to for love. He now secures one source of approval and if necessary sacrifices the rest—he moves from needing general popularity to needing general respect, just as earlier he moved from needing parental love to needing popularity. Respect too has its potential for conflict and it can be reflected upon, turned on itself to produce some more reflective response to a new risk, but most moral theory seems to have been produced by those at this respect-needing point in their moral development—they have elaborated and defended the cause which they have made their own, without much concern about the process by which that occurred (Rawls is an exception). They have rationalized and intellectualized their response to a common human predicament, that of reconciling, compromising, or selecting among the various conflicting disapprovers who function as forces in our lives. At each stage some possible response from others, be it withdrawal of love, of peer-recognition, or of respect, serves as a threat to train us to behave in certain ways, to cultivate certain virtues, certain habits and attitudes, as the hope of the opposite response, love, acceptance or popularity, respect, encourages those virtues. To the extent that we are loved, accepted, respected, we win some of the sweets of cooperation, and we also risk the evils of abandonment, betrayal, injustice. We begin wanting merely what one could call the first derivatives of the mother's breast—love, food, playthings, but we go on to want approval, justice, respect, and allegiance, all the higher derivatives.

I have sketched an *individual* development that in its own way is as oversimplified, overintellectualized, and hierarchical as the parody systems of norms I sketched earlier, and it owes much to Rawls. Because I looked only at the individual's response, not at the collective response of his family, his gang, his party, or his nation, I have distorted the picture. We would need to supplement the sequence of responses I have just sketched with one that begins from the parent's point of view, not the child's; proceeds to a reflection on parental influence, on school influence, on gang influence, on patriotism, on political parties; and then recall that at each point the two processes intersect. The parent has known what it is to be a child, and the child can, to some extent, see the parents' point of view; moreover, the child responds not only to parents but also to those forces which come about by reflection on and correction of parental guidance—to welfare officials, to schools, to television, and so on—at each point with a partial ability to see the rationale for whatever pressures are being put upon him. He anticipates his adult role as the adult recalls and still half-understands the child's outlook.

Moral development is at least as complex as psychologists who have studied it have claimed, but no *a priori* hierarchy captures its complexities nor represents all its possibilities. The sketch I have given is intended merely to show how new "moral" goods grow out of natural goods, not to display all possible moral goods nor to show the only possible form of moral growth. What form that takes in an individual person depends in part on the direction social reflective growth has taken, on whether the child grows up in a kibbutz or in a one-family home; in the care of parents, grandparents, or nurses; if in the care of parents on whether one or both are working outside the home, and, if both are working, on what sort of day-care facilities they have available, and so on. The direction taken by the social reflective development, as revealed in the history of childcare, schools, child psychiatry, juvenile courts and crime procedures, political and legal institutions, will in turn depend upon the sorts of persons who are designing and operating these, on whether one's schoolteacher is, say, a Marxist, or a born-again Christian, or a Kantian respecter of persons.

What I have tried to make persuasive is the suggestion that morality begins in a response to a natural response to a situation in which hope and fear are properly inspired by one and the same situation. Morality is a proliferating succession of responses, individual and collective, to those primitive responses to the risky adventure of interdependence. Morality then becomes a bootstrap operation. It starts from natural responses to aspects of our relations to others, aspects that are naturally feared or welcomed. These responses all involve risk and uncertainty; and moral training and criticism respond in ways which, if effective, decrease risk of evils of a variety of related sorts, and increase the chances of a family of goods but always at the cost of new risk. Morality is throughout responsive to already given responses, and its norms are reflective versions of natural responses to the risks and opportunities interdependence involves. If we see morality this way, I think we can keep that *critical* element which most normative theorists want to stress without making the critical morality one that cannot make constructive critical responses to the real situation. The role of morality as a criticizer of the real grows out of its more primitive role as a corrector of natural response. But instead of taking one possible higher form of correction, which occurs when we try to codify and justify our sense of right and wrong, and looking at its less intellectual ancestors as mere psychological preconditions of morality, on the approach I favor (which I take to be Aristotle's), we see that intellectualized version as merely *one* of the possible developments of a process of reflective conflict-resolving corrections of responses to ever-widening yet ever more discriminating sources of recognition and acceptance.

Correction always has some costs, but the correction of impulses and motives by the formative influences of parental encouragement and discouragement is, as Plato knew, far less costly than adult correction, and is so even when the psychological costs Freud explored are taken into account. Freud of course saw the costs of childhood acquisition of a set of deontological prohibitions, not of a set of Platonic, Aristotelian, or Humean virtues. As regulators of human tendencies, virtues may have less ugly psychic costs than those of a moral law which has to be burned in, and which tends to provoke return aggression, or more slowly working poisons.

What I have attacked is one way of doing moral philosophy, namely the articulation of a system of moral laws, vaguely anchored to intuitions about particular cases, laws that the theorist presents as valid or acceptable in conditions of strict compliance, hoping eventually to work back, from there, to the actual conditions (which, after all, generated the intuitions). I have charged that the variety of moral theories, and the absence of agreed criteria for choosing between them, make them all look like arbitrary constructions, and that in any case they are utopian constructions, since there is no point in our knowing what would be fair or what we should do provided everyone did likewise, when, whatever conditions we are in, we can be pretty sure that everyone is not doing likewise. Even as a way of representing a norm and of testing its coherence with others, imagining worlds with full compliance is, I claimed, useful only if the norms have a clear hierarchy that actual moral norms may lack, and only if we assume that the only good moral norms are the precise and definite ones.

Does this mean that we should live by our inherited fuzzy moral intuitions and do no moral philosophy at all? Only if there is no way to think about our morality except by attempting to contemplate a better world with its perfect moral system. There surely are other ways, and many great moral philosophers—Plato in *Meno*, Aristotle, Spinoza, Butler, Hume, Hegel, Nietzsche, Dewey—have shown us these ways. We can try to reflect on the actual phenomenon of morality, to see what it is, how it is transmitted, what difference it makes. We *may*, as a result of the resulting consciousness of what morality is, think we can make some improvements in it; however, these will come not from surveying abstract possibilities, but from seeing how, given the way it is, it can, by some move we can now make, improve itself, work better, correct its faults. Only when we think we know *what* it is, how it is now working, what it is doing, will we be in any position to see how it might really change, let alone know if that change would be for the better. I think we philosophers need to work with anthropologists, sociologists, sociobiologists, psychologists, to find out what an actual morality is; we need to read history to find out how it has changed itself, to read novels to see how it might change again. To feel any proper confidence that a possible change, a really possible change, a takeable step from here, is an improvement, we need of course not only to understand what it is that is changing, but to have some sense of direction, of where we are heading. We do not need a fully detailed vision of the perfect society to have that sense, and a sketchy vision may misdirect us. We need some sort of moral compass, but a compass that points to true north gives us neither a full nor a sketchy picture of the North Pole. A moral compass to guide us, not only in our individual actions but in our institutional or educational reforms and innovations, is not something we are likely to think up in an armchair, but something that will itself evolve by the testing of generations of people. The most we philosophers will do will be to see ways of tinkering with existing moral compasses, not ways of inventing them *ex nihilo*.

I suggested earlier that ordinary moral attitudes are learned responses to other people who present both a hope and a threat of destroying it, both a threat and a hope for averting it. Moral attitudes are corrections of spontaneous human responses of trust and love, fear and hostility, corrections encouraging some responses, altering others. If morality is, in its least sophisticated form, such an inherently responsive thing, a response to natural responses, then there is inbuilt into it a potential for self-correction, for including moral approval and disapproval, respect and contempt, among its own targets, without any discontinuity. The compass for moral change may be merely a natural development of the compass for morally acceptable action. Hume believed that all of morality was a matter of what he called reflection, turning natural responses, not just on their natural target, but on responses, turning self-interest on the workings of self-interest, turning sentiments on sentiments. Ordinary parental training, the source of all operative moral attitudes, is such a turning of responsive sentiment on the child's responses and expressed feelings. To extend moral reflectiveness we develop responses to such things as parental influence, responses that grow out of their own targets. Hume believed, perhaps overoptimistically, that increasing the inherent reflectiveness of moral responses would *not* lead to a wholesale rejection of moral control; but it is always a possibility not just that bourgeois morality, but morality as such, contains the seeds of its own destruction. The moral sentiment, just as much as that "reasoning" about morals which Hume tried unsuccessfully to dethrone, may subvert itself when it examines itself. I think we do not yet know whether that is so, because we have been so fixated on the *kind* of thinking about morality which Hume condemned as rationalistic and idle, but which Kant successfully revived, building in our heads systems of ideal moral laws or ideal institutions, that we do not yet know much about the direction in which the other sort of moral thoughtfulness would take us. We know that it can take a Marxist form. What Hume describes as the workings of moral sentiment is essentially a dialectical process. It might take other than Marxist forms, if we explored its possibilities. We need not believe that the real is the good or even the best, merely that actual moral processes are the place to start if we wish to determine the better. The utopian blueprint without any method of implementation is morally irrelevant, the utopian blueprint with no regulation of the method of implementation is a renunciation of morality. The unreal, the utopian vision, is at best morally irrelevant, at worst morally destructive.

What does this mean for courses in medical or business ethics? If they are not to be "applications" of Kantian "theories," systems of laws, what can they be? What some of them already are: attempts to understand the roles of doctor, patient, relative, advisory boards, to see what changes have evolved in those roles; what regulations or other controls have come into being and what difference they have made; what grievances are felt by whom, in the process as it is. If you want to call this sort of thing the application of a "theory" *about* morality to our procedures in health care, you are within your verbal rights these days when anything any professional thinker puts on paper tends to get labeled a theory. But it is not a normative theory in the Kantian sense, it is merely a framework for description and attempted understanding. If it links with any theory proper, it is with evolutionary theory, a theory of the costs and benefits of different forms of life, over many generations.

Since in business ethics and medical ethics we are dealing with institutions, where there are legal rights and powers and responsibilities attached to the various roles of, say, producer, entrepreneur, customer, consumer, courses in these fields will study the actual functioning of the recognition of these rights and powers, so will have a place for *essentially representable* moral and legal concepts. But they could also have a place for a study of the virtues of honesty and integrity, humanity and mercy. Beyond the rights, powers, duties, and responsibilities lie the convictions, sometimes inarticulate, of those who created those artifices, or who accept a life structured by them, convictions about the sort of *persons* who should fill these and other roles our society offers, the sort of person the roles themselves should help nurture. Some history of health care or business practices in different societies would give us a sense of the functions and possibilities of these professions. This will not give us any algorithm for the difficult case, the hard decision. We cannot and should not ever promise that, and we should beware of those who try to sell us any ready reckoner or decision-making machine. But we might help the decision-makers anticipate the reactions they should expect from different decisions, see the grievances of different parties, see all the actual and perceived interests involved. We can also make them aware of the categories of assessment we have for decision-makers, ourselves, and others—categories like fairness, integrity, considerateness, humanity, vision—the potential development of those categories, and their link with less specialized moral categories, applicable to those merely following good habits or routines, not facing hard cases or new dilemmas.

I have merely sketched an approach in ethics, which has been taken by some of the greatest moral thinkers, which is realistic in starting with functioning moralities, and which tries to understand those moralities—to discover, not prescribe, what *sort* of coherence they have, what links the bits together. I have used Hume's term *reflection* for the sort of thinking which can pick up a feature I think we do find in our least intellectualized moral responses, and can continue to develop that feature, reflective response itself. Reflectiveness about our practices requires at the very least noting whether they are counterproductive to their expressed aims. Teaching comparative normative theory at the introductory level is thus self-defeating, cannot bear reflective survey. We do not yet know whether trying to continue the sort of moral philosophy Hume and others practiced, reflecting on actual moral practices, will or will not end by destroying the things it reflects on. Darwin, who had read his Hume,[6] uses the term *reflection* for the ability we human animals have which gives us that moral conscience which most importantly distinguishes us from other animals. If, for better or worse, we want a philosophy of morality, reflection, continued and turned on itself, can give us that too.

---

[6]Charles Darwin, *The Descent of Man,* pt. 1, ch. 4. In n. 25 of this chapter Darwin quotes Hume.

3

Theoretical and Applied Ethics: A Reply to the Skeptics*

Ruth Macklin

SKEPTICAL CHALLENGES

Skepticism remains in many quarters about the value of bioethics for resolving moral problems in medicine. That skepticism takes a number of different forms. One line of attack focuses on the role of ethical theory, pointing out the inadequacy of theories for providing solutions to practical ethical dilemmas. Another criticism focuses on philosophers and their methodology, arguing that to analyze a problem down to the minutest detail is no substitute for giving an answer.[1] Still another skeptical challenge asks why ethics is needed when laws and policies must be in place anyway to govern the behavior of doctors and hospitals and to protect the rights of patients.

The first two challenges can be cast in the form of skeptical claims about the relationship between ethical theory and applied ethics:

---

*This essay first appeared in slightly shorter form in *The Nature of Clinical Ethics,* ed. Barry Hoffmaster, Benjamin Friedman and Gwen Fraser (Clifton, N.J.: The Humana Press, 1988).

[1] This and other criticisms of applied ethics are made by Cheryl N. Noble, "Ethics and Experts," *Hastings Center Report,* xii, 3 (June 1982). Replies to Noble's article are given in the same issue by Peter Singer, "How Do We Decide?"; Jerry Avorn; Daniel Wikler, "Ethicists, Critics, and Expertise"; and Tom L. Beauchamp. Parenthetical page references in the text to Singer and Wikler, as well as to Noble, will be to this issue.

1. Ethical theories are not especially useful in resolving the issues in bioethics.

2. The philosopher is not especially qualified to deal with issues in applied ethics.

It would be folly to assert that the enterprise of applied ethics is entirely without problems. But these skeptical claims miss the mark, casting the net too wide in their attempt to discredit the roles that ethical theory and philosophers can play. The skeptic who doubts the usefulness of ethical theories for resolving practical issues raises a larger challenge to rational inquiry concerning values. If ethical theories are useless, is it not likely that all attempts at rational analysis and systematic resolution of moral problems are doomed?

The core of truth in the first skeptical claim is that no one— philosopher, practitioner, or decision maker in any situation—can resolve practical moral dilemmas by a simple process of taking an ethical theory, applying it directly to a case, and coming up with a single right answer. If the first skeptical claim amounts to nothing more than the rather obvious point that ethical theories do not enable philosophers or moral agents to crank out automatic answers to troubling moral problems, it would hardly deserve the effort required for a careful examination of the relationship between theoretical and applied ethics. As any beginning student knows, philosophy does not supply answers to multiple-choice questions. It cannot offer a "how-to" guide to ethical quandaries. As Mary Midgley notes, "One of the jobs of philosophy is to find and formulate the rules which underlie sense, the inarticulate patterns by which it works, and to try and deal with their conflicts. The art of doing this used to be called wisdom, but we have got too prissy to use such words today."[2]

Fifteen years ago, when I first entered the fledgling field of bioethics, I wondered whether I or my professional discipline could be of any use in helping to resolve practical problems facing doctors. Even today, when I am called for an ethics consultation or confronted with a case presented at a regular conference in the hospital, I have some lingering doubts about my ability to help.

---

[2]Mary Midgley, "Philosophizing Out in the World," *Social Research,* LII (Autumn 1985), p. 449.

Struggling within myself over how to resolve the dilemma of a disabled, alcoholic, homeless woman who lived in a subway station and made a public nuisance of herself and who resisted hospitalization despite the efforts of psychiatrists to have her committed to a psychiatric institution, I was unable to resolve the conflict between her right to liberty and her medical and social "best interest." Contemplating the case of a mentally retarded girl from a Caribbean country visiting relatives in New York with her family, I couldn't achieve a definitive balance between the obligation to respect the parents' religious convictions when they refused recommended brain surgery for their daughter and the duty to override their refusal and perform a high-risk operation to try to save the girl's life. Conducting an internal debate about whether the higher obligation lay in preserving doctor-patient confidentiality or in informing the employer of an alcoholic train switchman about his impairment, I kept searching for an escape through the horns of that dilemma.

Now, however, I understand much better than when I began my work fifteen years ago just what it is I am doubting. Rarely does bioethics offer "one right answer" to a moral dilemma. Seldom can a philosopher arrive on the scene and make unequivocal pronouncements about the right thing to do. Yet, despite the fact that it has no magic wand, bioethics is still useful and can go a long way toward "resolving the issues," once that phrase is properly interpreted.

A thorough reply to the skeptical claim about the value of ethical theory for applied ethics must defend a series of related points: (a) if a theory is no good in practice, it is no good in theory either; (b) if the difficulty of resolving issues in applied ethics stems from ignorance, disagreements, or uncertainty about the facts, blame should not be laid at the door of ethical theory; (c) ethical theories should not be faulted for the fact that there exist fundamental value disagreements among human beings; (d) if ethical theories are not especially useful in resolving the issues in applied ethics, then neither is any other rational approach.

My experience as a philosopher working in a medical center has shown that many physicians and other health-care personnel faced with hard decisions and ethical dilemmas recognize that there is something we philosophers know how to do that they do not; or at least, that we can systematically and consistently analyze moral problems in a way that they can match only occasionally and imperfectly. That ability can be traced more directly to philosophers' competence in constructing well-reasoned arguments and justifications than to their command of ethical theories. Yet a knowledge of theoretical ethics is also crucial for being able to identify the source of disagreements and for arriving at a resolution of conflicts. Thus the two skeptical claims are not identical. Claim (1): that ethical theories are not especially useful in resolving the issues in applied ethics, requires a separate response from claim (2): that the philosopher is not especially qualified to deal with issues in applied ethics.

RESOLVING THE ISSUES

It would be surprising for a philosopher to tackle a controversial claim without first clarifying the question, or at least offering several interpretations of the meaning of the central claim. True to form, then, I shall begin by analyzing the first skeptical claim. The phrase 'resolving the issues' is vague. Additional confusion surrounds the notion of an ethical theory.

The phrase 'resolving the issues' can be understood in a strong sense that means "solving moral dilemmas" or "providing clear-cut solutions to ethical quandaries." On this strong interpretation, the skeptical claim asserts that the ability to arrive at correct or uncontroversial moral decisions is not aided by the use of ethical theories. If it is true—and I believe it is—that genuine moral dilemmas have no single right answer, then there is some merit in the skeptics' claim according to this interpretation of 'resolving the issues'. But this interpretation is not only too strong; it is also too narrow, since only a small percentage of the issues in medical practice and health policy have the characteristics of a genuine moral dilemma. I will argue a bit later that it is expecting too much of an ethical theory to settle controversial moral issues in cases where the controversies themselves can be traced to the disputants' commitment to different and often competing ethical principles. For now, let me note simply that this strong interpretation of 'resolving the issues' is neither the only nor the most appropriate way of construing the phrase.

An altogether too weak interpretation of 'resolving the issues' should also be rejected. That weak sense sees the philosopher's role as clarifying moral problems and structuring the issues. Although these tasks are part of what bioethicists do in the clinical setting and in their scholarly work, more is involved than mere clarification and structuring. Moral philosophy is not a form of "values clarification," getting people to recognize their own values and discover what they really think about perplexing ethical problems.

A third interpretation lies somewhere between the strong meaning—resolving moral dilemmas—and the too-weak notion of "clarifying the issues." What lies between these unacceptable interpretations? It cannot be captured in a neat phrase, but, roughly stated, it is the ability to produce a stronger argument for one position than for a competing alternative. Put another way, when no perfect solution can be found, it is still possible to arrive at the least inadequate or least implausible answer to the problem. It is obvious, however, that opponents in a moral debate are not likely to admit that their argument is less plausible or less adequate than their adversary's. Here is where ethical theory enters the picture.

A consideration of the role of ethical theories begins with the reminder that they contain more than simply a recitation of one or more ethical principles or moral rules. An important aspect of any ethical theory—at least any philosophically respectable one—is its epistemological component.

ETHICAL THEORIES

Every area of human inquiry has roots in epistemology. Whether the subject is science or ethics, technology, law, or art, questions of what truths exist, how we come to know those truths, and how they can be justified are bound to arise. Ethical theories embody normative principles, principles that set forth criteria for right and wrong, good and bad, just and unjust actions or policies. Normative principles are the key elements of ethical theories in their application to practical situations.

But theories also contain epistemological features important for the justification of the principles themselves. This is one reason why philosophers, given their background in areas of philosophy besides ethics, are better equipped than most to deal with issues in applied ethics. Although the heart of a moral theory is the fundamental moral principle or principles it embodies, the theory itself consists of much more than its normative content. There is at least as much controversy among philosophers over the foundations of ethics, about the theory of knowledge that lies behind an acceptance of one moral position versus another, and about the meanings of basic ethical concepts, as there is over the selection of the principles themselves.

This point is evident from a moment's reflection on the major differences between teleological and deontological theories of ethics, and between so-called "naturalistic" and "nonnaturalistic" approaches. The beginning student of philosophy is often struck by the fact that leading theories are in surprising agreement on the content of most substantive individual judgments. The rather small range of cases where they appear to disagree—for example, those in which an action that maximizes happiness is in violation of a moral rule—are not only few in number; they are often made to seem more significant by the fabrication of philosophers' examples, such as desert-island cases and that of the fat man stuck in the mouth of a cave in which ten people are trapped, along with some dynamite. The major differences among Western philosophical theories lie largely in their epistemological underpinnings and in what they take to be morally relevant factors. Although it is true that these latter differences render ethical theories quite distinct from a philosophical perspective, their distinctness is more often a function of these other theoretical differences than of the moral judgments yielded by an application of their normative principles.

The point is that 'resolving the issues' in applied ethics should be understood in a sense that takes into account the role of epistemological and conceptual features of ethical theories. There would be no need of ethical theories if all that was required were the normative principles that lie at the heart of such theories. Philosophy students would not have to read John Stuart Mill's entire essay, *Utilitarianism.* Teachers could simply point out the paragraph in which Mill states the "greatest-happiness principle." No one would have to plow through Immanuel Kant's tortuous *Fundamental Principles of the Metaphysic of Morals;* a half-page would be enough to list the three formulations of the categorical imperative. And why not just recite John Rawls's two basic principles which he finally arrives at near the end of *A Theory of Justice,* instead of wading through all 587 pages? A central aspect of "resolving the issues" in bioethics is attending to the conceptual, epistemological, and even metaphysical issues that philosophers deal with as their stock in trade.

In applied contexts, sometimes the issues are resolved by getting the participants or disputants to agree on what are the morally relevant considerations. Sometimes the issues are resolved by pointing out that the problem lies not in failure to assent to the same ethical principle, but rather in disagreement over the empirical facts or probable outcomes of alternative courses of action. It is a mistake to think that ethical theories are of no utility, since an important aspect of applying them is attending to their nonnormative features. It is on this point that replies to the first and second skeptical claims merge into one: philosophers *are* especially qualified to deal with issues in applied ethics, because they are skilled in addressing conceptual and epistemological matters as well as knowledgeable about ethical theories.

In addition to traditional, full-blown theories such as those of Kant and Mill, there is another legitimate category relevant to responding to the skeptics' challenge: smaller-scale theories designed to cover a more circumscribed range of actions than the whole of interpersonal conduct or all social institutions. For example, a concept that has received much attention in all areas of applied ethics is *paternalism*. Both in individual transactions such as the doctor-patient relationship and in public-policy settings governed by statutes or court decisions, a wide range of public and philosophical opinion exists about the justifiability of paternalistic interferences with individual liberty.

Popular sentiment as well as philosophical writings have tended to be rather critical of paternalism in individual, interpersonal relationships, but somewhat mixed in the sphere of legal or governmental paternalism, such as bans on saccharine or laetrile and laws regulating the wearing of motorcycle helmets or seat belts. Yet if debates about these matters are to be more than mere expressions of feeling about the permissibility of coercing individuals for their own good, there must be a theoretical framework for the discussion. A complete and fully worked-out theory of paternalism must include a view about the nature of persons and about the ability of people generally to know their own best interests. It requires an analysis of the meaning of the "best interests" doctrine, a discussion of the priority problem (individual liberty versus other values) and an account of the proper role of the state or community in preserving and furthering the interests of society as a whole.

Most writings on the subject of paternalism have not been so ambitious as to encompass all these concerns; yet philosophers such as H. L. A. Hart, Gerald Dworkin, Tom L. Beauchamp, Bernard Gert, and Allen Buchanan[3] have constructed small-scale theories of paternalism, analyzing the concept and applying it to a range of issues in law and ethics. A more comprehensive effort is made by Joel Feinberg in his recent books, which build on his earlier writings and seek to develop a full theory of paternalism, as well as an account of harm and offense to others.[4] In the absence of a theoretical framework, judgments about the desirability of paternalism in individual cases or regarding particular social policies reveal, at best, adherence to received wisdom or to dogmatically held precepts. A vague, antipaternalist sentiment is no substitute, in an argument that calls for a justification, for an appeal to underlying moral principles and related presuppositions.

The advantage of having a theory, as philosophers have argued at length, is that it enables particular judgments to be systematic and well grounded, instead of ad hoc. To the defender of an ad hoc approach or of decision making according to whim, the only reply is the same one given to the skeptic who asks, Why be rational? Skeptics who question the need for or value of ethical theories on the grounds that a systematic or rational approach to individual moral problems is unnecessary or undesirable will probably not be convinced by good reasons of any sort. Their skepticism extends beyond questioning the role of theory in doing applied ethics. If we include under the heading of "ethical theory" small-scale theories

---

[3]H. L. A. Hart, *Law, Liberty and Morality* (Stanford: Stanford University Press, 1963); Gerald Dworkin, "Paternalism," *The Monist*, LVI (1972); Tom L. Beauchamp, "Paternalism and Biobehavioral Control," *The Monist*, LX (1977); Charles Culver and Bernard Gert, "Paternalistic Behavior," *Philosophy and Public Affairs*, VI (1976) and "The Justification of Paternalism," *Ethics*, LXXXIX (1979); Allen Buchanan, "Medical Paternalism," *Philosophy and Public Affairs*, VII (Summer 1978).

[4]Joel Feinberg, "Legal Paternalism," *Canadian Journal of Philosophy*, I (1971), and the four volumes of his work *Harm to Others* (1984), *Offense to Others* (1985), *Harm to Self* (1986), and *Harmless Wrongdoing* (forthcoming) (New York: Oxford University Press).

of paternalism, of autonomy,[5] and privacy,[6] among others, it is hard to see how a justification of moral decisions could even be offered, much less adequately defended, in the absence of ethical theory. Theoretical underpinnings are needed to justify steps at any stage in a moral argument. The burden of proof lies with the skeptic to show how moral reasoning or ethical judgments can take place in a systematic or rational way in the absence of theory.

CLAIMS OF A LIVING SKEPTIC

To give some concreteness to my remarks, it is worth quoting some passages from a living skeptic, one who received a Ph.D. in philosophy and is now a practicing lawyer. This skeptic, then, cannot be faulted for betraying an outsider's ignorance of philosophical ethics, its methods or content, or for failure to understand the nature of philosophical inquiry.

In her article, entitled "Ethics and Experts," Cheryl N. Noble writes:

> Applied ethics attempts to use ethical theory in the solution of practical, moral and social problems of all kinds, including the morality of abortion, genetic research, euthanasia, capital punishment, warfare, pacificism, terrorism, and reverse discrimination and racism (p. 7).

Citing recent developments in ethical theory, notably the works of John Rawls, Robert Nozick, and Ronald Dworkin, Noble observes

---

[5]Gerald Dworkin, "Autonomy and Behavior Control," *Hastings Center Report*, VI (1976); and "Moral Autonomy," in H. Tristram Engelhardt, Jr., and Daniel Callahan, eds., *Morals, Science, and Sociality* (Hastings-on-Hudson, N.Y.: Institute of Society, Ethics and the Life Sciences, 1978).

[6]Many examples of small-scale theories of privacy exist in the literature in philosophy, political science, and economics. These pertain mostly to issues surrounding private property and what Rawls refers to as the notion of "private society." A different context is that of privacy and confidentiality in biomedical research and therapy, especially in the field of human reproduction. An example of such a theory addressed to issues in sex research and sex therapy is Richard Wasserstrom's article in W. H. Masters, V. E. Johnson, R. C. Kolodny, and S. M. Weems, eds., *Ethical Issues in Sex Therapy and Research*, vol. II (Boston: Little, Brown, 1980), pp. 42–60. A general analysis of the distinction between public and private morality is provided by Daniel Callahan in his "Minimalist Ethics," *Hastings Center Report*, XI (October 1981).

that "these theoretical developments encouraged the idea that there are 'methods' of evaluative thought that can be applied to particular practical 'issues' so as to produce specific answers" (p. 7). She also cites the journal *Philosophy and Public Affairs* as an instance of philosophers' reawakened interest in applied ethics. In the course of a critical discussion of Thomas Nagel's essay "War and Massacre," Ronald Dworkin's 1976 essay on reverse discrimination in the *New York Review of Books,* and a couple of other works published in the last decade, Noble expresses her distaste for these efforts in a number of loosely connected points. The main points can be recast in summary fashion as follows:

1. These efforts in applied ethics are abstracted from social realities; therefore, they are inadequate to deal with pressing moral concerns in our society.

2. The conclusions philosophers reach in these efforts are conventional and tame, drawn from a preexisting range of alternatives.

3. These efforts are little more than technical exercises in philosophy, no different in principle from what philosophers were doing before the dawn of the new age of applied ethics.

Noble accuses Nagel both of relying on his intuitions for his insights and of the quite different shortcoming of relying utterly on common-sense everyday notions and knowledge in order to arrive at his conclusions. She indicts Ronald Dworkin for using technical and quasi-technical notions drawn from contemporary theoretical ethics and of thus conveying the mistaken impression that the philosopher knows more than the lay reader about the principles that should govern society. While calling for a "concrete social analysis," which would presumably succeed where theoretical efforts fail, Noble gives no clue as to how that type of social analysis could succeed in drawing normative conclusions any better than the theoretical approach she criticizes. She says of all her chosen examples that "the principles used to 'justify' the social practices are only highly abstract descriptions of norms already embodied in those practices" (p. 9).

Hence her charge that the conclusions drawn by philosophers are "conventional and tame"—a charge that Peter Singer finds amusing. In a reply to Noble, he notes that he is regularly attacked "for arriving at conclusions so outrageous as to fly in the face of everything decent people believe in." These conclusions include the statements that we should become vegetarians, that a newborn baby has no more of a right to life than a fetus, and that infanticide is often justifiable (Singer, p. 10). Noble's accusation of Nagel is more devastating: he "ends up saying that the way things are is pretty much the way they ought to be" (Noble, p. 9).

It is at least odd, if not inconsistent, to charge philosophers who are doing applied ethics with failing to take sufficient account of social and historical realities and at the same time with deriving what ought to be the case in social justice from existing social norms and arrangements. Sometimes Noble appears to be attacking philosophers for pretensions to moral wisdom when all they possess is technical expertise in reasoning and a knowledge of classical moral theories and modern theory of value. Yet, apart from a jibe at Peter Singer for a remark in his *New York Review of Books* article of several years ago, Noble does not indict those whose works she explicitly criticizes for this fault. If anything, she accuses Dworkin and Nagel of the opposite—of demonstrating too little moral wisdom and too much reliance on mere technical expertise and conventional social norms.

In some places, Noble accuses philosophers of relying too much on common sense and on personal intuitions. In other places she complains that they simply draw on technical and quasi-technical notions from theoretical ethics. It appears, then, that she attacks both the use of ethical theory as a guide to applied normative judgments and what she deems the historical and political naiveté of writers in applied ethics. In this scattershot attack on selected writings, Noble fails to provide a superior alternative approach, either by way of example or by a sufficiently full description of what such an approach would look like. As Daniel Wikler observes, she "owes us a sketch of her rival account of morality. One difficulty with attacking conventional morality . . . is that the argument applies just as forcefully to any morality, including the critic's" (Wikler, p. 12). In the end, her account lacks a cogent picture of what is wrong with the activity of applied ethics as practiced by those schooled in ethical theory.

PROBLEMS IN APPLYING THEORIES

Of all the areas of inquiry philosophers have engaged in over the centuries, none has been intended as more "practical" than ethics. While always putting forward an ideal of some sort, moral philosophers have nonetheless conceived of their efforts as addressed to issues in the real world. If ethical theories are not especially useful in resolving issues in applied ethics, then moral philosophers have been misguided and have been misleading others for the past two thousand years or so. What would it mean to judge that a treatise in moral philosophy is good in theory but no good in practice? If the skeptics are right, that sort of judgment makes sense. Yet philosophers who object to the enterprise of applied ethics are not, for the most part, prepared to abandon the wholly respectable activity of constructing and analyzing ethical theories. If utilitarianism or Kant's ethics—to name only two—cannot be applied at all in real-life settings, why should we take them seriously as ethical theories?

It is, therefore, peculiar to maintain that ethical theories are impossible to apply, in principle. They are, however, very difficult to apply, for a number of different reasons. There is often a lack of sufficient information about relevant facts or future states of affairs. The probabilities of different possible outcomes may be unknown or only vaguely guessed. The problem of how to formulate a maxim governing an action is formidable. There is the difficulty of determining when the happiness produced by an action outweighs the unhappiness or which duty should take precedence when two or more come into conflict. Yet these problems, daunting as they are, have not led philosophers to abandon the study of ethical theory. We think sufficiently well of traditional and contemporary ethical theories to teach them to students, write scholarly treatises and publish articles on them in professional journals, and debate their respective merits on points where they conflict. If the skeptics are right, philosophers should cease misleading students and fooling themselves by paying so much attention to theories, which, if useless in practice, are no good in theory either.

What motivates skeptical claims of the sort under discussion? Two considerations in applied contexts are likely to give rise to skepticism about the application of ethical theories. The first consideration is evident in situations where there is an ethical problem or dilemma to be resolved and people disagree about what action to perform. In many (but surely not all) such cases, the dilemma exists precisely because two different ethical principles underlie the competing judgments about what to do. If a dilemma can be traced to a tension between two incompatible theories or to competing principles central to those theories, then of course the dilemma cannot be resolved by applying an ethical theory. The problem lies not in the difficulty of application, but, alas, in the unsettled metaethical problems of competing theories and disagreement over matters in the foundations of ethics.

The second consideration likely to give rise to skepticism about the application of ethical theories is the sheer difficulty of making the application. Even if all parties to a decision agree on which ethical theory is the correct one to apply, the empirical and methodological difficulties are still awesome. We need only recall the stock objections to a relatively straightforward theory such as utilitarianism, to be reminded of these difficulties.

There is uncertainty in being able to predict outcomes with any reasonable degree of accuracy. A range of problems surrounds measurement: whether interpersonal comparisons are necessary and, if so, how to make them. There are epistemological problems of assigning values to possible outcomes and determining whether individual preferences can be inferred simply from people's behavior. Debates persist over whether or not pleasures and pains are commensurable and about whether types of pleasures and pains can or ought to be weighted somehow. Some of these difficulties are functions of the stage of development of the social sciences. They reflect the fact that the sciences of psychology and sociology—if they are sciences at all—are in their infancy, as regards both the state of theory and its application in the spheres of prediction and control. If major difficulties in applied ethics can be traced to the state of the art in the social sciences, it is a mistake to focus blame on ethical theories or on the efforts of philosophers. What stands in the way of being able to apply ethical theory in this range of cases are shortcomings in social-science theory and practice.

Some problems of application, however, such as the conceptual and epistemological problems raised by utilitarianism, stem not from the primitive state of social science, but from the philosophical theories themselves. For those problems, the shortcomings lie not so much in efforts to apply the theory as in failure to work out the details of the theory in the first place. A theory that is impossible or exceedingly difficult to apply in practice is flawed in theory as well.

A factor that lends credibility to the skeptics' charge is that moral problems in everyday life rarely have the features of paradigms. Philosophers are notoriously clever at cooking up examples to illustrate their points—a cleverness exceeded only by their ability to think up counterexamples to destroy the claims of their opponents. Matters are fuzzy in real-life settings, though, and case examples do not neatly fit the theoretical precepts. The skeptic must recognize that, if these features make it difficult or practically impossible to apply ethical theories, they also make it difficult or impossible to arrive at any rational solution to the ethical dilemma. Decision makers ignorant of ethical theories are not, therefore, doing a better job in their ignorance than they would if they struggled to apply a theory. If it is difficult to arrive at a sound resolution of moral problems by using ethical theories, it is at least as difficult to reach ethical decisions in the absence of any theory whatever.

APPLYING ETHICAL THEORY TO BIOMEDICINE

One application of ethical theory to practice lies in the federal regulations in the United States that govern biomedical and behavioral research using human subjects. The overall moral standard embodied in current regulations of the Department of Health and Human Services is a blend of the utilitarian and Kantian theoretical approaches. Current regulations require that every institution engaged in federally funded biomedical and behavioral research on human subjects have an Institutional Review Board (IRB), whose task it is to review research protocols. One charge to the committee is to assess the risk-benefit ratio of all research protocols that come before it. All new drugs and devices must be assessed in this manner, as well as experimental treatments for diseases, new surgical techniques, and a wide variety of interventions that do not stand to benefit the research subjects themselves. In carrying out its function of protecting human subjects, the IRB is supposed to determine whether the benefits of the research will, in all likelihood, outweigh the risks of harm to the subjects. The regulations governing research require the IRB to determine that "risks to subjects are reasonable in relation to anticipated benefits, if any, to subjects, and the importance of the knowledge that may reasonably be expected to result."[7]

The moral standard embodied in this statement and in the risk-benefit assessment as a whole is clearly utilitarian. Even if there is some chance that research subjects will be harmed in the course of the study, the overall benefits (to themselves or to others) justify the

---

[7]45 CFR 46, *Federal Register* (January 16, 1981).

conduct of the research. The difficulties involved in weighing prob-able risks of harm against likely benefits, as well as the problems of predicting accurately, are considerable. But, on the assumption that making such calculations does not rest on an elaborate fiction, the use of risk-benefit equations to evaluate the ethics of biomedical and behavioral research is a good example of a public policy that adopts the utilitarian perspective.

But the utilitarian standard of morality is not the only standard evident in regulations governing biomedical and behavioral re-search. These same regulations require that, in all instances where human subjects are involved as individuals (in contrast to observa-tions of group behavior), their informed consent must be obtained. The doctrine of informed consent to research and treatment does not rest solely on the ethical principle that people deserve to be protected from undue harm. A strong Kantian strain underlies the practice of requiring a patient's or subject's informed consent—a strain expressed in language referring to "human dignity," "the need to respect personal autonomy," and the individual's "right to self-determination" in the medical setting. The items that must be disclosed to subjects in the process of obtaining informed consent are aimed at providing sufficient information to enable them to arrive at a rational, informed decision about whether to participate. Potential subjects must also be told that they have the freedom to refuse to participate in the research and to withdraw at any time.

Federal regulations governing research on human subjects thus contain a mix of elements from utilitarian and Kantian ethical the-ory, but no inconsistency need arise from the use of two different theoretical approaches. The utilitarian balancing required for mak-ing risk-benefit assessments applies to one aspect of research prac-tice, intended to protect research subjects from harm. The Kantian elements in the informed-consent process appear in a different pro-cedure, one designed to protect the rights of research subjects or patients. Aspects of both consequentialist and deontological ap-proaches to ethics are embodied in this public policy.

Yet, despite the fact that these two leading ethical theories are incorporated in this general way into federal regulations, a potential for conflict remains. This conflict has its practical expression in an ongoing debate surrounding the conduct of social-science research. Part of that debate has focused on the technical question of whether IRB review is necessary for all or some types of social-science research. Another aspect of the quarrel is addressed to the more general issue of whether government regulations ought to apply at all to various types of social-science research. The portion of the debate relevant to our concerns here has to do with the ethical standards that should govern informed consent to research of this type.

The debate begins with the fact that withholding of information and even outright deception of subjects has been widespread in social-science research. Some outspoken social scientists have argued that their research should be exempted from federal regulations, which were designed for biomedical experiments and have been applied to social-science research only as an afterthought. Others contend that it is all right in principle for such regulations to apply, but they should be modified to take into account the experimental design of much social and behavioral research, and the requirements for informed consent should be adjusted accordingly. Their argument is that much research could not be done without some measure of deception or without concealing the purpose of the study or the identity of the researcher.

Opponents in this debate over the conduct of social-science research have two very different conceptions of what factors should be morally relevant. Those who argue that the usual requirements for gaining informed consent should be modified or abandoned are appealing to utilitarian considerations. They claim that more benefit than harm results from doing the research, a claim that stands in need of empirical backing if it is to be accepted as a premise in the argument. Contributions to knowledge outweigh any likely harm that could come to research subjects from their having been deceived, they say, and the overall loss to humanity would be much greater if entire lines of research had to be abandoned than if less than fully informed consent was obtained. Furthermore, since all subjects are "debriefed" at the end of the experiment, deception occurs only for a short period of time, and the subjects end up being informed, just a bit later. The only factors held to be relevant are the benefits and risks of the research, and the only moral principle thought to be relevant is the principle of utility.

Their opponents, those who argue that the same requirements for informed consent should hold for social and behavioral research as for biomedical research, consider the autonomy of research subjects to be morally relevant. This side adheres to the "respect for persons" moral principle, adhering to the Kantian precept that people should never be treated merely as a means to the ends of others. This side in the debate is not moved by risk-benefit calculations that purportedly show that little harm is likely to befall subjects who are deceived in an experimental setting. Kantians are never moved by an appeal to consequences, unless they are closet utilitarians. For them, neither the loss of significant contributions to knowledge nor the benefits of possible future applications of the research are factors that should influence policy in this area. Even if no measurable physical or psychological harm is likely to befall research subjects, acts of outright deception, withholding information that might affect a subject's decision to participate, and disguised observation by researchers are violations of trust, privacy, or autonomy. The conclusion of the argument is that the proper criterion for moral rightness is respect for persons, not a balance of benefits over harms. Deception should be ruled out in all forms of research on human subjects.

Does this exercise in applying ethical theory resolve the issues? "No," under the strongest interpretation of 'resolve the issues', and "probably yes" under the more charitable interpretation. Although it is quite clear to philosophers who study the issue of deception in social-science research that the debate comes down to a conflict between two leading ethical principles, it is far from evident to the principal opponents in the debate. When the opponents themselves recognize that each adheres to a different moral principle from the other's, they may very well not budge an inch. But a deeper understanding of the nature of the conflict should emerge.

If skeptics who question the value or usefulness of bioethics still maintain that the issues are unresolved, they are demanding too much of the enterprise. When no single, rationally defensible ethical theory exists, it is misguided to expect that an appeal to theory can solve a conflict that stems from the application of incompatible theories.

As long as the debate between Kantians and utilitarians continues to rage and as long as the Western political and philosophical tradition continues to embrace both the respect-for-persons principle and the principle of beneficence, there can be no possible resolution of dilemmas traceable to those competing theoretical approaches. But the inability to make a final determination of which theoretical approach is ultimately "right" does not rule out the prospect for making sound moral judgments in practical contexts, based on one or the other theoretical perspective.

The choice between utilitarian ethics and a deontological moral system rooted in rights and duties is not a choice between one moral and one immoral alternative. Rather, it rests on a commitment to one moral viewpoint instead of another, where both are capable of providing good reasons for acting. Both perspectives stand in opposition to egoistic or selfish approaches, or to a philosophy whose precepts are grounded in privileges of power, wealth, or the authority of technical experts.

PHILOSOPHICAL ANALYSIS IN BIOETHICS

The skeptics' first claim remains problematic if we construe the phrase 'resolving the issues' to mean "solving ethical dilemmas" or "providing solutions to moral problems." But the skeptics' second claim: that philosophers are not especially qualified to deal with issues in applied ethics, is easier to rebut. This is because "dealing with issues" involves much more than applying ethical theories directly to concrete cases in order to solve moral problems. Few issues are "purely moral." Philosophical analysis of a more general sort is usually called for in applied ethics. This typically includes providing a conceptual analysis, as well as addressing a range of metaethical considerations: illustrating subtle distinctions between facts and values, clearing up ambiguities in key terms, and pointing out flaws in reasoning. Philosophers are likely to be more skilled than others in these pursuits, since, if there is any area of expertise that truly belongs to philosophers, it is mastery of techniques of reasoning and analysis.

A good illustration can be found in the cluster of concerns surrounding the beginning and end of human life. Many opponents in the ongoing abortion controversy have maintained that, if we only had an adequate account of when human life begins or when personhood emerges, we could then decide, once and for all, about the morality of abortion and set public policy accordingly. This view rests on the belief that there is a strong link between being a person and being the bearer of rights, especially the right to life. The philosopher Michael Tooley makes the equation explicit in his statement: ". . . in my usage the sentence '*X* is a person' will be synonymous with the sentence '*X* has a (serious) moral right to life.' "[8] The belief that there is a strong link between personhood and the right to life was further illustrated in a bill proposed in 1981 by anti-abortion legislators in the United States Congress, entitled "A Bill to Provide that Human Life Shall Be Deemed to Exist from Conception."[9]

However, a close look at the literature in bioethics reveals there is no consensus at all on the definition of 'personhood'. Writers who hold a feminist bias take the stance that at no stage of development does a fetus meet the criteria of personhood. And writers from religious traditions opposed to abortion offer a standard of personhood that even a zygote, a fertilized egg, can meet. My assessment of why it appears impossible for philosophers, theologians, feminists, and legal scholars to agree on criteria for personhood is that the position they already hold about the morality of abortion is imported into the definition of 'human life'. This is a sophisticated form of begging the question. Attempts to use the concept of a person as a means of resolving the abortion debate are bound to fail if they commit the age-old logical fallacy of *petitio principii*.

But the situation is even more complicated. Contributors to the literature surrounding the abortion debate cannot even agree on the relevance and importance of defining 'personhood'. Four distinct views can be discerned.

One view argues that settling the abortion issue once and for all depends crucially on coming to some agreement about whether the fetus is a person and, if so, when in its development personhood begins.

Another side maintains that settling the abortion issue has nothing to do with when personhood begins, since abortion may be morally justified even if it is acknowledged that the fetus is a person from the moment of conception.

A third view holds that whether the fetus is a person is irrelevant to whether it should have legal protection; concerns about the

---

[8]"Abortion and Infanticide," *Philosophy and Public Affairs*, II (Fall 1972), reprinted in Gorovitz et al., *Moral Problems in Medicine*, p. 309.

[9]U.S. Congress, Senate, *A Bill to Provide that Human Life Shall Be Deemed to Exist from Conception*, 97th Congress, 1st session, S.158 (Washington, D.C.: 1981).

health of the fetus create pressing policy issues regardless of whether or not the fetus is granted the status of a person.

The fourth position asserts that, since it is impossible to agree on criteria for defining personhood, this issue must be seen as entirely irrelevant to arriving at a solution to the abortion controversy.[10]

Defining 'personhood' may seem to many to be "merely a matter of semantics." Yet the question of what should count as a person, or what are the proper criteria for personhood, is a profound philosophical question belonging to metaphysics. Determining the relevance of that question to the abortion controversy is an epistemological matter. When issues of ethics and social policy are locked in perennial controversy, philosophy can illuminate those issues by showing how conceptual confusions and fallacious reasoning contribute to the problem. Although conducting a philosophical examination of these questions and issues will not succeed in resolving the debate over the morality of abortion, it does provide a deeper understanding of why the controversy remains unresolved and may even be irresolvable.

Similar problems arise for issues concerning the termination of life: euthanasia, the definition of death, and the ethics of withholding or withdrawing life supports. The leading court cases, including those of Karen Ann Quinlan, Brother Fox, Joseph Saikewicz, John Storar, William Bartling, and Claire Conroy, all revolve around the so-called "right to die." Yet conceptual confusions have added to ethical uncertainty in a number of these cases.

Initially, when the Quinlan case attracted public attention in the mid-1970s, there was a common misconception that, if only we had a medically adequate and morally acceptable definition of death, then the ethical problem of removing patients from respirators would be resolved. Some believed that the answer lay in adopting the criterion of brain death, cessation of electrical activity in the brain as measured by an EEG, electroencephalograph. According to this belief, if a brain-death criterion replaced the traditional heart-lung definition of death, then moral decisions would be easier.

---

[10]For the sources of these views and a full discussion of the concept of personhood in the bioethics literature, see my "Personhood in the Bioethics Literature," *Milbank Memorial Fund Quarterly/Health and Society*, LXI (1983).

But a look at the medical facts in the Quinlan case and those which followed reveals that Karen Ann Quinlan would not have been considered dead according to a brain-death criterion, although she was irreversibly comatose, with no hope of returning to a cognitive, sapient state. A much more radical departure from the standard heart-lung criterion would be needed before Karen Ann Quinlan and Brother Fox could have been considered dead while in a "persistent vegetative state."

Can bioethics resolve the issues? The answer is No if the question is taken to mean, Can philosophers supply unequivocal, right answers to all moral dilemmas in medicine? But, for other interpretations, the answer is Yes. When there is no single, correct answer to a substantive moral question, bioethics can still make a contribution. Ethicists can analyze actual or proposed policies and laws and address questions at the "metalevel," such as which moral problems should be candidates for laws and regulations and which are best left to informal resolution by the concerned parties. Another task at the metalevel is providing criteria of adequacy for a policy or a procedure designed to deal with ethical issues in health care.

In applied ethics, sometimes the issues are resolved by getting the disputants to agree on what the morally relevant considerations are. Doctors who come to recognize the right of patients to participate in health-care decisions no longer insist that their sole obligation as physicians is to bring about the best medical outcomes for their patients. Awareness that the public-health model governs medical practice in addition to the traditional clinical model leads to an acknowledgment that the physician's duty to keep confidentiality is not absolute. Coming to agree on what the morally relevant considerations are may not directly resolve a particular dilemma, but it shows with precision and clarity just what the residual disagreement is about. In this way, the issues are more fully understood, if not completely resolved.

4

Why Do Applied Ethics?*

R. M. Hare

It is becoming quite common nowadays to see writers, whether popular or academic, speaking of a happy period which has just dawned, in which philosophers actually try to say something relevant to practical issues. This rather patronizing pat on the back is not really intended as a compliment to our profession. It is intended, rather, as a rebuke to those in the recent past who, allegedly, did *not* say anything relevant to practice. As one who came into philosophy in the 1940s with the dominant motive of doing something to help us resolve practical moral problems, I may perhaps be forgiven for finding this a little irritating. My first published philosophical contribution to a practical issue (that of what the duties of citizens are when their governments are acting immorally) was delivered first in Germany, then on the BBC Third Programme, and published in *The Listener* in 1955,[1] and since then I have published many papers on practical topics. I do not think that I am alone in this among moral philosophers. It is true that some of them have confined their attention to ethical theory; but their theoretical contributions, none the less, may have been valuable indirectly in helping those of us who *were* applying theory to practice to improve the theory. On the other hand, they may not have been valuable, if the theoretical work was poor, as it may have been for

---

*This essay originally appeared in *New Directions in Ethics,* J. de Marco and R. Fox, eds. (London: Routledge & Kegan Paul, 1986, pp. 225–37); reprinted by permission of the author.

[1]"Ethics and Politics," *The Listener,* October 1955.

reasons I shall be discussing. But what the writers I am complaining about fail to say is that there can be no helpful intervention of philosophers, as philosophers, in practical issues unless the philosophy is well done. It is not easy to make any useful application of theory to practice unless one has a viable theory, or at least a firm and coherent grasp of the theoretical moves.

Why do people, and why do I, do applied ethics? One reason they do it is to make themselves more popular. They are in receipt of public money, and they think they will incur the public's displeasure if it can see no obvious helpful results from their researches. A better reason is that we want to find answers to moral questions and think that philosophy might help. I have found, since I first took up moral philosophy in the hope of tackling some acute moral problems that had confronted me during the Second World War, that it does help. It helps first of all by yielding clarifications on minor points of detail which, nevertheless, can generate major confusions. More importantly, it helps, if one does it well, by the clarification of moral language in general—its meaning, its uses and its logic. This is what I meant when I spoke of a viable ethical theory. I think I have one. Other theorists, I am sure, think the same of their own theories. The practical applications of these different theories are what make the theoretical disputes between us of practical importance. There are other theorists who are unlikely to say much that is of practical help. This can be for at least two different reasons. The first is that their theories are of an intuitionist sort which makes appeal to common moral convictions or consensus. These theories will be of little help because on any issue that is in the least contentious there are no common convictions and no consensus to appeal to. Try appealing to common intuitions about the abortion controversy, for example. I do not believe that even prolonged reflection on these intuitions will yield an equilibrium; what we need are firmly established rules of argument based on an understanding of the words we are using when we ask moral questions.

The second handicap which afflicts some moral philosophers can have the same consequence and worse. They may think that there is just no hope of finding an ethical theory—that is, an account of the logic of the moral concepts—which will yield rules of reasoning. In default of that, all we can do is exchange intuitions from our pluralist armoury; but then there is no reason why, failing any way of testing the intuitions in argument, the exchange should ever stop.

When there are conflicting intuitions battling for control of the conduct even of a single thinker, these philosophers can offer him no comfort or help beyond the armchair comment that such tragedies are one of the facts of life. Philosophers really would deserve a pat on the back if they succeeded instead, as they can if their theory is sound, in showing people how to sort out these conflicts.

There are, then, ways in which philosophers can help resolve practical issues by applying theory to them. But the benefit is mutual. Having taken part in a great many discussions, in working parties and seminars, with people from other professions who face moral problems (doctors and psychiatrists for example) I have been struck by the way in which, in trying to apply theory to these problems, one gains confidence in certain parts of the theory but sees the need for improvements in others.

It often happens in such discussions that I am not the only philosopher present. There may be, for example, somebody also who is, not a non-descriptivist Kantian utilitarian[2] like me, but a descriptivist intuitionist deontologist, perhaps pretending to be a Kantian. These theoretical differences are largely, though not wholly, independent of any differences on the practical issues. Before we start arguing, our unphilosophical opinions may or may not coincide. But when we do start arguing, it is likely to turn out that I am able to give Kantian utilitarian reasons for my opinions, and the other philosopher is not able to give any reasons at all. He just appeals to the consensus of those present, which, unless the working party has been stacked, may not be forthcoming. When he does produce reasons which seem to have any force with those who did not initially share his opinions, they turn out to be utilitarian reasons—appeals for example to the bad consequences of some policy.

A splendid example of this kind of thing occurring in a more august body is to be found in the report of the British Home Office working party on Obscenity and Film Censorship, chaired by Bernard Williams.[3] In his philosophical capacity, he is well known for

---

[2]For justification of the term 'Kantian utilitarian' see my *Moral Thinking* (Oxford University Press, 1981), p. 4.

[3]Home Office, *Report of the Committee on Obscenity and Film Censorship*, chairman Bernard Williams (HMS Cmnd. 7772, 1979). Reprinted without appendices by Cambridge University Press.

the single-minded integrity (in his eccentric sense of the word) of his persecution of utilitarians, which rivals St. Paul's of the Christians before his conversion. But the arguments of the Williams Report are utilitarian from start to finish, as has been pointed out by Ronald Dworkin in a review of the Report, and by myself.[4] The key chapter in the report is called 'Harms?', and is a masterly cost-benefit analysis of various proposed legislative measures for the control or decontrol of pornography. Whether this presages any Damascus-road conversion of Williams to utilitarianism I doubt; but it illustrates my point that when anti-utilitarians produce arguments on practical issues they are usually utilitarian ones. The Williams Report is a really excellent piece of work, and it is a pity that, being a bit in advance of public opinion, it has not been acted on.

I could not honestly say the same for the report of another British working party headed by a philosopher, the Warnock Report on Human Fertilization and Embryology,[5] which recommends new legislation for the regulation of in vitro fertilization and the treatment of embryos. My impression is that Mary Warnock and her working party, unlike Bernard Williams and his, did not set out to find solid arguments leading to conclusions that could be rationally defended. Rather, they looked around among the conflicting opinions that were current in the working party and outside, and tried to find recommendations which would arouse the least dissent. That, no doubt, is why Warnock had so much better a press than Williams, and is likely to be acted on by the legislature. But if one looks at the actual report, one finds again and again, in almost every paragraph, judgements which are mere affirmation without any argument. Many of these have struck the public, and have struck me, as perfectly sensible. But if one asks why they are sensible, one gets no answer from the report. It is significant that on the issues on which the report has been seriously challenged—that is, the issues which are most controversial and on which help would be most valuable—the disputes that have followed the publication of the Report have been left unresolved by anything in it. This illus-

---

[4]R. M. Dworkin, 'Is There a Right to Pornography', *Oxford Journal of Legal Studies* 1 (1981); R. M. Hare, 'Arguing about Rights', *Emory Law Journal* 33 (1984).

[5]Department of Health and Social Security, *Report of the Committee of Inquiry into Human Fertilization and Embryology*, Chairman Dame Mary Warnock, HMSO Cmnd. 9314, 1984.

trates very well what I said about intuitionists. The issues I am referring to are those concerning the legalization of surrogate motherhood and the time-period after which embryos should be given legal protection.

It might be claimed in favour of the Warnock approach that if philosophers want to influence public opinion, it is more likely to be successful than that of Williams. I am reminded here of what Plato says in the *Republic*[6] about the difficulties philosophers face in politics. And no doubt Mary Warnock did her usual marvellous job as a practical adviser to government. And she has shown elsewhere (for example in her writings on education) that she is capable of giving reasons (most of them broadly utilitarian) for her views. But she seems not to have made all the *philosophical* contributions to the report that she could have, although such help is badly needed in this area.

Williams, on the other hand, has not yet had much influence; but if anybody now or in the future wants to understand the issues on the control of pornography and make up his mind rationally what should be done about them, Williams has provided a wealth of genuinely philosophical assistance. I would say that his time will come. The only trouble is that events and technology do move on, and may require new discussions and measures; for example, 'video nasties' have come on general sale on the black market in Britain since the Williams Report was published.

I am sure that there will be some philosophers (perhaps the majority) who will claim that they fall into neither of the two classes I have mentioned: the Kantian utilitarians like me, and the intuitionists who cannot provide any reasons for their opinions. All I can say in reply is that in my reading of the philosophical literature on practical issues (although I have not read enough of it to speak with authority) I have found that nearly all writers appeal to moral intuitions to a degree which quite destroys their claim to rational assent; and that where reasons are given, they are either covertly utilitarian reasons, or are invalid (e.g., because of suppressed premisses), or else rest on foundations for which themselves no reasons are given. I could also, if space permitted, give my justification for discarding the prevalent dogma, emanating from recent *soi-disants* 'Kantians', and bottle-fed to nearly all beginner students, that Kant and the

---

[6]Plato, *Republic* 496a ff.

utilitarians are at opposite poles of moral philosophy and cannot mix. I have shown elsewhere how they can be synthesized.[7]

So, then, one of the main benefits that ethical theory can get from a dose of real practical controversy in the company of practitioners of other disciplines is that we are brought to see the poverty of intuitionism and the appeal to conviction and consensus. Some philosophers, however, react to this experience, not by trying to find a viable theory which *will* yield arguments that can be defended, but by doubting the practical value of theory altogether. They join the pluralist anti-philosophers that I mentioned earlier. This is even more likely to happen in the case of someone who has not had much serious down-to-earth contact with practical issues, but whose education in applied philosophy has been limited to the class-room. It is perfectly true that discussion of practical issues with students may be inconclusive. It may even be corrupting, if badly handled by a philosopher who does not know the theoretical moves well enough to guide students through them to conclusions which they can rationally accept. The students may come to think that absolutely *any* moral opinion can find *some* ethical theory to buttress it. That, to my mind, is not an argument for abandoning theory, but for seeking the best theory, which involves serious discussion of the theoretical issues with one's students. It might also be thought (wrongly) to be an illustration of what Aristotle says,[8] that the young are not a suitable audience for such lectures, because they lack practical experience. Certainly one does not find this happening with an audience of experienced practitioners, unless they have become too exasperated by the antics of bad philosophers. But nor, *pace* Aristotle, does one with the young either, if they are made acquainted in a serious way with the problems.

I may mention lastly another and even more pernicious kind of anti-philosopher, consisting of those whose motives for engaging in these discussions are not really philosophical at all. They have some deep unquestioned conviction, usually religious or political in origin, about, say, contraception or social justice, and, having learnt some philosophy, are prepared to make any eristical move they can think up, not to test the conviction, but to shore it up. To adapt the famous aphorism about politicians and statistics, they use logic as a

---

[7]See note 2 above and *Moral Thinking,* passim.
[8]Aristotle, *Nicomachean Ethics* 1095a 2ff.

drunkard uses a lamppost, not for illumination but for support. Some of these are good philosophers who have done excellent work in other fields; but when they come to applied ethics they are not prepared to expose to scrutiny opinions which they are certain are correct.

It might be thought from what I have said so far that my recommendation to philosophers engaged in practical discussion would be the following: discard all appeals to antecedent moral convictions; ascertain the facts from the practitioners; devise, by the theoretical methods available to the moral philosopher (essentially the methods of philosophical logic or conceptual analysis), a viable ethical theory yielding rules of sound reasoning on moral questions; and then reason from the facts in accordance with the rules and try to get the practitioners to follow the reasoning and accept its conclusions. This might be a possible approach to start with, but it suffers from certain disadvantages and is not what I am going to recommend. From experience I have come to see that a much more dialectical approach, in almost the true Platonic sense, is likely to be more fecund.

To begin with, the practitioners do not like to be given a theoretical lecture on moral philosophy, especially if they think you are trying to prove practical conclusions about which they have antecedent doubts. This difficulty will be increased if they are made aware, as they should be, that there are rival theories in moral philosophy which might not yield the same conclusions. But the biggest disadvantage of this procedure is that it cuts the philosopher off from a very important source of useful information. This is information about the moral opinions of those with experience of the issues. To paraphrase what Aristotle said about virtue, we have to examine it not merely in a logical way, but on the basis of what people say about it.[9]

It might be supposed that I would never think that important, after what I have said about the futility of appeals to convictions. But what I am now going to recommend is not an *appeal* to convictions, but rather a study of them in the hope that we might learn something about the concepts, including the moral concepts, that the practitioners are using. It was J. L. Austin above all from whom we learnt that those doing conceptual analysis will make fewer mis-

---

[9]Aristotle, *Nicomachean Ethics* 1098b 9 ff.

takes if they study the words whose use they are investigating in their proper habitat. I am sure that Wittgenstein would have said the same about the study of words *in use*. I have come to see that this is especially true in moral philosophy, but that in moral philosophy there is a peculiar hazard to be avoided. That is the hazard I was warning against when I said that we cannot usefully *appeal* to moral convictions however widespread, especially on issues which are controversial. The 'moral majority' does not have the last word.

What I am recommending is not that we should produce arguments of the following form, as many do: everybody but a few cranks and Buddhists thinks that meat-eating is all right, so it must be all right. I am recommending something quite different. This is that we should look at the opinions of people, and ask whether, if our theory about the uses of words and the rules of reasoning which they determine were correct, these are the opinions we could expect them to hold. The method is essentially that of Popper: It tests an ethical theory by seeing whether it yields predictions which are false. The predictions are about the moral opinions people will hold; and the basis of them is a series of assumptions about their preferences, their factual beliefs, including beliefs about other people's preferences, the meaning and thus the logic of the moral words they are using, and the correctness and clarity with which they follow this logic. People come to their moral opinions as a result of a number of factors, not all of them rational, and they may be led astray. But one of the factors is the meaning and use of the moral words they are employing; and these generate the rules of reasoning which, if they understand the words, they will follow, perhaps without articulating them.

There is a difficulty here which is common to all such hypothetico-deductive procedures. We are basing our prediction on a number of assumptions; and we can only test one of these assumptions at a time, by taking the others as given. In the present case what we are trying to do is to test the assumption about the meaning and logic of the moral words as people use them. We therefore have to take as given the other assumptions just listed. But in fact we may have other evidence for the truth of these, so this is not a fatal objection to the method. We may have evidence, that is, that the people we are examining have certain factual beliefs and preferences, and are to some degree clear-headed and logical.

Given these other assumptions, we can test the single hypothesis that their use of the moral words is as we have assumed. Thus, on the basis of purely anthropological facts and assumptions about the people we are examining, we can test a hypothesis in ethical theory, though not, of course, any substantial moral hypothesis.

There is, however, a possible objection to this procedure which we must now consider. We have been assuming that substantial moral opinions are one thing, and logical theses about the uses of moral words another. Ethical naturalists[10] deny this, but I shall not concern myself with them here. A more serious difficulty is posed by those who challenged us to say how we would discriminate between theses which people hold as a matter of logic (hold as analytically true) and their substantial moral opinions.[11]

If we were not able to make this distinction, then there would be a loophole in the procedure I have been describing. Given information on their moral opinions about particular matters, and the other assumptions I mentioned, we might be able to test hypotheses about (to put it vaguely at first) their ways of moral thinking. But which of these ways were logically imposed, and which of them were substantial moral theses or rules, we should not be able to say.

I propose to leave this difficulty for another occasion, remarking merely that even if we could not perform the required discrimination, as I think we can, we should still be able to make considerable progress in ethical theory by the method advocated. For, on the basis of information about people's opinions on particular matters, and the other assumptions mentioned, we should be able to test hypotheses to the effect that our subjects held some combination of rather high-level moral principles and rules for the use of words or the meaning of concepts. It would remain to sort out these two things from each other (which can be done). But at least we should have tested hypotheses in a combination of moral anthropology and conceptual analysis—hypotheses capable of shedding considerable

---

[10]On naturalism see my *The Language of Morals* (Oxford University Press, 1952). Chapter 5 and 'Descriptivism' (*Proc. of British Academy* 49, 1963), reprinted in my *Essays on the Moral Concepts* (London: Macmillan, 1972).

[11]On difference between moral and logical or linguistic theses, see my *Moral Thinking*, pp. 10ff. and *Freedom and Reason* (Oxford University Press, 1963), pp. 30 ff.

light in ethical theory. What we should not have tested, let alone proved, would be any substantial *moral* theses. This is what differentiates the proposed method from any form of intuitionism.

We might give the following as an example of the application of the method. Suppose we are trying to test the thesis of universalizability (part of ethical theory). We find that people (for example King David when reproached by the prophet Nathan)[12] do apply to themselves moral judgments which they have just been making about other cases they think similar in the relevant particulars. From the fact that they make these moral judgments, in conjunction with assumptions of the sort mentioned above, we infer that the thesis of universalizability (that is, the thesis that, as people use words like 'wrong' they hold it inconsistent to make varying moral judgments about relevantly similar cases) is compatible with the observed facts of usage.

If other instances are produced with which it is claimed that the thesis is incompatible, then the thesis will have to be tested again on those cases, and its defender will have to show that the cases are in fact not incompatible with it. This, in all the cases I have seen produced, can be done; the cases are only thought to be incompatible with the thesis because those who produce them are confused. But I am not here defending the thesis—only illustrating the method.

So the moral opinions of people are not a test of *moral* truth; they are, rather, a test of what I called a viable ethical (i.e., *metaethical*) theory. If we find people holding moral opinions different from what the rules of reasoning generated by the theory would justify, this does not in itself refute the theory. But it does raise the question of what *other* factor in their thinking could have led them to those opinions. As I said, the factor need not be a rational nor even a respectable one. They may simply have got their facts wrong, in which case, we hope, they will alter their opinions when they get them right. But it may be that they have deeply ingrained prejudices which are not amenable to reason, like some of the philosophers I mentioned earlier. I am sure that this is true both of some of the opponents of legalized abortion and of some of its defenders. Or it may be that they just have not thought very clearly and so have

---

[12]For David and Nathan, see 2 Samuel 12.

got into a muddle. All these factors, ignorance, prejudice and muddled thinking, can reinforce one another.

However, I am not so pessimistic as to think that people, especially educated people, will always fall into these traps. Of such people, the 'moral majority' is not actually a majority, even now. Let me give an example of how public opinion, by sound reasoning, albeit inarticulate, can come to reject a moral opinion that it rationally ought to reject. It is by no means the only example I could give. Before the First World War, the ruling classes of all the major European powers were swayed by a kind of nationalism (misnamed 'patriotism') whose outcome in action led directly to the war. The public, having seen the appalling sufferings caused, came to the conclusion that any set of moral principles that allowed such policies must have something wrong with it.[13] On the question of *what* was wrong, and what principles should take the place of those rejected, the public has not yet made up its mind. Some think they should be pacifists; others, like myself, think that there is a kind of patriotism which we can recommend to the citizens of all countries, not just our own (universalizing our prescriptions), and which will permit the use of force in resisting aggression, but not for national self-aggrandisement. That question is still being argued, as is the related question of what difference it makes that nuclear weapons are now available.

Nevertheless this is, so far as it goes, an example of how the public can, in the course of a generation, reach new moral convictions, or at least reject old ones, on rational grounds. And the grounds are ones which, when fully set out, are completely in accord with my own utilitarian ethical theory. I think that the application of the same style of reasoning could sort out the questions that remain, given more certainty about the facts than we yet possess. But for now all I want to claim is that this is an illustration of the mutual benefit that comes to theory and practice by their interaction. The conclusion (the rejection of nationalism) is one that we should expect people to come to, given their understanding of the

---

[13]On attitudes to war, see my "Philosophy and Practice: Some Issues about War and Peace," in *Philosophy and Practice,* ed. A. P. Griffiths, Royal Inst. of Philosophy Lectures 18, Supp. to *Philosophy* 59 (Cambridge University Press, 1985).

moral concepts as set out in the theory, and given also their knowledge of the facts, a reasonable freedom from muddle and prejudice, and their ordinary non-moral preferences, such as the preference not to undergo the kind of sufferings that the two world wars entailed. So the theory has to that extent been tested. That is the benefit for theory. The benefit for practice is that, having provisionally, in Popperian style, tested the theory, we can go on using it in trying to solve the problems that remain.

So then the approach that I favour when discussing moral questions with the practitioners of other disciplines is not the somewhat condescending one that I described earlier, but rather something like this. First of all, find out from the practitioners as much as they know about the facts which generate the moral problems. Then discuss the moral problems with them in a perfectly open way, trying to find out what they think, and the reasons they give. It is my experience that one learns a lot by doing this. The practitioners may not be moral philosophers; but they have had in the course of their work to grapple with the problems; they do understand how to use the moral words, though they may not be able to give a philosophical account of their use that will stand up. So they can be expected to have thought rationally about the problems to the extent that they were free of prejudice and muddle (it would be implausible to accuse them of ignorance, because it is their own field and they have their noses in the problems). The doctors, for example, that I have met on working parties measure up very well to these expectations, unlike many people outside their disciplines who pontificate publicly about such questions. Admittedly, one occasionally meets very prejudiced irrational people; but I have not met them in the working parties I have served on.

Having elicited the opinions of our colleagues and the reasons they give for them, we can then ask to what extent a sound process of reasoning, based on the logic of the concepts that they are using, would yield those opinions. If opinions differ, as they will, then we can go further, and ask which of the opinions would be supported, and which rejected, by such a reasoning process. By the time the argument has reached this stage, it should be possible to explain one's reasoning to the non-philosophers, because they will have learnt something about philosophy in the process, just as the philosopher will have learnt something about medicine. Ideally, opinions will at this point start to converge as the reasons for them become clear, and you may even be able to present a unanimous report.

To sum up then, the chief benefits that ethical theory can get from an immersion in practical issues are two: first, the exposure of the pretensions of intuitionists (whether they call themselves that or not), who think that appeals to convictions or to consensus can carry any weight; and secondly, the testing of ethical theories about the meanings of moral words and the rules of moral argument which they generate, by seeing whether people's actual conclusions, when they are reasoning in favourable conditions, free from ignorance, muddle and prejudice, tally with what sound argument, in accordance with these rules, would justify. In this way we can hope to establish, at least provisionally, a theory which can then be applied to new problems. Since the testing of the theory will have involved no appeal to any substantial moral convictions, but only to the empirical, non-moral (if you like, anthropological) fact that people hold them, we can retain the hope that the same kind of application to new problems, in addition to shedding light on the problems and so helping with practice, will also further test the theory. It is a virtuous spiral.

5

How Can We Individuate
Moral Problems?*

Onora O'Neill

To do applied ethics at all we need, it seems, not only adequate moral theories but something to which they can be applied. The likeliest candidates may seem to be moral problems which are unresolved, or inadequately resolved. On inspection this answer does not seem quite satisfactory. One way in which it can unravel is this: when we ask people what the most important moral problems are we will get varied lists. A little historical or anthropological reflection reminds us that what now seem major problems have not always struck thoughtful people that way. The concerns of feminists have been marginal in past ethical thinking, and in many societies abortion has seemed a trivial issue. Concern about animals has been a recurrent but not a constant theme in ethical writing. Concern about collaboration, resistance, keeping hands clean and civil disobedience has been prominent during wars, including cold and civil wars; but less so at other times.

An initial reaction to these reminders might just be the comment that moral problems do indeed vary, and so different problems are discussed at different times. But this is only part of the story. Slavery, serfdom and forced labor were not new problems, but

---

*Appeared originally in *Social Policy and Conflict Resolution: Bowling Green Studies in Applied Philosophy,* vol. VI (1984), pp. 104–19, Thomas Attig, Donald Callen, and R. G. Frey, eds.; reprinted by permission of the author and the editors.

newly perceived as moral problems. Behavior to distant kin may not seem to us a domain of acute moral problems, but others might see in this our moral blindness rather than lack of problems they took seriously. It seems that moral problems can exist unperceived and unheeded. A great deal of the effort of moral reform is to make others aware of and responsive to problems rather than solutions. The anti-slavery movement had first to show that there was something to discuss. It is always a move forward to get others to see matters in a different light and so "on the defensive."

The thought that moral problems can exist unperceived suggests, perhaps, a picture of incomplete discovery. Just as islands or rivers may exist uncharted, so perhaps there are undiscovered moral problems waiting to be entered on the map of applied ethics. But this analogy can mislead. Rival cartographers use different projects and conventions but do not disagree about the major topographical features of the region to be charted. But rival moral theories and outlooks may differ about what problems there are. The point is not merely that observation will pick out items only in terms of the categories brought to an inquiry. In that sense even the data of geography are theory led. Moral problems are theory led in a deeper way. The features physical geographers survey and map are agreed upon between them and are in many cases salient for non-specialist observers. The range of problems picked out by one moral theory may not be problems for adherents of different theories, and are not generally salient for non-specialist observers. It is hard to think of relatively specific situations that would be universally seen as moral problems; at most there may be universal agreement that problems arise in various broad areas of human life.

In the light of a moral theory concerned with rights, violations of privacy may seem serious problems; yet some may be invisible in the light of a theory concerned with costs and benefits rather than rights. In the light of one account or autonomy, relationships between "clients" and either prostitutes or social workers may seem standardly unproblematic unless we suspect failure of informed consent. In the light of other views it may seem that relationships with prostitutes or social workers, in their professional capacities, would always be morally problematic. It seems unlikely that there is any theoretically neutral way to establish a list of moral problems or even of the moral problems of a given period or society or of a specific domain of life. Rather any listing of moral problems will be theory led in at least two respects. Problems will appear on the list only in the light of theories which include appropriate concepts and will not be salient in abstraction from such theories.

There are those who claim that moral problems are theory led in a third and more fundamental way, in that they are not merely selected and made salient to us by theories, but exist only when the adoption or dominance of a certain moral theory or outlook establishes an agenda of moral problems for a given society. Such views may see moral discourse and the problems, arguments and solutions which such discourse permits and generates either as reflecting dominant ideologies or as a human invention. In these perspectives it would be senseless to claim that the same moral problem might be addressed by any of a variety of theories, or that certain moral traditions were blind to a particular sort of moral problem or that there is any objective list of "the moral problems" faced by any individual or society. All such claims make sense only if moral problems are to *some* extent independent of theories, even if our apprehension of them is theory dependent. They lack sense in a perspective which sees moral problems as constituted by a mode of discourse, and so not individuable in abstraction from that discourse. To those who hold such perspectives the current preoccupations of writers in applied ethics reflect no more than the internally generated difficulties of certain ethical positions which have come to dominate public discourse in certain societies. Liberal theorists debate the fine points of liberal ideology in a new scholasticism, and like earlier scholastics mistakenly see their debates as having a universal significance. But the problems they debate are only shadows of received theory and lack autonomous reality. While such perspectives localize others' moral debates, claiming that they lack sense beyond the context of locally received theories, they leave fundamental practical and moral questions formulated but not readily resolvable. For those who do not embrace a radical conceptual relativism it makes sense to ask whether one rather than another mode of moral discourse ought to be adopted, and to wonder whether certain theories are deficient because they fail to select or make salient problems of various sorts. For present purposes I shall set aside positions which embody a radical conceptual relativism and consider some of the implications of the claim that moral problems, even if not theory-constituted, are nevertheless only selected and salient in the light of some moral theories.

Even this limited sort of theory dependence has interesting implications for methods that can appropriately be used in moral reasoning. For example, it suggests that it is suspect (though it seems to me common) to start with some moral problem which is taken as "given" and then cast around for a fitting theory. A moral problem is not like an awkwardly shaped child, all too solidly there, while the parent casts around for a garment that will fit. When we find that utilitarianism sits awkwardly on a problem it is not enough to reach for a Rawlsian or a human rights outfit. For if we find that one of these is better suited, it may reflect only a match between the terms in which the problem was tailored and the terms of the theory. It might yet be that different articulations of the problem would fit it to be handled by other theories. Whereas a child has a given shape and clothes must be found which fit (more or less) well, a moral problem may be rearticulated to fall within the scope and terms of a theory to which it was initially ill-suited. But children cannot be reshaped to the clothes that are to hand.

But if moral problems are not "given" in a way which would make such patterns of reasoning possible, then a central problem of applied ethics must be to pick out the most important problems for applying moral reasoning. We cannot just wait for moral problems to "crop up" but must try to see whether those problems which strike us as important are indeed so, and whether current debates neglect other problems of moral significance. What reasons can we give ourselves for thinking that we are not overlooking central moral problems, as we now may think the generations who interpreted the rights of man as the rights of men or overlooked the iniquities of slavery did?

One reason that could suggest that we are no longer so myopic is that we now have a flourishing tradition of debate in applied ethics. If ethical theory is already being applied to moral problems, then we must already have methods for picking them out and for settling disputes about rival specifications of the moral problems of a domain. Only given such methods, as well as adequate ethical theories, could the enterprise of applying ethics take place. With this hope in mind I shall consider whether recent writing in ethics provides us with models for individuating moral problems.

HYPOTHETICAL EXAMPLES IN CONTEMPORARY ETHICAL WRITING

The surface of contemporary ethical writing is studded with detailed accounts of moral problems. Few writers now illustrate their theoretical claims with minimal accounts of the relations and transactions between A, B and C. Even Smith, Brown and Robinson, who used to serve so frequently, have been retired, sometimes with complaints about gender and class bias. Elaborate and detailed examples are employed in their place. I shall consider a sample of contemporary uses of examples in ethical writing to discover whether any offers or suggests a model (or an account) of how we might individuate moral problems. This section will be concerned with hypothetical examples, and the next with actual cases.

Sartre is often acknowledged as a pioneer here. His famous example of the young man torn between joining the Free French and staying to care for his mother ostensibly shows that moral codes and theories can neither make our decisions for us nor guide those decisions. The example is rich and detailed; but for all that, it is not independent of moral theory. Rather, it is constructed to make vivid the claims both of personal devotion and of wider public duty. The point of the example would be lost on anybody who did not appreciate both codes. The example is indeed not merely illustrative, but rather specifically illustrative of two codes which in this situation generate incompatible prescriptions. Here illustration is used to criticise the codes and more abstract theories it illustrates. Certain moral theories are shown to generate problems which they cannot solve. Sartre's aim is to cast general doubt on the adequacy of moral theory; yet his thought depends on the theory which provides the method of discerning and making salient the predicament discussed. The example shows at most that moral theories are incomplete and not that they can be jettisoned. For those who reject or do not understand the two codes to which Sartre's protagonist is drawn there is no moral problem here. Rich and poignant examples too are theory led. If Sartre's discussion leads us to doubt certain theories, it may also lead us to doubt the principles of individuation by which his crucial example was generated.

Rich and detailed examples have also been demanded and discussed in much Wittgensteinian ethical writing. Winch has even suggested that examples rather than theories are fundamental for moral thought: "All we can do, I am arguing, is to look at particular examples and see what we *do* want to say about them."[1] Curiously, the "particular examples" of much Wittgensteinian ethical writing are not usually examples of actual cases at all, but rather hypothetical, usually literary, examples of moral vicissitudes. There is, perforce, little we can do about such examples except "see what we do want to say about them." We cannot be guided just by looking at literary or other hypothetical examples for two reasons. First, if we have reason to think that moral problems are not salient in abstraction from theory, the results of looking will vary with the ethical theory or code or outlook through which we look. Secondly, focus on examples cannot guide our judgment of the fit between actual cases and supposedly relevant examples.

The first of these points is accepted by some Wittgensteinian writers.[2] They take it that whatever moral theory is embedded in current social and moral practices provides categories which select and define moral problems and considerations and render them salient. But if current practices determine the selection of moral problems, there is much less to insistence on detailed examples than the passage above suggests. Examples are not replacing theory in moral reasoning. Rather theory is present from the start, embedded in current practice. But if we think it possible to criticise current practice, we will not be likely to take it as defining what moral problems there are. Only a strong relativism which holds that current practice constitutes the domain of moral concern (rather than rendering one or another aspect of that domain salient) can take for granted whatever specification of moral problems current practices offer. Yet Wittgensteinian writing, even when it repudiates relativism, has said little about ways in which disputes about what moral problems there are might be resolved. Clearly no mere appeal to examples can avoid relying on some theoretical claims to justify a particular construal of the domain of moral problems.

---

[1] Peter Winch, "Moral Integrity" in his *Ethics and Action* (London: Routledge and Kegan Paul), p. 182.

[2] Wittgensteinian writers who make this move include D. Z. Phillips and H. O. Mounce in *Moral Practices* (London: Routledge and Kegan Paul, 1970); R. Beardsmore in *Moral Reasoning* (London: Routledge and Kegan Paul, 1969); Rodger Beehler, *Moral Life* (Oxford: Blackwell, 1978). I have discussed their approach more fully in "The Power of Example," *Philosophy*, forthcoming.

Detailed examples have also been much discussed in post-Rawlsian writing in applied ethics. Appropriately in this genre of ethical writing we find discussion not only of hypothetical and literary examples, which are evidently theory led, but of actual case histories. The implications of introducing actual cases will be discussed in the next section. The special role of hypothetical examples in the Rawlsian method of reflective equilibrium once again offers us no method for individuating moral problems. Reflective equilibrating requires us to weigh a (tentative) ethical theory with "our considered moral judgments." In the process both theory and considered moral judgments may need revision. But considered moral judgments are themselves theoretical. They do not reflect direct access to an objective construal of the domain of problems. Rather reflective equilibrating is a method by which we can achieve coherence between our more specific and more general principles. Even when coherence has been achieved we may still worry whether the resulting theory fails to select certain types of moral problems, or gives undue prominence to others. Only if we thought that our initial, pre-reflective moral judgments embodied some direct intuition of moral reality could we be sure that the theoretical position reached with their help was neither blind to some moral problems nor hypersensitive to others. Reflective equilibrating is a method for constructing moral theories and not a guarantee that the most important moral problems have been picked out.

A focus on hypothetical examples is not a theory of moral individuation or of moral judgment; still less is it a way of breaking free from moral principles, codes or theories. Examples may be used to illustrate or to question moral theories, or to present them in less abstract and more socially contextualized ways. But no amount of vivid illustration or sensitivity to the contexts of moral reasoning can substitute for an account of why certain (but not other) situations are thought of as moral problems. The change in flavor of much modern ethical writings has been more like the shift from cookery books with black and white illustrations to cookery books with glossy colored photographs of meals that might be made. But the aim of applied ethics is not to illustrate recipes. It is more like helping a cook who has to decide what meals to produce when faced with actual utensils and ingredients, so needs to begin with an inventory of a particular kitchen and larder. Vivid illustrations are no guarantee of substantial results—especially when the utensils and ingredients illustrated are lacking.

ACTUAL CASES AND IDEOLOGY

Each of the moves towards more determinate and vivid ethical writing considered in the last section uses *hypothetical,* unavoidably theory led, examples for theoretical purposes. These moves neither show how we can justify a particular way of specifying a domain of moral problems, nor how theory is to be applied to the resolution of actual cases. So it may seem that if we are to consider how applied ethics is to be done we should look at actual rather than hypothetical examples and perhaps try to contribute to the resolution of actual moral problems. A good part of post-Rawlsian activity in applied ethics especially in the United States has been involved with actual, especially public, problems. William Ruddick has described some of these activities:

> In the last decade many academic philosophers in the United States have "gone public". In television interviews, newspapers and neighbourhood meetings they have discussed misuse of animals, whistle-blowing and world hunger. Philosophers sit on presidential commissions on medical experimentation, on scientific research review boards, on committees to draft codes of conduct for trial lawyers, social workers and senators. They consult with town planners, prison officials and inmates, generals, corporation executives, and hospital staffs. They run for political office, serve as congressional legislative aides, cruise in police cars. . . .[3]

Philosophers who join in these activities appear to have no difficulty individuating moral problems; they have begun to work for morally adequate resolutions. But we may still wonder whether applied *Rechtsphilosophie* will be helped by cruising in police cars, or more generally by "going public." One result of such involvement is that the preoccupations of various practitioners may be taken to define the domain of moral problems. Applied ethics then runs the danger of allowing its agenda to be defined by the concerns of various interest groups and bodies of professional opinion. An agenda

---

[3]William Ruddick, "Philosophy and Public Affairs," *Social Research,* 47 (1980), pp. 734–48, esp. 734 and 744.

constructed on these principles may make some problems more sali-ent than they would otherwise have been and may leave others in-visible. Ruddick points to the danger of the "legalization of philosophy," which is revealed not only by the extent to which "public issues are defined by current court concerns," but also by a preoccupation with rights and violations of rights and relative lack of concern for matters such as the virtues of public life. The worldly success of applied ethics in the United States has to some extent been achieved at the cost of the restriction of focus which working with practitioners requires. It has also produced in some other parts of the English speaking philosophical community an uneasy sense that a great deal of the literature in applied ethics is either openly or subliminally structured by legal and social categories that are at home mainly in the political and ideological setting of public life in the United States.

A case can be made for accepting this restriction of focus. Many moral decisions, above all those of public life, must address prob-lems as conventionally defined. They cannot await social transfor-mations or revolutions which would reconstrue these problems. *Rechtsphilosophie* is unavoidably concerned with problems that arise under morally imperfect conditions, so must accept that the solu-tions it seeks are restricted in certain ways.

But there is also a good case for not accepting this restriction and so for not becoming too involved with practitioners. Conven-tional ways of specifying the problems of a domain are bound to miss problems which reflect the conventions themselves. For ex-ample, bureaucratic structures and the corresponding official dis-course will not pick up problems which arise from the moral distancing of officials from cases with which they deal. Such distancing is basic to bureaucratic culture—the guarantee of impartiality—and its moral cost will therefore be little stressed within bureaucratic discourse. Yet this very distancing transforms other human beings into "cases" or "clients," which is surely not morally insignificant. Sometimes sharing practitioners' perspectives may be question begging or even corrupting. This may be the cost of allowing the agenda of public moral problems to be determined by the discourse and interests of practitioners.

One response to these difficulties might be to seek involvement not only with "establishment" practitioners in a given domain, but also (perhaps primarily) with those who dispute professional or official construals of some domain of problems. For example, some feminists have objected to the construal of childbirth as a standard medical episode in which patients are dealt with by professionals. They insist that women giving birth are not passive, hence not patients, and that they need medical help in the way that those attempting hazardous sporting or endurance records need medical help—that is on stand-by. This external critique has affected some medical practices; for example, women in labor may be seen less as patients and less often obliged to adopt the prone and painful position needed by patients on operating tables, and may be allowed more choice and more information about their treatment and less social isolation than used to be thought necessary.

Involvement with practitioners does not have to be only with established and official practitioners and their perspectives. But it is unclear whether involvement with any or with multiple groups of practitioners can guarantee adequate specifications of the problems of a domain. May not involvements with practitioners yield rival specifications of the problems of a domain where practitioners are ideologically divided? And when there *is* consensus among practitioners, may it not still reflect an ideological position which is incompatible with whichever moral theory is being advanced as the most adequate approach to the resolution of problems? And may this moral theory not then also come to be thought of as one more contender in the ideological arena, which affords no privileged vantage point on the specification of problems or on their resolution? Such a line of thought might lead to the view that political activity must always not only supplement but precede moral reasoning, since we cannot rationally arbitrate between alternative modes of moral discourse, nor between alternative accounts of what problems there are. Once one or another ideology is established as dominant, applied ethics will be possible, though confined to the framework established by this ideology. If liberal modes of thought remain dominant in some places we can expect an applied ethics concerned with violations of rights; if liberal ideologies lose their dominance, concern with rights and their violation may fade from the agenda of applied ethics to be replaced by concern for whatever problems are made salient by the newly dominant mode of discourse. If such an account is correct, applied ethics is neither impossible nor unimportant, but is always less fundamental than political activity. Only political activity can establish a context in which certain moral

problems become salient and certain solutions defensible or reject-
able. Further, moral reasons could not then be given for activity
that aims to reinforce or to undermine the position of any such
framework of thought. If discourse (or ideology or received practices) constitute moral frameworks, moral reasoning can say nothing for or against imposing or seeking to impose a particular mode
of discourse.

This picture of applied ethics as ancillary to dominant ideologies would not be widely shared by those who write in the field.
The reason why philosophers have sought public involvements has
not been (merely) so that they could join in political struggles or so
that they could elaborate the ethical implications of dominant ideologies. The hope has rather been to resist any claim that moral
theory is just one of multiple contending ideologies, and to offer a
distinctively philosophical contribution to the resolution of moral
problems. But it is not enough for writing in applied ethics to seek
reasoned resolutions of problems, while assuming that the specification of problems is given. It is also necessary to offer reasons for
accepting a specific account of the morally significant problems of a
domain. In the next section of this paper I shall offer some comments on what the reasoned specification of moral problems might
minimally require.

STRATEGIES OF REFLECTION

If the enterprise of applied ethics is to do more than clarify and
resolve problems raised by whatever ideologies become dominant
from time to time, we must have at least some ways of questioning
and revising proposed lists of moral problems. This need may seem
easily met if we assume as our own starting point a particularly
strong moral theory. For example, utilitarianism includes principles
for individuating acts (in terms of expected consequences) and for
individuating acts of moral significance (in terms of the expected
utility of consequences). Given this theory we might expect a few
difficulties (of principle) in discerning the moral problems of some
domain, or indeed in calculating morally required solutions. Utilitarians do not generally need to consider or debate others' views of
what the morally significant problems are; ideological divergences
are of import only if they affect expected utility; their discussion is
morally required only when such a debate will have beneficial con-

sequences. But this absence of difficulties of principle is matched by difficulties in the practice of applying utilitarian thinking in actual situations, and framed by a lack of reasons for those who do not find themselves at utilitarian starting points to think utilitarianism itself more than a sporadically dominant ideology.

For those who cannot accept or justify utilitarian starting points there is no ready chart of the problems to which moral thinking should be applied. The difficulty arises, I think, from two quarters. First, without consequentialist principles of act individuation we are immediately faced with multiple distinct ways in which the situations and available acts of any domain can be picked out. Second, even when we can agree which situations obtain and which acts have been or might be done, we may still disagree over which are morally significant. Applied ethics needs moral theories which not merely pick out acts and aspects of situations as morally significant, but offer grounds for thinking that what the theory picks out is indeed morally significant. Adequate moral theories must include a critical appraisal of their own strengths. Without such theories we risk merely *accepting* or *positing* what moral problems there are, and do nothing to overcome the suspicion that applied ethics is only the under laborer or handmaiden of some possible ideology. To overcome this suspicion we need some account of what it would be to specify a domain of moral problems in ways that could be defended beyond circles to whom these problems are immediately salient. I shall offer a tentative sketch of some standards for such a critical moral theory.

First, it seems to me, any principles for picking out moral problems which are relevant in practical reasoning must *start* from the ways in which the agents who are mainly involved would construe the problems. (This suggests that it *might* be important to ride in police cars: but also to listen to those who commit, suffer or fear crimes). Construals of problems which neglect agents' views risk being unintelligible to those who may have to act. Our "moral starting point," to use a phrase of MacIntyre's, must include construals of acts, situations and problems which are intelligible to agents whose construal of problems may seem deficient or ideologically biased.

Second, it seems to me, rationally defensible principles for picking out moral problems need not pick out just those problems which those most affected or those best placed to act would initially and unreflectively pick out. A mafioso might view his main problems as those of enforcement and loyalty within the "family." Few would share his view. If applied ethics is not to be subservient to local or dominant ideologies it must sometimes reject both agents' and more generally received construals of problems as deluded or inadequate. But such rejections will carry weight only when alternative construals of problems are in principle rationally defensible to agents who may initially have been gripped by some ideology which rendered the proposed revised account of a domain of problems invisible or irrelevant. If we cannot sketch what such a defense of a way of construing the moral problems of a domain would be, and how it might be presented to those who face these problems, then we must, I think, concede that applied ethics can be conducted only within whatever ideological framework is taken to set problems and to define what would count as solutions. However, we may not always convince those who initially reject a revised construal of a domain of problems.

The task of defending one rather than another construal of moral problems need not, however, be that of establishing one rather than another fundamental categorical framework. It requires that an ethical theory, its fundamental moral categories, and the resulting specification of a domain of moral problems be defended in terms accessible to those who do not initially hold this theory. But such a defense may need no bridge between incommensurable conceptual frameworks. The task is rather to show that a group of human actions, relationships and possibilities, should be seen as constituting one rather than another sort of moral problem. It therefore seems that applied ethics needs something like what Kant called "reflective judging," where "the particular is given and the universal has to be found for it."[4] The first step in applying any moral theory is to reappraise or reconstrue not some indeterminate, conceptually alien, subject matter, but rather human situations which are already seen in certain light. It is because human situations are already, pre-reflectively, described in specific (no doubt partly ideologically determined) ways, because we have moral starting points, that it is possible to aim for a reasoned defense of one

---

[4]Immanuel Kant, *Critique of Judgment,* tr. James Meredith (Oxford: Oxford University Press, 1978), p. 179. For further discussion of strategies of reflection see the last section of "The Power of Example."

rather than another construal of moral problems, and for a reasoned revision of initial views.

Such a reasoned account of the moral problems of some domain must do more than offer a prepackaged (official or countercultural) construal of problems. The dominance or obscurity of the conceptual framework in which a problem is construed can be relevant to the ease with which a particular construal of some domain of problems can be communicated; but dominance neither confers nor precludes authority. Standards for reflective judging cannot be read off received outlooks or accepted practices or individual convictions and attitudes.

Rather reflective judging "stands in need of a principle." According to Kant when we judge a given particular reflectively we aim to discern the "coherence of experience with our own and others' cognitive capacities."[5] This provides some indication of ways in which construals of problems might be rationally defended even to those of differing outlook and ideology. To show a construal of some moral problem acceptable we have to show that it coheres not with the actual views but with the cognitive capacities of all who are party to the situation. The enterprise of revealing coherence demands an account which recognizes disagreements between rival ways of picking out moral problems and provides a background against which such discrepancies are themselves comprehensible. But this background does not have to include any Archimedean rational standpoint from which all possible disagreements can be resolved to the satisfaction of all possible parties. What is (minimally) needed is some shared strategies, to which all actual parties are committed in their own debates about the construal of problems within their own preferred ideological frameworks. Given this much we can make some moves forward. For example, if certain psychoanalytic construals of patients' behavior are to be preferred to patients' own accounts, it is because we can give some account in which both the subjective and the psychoanalytic account and the discrepancies between them are intelligible, and potentially intelligible to the patient. Or if we reject a construal of some family problem in terms of conflicting parental rights and children's claims, in favor of a construal which sets the matter in the context of

---

[5]Immanuel Kant, *First Introduction to the Critique of Judgment*, tr. J. Haden (Indianapolis: Bobbs Merrill, 1965), p. 220.

a developmental account of the shared life of a family, this could be argued for only in the context of a larger picture within which the adversarial, conflicting rights model of family life is shown less coherent with what all parties can understand than the developmental approach. Ideological starting points are on this view essential to applied ethics, not because they constitute frameworks to which moral problems and their solutions are confined, but because a rationally defensible account of the moral problems to be faced must acknowledge and judge between the alternative construals of problems and situations from which those who have to act begin their debates.

If we were faced with *radical* conceptual relativism there might be no ways in which the discourse of those with rival ideologies could mesh, and so no strategies of reflective judging by which to tackle points of disagreement. But in the arena of human action this is not our situation. Gellner has recently commented:

> The incommensurability thesis owes something of its plausibility to a tendency to take too seriously the self-absolutizing, critic-anathematizing faiths of late agrarian societies, which indeed are generally so construed as to be logically invulnerable from outside and perpetually self-confirming from inside. Despite these notorious traits . . . the adherents of these faiths have, in practice, known how to transcend their own much advertised blinkers. They are and were conceptually bilingual, and knew how to switch from commensurate to incommensurate idioms with ease and alacrity.[6]

Radical conceptual incommensurability is not mainly a practical problem. Even when we come closest to it, and suspect others' sanity or our own, strategies of listening to the other may reveal levels of interpretability and decipherable communication. We can reserve our practical worries about radically incommensurable views of human action and moral theory for the arrival of genuine aliens; and if they arrive, they may turn out to be kin to E.T.

In calling the various strategies of reflective judging on which we may find agreement and the possibility of communication with others of disparate ideology *rational* processes, I do not mean to suggest that they are mechanical or algorithmic or that they guarantee any form of completeness or closure in our moral thinking. Pre-

---

[6]Ernest Gellner, *Nations and Nationalism* (Oxford: Blackwell, 1983), p. 120.

sumably the very fact that alternative descriptions of situations are indefinitely many and that we have no calculus of descriptions means that reflective judging cannot be reduced to a set of algorithms. Strategies of reflective judging are no more than ways of revising initial construals of moral starting points to achieve greater intelligibility to the parties involved. The test of adequacy in such revisions is coherence with the cognitive capacities (not the actual cognitive performance) of those involved. If we follow such strategies we have no guarantee that we will start with any common agenda of moral problems, but some reasons to think that we may be able to move towards one, while acknowledging and making sense of discarded and rejected construals of the domain of problems we confront. If this is the case, then practical reason cannot neglect ideology, but need not be only its underlaborer or handmaiden. The specification of moral problems is no more in principle immune to rational criticism than is the formulation of moral theories.[7]

---

[7]Earlier versions of the paper benefitted greatly from comments by R. M. Hare, William Ruddick, Richard Lindley, Keith Graham and Jan Narveson. I am grateful to each of them and well aware that the present version does not answer all the questions raised.

6

Is There a Problem about "Applied" Ethics?

Jan Narveson

Every "applied" science has its difficulties in practice. Is there anything special about ethics in this regard? Have we reason for thinking that what has lately been called "applied ethics" is impossible, that philosophy must be quite particularly impotent in this domain? That is the question I will be considering here. My answer will be that we do not. Difficulties we have always with us, but there are no peculiarly intractable, let alone fatal, problems in pursuing applied ethics.

My plan in this brief investigation will be to distinguish a number of different objections that might be taken to pose the special problem we are concerned with here—eight, in fact. And I conjecture that the feeling that there is something special about applied ethics in this respect may be due to failure to appreciate the differences among these possible objections. We will move, approximately, from the most general in scope to the most specific.

I

A very long time ago in this century a view developed to the effect that philosophical ethics as a whole was powerless to arrive at practical conclusions. A distinction was made between "metaethics" and "normative" ethics, the former consisting, as the word suggests, in propositions "about" ethics, propositions "mapping the conceptual geography" of the subject, the latter in real judgments about actions and characters, policies, and principles. And the philosopher's peculiar domain, it was held, was confined to the former. [A historical note: I have observed a tendency in recent philosophical literature to talk as though the view in question was absolutely standard in the field up until *very* recently—shortly before the moment of writing, one inferred. So perhaps it will add perspective to note that virtually all the work in philosophy that this writer has ever done, including my Ph.D. thesis (1961), was in normative rather than "meta" ethics—insofar as one can distinguish these two—and that a careful perusal of the philosophical literature in America, at least, will reveal that the view in question was *never* the monopoly view.] Since this idea is now generally exploded, there is no need to go on at length about it, but, because they have some bearing on what follows, I shall briefly summarize the two main points to be made against it.

In the first place, the proposed distinction is not going to do what was wanted anyway. This is partly because it surely presupposes another distinction between analytic and synthetic which in turn has been abandoned by most philosophers as possessing any ultimate theoretical significance. But, even if that were not so, it is hard to believe that it would make no difference in practice *which* analytic theory of ethics was correct. If theory *A* is correct, then what people are doing when they make ethical judgments and decisions is one thing; but, if *B* is correct, then they are doing quite another. And which they are doing will determine what kind of further cognitive inputs are in order and will have what effect. It is not credible to suppose that the effect on practice of one theory's being right rather than another is zero; but this must, presumably, have been what was being maintained.

In the second place, even if we accept the distinction, how do we move from the premise that there are these two quite different kinds of activities, one "purely conceptual," the other "normative," to the conclusion that philosophers get to do only the former? Philosophers have a nose for distinctions, and a keen eye on the lookout for fallacies, on the one hand, and for good arguments on the other. Unless one took the extreme view that thought in general is irrelevant to ethics, one would expect that philosophers had a natural advantage when entering the domain of practice. There is, it seems to me, something absurdly "scholastic" (in the pejorative sense of that term) about excluding those who in certain respects are obviously more than usually well qualified from the domain in question. The objection seems to envisage some kind of all-powerful trade-union rules of a more than ordinarily arbitrary and self-defeating kind. (Fantasy: some government makes a momentous decision, affecting millions of people for generations to come; it adopts this policy, a bad one, for patently fallacious reasons. Some philosopher happens to point this out at a cocktail party after the damage was done. "But why didn't you say so before?", says the incredulous official. "Oh, that wasn't in my department, you know" . . .)

II

A very different—and in its own way extremely important— objection that we often hear stems from the *disagreement* that we continually encounter among different thinkers. The complaint is of the form, "*Philosophy* has nothing to say about such and such"; and, on one obvious understanding of the claim, it is very likely to be true: Philosophy doesn't say anything in particular, because each different philosopher says something slightly or even radically different from the next. One has but to consult any of the current journals dealing with public affairs to see the truth of this complaint. It *is* true; but is it relevant? For one thing, this is hardly a complaint peculiar to philosophy. Experts often disagree with one another about practical matters. Does this show that they were not, after all, experts? Does it show that we should not bother consulting experts on the matters in question? Obviously it does not. Apparently contrary pieces of advice may, for one thing, sometimes both be right: we may do better following either piece of advice than none at all. What you may get from both advisors is a coherent and well-reasoned plan, in the absence of which you might have acted haphazardly or stupidly. And the same might be true where the advisors are philosophers. Nevertheless, the point is a fair one. If we disagree about what to do about *X,* then at least one of us is likely to be wrong. But how are we going to determine which unless we keep at it? It is here that the complaint is seen to misfire. If it were well taken, its effect would be that we ought to *stop* doing these things.

That would be like inferring from the fact that different doctors give you different diagnoses that the medical profession should close its doors! But, obviously, a more rational response is "Well, back to the drawing board; we clearly don't have this all figured out yet."

III

Still another quite different kind of objection consists in citing certain prominent theories and accusing them of being indeterminate in their implications for action. For example, consider the principle of Utility, as advocated by a procession of philosophers since Jeremy Bentham. It is a particularly interesting case in point because it was introduced by Bentham with an avowedly practical aim. Moreover, Bentham's practical archenemy was, in a perfectly respectable sense of the word, a theoretician. Sir William Blackstone—of Blackstone's *Commentaries*—was the enemy, and to improve the laws of England—drastically as Bentham saw it—by freeing them from the shackles of Blackstone was Bentham's explicit purpose. Moreover, his labors were not without success. All of this is interesting because the precise interpretation of the principle of utility is among the knottiest tasks of ethical theory. It calls for cardinal, interpersonal comparisons of utility, which some theorists want to insist is absolutely impossible; in principle it takes to be relevant events that happen in the remote future; and it raises the deepest kind of difficulties about the notions of 'act', 'consequence', and 'cause' (among others). In the face of all these difficulties, it is a rash philosopher who will say without qualification that "utilitarianism implies that we should do *X*," where '*X*' refers to some concrete policy or action.

But what are we to make of this? As I say, the general historical perception is that Bentham did not labor in vain; it is hard to disagree that some of the changes that undoubtedly came about in considerable part because of the work of Bentham and his associates *were* changes in the direction of "increasing utility on the whole." On the other hand, we can think of innumerable cases where it would be possible to argue either way, to argue for any number of seriously differing actions or policies as constituting what would maximize utility. Even if we all agreed that the principle of utility is the supreme court of appeal on all moral issues, we would, in short, be very far from agreed about *what to do!* And it would be a rare ethical theory of which the same was untrue. In virtually every case—and surely in all the plausible cases—there is a considerable gap between the principles of the theory (even if we were all agreed that that was the right theory) and concrete decisions. In substance, therefore, the reply again is: objection sustained. But again, we have the question, What has been proved? At least two things, I think.

First, if some ethical theory should prove to be genuinely inde-terminate at some point where determination is needed, then there is nothing to say except that that is a fatal objection to that theory as it stands. It would have to be supplemented, patched up, or dis-carded. If, for example, it could be established that the whole idea of cardinal utility is in principle incoherent, then that is a blow from which utilitarianism, as usually understood, could not recover. The point here is that we must not identify the whole enterprise of moral philosophy with any particular theory within it. But why should there not be progress? Old theories will fall into disuse or simply die from fatal conceptual diseases; new theories will replace them. So it goes. None of this has any tendency to establish that the enterprise is unfounded or that we can never expect any definite results.

Second, there is the intriguing possibility that the division of labor needs further elaboration. Consider the various engineering disciplines: in addition to theoretical chemistry, there is chemical engineering, in which the relatively abstract results of pure chemis-try are applied in innumerable practical problems. Why should not the same be true in ethics? Perhaps the fundamental principles of ethics are a matter of much greater dispute than those of theoretical chemistry—probably layman's naiveté moves me to suppose this, I admit—and some might think that this wrecks the analogy. But I think not. For one thing, contributions to chemical theory are made at the chemical-engineering level and not exclusively by those officially engaged in pure chemistry, and we should expect some-thing similar in ethics. We should expect that the detailed focus on concrete issues will provide "data" for general theory, and not that inquirers in these concrete fields will only "apply" preexisting gen-eral theories to particular cases. Secondly, general theories urgently need applying if we are to get a clearer view of their implications—and this is something that can be done without waiting for a deci-sion by The Philosophical Profession concerning the fundamental correctness of those theories. Indeed, to represent the situation as if the latter were the appropriate procedure would be grotesque.

IV

This and the next items to consider are closely related and quite different from any of the foregoing. The first of these has it that ethical theorizing is *futile,* futile because no ethical theory will ever be persuasive. People have their fixed ethical beliefs, perhaps those inherited from childhood, and philosophers can do nothing to change them, nothing to get those who hold them to act on any other bases of decision whatever. This view, indeed, is by no means confined to areas outside the walls of philosophy; in fact, the intuitionists, or some of them, held essentially this view. The philosopher, they agreed, is quite incapable of supplying the ordinary man with "the correct" principles of action, in part because ethics is not a matter of "principles" at all and in part because ethical directives stem from within the soul, from places in it that are inaccessible to the discursive reasoning of the philosopher.

The reply to this is quite different from the replies appropriate to the earlier objections considered above. In those cases, my reaction, essentially, was to concede the substance of the objection, but deny its relevance, or at least its sufficiency, as a complaint about the possibility of applied ethics. But one can hardly make that reply to the present objection. The very essence of "applied" ethics, one would think, is to assist people in resolving ethical problems, to come up with better ideas to guide conduct. If better ideas *cannot* guide conduct, this essential object is lost; "applied" ethics would become purely academic, which is as much as to say that it cannot be applied. What we can do, however, is deny the substance of this claim outright. It is simply untrue that no one has ever had his or her principles affected, even drastically affected, by philosophical reflection. In the absence of philosophy, would Socrates have meekly accepted the hemlock, or Diogenes taken to his tub? Or consider the inordinate supply of revolutionaries operating in today's world: is it remotely plausible to think that these people were wholly unaffected by theories in taking to their campaigns of terrorism and assassination?

It is not clear what we are to count as theory or precisely what we are to count as persuasion. But it seems to me that the very facts trotted out to support this cynical hypothesis contribute to its incredibility. On the view before us, one supposes, we get our principles from our parents, early teachers, and peers. Or rather, we get a repertoire of behavioral guides, some of which would qualify as "principles," others as very rough rules of thumb, and still others as fairly arbitrary dicta on very specific points of conduct. But if we are incapable of having our behavior affected by principles, then how is this process to get off the ground, as it manifestly does? And if it is admitted that we can be influenced by principles at early stages, then why on earth should we cease to be amenable to such influences in later life?

V

A more radical version of the same idea is the thesis that we are not amenable to any kind of moral influence at all: not merely are *principles* without force in human life, but neither are any directives for improved conduct, however specific. This view is, of course, subject to the same rejoinder as the foregoing: it simply is not true. Some people may, indeed, not be amenable to any sort of behavioral influence from moral criticism, but typical people are; and a good many people are extremely sensitive to it. Beyond that, it must be pointed out that an objection on this level is too much like a solipsist's objection to sociology. It would be pointless for sociologists to take solipsists seriously (except perhaps as special cases of some kind of dysfunction), even though it is not pointless for philosophers to do so. And it is pointless for those seriously concerned about the possibility of applied ethics to base any worries about that on the possibility that the *entire* subject of ethics may not exist.

VI

We come now to two more sources of doubt which, unlike the preceding two, must be taken very seriously indeed. The first of these is the general thesis of *intuitionism*. According to what I here mean by this theoretical syndrome, theorizing of the kind to which philosophy is confined is not capable of guiding our judgment about specific cases and situations. On the contrary, such judgments provide the "data," the touchstones by which we assess theories when they are put forward. The theorizer, on this view, is essentially a secretary, or perhaps a librarian—or perhaps a scientist, on the understanding that scientists are passive observers of facts. Just as the scientist's theories are tested against the facts, and not vice versa, so the moral philosopher's theories are tested against the hard core of our particular judgments, and not vice versa. What are we to make of this set of contentions?

This can hardly be the place to undertake a full-scale discussion of the merits of intuitionism in its "methodological" form; and, fortunately, others have written to good effect in any case. I would here add only three observations.

In the first place, any kind of intuitionism (including this one) is in for embarrassment if it should turn out that intuitions conflict. And the force of this point is greatly increased when we realize that not only conflicts within a single person's set of judgments, but also conflicts between one person and another are problems for him. Intrapersonal conflicts are obviously a problem; how can judgments J_1 and J_2 both serve as touchstones of moral truth if they conflict with each other? But interpersonal conflicts, it has to be appreciated, are also a problem. Only a raving egotist can comfortably take the position that these are not problems because, whenever they arise, it is simply because the others are wrong—their moral vision is defective. (In saying this, I realize, I am no doubt delivering an intuition; but will anyone seriously disagree?) Perhaps some who are inclined to intuitionism will dig in their heels and insist that intuitions do not *really* conflict. If we look long and hard enough and make enough distinctions, they may say, we shall eventually discover that our intuitions do, after all, form a consistent set. Indeed? But now two thoughts press themselves forcibly upon us. What is all this lengthy and exhausting analysis and reflection if it is not, in truth, moral philosophy? And further, consider the very claim that two particular moral judgments might be inconsistent. For example, we say that Jasper, on Tuesday, was wrong to deny extra time to the opposing speaker, whereas Martin, on Wednesday, was right to do the very same thing. In order even to suspect inconsistency here, we must be thinking of both of these entirely distinct particular situations as exemplifying a common type which is, or should be, subject to a single rule covering all cases of that type. And just what is that type, and which rule are we to adopt? Answers to this question are necessary, if we are to get anywhere at all;

but thinking about those questions is, surely, theorizing. Theory, in short, is inescapable.

Secondly, there are intuitions and there are intuitions. The intuitionist in moral theory presumably meant to hold that the moral philosopher must test his theories by reference to preexisting *moral* intuitions. But, apart from the fact that recognizably moral intuitions themselves come in many varieties and all shades from highly specific to highly general, what if we find that our set of intuitions in some area appear, when looked at all together, to be a chaotic mess, whereas what we would have if we made a few important changes in certain of them would appear highly coherent and beautiful for the intellect to gaze upon? Here we have *theoretical* intuitions set against specifically moral ones. But why isn't one intuition as good as another? Why must moral intuitions always be catered to, should other very strong ones conflict with them? It is, I suggest, endemic to the intuitionist's position that he cannot defend this.

Finally, there is a point to be made about the character of practical decision making which might easily be mistaken for an overwhelming argument for intuitionism although closer inspection will reveal that it is nothing of the sort. The point is this: when acting, we *must* act on those judgments which we at that time accept as best. And the point is, surely, irrefutable. What could it mean for me to say, truthfully, "All things considered, X is what I ought now to do" and yet quickly add, "but of course, Y is the right thing to do, so of course I shall do that!" There is no way for an agent to distinguish between the truth and what he takes, at the time of acting, to be the truth. But this proves nothing at all regarding the possible relevance of theory to his situation. Nor does it prove that his then set of beliefs is sacrosanct in any way. Action is, and of course must be, compatible with the realization that one might be acting wrongly. There is nothing for it but to hope that one has done one's thinking well, and press on. Acting on a belief does not make it true, alas. And the possession of what one believes to be a solid theoretical basis for one's decision may promote confidence as much as a quite spectacular "intuition."

VII

Perhaps it is another side of the same coin to insist that, really, "applied" ethics is nothing more than getting at the facts, in that sense of 'fact' in which the experts, the scientists for instance, are preeminently the people who have or know how to get them. More fully: in "applying" ethics, what, after all, are we doing if not deducing the implications for particular cases of general ethical precepts? Now the form of the argument—so this objection has it—consists of a major, "ethical" premise, which is general, and a particular evaluative judgment as conclusion; and therefore, in between these, there needs to be a "factual" premise showing that the particular case in question falls under the general principle in question. The major, or ethical premise is general and abstract—no room for "applied philosophy" there! And the minor premise is purely and solely a matter of fact—no room for "philosophy" of any kind *there*. But that's all there is! So "applied philosophy" turns out to be a misnomer, a nonsense-idea, or an illusion.

That this may be merely the other side of the coin from intuitionism suggests itself when we ask, to begin with, concerning those "major premises," how we are to know which ones to employ. For the view, if its criticism were correct, would appear to require that there be a fixed, definite set of "ethical major premises." Otherwise, the thought might loom before us that there is some need to devote hard thought to the matter of just which premises to use and just how "general and abstract" they are to be when we focus on the area in question. For that matter, which "facts," figuring in the minor premises, are the relevant facts? Is the scientist, as such, to know that too? How?

The fact is, of course, that when we think about fairly complex concrete ethical issues, the situation does not come packaged neatly into an "ethical" and a "factual" component. Considerable reflection might lead us to the conclusion that for a certain range of cases, the decision does really turn on certain quite definitely factual questions, and those questions really are amenable to specific expertise of the kind that some scientist might have and most of us do not. But that conclusion, as I say, is likely to emerge only *after* serious thought has been focused on the matter; it may have been anything but obvious beforehand that just those are the facts it would turn on. Similarly with any really usable "major ethical premises." In the areas worth investigating, think how unhelpful, how jejune it would be to announce as one's grand premise that "murder is wrong"! But the whole issue may be whether this is to be reckoned a case of "murder" at all, or whether some other concept—

manslaughter, culpable negligence, or even something within the agent's rights—is appropriate instead. We cannot usefully start with global ethical "premises" because they have the conclusions already tucked away inside them, and so we have to sort through the problem and work our way back to major premises that will prove to be the appropriate ones for the cases we are considering.

None of this is to deny that we may usefully set up moral arguments as sets of premises leading logically to practical conclusions about the range of cases we are concerned with. Some have objected to the "deductive model," but that is not my complaint. Rather, the point is that a tight deductive argument is what we will end up with, if all goes well; it is not what we start with. Or rather, we start by formulating various possible deductive arguments and then criticize them in the light of further thought about the issue in question.

Nor do I wish to deny that there are "ultimate principles" in ethics, of very general reach, or that such principles really are relevant to concrete issues. What we must deny is only (a) that there are, available early in the game, very general principles that are both interesting and self-evident, and (b) that very high-level principles apply themselves easily to relatively concrete situations. But just this, probably, is what those who deny the propriety of "the deductive model" are really affirming. For how can we doubt that, if some relatively concrete type of act is really right or wrong, then there is some reason why it is, a reason that can appropriately be formulated as a general principle? Those who deny such things, it seems to me, leave ethics in a state of mystery which is both unintelligible theoretically and likely to be inimical in practice.

VIII

This brings us to the final challenge. Real life, it will be said, consists of fully concrete situations, infinite in their complexity. As such, they cannot be reached by abstract principles of the kind that philosophers endeavor to frame. The full concreteness of real life must ever elude us, however hard we try. Is there a problem here?

The brief answer is: No. Or rather, that no *general* problem, no problem of a kind that threatens to sweep away the whole endeavor, can coherently be thought to stem from this quarter. In any case, the charge involves a misconception. Let us consider each of these points in turn.

There are two rather contrary ways to understand the general claim about concreteness. On the one hand, we have the suggestion above, that the concrete is terrifically, perhaps even infinitely, *complex.* On the other, however, it might be insisted that reality is *unanalyzable,* that in real experience everything flows into everything else in such a way that one simply can't detach anything from anything. These are, however, very different claims. And the second, if it were true, would indeed cut very deep. Absurdly deep, in fact; for if this were really true, then no intelligent decisions about anything could be made. To make a decision, one must choose among alternatives and be able to bring reasons to bear on behalf of one or another or all of them. But if nothing can be distinguished from anything else, we cannot even identify the alternatives, let alone marshal considerations telling in favor of one as opposed to others among them. In any case, the claim may be dismissed as nonsense. Those who insist on any such characterization may be suspected of secretly assuming that real reality is present only to the minds of newborn infants, who indeed can scarcely distinguish anything from anything—not a very sensible point of view when one is addressing thinking adults.

However, the thesis that reality is complex and even, perhaps, infinitely so is clearly not to be dismissed so readily; indeed, perhaps not at all. One need only take a quick look around to appreciate the incredible amount of information that is in principle statable regarding one's immediate environment, not to mention the great universe beyond. So if all of this goes into the "concreteness" of real life, then the claim may be granted, straight off. But there are two questions to ask. In the first place, *does* all of this clutter of fact count as belonging to one's "real situation"? Not obviously. Surely almost all of these facts would normally be dismissed as irrelevant, especially if one has in mind—as we should here—one's "situation" as a practical being, an acting agent. Immersed though we are in the infinite clutter of reality, only a tiny bit of it all is relevant to our practical situations. If one has just received a pink slip from one's employer, the fact that the wall before one is absolutely crammed with silicon atoms isn't part of one's situation, even though those atoms are no doubt as perfectly and entirely "real" as you like. This is not to deny that situations are typically complex, and sometimes horrendously so. It is to deny that they are so by virtue of the sheer concreteness of them. Their complexity in the sense in which it is relevant to describe them thus may still be mind-boggling, for all that. But it does not follow that the situation is unmanageable. Roughly, we can say this: that, in real life, unanticipated but fully relevant facts have a way of cropping up, and it is not reasonable to assume that one has everything nailed down tight at every turn one takes. One must simply do one's best; with luck, that will often be good enough. And, meanwhile, the possibility of useful practical advice is by no means precluded by such complexity as there is. Good advice, like wise decision, is difficult, yes; but not impossible.

This brings us to the second and more basic point, which is that it is quite wrong to think of "applied ethics" as if it were concerned with psychiatric counseling, for example. We need to distinguish, here, between the particular and the (merely quite) specific. Particular acts, taking place at identifiable times and places, obviously lie beyond the purview of philosophy: we are not as such concerned with them. Applied ethics is, nevertheless, concerned with relatively specific kinds of acts: e.g., the proper distribution of scarce life-sustaining equipment, the rights and wrongs of premarital sex, and so forth. What is the difference? Particular acts take place at definite places and times and are done by identifiable, particular persons. "Relatively specific kinds of acts," on the other hand, are universals, not particulars: an indefinite number of particular acts can exemplify even the relatively specific description under which applied ethics is concerned with them. Should there happen to be but one such act in the history of the universe, that would be surprising, but logically accidental. Nevertheless, applied ethics occupies a region not necessarily reached in general ethical theory. At that level, we seek the ultimate criteria of right and wrong, good and bad, etc. Now, these criteria may be of such a kind that no act, as we ordinarily identify act-kinds, would be said to be identified by them. I cannot simply maximize happiness: I must perform some concrete kind of act the effect of which, hopefully, will be to exemplify that description. Applied ethics is concerned with classes of acts which we can identify, among our choices, as being directly of that description or not. Such, at any rate, is the kind of difference we are looking for. Nevertheless, one might save someone's life *by* throwing him a life ring. Is "saving a life," then, not something we can as such do? It seems we have here a distinction in degree, essentially. But that is all right. It is, I would think, unnecessary, as well as probably impossible, to put a tight definition on the class of act-descriptions under which ethical concern with them would be "applied" rather than "theoretical."

IX

The brunt of this paper has been negative. Arguments from many different directions, purporting to show that applied ethics is impossible, have been considered and rejected. Often the rejection has taken the form of accepting the substance of the proposed criticism, but rejecting its relevance to the conclusion on behalf of which it was offered. In a few cases, I flatly rejected the premise. But this may seem unsatisfying. Is there something positive to say, something that clearly establishes the legitimacy of this category?

One obvious thing to say, of course, is that applied ethics is actually done, so it must be possible. But it is not entirely clear that this is a good argument. An old teacher of mine told the following anecdote: A: "Do you believe in baptism?" B: "Of course I believe in it—I've seen it done!" Luckily, the claim that it "is actually done" is rather better taken regarding applied ethics than it was in the baptism case. One can look into any of a half-dozen journals (at least; probably far more) over the past decade and find dozens of articles on such topics as abortion, civil disobedience, vegetarianism, reverse discrimination, and so on; and among these are many that, in the judgment of any competent and unbiased observer, would have to be agreed to be illuminating, stimulating, perceptive, and persuasive—or, where not persuasive, provocative in such a way that we may be sure of the appearance in later issues of interesting and helpful commentaries. Moreover, I would likewise be prepared to say that this literature in philosophical journals is, so far as attacking the specifically moral issues involved is concerned, almost uniformly *better* than what one finds on similar topics in more popular literature or in those portions of the literatures of other academic disciplines that touch on these matters. (In saying all this, I am of course making a value judgment, and, since I am a member of the academic philosophical profession myself, one that is obviously liable to a charge of bias. The only reply here is: look and see for yourself. It is clearly of importance that this large body of literature contains much that is worthwhile, for that is surely enough to justify all this activity even if we had nothing but puzzlement about the conceptual status of the whole enterprise.

Looking into this literature, however, also supplies some firmer support for optimism about the general issue. Provided we are not hung up about strict dividing lines between "theoretical" and "applied," what we find from a decent survey of this work is, in the first place, that focusing on relatively concrete issues is enormously valuable for those of us who are interested in fundamental theory. To take a case of special interest to this writer, consider the issue of animal rights. Here is a splendid issue for getting clearer on the notion of a right and on the foundations of rights. This issue is admirable too for trying to assess the implications of utilitarianism; it is important, for instance, to realize that different versions of utilitarianism seem to give drastically different results and that strong cases can be mounted within utilitarianism on both sides of the controversy. In the absence of a climate in which it was considered legitimate and worthwhile to delve into such issues, we would surely have a lesser appreciation of that theory. And the same can be said for almost any of these issues.

In the second place, we ought surely not to overlook the fact that this volume of work that has been done is getting results. We do have a better handle on many of these issues than we would have otherwise. In some few cases, we perhaps are even approaching agreement; and, in any case, we have pretty substantial agreement about what *won't* work. The cynic may say that these "results" don't have the proverbial snowball's chance in hell of being put into practice. But the cynic is, to start with, wrong. They will not, of course, be adopted tomorrow; nor should they. Even those who are utterly convinced of the correctness of some important conclusions on these matters are likely to agree that they need to be thoroughly considered, reflected upon, and shown resistant to refutation before being "put into practice" in whatever sense they can be. Indeed our terms of reference, so to say, just do not include "putting results into effect," except of course in our own personal practice. The "applied" philosopher is still a theorist, still essentially performing a cognitive, intellectual task rather than a political or social-activist one. Even the proponents of "praxis" are to be supported or refuted in print, not on the barricades. And in fact, if they are refuted in print, we shall not need ever to get to the barricades—which is illustrative of the general point.

From all of which I conclude that "applied ethics" is not only legitimate, but a downright good thing. Like many another discipline, its boundaries are uncertain and disputed, its results and ways of proceeding anarchic, and its practitioners continually embroiled in disagreements. Long may it live!

7

Is Applied Ethics Worth Doing?

Dale Jamieson

Throughout most of this century philosophers have sharply distinguished moral theory from moral practice, and many have held that moral theory has little or nothing to do with acting morally. It was commonly said that the proper domain of moral philosophy is moral theory: moral practice is the province of Everyman. The following passage from C. D. Broad is a characteristic expression of this view.

> We can no more learn to act rightly by appealing to the ethical theory of right action than we can play golf well by appealing to the mathematical theory of the flight of the golf-ball. The interest of ethics is thus almost wholly theoretical, as is the interest of the mathematical theory of golf or billiards.[1]

Anticipating the disappointment some might feel about the irrelevance of moral philosophy to practical concerns, Broad quotes the following Latin phrase, *Non in dialectica complacuit Deo salvum facere poplum suum*, commenting that "salvation isn't everything."

Although salvation may not be everything, it is certainly something, and something quite important. It seems inevitable that sooner or later philosophers would again try to bring their methods to bear on matters of salvation. What was needed was a spark, and

---

[1] *Five Types of Ethical Theory* (Paterson, N.J.: Littlefield, Adams, 1959), p. 285. The most striking exception to the dominant view is John Dewey and the pragmatist tradition.

it was provided by the civil rights and anti-war movements of the 1960s. By the 1970s philosophers were, for better or worse, "back on the job."[2]

I first became acquainted with this new work in applied ethics when I heard Roger Wertheimer read "Understanding the Abortion Argument."[3] Wertheimer's paper had not yet appeared in *Philosophy and Public Affairs,* and indeed that journal had not as yet published a single issue. I was both intrigued and irritated by Wertheimer's paper. On the one hand he was using his philosophical skills to address a real issue in people's lives. On the other he seemed to conclude in a fit of Wittgensteinian despair: we could and should appreciate both sides of the abortion argument, but there was little or nothing that philosophers could do to help bring it to a rational conclusion. It seemed to me that, if philosophers could only kibitz while real people had it out, then we might as well stick to the Problem of Universals.

Wertheimer's article was just an opening shot in what soon became a deafening barrage. Undoubtedly different pieces moved different people in different ways. For me the crucial year was 1975. The first publications that made me think that there might be a place for philosophers in the real world were Peter Singer's *Animal Liberation* and Tom Regan's "The Moral Basis of Vegetarianism."[4] It is no doubt true that, in part, the power of these works comes from their vivid portrayal of animal suffering. Before 1975 most of us thought of happy chickens and contented cows rather than of battery hens and totally confined, anemic veal calves. Probably we also thought that all or most experimentation on animals was necessary and carried out in the most humane way possible. But, in addition to confronting us with the facts of animal exploitation, itself an important departure from mainstream ethics, these works were also solid pieces of "analytic" philosophy. What was striking was that

---

[2] "Philosophers Are Back on the Job" is the title of an influential article by Peter Singer that appeared in the *New York Times Magazine* for July 7, 1974.
[3] *Philosophy and Public Affairs,* I, 1 (Fall 1971): 67–95; reprinted in Joel Feinberg, ed., *The Problem of Abortion* (Belmont, Calif.: Wadsworth, 1973).
[4] Singer, *Animal Liberation* (New York: New York Review Books, 1975); Regan, "The Moral Basis of Vegetarianism," *Canadian Journal of Philosophy,* V (1975).

they arrived at utterly unintuitive conclusions about how we ought to live. When I first read them I didn't think there was a chance in a hundred that they could be right. A year later I concluded, with lots of minor quibbles and qualifications, that they *were* right.

I mention the work of Singer and Regan and its effect on me for one reason. If it is the case that philosophers can construct sound arguments about how people ought to live which lead to conclusions that would seem ludicrous to most people who have not studied moral philosophy, then it must be the case that, in some sense and to some degree, there is some connection between being a moral philosopher and being a moral expert. And, just as there is reason for architectural experts to do architecture, so there is reason for moral experts to do applied ethics.

In a remarkably short period of time the view that moral philosophers are moral experts has become very prominent, and applied ethics is one of the few growth areas in a depressed academic job market. A glance at *Jobs for Philosophers* shows that virtually every philosophy department in the country wants someone in applied ethics. Several universities, like my own, have established new centers for research in applied ethics or in the philosophical foundations of social policy. Philosophers have also successfully insinuated themselves into schools of public policy, medicine, law, engineering, business, journalism, environmental science, and so forth. They have also done well with funding agencies. During the Carter Administration the National Endowment for the Humanities looked upon programs in philosophy and public policy with great favor, and many private foundations continue to do so.

Undoubtedly many of our patrons in government and business have affection for us for all the wrong reasons. They think of us as secular priests or as technocrats whose field is ethics rather than, say, public finance. Many of us have probably felt all along that, when and if our patrons find out what we really do, the jig will be up. But our severest critics have been not professionals in business or government, but rather ideologues of the political right and left. The right dislikes us because we are left-leaning irreligious college professors who are usurping the role of the church and family in moral education. The left dislikes us because we treat individual morality as if it were important, instead of focusing on the economic structures and class divisions which are the real forces of history.[5] Some of our colleagues are also dubious about what we do. Worldly success is viewed with suspicion in a discipline whose founding father was rewarded for his work with execution.

Most of the criticisms of applied ethics that I have heard have been expressed in conversation. It is only recently that articles critical of this field have begun to be published in professional journals. Still, it seems clear that times have changed and reaction has begun. There are signs all around us: the shift in direction at the National Endowment for the Humanities away from public policy toward more traditional concerns; articles critical of applied ethics in such journals of opinion as *Commentary* and the *Public Interest;* the revival of virtue theories in the philosophical literature. It would not be too surprising if applied ethics, which had a meteoric rise in the 1970s, suffered an equally meteoric decline in the 1980s.

This might make us wonder whether the decline and fall of applied ethics would be lamentable. I think it would indeed be lamentable, even though applied ethics as it is usually practiced is open to well-founded criticisms. But, before I discuss some criticisms of applied ethics, well-founded and otherwise, some misunderstandings about it should be put to rest.

First, much of what is said about applied ethics, and probably much of what I have said so far, suggests a picture in which the distinction between the theoretical and the applied is very sharp and clear. Unfortunately life is more complicated than that. Still, the difference between the theoretical and the applied can be illuminated to some degree in the following way. Theoretical and applied ethics have the same subject matter: the moral lives of agents and patients. What is different about them is their perspective on this subject matter. Theoretical ethics takes the broad view; it is the telescope through which we observe the phenomena. Applied ethics views a narrow band of the same terrain in greater detail. It is the microscope through which we examine our moral lives.

A second misunderstanding concerns the relationship between applied ethics and the history of moral philosophy. Some people write as if applied ethics were something very new and different

---

[5]For criticism from the right, see Mark Lilla, "Ethos, 'Ethics,' and Public Service," *Public Interest,* LXIII (1981); from the left, see Cheryl N. Noble, "Ethics and Experts," *Hastings Center Report,* XII, 3 (June 1982).

which appeared from out of nowhere about 1970 and as if, before this time, ethics just *was* theoretical ethics. Such a view cannot survive even a casual reading of the history of moral philosophy.

The *Groundwork of the Metaphysics of Morals* is certainly a paradigm work in theoretical ethics; yet Kant applies his theory to such practical matters as capital punishment, suicide, and the duty to tell the truth. Both Bentham and Mill move quickly from discussions of fundamental principles to disquisitions on particular cases, and back again. There is nothing new about applied ethics as a subject of philosophical concern. The banishment of applied ethics in this century, a position for which I invoked Broad as a spokesman, was a relatively brief and novel interlude in the history of moral philosophy. What is new about the recent revival of applied ethics is the way in which it has become entrenched in our educational and cultural institutions, but that is part of the larger social and cultural history of philosophy rather than the history of moral philosophy proper. Kant, Bentham, and Mill discussed practical matters in the same breath as theoretical issues because they understood that doing ethics in the full sense involves both. Applied ethics requires theoretical ethics as a foundation for its claims and arguments. Theoretical ethics is vacuous if it does not bear on human conduct. To paraphrase something Kant might have said but didn't: applied ethics without theoretical ethics is blind; theoretical ethics without applied ethics is empty.

Finally, we should be aware that many different things go on under the rubric of applied ethics. My work in this area centers on teaching courses in environmental ethics and contemporary moral problems and on doing research on the morality of killing. I am also involved in trying to bring the results of philosophical investigation to bear on issues of social policy. Other practitioners of applied ethics do not teach in philosophy departments, but work in a variety of other settings, some of them nonacademic. Some practitioners even wear white coats and beepers and help make life-and-death decisions in clinical situations. Quite obviously, my problems are different from theirs and theirs from mine. In what follows, my remarks will be from the perspective of one who does "academic" applied ethics rather than the "clinical" version.

I shall discuss six criticisms of applied ethics. Some of these criticisms are good ones, and I shall try to say what we should learn from them. Others are not so good, and I shall try to say why. In the concluding section I shall say why I think applied ethics is worth doing.

RELATIVISM AND SUBJECTIVISM

Much of the hostility toward applied ethics is rooted in metaethical views concerning the possibility of moral knowledge. A class of freshmen, asked whether it is wrong to let people starve in the Third World while we destroy most of our vegetable protein in the process of converting it into meat, all too often will not say "yes" or "no" or even plead agnosticism. Instead their response is: "Who's to say what's right or wrong?" Although this response has the grammatical form of a question, it is meant as an assertion: the only conceivable answer is that no one can say what's right or wrong. This is a depressing experience for an ethics teacher, but there is a bright side. Freshmen are in college in order to learn, among other reasons, and usually by the end of the semester this particular response has been purged from their behavioral repertoires. What is more depressing is that the views of untutored freshmen on the subject of morality are often no more or less sophisticated than the views of social scientists and nonacademics. Even many people who favor the teaching of ethics in professional schools do not believe in the possibility of moral knowledge. They have the peculiar view that it is a good thing to spend one's time trying to answer questions that are in principle unanswerable. Although there is no right answer about, say, whether or not it is permissible to take a bribe from Lockheed, reflection upon the question functions as ersatz justification. From this it is a short step to the view that it doesn't matter what you do so long as you know what you are doing. By this process the callous and calculating are transformed into the virtuous.

The position that drives the question, "Who's to say what's right or wrong?", is what I shall call the *denial of moral expertise*. On this view ethics is importantly different from accounting, surgery, carpentry, and so forth. In these areas there are experts. In matters of morality there are not. We are all equal. I take it that research and teaching in applied ethics is directed toward the development of moral expertise, at least insofar as that is taken to mean greater understanding of moral truths concerning practical issues. If moral expertise is not possible, then applied ethics is not worth doing.

There are at least two bases for the denial of moral expertise. One is subjectivism, and the other is relativism.

Subjectivism can take at least two forms. One holds that ethical "statements" are the expressions of nonpropositional inner states. They do not have truth conditions, so the concepts of verification and proof do not apply to them. A second version holds that ethical statements really are statements, but they are about the beliefs, desires, feelings, and attitudes of the speaker. On both views an apparent dispute about the morality of suicide, for example, is not really a dispute about suicide, but at best a dispute about the sincerity of those who are arguing.

Relativism holds that ethical statements are true or false only relative to particular cultures. Just as 'Snow is white.' is true in English, so 'Murder is wrong.' is true in England. Unsophisticated relativists think of cultures as very small, perhaps constituted by the speaker and his friends. When a "culture" has only one member relativism collapses into subjectivism, or at least is pragmatically indistinguishable from it.

We should see first that, if subjectivism or unsophisticated relativism can be sustained, then not only applied ethics is threatened but also theoretical ethics in the grand tradition of Aristotle, Kant, and Mill. If either of these views is correct, the task of the moral philosopher is just to pick up the pieces that are strewn about by the moralist and the casuist, who, unencumbered by philosophical knowledge, can continue to claim the authority to tell people what to do. Neither of these positions, then, provides the ground from which critics of applied ethics can mount an attack, if they also wish to defend theoretical ethics as it has traditionally been conceived.

For familiar reasons which I shall not rehearse here, both subjectivism and unsophisticated relativism are false.[6] Still it is striking that, despite our best efforts to keep them down, these views keep bouncing back. I believe that part of the reason it is so difficult to exterminate them completely is that, though false, they are based on real insights. Morality is *subjective* in that moral rules, principles and judgments are ultimately validated by reference to the welfare of individual beings. Morality is *relative* in that there is a class of

---

[6]Refutations of subjectivism and unsophisticated relativism occur in almost every introductory ethics book. See, for example, Bernard Williams, *Morality: An Introduction to Ethics* (New York: Harper & Row, 1972).

possible moralities for societies of intelligent social animals such that all members of the class are adequate and all can be defended on rational grounds. What is important to see is that we can give both subjectivism and relativism their due without being driven to the denial of moral expertise.

Thus far I have claimed that the denial of moral expertise is often based on subjectivism or relativism and that both of these views, at least in the forms that directly support the denial of moral expertise, are false. Moreover, I have argued that these views can be espoused only by those who are also prepared to reject theoretical ethics as it has traditionally been conceived.

VIRTUE CANNOT BE TAUGHT

Another reason often cited for believing that applied ethics is not worth doing is that virtue cannot be taught. Put this way, however, the claim is overstated. What people who say this usually mean is that virtue cannot be taught by the classroom methods of the moral philosopher with their emphasis on reason and argument. This view is not new. We can find its origins in the work of Aristotle and the eighteenth-century Scottish philosophers. The following passage from C. S. Lewis expresses it eloquently.

> It still remains true that no justification of virtue will enable a man to be virtuous. Without the aid of trained emotions the intellect is power-less against the animal organism. I had sooner play cards against a man who was quite skeptical about ethics, but bred to believe that "a gentleman does not cheat," than against an irreproachable moral phi-losopher who had been brought up among sharpers.[7]

Much of what Lewis says in this passage is true, but it does not show that applied ethics isn't worth doing. To suppose otherwise is to misunderstand the role of applied ethics in moral thinking. R. M. Hare's distinction between two levels of moral thinking, the "intuitive" and the "critical," can help us see that this is true.[8]

The intuitive level is characterized by deeply entrenched dispo-sitions and the feelings that go along with them. We are trained not to cheat at cards, and we may have feelings of guilt at the mere thought of cheating. Most of our moral life is conducted at the

---

[7] *The Abolition of Man* (New York: Macmillan, 1947), pp. 33–34.
[8] *Moral Thinking* (New York: Oxford University Press, 1982), part I.

intuitive level. We do not ordinarily reason about what to do. We follow our heart's command. But there is also a role for critical thinking, and that is the level at which we do applied ethics.

The first reason why critical thinking is important is that sometimes the head should overrule the heart. Lewis seems to suggest that this is impossible, but that is surely wrong. It may well be my duty to cheat at cards, if it would not seriously harm my victim and my family would otherwise starve. That this is my duty could be shown only by reasoning about this particular case in conjunction with some knowledge of moral theory. Our emotions are not likely to be convinced, however. We might feel as sickened by cheating in a good cause as by cheating in a bad one.

A second reason why critical thinking is important is that we need to know which moral dispositions to encourage in ourselves and in our children. Perhaps southern plantation owners did not feel remorse for the pain they caused their slaves. Perhaps they raised their children to feel remorse when they harmed whites but not when they harmed blacks. Critical thinking could show them they were wrong.

A third reason why critical thinking is important is that many of the moral problems we face today are novel; we have no deeply entrenched dispositions to guide us. It may well be wrong to keep alive for years someone with no hope of recovery who is barely conscious and in pain, but the opportunity to do this is so recent in our history that it is not surprising that our dispositions concerning cases like this tend to be contradictory, vague, and ill focused.

Finally, critical thinking is important because some practitioners of applied ethics are interested in evaluating alternative social policies as well as in providing moral advice about personal problems. Our moral psychology, however, is remarkably unresponsive to complicated large-scale issues, especially those which involve people and events that are not close at hand. We do not respond strongly to the suffering of distant strangers in Assam or to issues like the New Federalism. Yet there are important moral dimensions to these issues which can be appreciated only by reason, since they outrun our capacity for heartfelt response.

There is another point that should be made, though too much should not rest on it. A professor of philosophy is not just a machine for producing and evaluating arguments. He is also a person whose behavior while teaching and lecturing reveals his conscientiousness, his intellectual honesty, his willingness to treat others with respect, and his commitment to his ideals. For these reasons he, like all people, is continually involved in moral education by example as well as by argument. Because of the nature of the subject and the fact that he is guaranteed an audience, a moral philosopher is often an especially important role model for his friends and students.

Although not everything important to behaving morally can be taught in a classroom by a moral philosopher, some of it can be. Applied ethics is worth studying and teaching even if it is only part of a complete moral education.

DIVERSITY OF OPINION

A third argument against applied ethics is really a moral argument. Virtually everyone has moral beliefs. These are obtained from our interactions with parents, schools, religious institutions, and so forth. These beliefs do not always, or perhaps even usually, form a consistent set. Nor can most of us articulate the reasons we have for holding the beliefs we hold. Despite this, we succeed in muddling through with a fair degree of success. There is of course plenty of room for improvement in our moral thinking. But the problem is that applied ethics is not conducive to such improvement. Indeed, it is often harmful.[9]

When a student takes a course in applied ethics he immediately finds that his moral beliefs are under attack. They are shown to be inconsistent, and he discovers that he cannot do a very good job of defending most of them. Simultaneously he is confronted with a whole cafeteria of competing moral theories and beliefs. Some august thinkers say that acts are justified by their consequences; others vigorously disagree. Some speak of natural rights; others condemn such talk as "nonsense upon stilts." Some claim that the fetus's potential is sufficient for ascribing to it full moral rights; others hold that killing fetuses is morally equivalent to killing fish. This maelstrom of radically different conflicting views emanates from the very people who are supposed to be moral experts. If they cannot get their act together, is it any wonder that an intelligent student who has been argued or perhaps browbeaten out of his naive morality

---

[9]William J. Bennett makes this argument in "Getting Ethics," *Commentary*, LXX (1980).

retreats to skepticism? His old views have been discredited, and the new ones have committed "fratricide." He is left with nothing, and it is the fault of the practitioner of applied ethics, who turns out to be responsible for contributing mightily to the thing he abhors: the denial of moral expertise. In order to save theoretical ethics from skepticism and in order to preserve a society in which people have moral beliefs and ideals, we should jettison applied ethics.

There are really two arguments here. One is that widespread disagreement among practitioners of applied ethics is sufficient for thinking that applied ethics isn't worth doing. The other is that widespread disagreement among practitioners of applied ethics has pernicious consequences, and that is sufficient for thinking that applied ethics isn't worth doing. We shall examine the first argument first.

The problem with this argument is that it underestimates the amount of agreement among people working in applied ethics, overestimates the disagreement, and makes too much of both. There are probably few important propositions to which every moral philosopher assents, just as there are probably few important propositions to which every physicist or chemist assents. Still, there are propositions about which there is considerable agreement. Perhaps more importantly, the views of moral philosophers on many issues diverge sharply from those of most ordinary people. Consider some examples. Most moral philosophers reject the view that moral problems can be resolved by appeal to divine commands. They know that justifying ultimate ends is very different from justifying instrumental ends. They know that pleasure is not a sensation and that no simple version of hedonism is true. Concerning more practical issues, most moral philosophers agree that abortion is not murder. Most would deny that life itself, independent of its quality, has value. Most would hold that the distinction between acting and omitting is without moral significance in a broad range of cases. They would say that we should do more to help desperate people even if they are not citizens of our country. And most would agree that the interests of nonhuman animals should be taken more seriously than they are usually taken. Let me say again that I do not mean to suggest that every person working in applied ethics holds these views. Philosophers are cranky by profession, and any statement of the form "Most philosophers believe that *P*" is certain to provoke a flurry of activity on behalf of not-*P.* My claim is just that there is some consensus among people working in applied ethics and that this consensus is unlikely to be mirrored in the thinking of nonphilosophers.

But even if I am wrong in supposing that there is consensus about some issues in applied ethics, the fact of widespread disagreement would not be sufficient for thinking that applied ethics is not worth doing. Such an argument, if it proves anything at all, proves too much. There is no unanimity among interpreters of Plato. Metaphysicians and epistemologists do not speak with a single voice, nor do physicists or biologists. Perhaps it is true that moral philosophers disagree more among themselves than physicists do, but, if that is so, one reason is that in certain respects moral philosophy is harder than physics. Whether an action or a policy is right depends on many things: the welfare of those affected by it; how it is institutionally embedded; the prevailing beliefs, desires, and expectations of those in the affected community; the intentional states of the actor; and undoubtedly much more besides. Regularities concerning these matters are very difficult to discover because they involve the behavior of intelligent social animals. Secular moral philosophy is in its infancy. It is a wonder that we know as much as we do.

The second argument is more interesting. It claims that widespread disagreement among those who do applied ethics has pernicious consequences and that, for that reason, applied ethics is not worth doing. We might formulate this as the charge that the practitioners of applied ethics are guilty of corrupting the youth.

Note first that the question of whether or not applied ethics is worth doing is itself a question in applied ethics, for it concerns the value of one of our everyday activities. Perhaps applied ethics can be avoided only by remaining silent.

More importantly, I doubt that applied ethics has the pernicious consequences that this argument attributes to it. I have seen many cases in which study and research in this area improves the moral sensibility of those who undertake it. I have even seen people's behavior change radically for the better when they became convinced of the soundness of an argument. When the study of applied ethics does have pernicious consequences I think it is almost always because of the way in which the subject is taught and studied. But, ultimately, I and the critic are at a standoff on this point. The question of whether or not studying applied ethics is conducive to moral improvement is an empirical question which is not easily settled. For its answer depends in part on what our conception of moral improvement is, which is itself a moral question. But there is another point that I think is telling against the argument. Other things are valuable besides maintaining a culture in which people believe in the possibility of moral knowledge. One of them is the attainment of moral knowledge. If the price of such knowledge is the creation of some moral skeptics, that is a price we should be willing to pay.

SINGLENESS OF OPINION

A fourth argument against applied ethics denies a crucial premise of the previous argument. This fourth argument holds that applied ethics is worthless because only a narrow range of views is usually countenanced. It is not worth our while to study a field that, after a lot of hot air and bother, merely reinforces our prior beliefs. Cheryl Noble has claimed: "Starting from a position of political and historical naiveté, they [applied ethicists] inevitably arrive at conventional and tame conclusions, drawn from a preexisting range of alternatives" ("Ethics and Experts," p. 8). It is hard to see how someone could believe this. In the last ten years philosophers have defended a host of views that most people would consider shocking. Here are some examples. Peter Singer has argued that we should give until it hurts to relieve world hunger; Tom Regan that it is wrong to harm any animals at all in the course of scientific research; Holmes Rolston that even a smallpox virus has intrinsic value; Michael Tooley that infanticide is often permissible; Hugh LaFollette that parents should be licensed.[10] Noble has responded to such obvious counterexamples by claiming that most of them "could be joined together to form a good profile of one garden variety liberal."[11] This claim is

---

[10]Singer, "Famine, Affluence and Morality," *Philosophy and Public Affairs*, I, 3 (Spring 1972): 229–43; Regan, *The Case for Animal Rights* (Berkeley: University of California Press, 1981); Rolston, "Are Values in Nature Subjective or Objective?", *Environmental Ethics*, IV (1982); Tooley, "A Defense of Abortion and Infanticide," reprinted in Feinberg, *The Problem of Abortion;* and LaFollette, "Licensing Parents," *Philosophy and Public Affairs*, IX (1980).

[11]Noble, "Response," *Hastings Center Report*, XII, 3 (June 1982): 15.

just false. Peter Singer's prescriptions concerning our duties to the Third World go far beyond those of anyone who could reasonably be called a liberal. The reordering of our relationships to the natural world that Regan and Rolston advocate would be as shocking to Steward Udall as to James Watt. And only the most extreme feminists have gone as far as Michael Tooley in defending infanticide as well as abortion. Still, much work in applied ethics is open to serious criticism, and there is something important that is on Noble's mind, as we shall see in the next section.

PROBLEMS OF METHOD

Work in applied ethics has often been criticized for placing too much weight on moral intuitions. The critics echo Mill's attack on those who make "ethics not so much a guide as a consecration of man's actual sentiments."[12] Noble takes Thomas Nagel as an exemplar. He defends the "conventional, modern Western view of how wars should be fought" on the basis of intuited absolutist principles. "Whether he is discussing war or equality, Nagel ends up saying that the way things are is pretty much the way they ought to be." He lays out "general principles of fairness and represent[s] them as independently derived and justified" when they are not ("Ethics and Experts," p. 8). Phillip Abbot similarly criticizes philosophical treatments of abortion: "[D]espite their [philosophers] flaunted independence from moral convention, they may only be intuiting conclusions already determined by an increasing atomistic society."[13]

These criticisms raise difficult questions about method in moral philosophy. These questions are some of the most vexing in all of philosophy. They are especially problematical for applied ethics because it is the nature of the enterprise that they are not often confronted or even acknowledged, yet everything that is said or written about practical moral problems rests on some presuppositions about method.

---

[12]John Stuart Mill, *Utilitarianism* (Indianapolis: Hackett, 1979), p. 3.
[13]"Philosophers and the Abortion Question," *Political Theory,* VI (1978): 331.

R. M. Hare is one of the few philosophers working in applied ethics who has explicitly discussed these problems. He has argued that appeal to moral intuitions is always illicit and that only linguistic intuitions can provide the bedrock for moral theory (*Moral Thinking*, ch. I). I have serious doubts about Hare's positive view. I don't believe that his sharp distinction between moral and linguistic intuitions can be sustained. Nor do I see how linguistic intuitions can be pure so long as moral ones are tainted. Nevertheless, he and Noble are right in thinking that too much work in applied ethics is just a restatement of the writer's prior beliefs in the guise of something else. Arguments must rest on some unargued assumptions, but we have been too permissive in granting controversial assumptions that are quite fundamental.

The appeal to intuition takes many forms. Sometimes moral intuitions provide the limits beyond which the conclusions cannot stray. If a theory implies that animals have rights, then some would say that the theory must be rejected. Intuitions also enter arguments in response to imagined cases that bear only the slightest resemblance to anything we have ever experienced. We are then instructed as to what our intuitions are, and the conclusion is drawn. Sometimes we are given cases that are close to our actual experience, but we are told to purge our minds of all the contingent associations we are likely to have with such cases. If we drag any of these real-world assumptions into the conversation we are told that we are not thinking philosophically.

Despite the dangers, it is doubtful that moral philosophy can be done without relying on a stock of prior moral beliefs or "intuitions." We must always begin from where we are, and we are always somewhere. This is true of epistemology in general, not just of moral epistemology. There is no harm in relying on prior beliefs and intuitions, however, so long as each individually is open to revision. When we think about moral questions, it is also important that the route from the stock of prior beliefs to the conclusion of an argument not be too direct. Although this point cannot be pursued further here, I hope that enough has been said to make plausible the view that problems about the role of intuition in moral philosophy are not different in kind from problems that arise in general epistemology; and just as these problems do not lead us to the conclusion that epistemology is not worth doing, neither should they lead us to the conclusion that applied ethics is not worth doing.

Another methodological trap for the practitioner of applied ethics is baited by the very name of the field. The expression 'applied ethics' suggests a field in which ethical theories are applied to particular cases in much the same way that a mechanic applies automotive theories to the transmission of a Volvo. Inspired by this picture, classes in applied ethics often center on laying out the deontological, consequentialist, and contractarian views of various contemporary problems. Although it is undeniable that some moral theories are more at home with some conclusions than with others, this simple-minded way of "applying" theories to cases is indefensible. It ignores the fact that these are all families of theories. 'Consequentialism' refers to a class of theories of which utilitarianism is a member. But utilitarianism too admits of many varieties. There is no unique utilitarian view of affirmative action, euthanasia, or abortion. All the great moral theories are too complicated for that, and so are the practical issues to which they are "applied."

Although there are dangers and temptations that the practitioner of applied ethics must seek to avoid, this is true in all areas of philosophy. Applied ethics can be done badly, but so can epistemology or metaphysics. These considerations concerning method do not show that applied ethics isn't worth doing.

APPLIED ETHICS AND THE REAL WORLD

Most of the work that has been done in applied ethics has focused on individual rather than societal responses to ethical problems. The main concern has usually been to say what individuals should do about various problems like world hunger and abortion. Questions about what social policies we should adopt or what individuals should do as members of a democratic society hardly ever get addressed. This is especially striking in the literature on professional ethics. Philosophers have written voluminously on various aspects of the physician/patient relationship while virtually ignoring questions about the role of medical institutions in the life of society. Although philosophers have written quite a lot about the difficulties faced by individual doctors and hospitals in the distribution of resources, they have said little about the larger problems concerning the proportion of our total resources that go to the medical sector or about the problems of justly distributing those resources across the entire population. Similarly, the literature on engineering ethics exemplifies a single-minded devotion to the problems of the whistle-blower while saying very little about the role of engineering in society.

One reason why philosophers tend to avoid the social dimensions of ethical issues is their reluctance to appear politically and socially committed. Applied ethics is welcomed into the halls of government and business because it seems to be another specialization. An employer might say: We have someone who does economic analysis, someone who does policy analysis, and someone who does systems analysis; why not hire someone who does ethical analysis? It is very easy for philosophers to adopt the role of the technocrat, since much of our recent history has conceived of the philosopher as the disinterested analyst, sorting out conceptual muddles. Some people are soil engineers, others are electrical engineers. We are conceptual engineers. After all, what is letting the fly out of the fly-bottle but a low-level engineering job? I am not sure to what extent this model was ever a viable description of what anyone did in any area of philosophy. I do know, however, that it is not a viable model for someone in applied ethics. The positions we take in our work have political and social consequences, and it would be dishonest to pretend otherwise.

A better reason why philosophers have focused on the individual dimensions of moral problems while neglecting the social is that philosophers are primarily college professors. They speak to students rather than to presidents or legislators. They write mainly for other professors. Even those who wear white coats and beepers typically address medical students and individual physicians. Given the institutional location of most philosophers, writing about individual responses to ethical problems makes good sense. We might succeed in changing the behavior of a few students and colleagues, but, if our goal is to change the world, our prospects are bleak. As philosophers fan out into policy-making contexts they will begin to write for different audiences, and the character of their work will change. Already this is occurring.

But this response will take us only so far. Even if we take into account the institutional background in which philosophy is embedded, it still seems to many people that philosophical writing on most contemporary issues usually misses the heart of the matter and, for that reason, is less effective than it might otherwise be.

Thomas Nagel seems largely to agree with this, but he doubts that it could be otherwise. He writes:

> I am pessimistic about ethical theory as a form of public service. The conditions under which moral argument can have an influence on what is done are very special, and not very well understood by me.
>
> It certainly is not enough that the injustice of a practice or the wrongness of a policy should be made glaringly evident. People have to be ready to listen, and that is not determined by argument. I say this only to emphasize that philosophical writing on even the most current public issues remains theoretical, and cannot be measured by its practical effects. It is likely to be ineffective; and if it is theoretically less deep than work that is irrelevant to the problems of society, it cannot claim superior importance merely by virtue of the publicity of its concerns. I do not know if it is more important to change the world or to understand it, but philosophy is best judged by its contribution to understanding.[14]

It is certainly true that most of us would not know how to make our words change the world even if that were what we wanted. The gap between individual morality and public policy is awesome, as Nagel suggests. It is not even easy to grasp what makes a society lurch in one direction rather than another. Nagel is also right in saying that philosophical work should not be judged by its influence on public life. To suppose otherwise threatens to collapse the distinction between philosophy and advocacy journalism. Still, I am disquieted by Nagel's words. He does not seem disappointed that "philosophical writing on even the most current public issues remains theoretical;" but this, perhaps more than anything else, is what has disturbed the critics of applied ethics, and it deserves a sympathetic response.

Consider first the words of Mark Lilla:

> We have always been a moralistic nation, but seldom before have we conducted our political arguments in full academic regalia . . . [t]his sort of moral discourse is now so pervasive that even the moral obligations of government officials . . . are now discussed in the obscure and formal analytic language of the contemporary theoretical philosopher . . . While angels dance on pins, these thinkers ponder such questions as: if a group of people are hopelessly trapped in a tunnel by a fat man stuck in the opening . . . is it right to blow the

---

[14]*Mortal Questions* (New York: Cambridge University Press, 1979), p. xiii.

man to bits to save the group? ("Ethos, 'Ethics,' and Public Service," pp. 10–11.)

Cheryl Noble has written that recent work in applied ethics is

"devoid of interest in other traditions of social and cultural criticism—historical, social, scientific, literary, or psychological."

Because of this, she believes that its

"conception of the kind of knowledge and insight needed to shed light on moral issues is unavoidably inadequate" ("Ethics and Experts," p. 8).

To a very great extent the remarks of Noble and Lilla are unfair, and based on serious misunderstandings. As I suggested at the outset, theoretical and applied ethics are complementary; good work in one requires the other. And it is not surprising that the methods and approaches of theoretical ethics strike many nonphilosophers as "formal" and "obscure." Still, there is something important that Lilla and Noble are on to.

Much recent work in applied ethics is not really about the problems it seems to address. Some philosophers write about animal rights because they are concerned with the nature and scope of rights in general. Other philosophers address the physician/patient relationship because of their interest in arguments for and against paternalism and coercion. Problems of world hunger provide a convenient backdrop to discussions of action theory and its relation to moral responsibility. The list could go on. I do not mean to suggest that everyone working in applied ethics has a hidden agenda, only that much of the work that seems to be about "real issues" is not. All too often we have tried to have it both ways. We have wanted the public support and attention that comes from addressing issues of real public concern; at the same time we have been more interested in impressing our peers than in making a difference in the world. To put the point in another way: some of the critics of applied ethics have noticed, perhaps obliquely, that most work in *Philosophy and Public Affairs,* for example, is really about philosophy rather than public affairs.

To some degree this can be explained by the defensive position of applied ethics within professional philosophy. Although most philosophy departments have created courses in applied ethics within the last ten years and many have hired specialists in this area, often this has been a grudging concession to student demand or administration pressure to increase enrollments. Running hundreds of students through courses in contemporary moral problems has become a popular strategy for trying to save "real" philosophy courses—logic, philosophy of science, philosophy of language—in an era of shrinking budgets. Although applied ethics has become institutionalized in philosophy departments, to a great extent the relationship is very much like the result of a shotgun wedding. Given the widespread skepticism about applied ethics within the profession, it is not surprising that practitioners of applied ethics have been anxious to demonstrate their philosophical *bona fides;* and this can be done only by writing articles directed toward philosophers and relying on philosophical sources published in philosophical journals. Two results of this have become apparent.

First, while practitioners of applied ethics have been concerned to show that they are real philosophers rather than half-breeds, their colleagues in philosophy of science have been busily studying physics, biology, psychology, and cognitive science. It is ironical that, although most philosophers are willing to admit that a logician has more in common with some mathematicians than he has with many of his fellow philosophers, they resist the view that in order to do applied ethics well it might be necessary to spend more time talking to economists, sociologists, activists, and street people, than to other philosophers.

Second, it is becoming increasingly clear that much work in applied ethics exemplifies the worst of both worlds. Writing traditional philosophical articles under the guise of doing applied ethics will never satisfy traditionally minded philosophers. For they understand that, for the most part, the deepest and most interesting philosophical work will be done by people who honestly and directly take on the fundamental problems. Nor, as we have seen, does this hybrid work satisfy those who are concerned with the real issues. For they rightly see that much of this work consists in a dance between philosophers rather than a conscientious attempt to address the issues.

Philosophers are moving in the direction of the real world, but they have not yet landed. For reasons I will discuss in the next section, I believe that philosophers can do important work on issues of great public moment. Ultimately, however, this belief will stand or fall on the basis of our attempts. So far we have barely tried. We have isolated ourselves by ignoring the social dimensions of ethical problems. As to our ultimate effectiveness, the jury is still out.

WHY PHILOSOPHERS SHOULD DO APPLIED ETHICS

Thus far my project has been mainly negative. I have resisted the view that applied ethics is by its very nature so deeply flawed that it is not worth doing. I would like to conclude by briefly saying why philosophers should do applied ethics. My claim is really very simple: philosophers have advantages that most people do not have which make philosophers natural candidates for the role of moral expert.

First, philosophers are trained in logic. They can detect fallacies and separate good arguments from bad. They can identify premises and point to those which require additional support. Anyone who reads the newspaper knows how ubiquitous logical mistakes are in the discussion of public issues. Often it is an important contribution just to identify the logic of the arguments that people employ.

Second, philosophers are trained in thinking about moral concepts. We know, for example, the difficulties involved in negotiating the supposed chasm between "facts" and "values." It can be a great service to point out those premises that people employ which spring from deep value commitments, since their adherence to those premises is unlikely to be sensitive to new factual information. Consider an example. Many people are in favor of capital punishment because they believe that murderers deserve to die. Any rational discussion of their views must engage this value commitment. No number of studies about the inefficacy of capital punishment as a deterrent will move them. Although analytically this point is very simple, it is often obscured by the rhetorical flak that surrounds real arguments. Philosophers also know that the relationship between the good and the right is really very complicated. Ordinary people often think it is quite simple: if something is good then it is right to bring it about. Sensitivity to the full range of possible relationships makes philosophers specially qualified trail guides on the road from the good to the right.

Third, philosophers have knowledge of moral theories. Although, as I have suggested, these theories cannot be trotted out and "applied" to real problems, they do provide a storehouse of sophisticated thinking about how particular judgments may be unified into a larger framework. This is important because people often make moral decisions on a piecemeal basis. (For example, it is sometimes said that, for a policy maker, the time horizon is the next five minutes.) The result is that people often hold obviously inconsistent views about what ought to be done. The knowledge of moral theories which philosophers have can influence people to recognize the necessity of thinking about the fundamental principles that underlie their particular judgments.

Fourth, philosophers have the leisure to think about real moral problems, whereas many other people do not. The thinking of ordinary people usually remains at the intuitive level because the press of circumstance does not allow the time for the hard work that critical thinking requires. Most people rightly believe that it is better to rely on one's intuitions than to do a poor job of working out all the complications involved in a difficult issue. Philosophers are moral experts, in part, for the same reason that physicians are experts in medicine: both moral philosophers and physicians devote themselves full-time to their areas of expertise.

Finally, philosophers are sufficiently insulated from the pressures of ordinary life that they can think about moral issues in a relatively impartial way. Very few people in any society can follow their thinking about practical issues wherever it might lead, without fear of reprisals. Many people avoid moral crisis by avoiding moral thinking. Since moral philosophers are paid to think through moral questions, they are less likely to be threatened if they come up with the "wrong" answers. We should not be too sanguine about this, however. There is a history of political interference in American universities. Moreover, as philosophers increasingly work outside of universities and as support for universities becomes more politicized, this advantage will erode.

These, then, are the advantages that philosophers have in thinking about real issues. It adds up to a kind of moral expertise. Applied ethics is worth doing for philosophers because philosophers are moral experts. This does not imply, however, that philosophers should be the only ones to do applied ethics, that people should always defer to philosophers, or that philosophers always do applied ethics well. Nor does it imply an excessively optimistic view about the place of reason in ethics. When all is said and done, people will

continue to make difficult decisions about real moral issues. They
will consult policy analysts, theologians, astrologers, physicians,
politicians, and bartenders. Philosophers may not be ideally suited
for the role of moral advisor, but they are better suited than their
rivals. For this reason applied ethics is more than worth doing.
Philosophers have a duty to bring their expertise to bear on the
problems of real life.[15]

---

[15]This essay was largely written in 1983. For this reason some of the
examples may seem dated, though I believe that the substantive points they
are meant to illustrate still hold. Since this essay is a kind of personal
apology, it seemed natural at the time I was writing it to use male pro-
nouns to refer to the applied philosopher. I hope that this will not give offense to any of my readers. I am heavily indebted, especially in Section I,
to Richard Sharvy's underground classic, "Who's to Say What's Right or
Wrong? People Who Have Ph.Ds in Philosophy, That's Who." Section 7
largely follows Peter Singer's "Moral Experts," *Analysis,* XXXII (1972). In
addition, I have benefited from the suggestions of Nancy Davis, John A.
Fisher, James W. Nickel, Elizabeth Robertson, David M. Rosenthal, Anita
Silvers, and especially Tom Regan.

8

Philosophy and Policy

James W. Nickel

The methods and results of the philosophy-and-public-affairs movement have frequently been questioned—sometimes in a spirit of
philosophical inquiry, but more often in bitter political polemic.[1] In
my opinion one cannot reasonably doubt that philosophers have
had interesting and useful things to say about policy issues. In support of this claim one could cite many examples, including Irving
Thalberg on racism, Ronald Dworkin and Richard Wasserstrom on
reverse discrimination, Henry Shue on human rights, Charles
Fried and Norman Daniels on access to medical care, Mark Sagoff
on environmental issues, and Judith Jarvis Thomson on abortion.[2]

The interesting question here is whether useful philosophical
discussions of policy issues are the product of distinctively philosophical skills and knowledge. If so, what philosophical knowledge
and which skills are these, and does possession of them confer moral
expertise?

As a way of addressing these questions, I will survey some types
of philosophical skills and knowledge which are likely to be relevant
to policy deliberations. In doing this I will move from the less to the
more controversial and from the less to the more distinctive. My
conclusions will be, first, that moral and political philosophers have
some useful—if not utterly distinctive—knowledge and skills to offer
to discussions of policy, and, second, that this remains largely true

---

[1]See for example, Philip Abbot, "Philosophers and the Abortion
Question," *Political Theory*, VI (1978): 313–335; William J. Bennett, "Getting Ethics," *Commentary*, LXX (1980): 62–65; Mark T. Lilla, "Ethos,

even if values and norms lack "objectivity" or if all existing theories of normative ethics are inadequate. If my arguments for these conclusions are persuasive, they will provide not only a defense of philosophical work on policy issues, but also a rationale for including philosophical study in interdisciplinary policy programs.

PHILOSOPHICAL SKILLS

Socratic Doubt

This is a willingness to identify and challenge key assumptions that others wrongly take to be unproblematic. Socratic doubt does not deny the possibility of genuine knowledge; it is targeted rather than wholesale skepticism. A practitioner of Socratic doubt may be thought of as a gadfly, a buzzing presence that whispers "You know less than you think" in the ears of politicians, scientists, economists, and moralists. To defend what he or she whispers, the gadfly may need—like Socrates—to deploy philosophical skills to demonstrate the absence of knowledge or the presence of confusion. A good

---

'Ethics,' and Public Service," *Public Interest*, LXIII (1981): 3–17; Cheryl Noble, "Ethics and Experts," *Hastings Center Report*, XII (1982); William Ruddick, "Philosophy and Public Affairs," *Social Research*, XLVII (1980): 734–48.

²Thalberg, "Visceral Racism," *The Monist*, LVI (1972): 43–63; "Justifications of Institutional Racism," *Philosophical Forum*, III (1972): 243–63.

Dworkin, "Reverse Discrimination," *Taking Rights Seriously* (Cambridge, Mass.: Harvard University Press, 1977): 223.

Wasserstrom, "Racism and Sexism," in *Philosophy and Social Issues: Five Studies* (Notre Dame, Ind.: Notre Dame University Press, 1980), pp. 11–50.

Shue, *Basic Rights* (Princeton, N.J.: Princeton University Press, 1980).

Fried, "Equality and Rights in Medical Care," *Hastings Center Report*, VI (1976): 29–34.

Daniels, "Health Care Needs and Distributive Justice," *Philosophy and Public Affairs*, X (1981): 161.

Sagoff, "Economic Theory and Environmental Law," *Michigan Law Review*, 79 (1981): 1393–1419.

Thomson, "A Defense of Abortion," *Philosophy and Public Affairs*, I (1971): 47–66.

example of Socratic doubt is provided by the challenges of philosophers and others to the pretensions of cost-benefit analysis, particularly as it is used in the environmental area.[3]

Skills in Conceptual Analysis and Reconstruction

Disagreements about policy, like disputes about other things, often turn on ambiguities and confusions. Analysis of central but troublesome terms can be helpful in making clear exactly what is under dispute and explaining where particular arguments do and do not apply. Much work on the reverse-discrimination debate, for example, attempted to clarify concepts such as "discrimination" and "racism." Thalberg and Dworkin, for example, saw racism and racial discrimination as complex phenomena, not definable simply in terms of "assigning benefits or burdens on the basis of irrelevant characteristics." They offered alternative accounts which emphasized the institutional and ideological dimensions of racism and sexism.[4]

Conceptual work need not be a matter of particular concepts alone; it applies to conceptual frameworks as well. In *Basic Rights*, Henry Shue provided a helpful framework for thinking about the complicated interdependencies that emerge in the implementation of human rights (see fn 2, above).

Conceptual analysis is sometimes directed to destruction rather than reconstruction. Distinctions are often drawn because two apparently similar things are thought to require different moral appraisals. Philosophical work may attempt to undermine these differences in appraisal by undermining the underlying distinction. Good examples of this can be seen in recent philosophical work on

---

[3]See note 2 above. See also Laurence H. Tribe, "Policy Science: Analysis or Ideology?," *Philosophy and Public Affairs*, II (1972): 66–110; and "Ways Not to Think about Plastic Trees: New Foundations for Environmental Law," *Yale Law Journal*, 83 (1974): 1315.

[4]See Thalberg and Dworkin in note 2 above. See also my "Preferential Policies in Hiring and Admissions," *Columbia Law Review*, 75 (1975): 534–58, reprinted in Gross, ed., *Reverse Discrimination* (New York: Prometheus, 1976).

actions and omissions and in the related work on negative and positive freedom (duties, rights).[5]

Dialectical and Methodological Skills

These are highly developed abilities to argue well, to construct interesting arguments, and to identify fallacies and weak premises. Perhaps we should also include here skill in the analysis and interpretation of statistical data. In some cases this is more like "applied philosophy of science" than "applied ethics." As philosophers have turned to issues such as risk assessment and the morality of nuclear deterrence, subjects such as probability theory and decision and game theory have become more important to the philosophy-and-public-affairs movement.[6]

Broad Vision

This is an insistence on seeing all dimensions of a problem, particularly those which are likely to be neglected by existing institutions and methodologies. For example, cost-benefit analyses of environmental problems sometimes neglect or give limited attention to values that cannot easily be assigned market prices. In taking a broader perspective, philosophers may insist that these values not be slighted and attempt to explicate their implications for policy. This should not, however, merely be a matter of philosophers saying "We'll specialize in value issues while social scientists attend to the economic, political, and social impacts." It should rather be a matter of joint work to develop a comprehensive view that considers and gives reasonable weights to the full range of relevant considerations. Focusing attention on norms and values while ignoring so-

---

[5]For example: James Rachels, "Active and Passive Euthanasia," *New England Journal of Medicine,* 292 (1975): 131–37 [(reprinted in Bonnie Steinbock, ed., *Killing and Letting Die* (Englewood Cliffs, N.J.: Prentice-Hall, 1980)]; and Henry Shue, *Basic Rights,* pp. 35–55.

[6]For example, see Ian Hacking, "Culpable Ignorance of Interference Effects" in Douglas Maclain, ed., *Values at Risk* (Totowa, N.J.: Rowman & Allenheld, 1986), pp. 136–54. For a more general discussion of bargaining and cooperation, see David Gauthier, *Morals by Agreement* (Oxford: Clarendon Press, 1986).

cial, economic, and political considerations is at least as bad as doing the opposite.

MORAL EXPERTISE

So far, we have identified skills rather than propositional knowledge that can be used in arguments justifying particular decisions. The skills discussed are not uniquely possessed by philosophers, and using them does not require one to reject moral skepticism, to believe that humans have available to them a reliable method of justifying moral propositions. The skills discussed so far are useful even if values and norms are nothing more than matters of social convention or personal choice. The idea of moral expertise takes us beyond these skills and suggests knowledge of general or particular moral truths. It is useful, however, to divide moral expertise into distinct elements; we will find that, as before, these elements do not all stand or fall together.

Knowledge of Human Moralities, Moral Concepts, and Moral Theories

One kind of moral expertise involves extensive knowledge of human moralities, their key concepts, and their historical development, and of philosophical theories about the nature of morality and moral judgments. Knowledge of these sorts can be divided into (1) historical, anthropological, and sociological material on human moralities at different times and places, and (2) knowledge of philosophical theories about the nature, fundamental principles, and grounds of morality—as well as knowledge of the historical development of these theories.

A person with the latter sort of knowledge would know moral philosophy, have spent time reflecting on widely accepted moral norms as well as on the nature of morality, and hence have interesting things to say in response to questions such as When is consent informed and meaningful? or What are some of the plausible, but different, understandings of distributive justice?

Ability to Test Moral Beliefs by Uncovering Inconsistencies and Posing Insightful Analogies

Philosophers are likely to be good at testing general moral claims or principles by looking for inconsistencies, posing hard cases, or suggesting analogies from less problematic areas. This is a matter of using imagination and argument to arrive at what Ronald Dworkin calls "articulate consistency, or what John Rawls calls "reflective equilibrium."[7] Part of this process is formal; it involves logical skills and the examination of possible meanings. More substantive matters are also involved, however, since posing insightful analogies is likely to require moral sensitivity and understanding. To understand the implications of the right to life, for example, one might ask whether there are limits to the burdens that this right can impose on others. Pursuing this might involve following Judith Thomson in imagining particular scenarios involving such burdens and seeing what kind of intuitive response people have to these situations when they are described in detail (see fn 2 above).

Possession of a Critically Examined Moral Perspective

If one had applied the procedures just described in a sincere and thorough way to one's own moral beliefs, the result would be a critically examined moral perspective. This would be a matter of having beliefs about values and moral norms which have been critically examined, tested for consistency, and systematized to some degree. One might hope that such beliefs are more reliable than purely intuitive ones. However, if two people start a process of examination and systematization with substantially different moral intuitions, their deliberations may lead them in different directions rather than toward agreement. It is far from certain that engaging in critical examination will lead everyone to the same moral outlooks and conclusions or that critical examination will make one's beliefs wiser or more justified. Nevertheless, a person with a critically examined morality may be able to play a helpful role in the choice of normative grounds for policy decisions. It is sometimes helpful to policy makers to be able to discuss a problem or a dimension of a problem or a proposed solution with someone who has thought through in great detail the moral dimensions of that problem, particularly if important implications and consequences are not obvious. This is a service that philosophers who have critically

---

[7]Dworkin, "Hard Cases" in *Taking Rights Seriously* (Cambridge, Mass.: Harvard University Press, 1977), p. 81; Rawls, *A Theory of Justice* (Cambridge, Mass.: Harvard University Press, 1971). See also Virginia Held, *Rights and Goods* (New York: Free Press, 1984), pp. 264–79.

examined the moral dimensions of a policy issue may be able to provide.

The Ability to Give Persuasive Formulations of Widely Held Moral Principles and to Argue Cogently from These to Interesting Results about Policy

One widely used way of defending policies is to show that they are permitted, endorsed, or required by plausible formulations of accepted moral principles. For example, in "Famine, Affluence and Morality," Peter Singer defends aid to hungry people at home and abroad by appealing to the plausible moral principle that one should aid people if preventing a great loss to them can be achieved at only a slight cost to oneself.[8] In this particular paper, at least, Singer does not derive this principle from a moral theory such as utilitarianism; he simply endorses it as a moral principle that is and ought to be widely accepted.

This approach can also be used in a negative way, that is, by trying to show that a particular conclusion does not follow from and so cannot be defended by appeal to a certain moral principle. For example, Nancy (Ann) Davis argues in "Abortion and Self-defense" that it is doubtful that one can defend abortion, even in cases in which the woman's life is clearly at stake, by appealing to a right of self-defense alone.[9]

Weak Applied Ethics: Using Ethical Theories to Illuminate Policy Questions

Many have hoped to connect philosophy and policy by using ethical theories to suggest the normative grounds for policy. We might call this *applied ethical theory* or *applied ethics*. It involves the application to policy issues of moral theories such as utilitarianism or Kantianism. Unlike the previous approach, appeals to ethical *theories* offer something distinctively philosophical.

---

[8] *Philosophy and Public Affairs*, I (1972): 229–243. See also the "Postscript" to the reprinting of this essay in William Aiken and Hugh LaFollette, eds., *World Hunger and Moral Obligation*, (Englewood Cliffs, N.J.: Prentice Hall, 1977), 22–36.

[9] *Philosophy and Public Affairs*, XIII (1984): 175–207.

There are weak and strong versions of "applied ethics." *Weak applied ethics* is simply the attempt to find illumination for policy by investigating the implications for particular issues of ethical theories that many philosophers accept or find interesting. It does not assume that any of these theories is fully adequate or authoritative. *Strong applied ethics,* which I will discuss in the next section, takes some particular ethical theory to be true, well founded, or authoritative and asserts that it is possible in principle to settle some policy issues by deriving a prescription from that theory.

Weak applied ethics pursues better understandings of policy problems and alternatives by looking at them through the lenses that different ethical theories provide. A person who was uncertain about the justification of a policy of providing free health care to low-income people might be interested to learn what, if anything, well-known ethical theories—when conjoined with plausible empirical premises—imply for this issue. Even if this person was not prepared to endorse a particular one of these moral theories, she might still hope to find illumination and guidance by seeing their implications for this issue.

Much work in philosophy and public affairs has taken this form. Norman Daniels, for example, defends the distribution of health care on the basis of need by appealing to Rawls's principle of fair equality of opportunity. In applying this Rawlsian principle to health care, Daniels explicitly asserts that his argument does not presuppose the acceptability of Rawls's general theory; other normative theories might endorse the same principle (see fn 2 above). As Daniels's essay illustrates, normative theories often contain subordinate moral principles—such as a principle of equal opportunity—that are widely accepted on their own. Hence, Weak Applied Ethics is sometimes hard to distinguish from the previous category.

Strong Applied Ethics: Applying a Well-Founded Ethical Theory to a Policy Issue to Yield Well-founded Prescriptions

This approach to policy questions suggests that we figure out which ethical theory is most nearly correct and use it to provide normative premises for policy making. It presupposes that there is, or will someday be, at least one ethical theory that is sufficiently correct to be able to confer correctness, or some approximation thereof, on its implications for policy.

Those who endorse strong applied ethics are likely to hold, first, that philosophical treatments of policy issues should attempt to show how prescriptions concerning particular policy issues are derivable from true or plausible theories of normative ethics, and, second, that such derivations can provide full or partial justifications for particular policy positions.

These claims can be viewed as prescriptions for present practice or—more modestly—as goals to be achieved by improving theories of normative ethics. The modest view, which we might call the *aspirational version,* seems to be held by Derek Parfit. He holds that secular moral theory is at an early stage in its development and, hence, thinks of existing ethical theories as primitive and inadequate.[10] As such, these theories would provide very imperfect guidance to practice.

The more ambitious view holds that we now possess well-founded theories of normative ethics and that these theories can play a useful prescriptive role in policy making. We might call this the *achievement version.* R. M. Hare, for example, holds the more ambitious view.[11] He seems to think that only minor improvements will be required in the ethical theory he advances and, hence, that this theory can now lend authority to the moral positions it implies.

The achievement version claims to offer guidance to policy makers here and now—and this makes it attractive. The aspirational version offers only the hope that someday such guidance will be available. If we don't have an adequate theory in hand now, we can offer only those pieces of such a theory which we think are adequate or drop back to relying on a critically examined moral consciousness or appeals to widely accepted moral principles.

I am dubious of the claim that existing moral theories are now sufficiently penetrating and sophisticated to serve as a source of guidance in selecting the normative grounds for policy. Philosophers do not agree on which ethical theory is correct; hence, even if one of them is correct and authoritative, it is not clear which one it

---

[10]"Future Generations: Further Problems," *Philosophy and Public Affairs,* XXII (1982): 172.

[11]*Moral Thinking* (Oxford: Clarendon Press, 1981), pp. 25–64.

is. Because of this disagreement, along with the presence of grave flaws in all the existing theories, it would not be irrational for a person to prefer guidance from his own intuitive moral beliefs to guidance from an ethical theory. I am open-minded about the future prospects of moral theorizing, but I doubt that we have much moral theory in hand that can be offered with confidence as a guide to policy in hard cases. As guides to policy, I am much more comfortable with middle-level moral principles that are widely accepted than with grand principles such as the principle of utility or Rawls's difference principle.

CONCLUSION

Since only the aspirational version of strong applied ethics seems plausible at present and since it offers no immediate guidance to policy makers, I doubt that strong applied ethics—as I have defined it here—has much to offer at present as a way of connecting philosophy and policy. If this were all that philosophy had to offer to policy, we should prescribe the demise—or postponement—of the philosophy-and-public-affairs movement. But my exploration has shown, I believe, that useful roles for philosophers—and philosophical skills—in discussions of public policies are not closely wedded to cognitivist theories about the objectivity of moral values and norms or to faith in the correctness of some particular ethical theory. Perhaps this conclusion makes what philosophers have to offer less distinctive; some lawyers or economists may be able to offer many of the same skills. A less distinctive role for philosophers may be a good thing, however, if it results in their being less constrained by disciplinary boundaries and by traditional assumptions about what philosophers do.

9

Ethical Experts in a Democracy*

Peter Singer

I

Twenty years ago there was a general consensus among philosophers that there was no such thing as an expert in ethics. There were, of course, philosophers who prided themselves on their expertise in metaethics—that is, the meanings of the moral terms—but these same philosophers were the first to deny that their knowledge in this area gave them any edge over anyone else in deciding what ought to be done. Thus A. J. Ayer wrote:

> It is silly, as well as presumptuous, for any one type of philosopher to pose as the champion of virtue. And it is also one reason why many people find moral philosophy an unsatisfactory subject. For they mistakenly look to the moral philosopher for guidance.[1]

and C. D. Broad bluntly stated:

> It is no part of the professional business of moral philosophers to tell people what they ought or ought not to do . . . Moral philosophers, as such, have no special information not available to the general public about what is right and what is wrong.[2]

---

*This paper was written for the present volume in 1981 and, accordingly, reflects the situation in applied ethics at that time. It was not possible to revise it before publication.

[1]"The Analysis of Moral Judgments" in Ayer, *Philosophical Essays* (London: Macmillan, 1954).

[2]*Ethics and the History of Philosophy* (London: Routledge & Kegan Paul, 1952).

The prevalence of these opinions among philosophers was matched by the attitudes of thinking people generally, including those working in ethically sensitive areas such as medicine and biological research. In ethics, it was widely believed that no one's opinion was any better than anyone else's. Indeed, it was often assumed that this attitude to ethics was an essential element of a democratic society. The contrary view—that some people are better able to tell right from wrong than others—was seen as elitist and intolerant, a first step toward taking power from ordinary citizens and vesting it in a small group of self-proclaimed experts who would tell us all what we ought to do; it was thought of as a view fitting for a theocracy or a totalitarian state based on a single ideology, but not for a pluralist society.

During the 1970s these attitudes changed. Gradually it became an accepted part of moral philosophy to discuss the rights and wrongs of abortion, civil disobedience, euthanasia, overseas aid, the redistribution of income, and reverse discrimination. Though philosophers started by analyzing the concepts involved, they soon began to argue over the normative issues. So it has become difficult for philosophers to deny that their discipline has something special to contribute to ethics. If the articles moral philosophers now contribute to their academic journals reflect their professional training and their specifically philosophical abilities—that is, if they are not articles that *any* intelligent thinking person could write—then there is no escaping the conclusion that these philosophers possess some form of expertise in ethics.

Parallel to this change in academic philosophy was a change in the community view generally and in medical ethics in particular. Whereas in the past doctors and medical researchers had relied on established practices and precedents to tell them what was or was not ethical, the rapid growth of new techniques showed up the inadequacy of relying on what had been done before. Legalizing abortion, for example, created entirely new questions about the ethics of research on the aborted fetus. In the U.S., in order to answer these and other new questions, Congress created the National Commission for the Protection of Human Subjects of Biomedical and Behavioral Research. Though the device of a national commission to handle a tricky issue is not new, this commission was charged with resolving questions that were specifically ethical. Inevitably it came to be regarded as a commission of ethical experts, an impression that continued as the original commission was succeeded first by the HEW Ethics Advisory Board and then by the President's Commission for the Study of Ethical Problems in Medicine and Biomedical and Behavioral Research.

Have we now entered an era in which the idea of ethical expertise has lost its disturbing overtones? To jump to this conclusion would be premature. There are still some who are uncomfortable with philosophers' doing applied ethics, and rather more who view with disquiet the perpetuation of an Ethics Commission. Writing in *The Public Interest,* Ithiel de Sola Pool has described proposals for guidelines on social research which arise from recommendations of the original National Commission for the Protection of Human Subjects, as "the new censorship." The merits or otherwise of the particular proposals do not concern us here, but there is a broader objection that underlies what Pool is saying. Noting that Congress charged the Commission with the task of conducting "a comprehensive investigation and study to identify the basic ethical principles which should underlie the conduct of biomedical and behavioral research," Pool condemns this as "a charge better suited to Iran's 'Revolutionary Council' than to an American political commission." Here then is precisely the attitude to which I referred earlier: that the investigation and identification of the basic ethical principles that should underlie conduct in any area is a task for clerics in a theocracy, not for any political commission in America.[3]

For those of us working in applied ethics, there is a temptation to dismiss this kind of objection as a leftover from the days, now fortunately past, when serious thinkers devoted themselves to supposedly neutral tasks like fact gathering and linguistic analysis, while value judgments were left to religious leaders or to anyone's subjective feelings. This would be a mistake, because there are serious questions behind the doubts about ethical expertise in general and about the role played by ethics commissions in particular. These questions are the subject of the rest of this essay.

---

[3]Ithiel de Sola Pool, "The New Censorship of Social Research," *The Public Interest* (Spring 1980): 57–66. For a more general criticism of the idea of ethical expertise, see Cheryl N. Noble, "Ethics and Experts," *Working Papers for a New Society* (July/August 1980): 57–60, reprinted (with replies) in the *Hastings Center Report,* XII, 3 (June 1982): 7–9.

II

First it is necessary to consider the extent to which there can be such a thing as an ethical expert. Since I have written on this topic before, I shall confine myself to a brief statement of the main points.[4]

In most areas in which we accept a division between experts and those who are not experts, we can point to specific advantages that the experts have over the others. Expert mechanics know a lot about how cars work and what can be done to repair them when they go wrong. When my car won't start and I have exhausted my meager list of remedies, expert mechanics can apply their superior knowledge to get my car running again. To distinguish expert mechanics from those who are not expert is, therefore, relatively straightforward (in theory). But what kind of superior knowledge do experts in ethics have, and how do we distinguish those who are expert from those who are not? I can tell when my car has been fixed properly, but how do we tell when our moral problems have been properly solved?

The question is not simple, and to answer it adequately would take us deeply into the nature of ethics. It can be answered only on the premise that reason and logical argument have *some* role to play in ethics. If we abandon this premise, if we accept the view that ethics is entirely a matter of subjective feelings or intuitions in which anyone's feelings are as good as anyone else's, then there really is no role for expertise in ethics. This is, however, an extreme view, and even those moral philosophers who call themselves "subjectivists" are ready to admit that subjectivism does not close the door on argument in ethics and that there is something wrong with—to give a crude example—claiming that all human life is equally valuable and yet agreeing that a defective baby who contracts pneumonia should be left to die, when a normal baby would be given antibiotics. Thus subjectivism at the most fundamental

---

[4]See my "Moral Experts," *Analysis*, XXXII (1972): 115–117; "Bioethics: The Case of the Fetus," *New York Review of Books*, August 15, 1976; and my reply to Cheryl N. Noble in the *Hastings Center Report*, XII, 3 (June 1982): 9–11.

level of ethics is still compatible with reason and argument playing a significant role in debates over ethical issues.[5]

Once a role for reason and argument has been acknowledged, it follows that the first essential for an ethical expert is simply the ability required of all experts in any area that involves reason and argument, namely, the ability to reason well and logically, to avoid fallacious reasoning in one's own arguments, and to detect fallacies when they occur in the arguments of others. These abilities are not, of course, limited to any small band of people with a specific kind of training. A training in philosophy usually does try to develop these abilities, perhaps more directly than most other forms of training since it has logic as one of its branches; but obviously a proper training in law, for example, would have similar aims, and there are some whose nose for a bad argument needs no training at all.

A second requirement for expertise is some understanding of the nature of ethics and the meanings of the moral concepts. Those who do not understand the terms they are using are more likely to create confusion than to dispel it, and it is only too easy to become confused about the concepts used in ethics. Here there is a specific kind of training that can provide this element of expertise, namely, a university course in ethics. Again, though, this training is not the only way in which one can become clear about moral language.

Thirdly, an expert in ethics ought to have a reasonable amount of knowledge of the major ethical theories, such as utilitarianism, theories of justice and of rights, natural-law theories, and so on. These are, of course, also discussed in university courses on ethics. In saying that an expert in ethics ought to have some knowledge of these theories, I am not denying that one could come to well-argued and sound conclusions on ethical issues without such knowledge; I am saying only that to decide these issues in a theoretical vacuum, without awareness of fundamental theories that bear on them, is in the long run not likely to be as satisfactory as deciding them against a background of knowledge of these theories. To adapt Santayana,

---

[5]For examples of ethical subjectivists or noncognitivists who still accept an important role for reason and argument in ethics, see J. J. C. Smart, *Utilitarianism, For and Against* (Cambridge: Cambridge University Press, 1973) and J. L. Mackie, *Ethics* (New York: Penguin, 1977).

those who do not know the work already done in their field are likely to waste a lot of time repeating it.

Fourthly, an expert in ethics must be well informed about the factual matters that are relevant to the ethical issues being discussed. This means that an expert in medical ethics has to know or be capable of learning a certain amount of medicine. Since no one can be expert in all areas of medicine, let alone in all the other areas in which ethical questions arise, the ability to make oneself familiar with a new field of knowledge may be as much as can reasonably be expected.

Last but not least, time to think and reflect about ethical issues is essential. It is difficult to develop and display expertise in ethics if one works full-time as a neurosurgeon and thinks about ethical issues only in one's spare time.

Looking over the five points that I have mentioned, the reader may be struck by the fact that many people could satisfy these qualifications for expertise. Unlike, say, expertise in nuclear physics, expertise in ethics is open to any reasonably intelligent person who is prepared to put some time into it. This is certainly true, and to this extent expertise in ethics is more widely spread and more easily gained than expertise in nuclear physics. All the same, the points I have mentioned allow for degrees of expertise. Although many people will be able to put together some arguments for an ethical view without committing any logical fallacies or showing confusion over the meanings of the terms they are using, some will be able to do this more consistently than others. It may not always be easy to decide who is doing it better, since, once we get away from obvious logical fallacies, it becomes controversial what makes one argument more persuasive than another; but some agreement on this can be achieved. The existence of this agreement is what enables the editors and referees of journals like *Ethics* and *Philosophy and Public Affairs* to decide, in a manner that is not entirely arbitrary, that, of several papers submitted on a controversial ethical issue, one or two should be published and the rest should be rejected. It is also what enables those teaching applied ethics to grade essays in a way that reflects more than their own whims. In other words, although almost anyone can become a bit of an expert in ethics, some will become much more expert than others.

If I am right about this and if there are specific problems in, say, medical research, that raise novel and complex ethical issues, it would seem reasonable to get together a few of the members of our community who have a high degree of ethical expertise to consider these issues and to advise those responsible for the use of public research funds. Is this elitist? Is it something that should have no place in a democratic, pluralist society? That is the next question I shall discuss.

III

Why is it that the idea of expertise in ethics should appear undemocratic, whereas the idea of expertise in nuclear physics does not?

The standard view is that experts in nuclear physics, or in any other scientific field, may properly advise governments on factual questions (such as the consequences of a 10-megaton nuclear bomb exploding over New York City), but that it is then up to the government to decide the policy questions (such as whether to seek peace). One reason that expertise in ethics may seem undemocratic is that it blurs the distinction between factual and policy questions.

Of course, the neutrality of the factual advice offered to government is open to question; but, even if we grant that there is a distinction to be drawn between what we might call "factual expertise" and "policy expertise," it is not clear why this should be a reason for rejecting the latter as undemocratic. It cannot be because elected leaders in a democracy are expected to make all their own decisions, free from any advice except neutral advice about the facts. Elected leaders in all major nations listen to advice about what they ought to do before they make up their minds, advice not just from their constituents but also from their own appointed advisors. If this is not undemocratic, why should it be undemocratic for elected leaders to seek the advice of a body of people who have more expertise in ethics than they themselves have?

It is important that it is advice we are talking about here, and not binding pronouncements. To grant an ethics commission the power to make its own laws or regulations without further recourse to any elected person or body would reduce the scope for democratic decision making. But elected leaders are free to reject the advice of their commissions, even of those commissions with ethical expertise, and voters are free to vote against elected leaders who do not reject the advice of commissions whose findings they dislike.

Thus democracy and a commission with ethical expertise can co-exist.

Perhaps it is not so much democracy as pluralism that lies behind the idea that an ethics commission is somehow out of place among American political institutions. For, whereas nuclear scientists do not differ significantly in their views about nuclear physics whether they are Protestants or Catholics, atheists or Jews, black or white, Hispanic or Chinese, these religious and ethnic differences certainly do affect people's views about ethics, even the views of those who seem to meet the requirements for ethical expertise set out in the previous section. Now, if America is a pluralist society, it would seem that the members of an ethics commission should be drawn from a range of the different groups that make up American society—that there should, for instance, be at least one Catholic, at least one black, at least one woman, and so on. (This practice does appear to have been followed in selecting members of the commissions that have existed so far.) But, given this diversity of membership, how will the commission reach its decisions? When the National Commission was first set up, F. J. Ingelfinger, the influential editor of the *New England Journal of Medicine,* commented: "One may wonder if the diverse elements of the Commission really can reach a consensus. Or will eternal ethical verities be decided by 6 votes to 5?"[6]

In theory, this objection looks serious. Though experts may disagree in any area, and a committee of nuclear physicists might be as divided about the feasibility of using nuclear fusion to generate electricity as a pluralistic ethics commission would be over the morality of abortion, it has to be conceded that disagreement over the correct approach to ethics goes deeper than disagreement over the correct approach to most scientific questions. Moreover, fundamental disagreement in ethics seems in principle harder to resolve than scientific disagreement, since we cannot even imagine any tests or experiments that would show who was right.

Yet in practice the objection has not been as insuperable as its theoretical basis would lead us to expect. In a survey of the first two years' work of the National Commission, Ingelfinger himself ad-

6"Ethics of Human Experimentation Defined by a National Commission," *New England Journal of Medicine* (Jan. 6, 1977): 44–45.

mitted that: "the skeptics have had to swallow most of their doubts. In the context of the formidability of its assignments, the Commission has been remarkably successful" *(ibid.).* This retraction was prompted by the work of the Commission in the areas of fetal research, research on prisoners, and psychosurgery. In many of these areas the Commission was able to make unanimous or near-unanimous recommendations; close votes were rare.

The degree of consensus reached by the Commission is at least in part testimony to the extent to which ethical expertise does, after all, cut across the differences between groups in a pluralistic society. Select from among the most open-minded members of each group; provide them with an expert staff to prepare fact-finding and background papers; sit them around a table with a specific problem to solve; and they will find themselves in agreement often enough to give a useful answer.

That is part of the story—the more positive part. Less positive is the fact that the agreement is often reached at a price. Fundamental ethical issues on which agreement would not be possible are evaded. Other disagreements are papered over by meaningless rhetoric at odds with the content of the specific recommendations made or by language so vague that each side can see it as an expression of its own view, although the views of the different sides are really incompatible.

Examples of all these techniques for avoiding disagreement can be found in the reports and recommendations of both the National Commission and the HEW Ethics Advisory Board. For instance, when the National Commission studied the ethics of research on fetuses that are either about to be aborted or have been aborted but are still alive (though not viable), it might have been expected to proceed by deciding whether it regarded the fetus as possessing the moral status of a normal human being and then either allowing or prohibiting research accordingly. Instead, the Commission took a most circuitous route to its conclusions. It first declared that the fetus is a human being and, therefore, broadly entitled to the same protection as other human beings. The Commission then affirmed the general principle that "manifest risks imposed upon nonconsenting subjects cannot be tolerated" and only research involving minimal risk or no risk is permissible when the subject cannot consent. It added that the same principles apply even when a fetus is about to be aborted.

At this stage a reader might have jumped to the conclusion that the Commission was about to boldly prohibit all potentially harmful research on the fetus; but then it took back much of what it had said by stating that some members were of the opinion that the decision to abort does make a difference, not to the status of the fetus, but to what constitutes "minimal risk." For instance, it is one thing to administer a drug with unknown long-term effects to a fetus undergoing abortion, and quite another to administer it to a fetus likely to develop into a child.

Clearly, this makes the definition of 'minimal risk' absolutely crucial to the issue of how much research will be permissible. Unfortunately, the Commission found itself unable to reach agreement on how to define this term, and so recommended that a "national ethical review body" be set up, to which this and other questions of interpretation could be referred. Here consensus was achieved only by passing the most difficult buck to another—then nonexistent—body."[7]

For another example, consider the report of the HEW Ethics Advisory Board into the ethics of in vitro fertilization and embryo transfer (better known as "test-tube babies"). Here again the moral status of the fertilized human embryo was the most fundamental question raised. Since some research proposals involved fertilizing eggs that were not to be transplanted into the womb, approving the research effectively meant approving of the disposal of human embryos—embryos only a few days old, to be sure, but human embryos nevertheless. So it seems scarcely possible to pass judgment on the propriety of this kind of research without taking sides on the issue that has dominated the abortion debate: whether human life is sacrosanct from the moment of conception. Yet this is what the Board managed to do, after its fashion. Although the Board recorded its agreement that "the human embryo is entitled to profound respect," it added cautiously that "this respect does not necessarily encompass the full legal and moral rights attributed to persons." Indeed, when one reaches the Board's specific conclusion

---

[7]*Research on the Fetus: The Report of the National Commission for the Protection of Human Subjects of Biomedical and Behavioral Research,* U.S. Dept. of Health, Education and Welfare, Federal Register, August 8, 1975, with a separately published Appendix, DHEW Publication No. (05) 76–128. For further discussion, see my review in *The New York Review of Books,* August 15, 1976.

to the effect that research on in vitro fertilization, even without transfer of the embryo to the uterus, is "acceptable from an ethical standpoint" provided specified conditions are met, one wonders whether this "profound respect" means anything at all. Does it mean that the unwanted embryos should be given a decent burial, instead of being tipped down the sink? The Board did not say. On the other hand, when one reads its own gloss on the meaning of the key phrase 'acceptable from an ethical standpoint', its recommendation becomes less certain. The phrase does not mean, the Board says, "clearly ethically right"; rather it means "ethically defensible but still legitimately controverted." In particular the phrase does not mean, the Board emphasized, that the ethical considerations against such research are insubstantial.

Put all that together and we have a masterpiece of consensus drafting. The human embryo is entitled to profound respect, but it is ethically acceptable to do research designed to create an embryo that will be watched for a short period and then disposed of; but then again, though this is "ethically acceptable," it may still legitimately be controverted, and the ethical considerations against it may well be substantial.[8]

That is one way in which an ethics commission can function in a pluralist democracy. Is it the only way?

IV

An ethics commission chosen to provide a balance between members of different religious and ethnic groups may, by careful drafting, be able to write a report that all its members can support; it is less likely to be able to write a report that sets out a clear, well-grounded, and consistent answer to a difficult ethical question. Thus the better an ethics commission satisfies what are often thought to be the requirements of pluralist democracy, the worse it satisfies the requirements of clarity, precision, and coherence. Or so I would speculate. If I am right, we have to choose between these two conflicting sets of requirements.

Up to now, both the selection of members and the subsequent reports of the National Commission and the Ethics Advisory Board

---

[8]See Margaret O'Brien Steinfels, "In Vitro Fertilization: 'Ethically Acceptable' Research," *Hastings Center Report*, IX, 3 (June 1979): 5–8. The full report is in the *Federal Register*, June 18, 1979 (vol. 44, pp. 35033–58).

suggest that a good deal of weight has been given to the requirement that the reports should reflect a consensus among the principal groups that make up American society, and rather less weight has been given to the requirement that the reports be intellectually rigorous. Suppose we were to reverse this order of priority, by making expertise in ethics—as defined in Section II of this essay—the essential qualification for appointment to the commission, with diversity no more than a secondary consideration. It might also help to make the commission smaller; for anyone familiar with committees knows that once the size of the committee grows beyond five or six, effective discussion becomes difficult and clear, direct reports unlikely.

The aim would be a better standard of report—the kind of report that would question widely held but ill-founded moral beliefs in a way that cannot be done if consensus is the name of the game. (It might also, incidentally, be the kind of report that would stand some chance of publication in a journal with referees who look for clear opinions supported by solid argument.) Admittedly, whether any change in the membership of the Commission would bring this about is problematic, and if the changes I have proposed failed to do so, they would have sacrificed consensus for no gain at all.

There are two obvious objections to the proposal, each related to a point we have discussed earlier. The first is that the proposal represents a turning away from the principles of democratic pluralism and toward government by experts. The second is that even a commission appointed on the basis of expertise in ethics might come up with conclusions that in time come to be seen as horrendously wrong.

I have already indicated that I do not think an expert advisory commission is in itself a threat to democracy. The kind of commission I have proposed may indeed represent a turning away from pluralism, but democracy and pluralism are distinct. Pluralism is in any case desirable only within limits. We don't insist on having a Catholic, a Protestant, a Jew, a black, and a woman on expert committees looking into fusion power. That is because we have independent standards of expertise in this area. If I am right in claiming that there is such a thing as expertise in ethics, perhaps we do not need to pick our ethics commissions on this basis either. It is, in any case, political window dressing rather than real pluralism that produces such carefully contrived membership lists. Does anyone really believe that the female point of view, or the black point of view, or even the Catholic point of view, is so universally accepted by all members of each group that it can be represented by one person?

As for the objection that even a commission of experts can make bad decisions, that is no doubt as true in ethics as it is in any other area. It would be reasonable to expect that the more expert a committee was, the fewer bad decisions it would make. That is not, however, the only possible reason for preferring a more expert ethics commission. In the long run, it could be even more important that the reports of the ethics commission be well reasoned than that they come to the right conclusions. The general level of discussion of matters ethical is not high, as the Letters to the Editor columns of our daily newspapers show whenever euthanasia, abortion, genetic engineering, or other controversial matters are in the news. Intelligent, literate people readily abandon all rational standards of argument when they get into the area of morality. There is an urgent need to convince people, from the upper echelons of our society downwards, that there *are* ways of reasoning about complex ethical issues, that this is an area in which clear thinking, dispassionate reflection, and careful argument can get us somewhere. An expert ethics commission could show, by its example, that this is the case. In doing so it would be doing something of immense educational value.

10

Ethics, Applied Ethics, and Applying Applied Ethics

Frances Myrna Kamm

Insofar as ethical theory is thought of as involving substantive normative doctrines (e.g. utilitarianism, deontological views) rather than merely as metaethics, it seems that ethical theory, in some sense at least, *itself* requires its own application to everyday life. That is, the theory says that we are supposed to be ethical in our actions, not merely think about ethics. (By contrast, it is possible to have a theoretical physics without ever applying it to construct mechanical devices.) Yet various problems can arise concerning the relation of theory to applications, in general, and also in various particular settings. In this article I shall first describe in outline a conception of applied ethics and some ways in which theory might be thought to be related to application in particular cases. I shall then consider three broad types of questions about the model(s) of applied ethics I have presented: (1) amplifications of and narrow objections to the model; (2) basic objections to the model; and (3) problems about *applying* applied ethics. Most of the particular examples I use will be derived from my work in the medical-ethics context.

SKETCH OF A MODEL

Applied ethics as it has been or could be practiced can be represented in a brief sketch of several components. The first is that philosophers *think* about problems in the "real world," usually the world of public events, which have been recognized as having a moral aspect to them, in an attempt to prescribe a course of action. Second, applied ethics is not to be identified with popular philosophy; i.e. its discussions need not be accessible to the general public. Theoretically, they might be accessible only to other philosophers who, as citizens, wish to decide about public issues, but, in fact, there is an attempt to be accessible to, and work with, professionals in whose area of interest the problems arise.

Third, the method used to solve practical problems is the application of general ethics and philosophical reasoning.[1] (The latter includes metaphysics, philosophy of mind, rational decision making. For example, the partly metaphysical issue of whether the conceptus is a person is relevant to abortion.) The application of general ethics and philosophical reasoning could take at least the following forms:

(a) We could use a theory, e.g., utilitarianism, or perhaps veil-of-ignorance reasoning, that has a definite, almost mechanical, decision procedure for deciding on almost every occasion what the morally best act or policy is. These theories may be applied directly to a problem situation, or else indirectly; i.e., they may be used to justify general rules, which are then applied to a problem. Furthermore, they may determine a range of answers to a problem, all of which are equally good.

(b) We could have a very firm core concept, e.g., of the person or of society, from which particular decisions should follow, e.g., the idea of the individual as a rational, autonomous agent who may not be used merely as a means.

(c) We could have a list of factors that are considered ethically relevant and not reducible to other factors and use these to decide problems. Such a list typically includes various specific duties and rights, vices and virtues, utility, fairness, justice, etc. Some philosophers do not consider this a theory at all. Alasdair MacIntyre criticizes such a potpourri of considerations as the remnants of once

---

[1]Alternatively, it might be suggested that, rather than apply general ethics to professional problems, philosophers should accept the concepts the professionals themselves accept as guiding their profession and make clear what these concepts entail. This approach would imply that if, e.g., a doctor's code did not already include a commitment to honesty with a patient, it would be inappropriate for a philosopher to criticize the code. This approach to applied ethics is far too narrow.

viable traditions which we no longer really understand.[2] The more positive view is that, having gone through several moral traditions (or theories), we have collected the best of each and corrected for the inadequacy of one by complementing it with something good from another. Or, uncorrupted by any one theory, we can see that there are multiple irreducible values.

Philosophers can be useful to professionals whose work typically leads them to focus almost exclusively on one or another factor, by constantly reminding them of all these factors. For example, in discussion of euthanasia, concern for the good of a patient may lead a doctor to forget the rights of a person who does not want a death that is good for him. Although there may be mechanical procedures for deciding about some of these factors (e.g., utility), individually there need not be any mechanical procedure for deciding how to weigh them against each other and ultimately deciding what to do. The weighing process may simply require sensitivity and good moral judgment.

(d) Instead of just factors, we could have a set of general principles to guide us in cases. These principles are essentially detailed descriptions of the relations that should hold between such factors as (c) describes.

(a), (b), (c), and (d) represent different ways in which decisions about cases derive *from* theories. This unidirectional flow, however, may or may not be absolute. If one is committed to a theory, then any result derived from it is the correct result. If one holds the theory tentatively only, then one can derive results from it and, using some independent standard, judge whether the results are acceptable. If they are not, one can revise the theory. (The question then arises, what this other standard used to judge cases is.) It should be noted, however, that "real-life cases" are not necessarily the ideal sorts of cases with which to test and revise a theory, since they tend to involve detail inessential to a theoretical point; unrealistic hypotheticals are often better. Doing applied ethics, may, therefore, often interfere with rather than aid the theoretical pursuits.) An approach which I shall now describe shifts even more the flow between theory and decisions about cases.

---

[2]In *After Virtue* (Notre Dame, Ind.: University of Notre Dame Press, 1981).

(e) We could make decisions in cases and *then* make explicit to ourselves the general principles, factors, concepts, or decision procedures that lie behind our particular decisions. Method (e), more than (a)–(d), also emphasizes the examination of many particular cases with subtle distinctions between them, as a way of increasing people's capacities to note morally significant differences and to consciously systematize these differences.

In fact, what would usually be done in considering a practical problem, whether one had a complete list of morally relevant factors or not, is first to survey the problem and reach a tentative decision. No doubt this would involve responding to morally relevant factors in a case, but one may not yet be consciously aware of what these are. Consciousness may come only once one looks for reasons for one's decision. To start with a list of moral factors or principles, as in (c) and (d), and check a situation for them, could result in never seeing the forest (all the factors properly weighed) for focusing on the trees. Most importantly, it may also limit the ability to see *new* morally significant factors not yet on the list. So, often we start not by using a theory, but rather just by thinking in accord with it.

Pinpointing what lies behind our decisions may lead us to change our decision, if we cannot accept a principle or procedure the decision reflects as in itself compelling. If being explicit about the general idea or principle behind our decision ever does lead us to *change* our decision or if a theory ever yields a decision we would not have made without it, then this alone will show that theorizing or thinking in general terms is relevant to finding a solution to a practical problem. Furthermore, theory is important even if no new decisions are ever forthcoming (i.e., if we had good intuitions about every case), for the more we can point to decision procedures, essential conceptions, morally relevant factors, or principles based on an analysis of a decision or available before a decision, the easier it is (1) to justify our decision to others in the public arena, (2) to understand our own acts. Should we find it hard to exercise any ability we have to decide issues without explicit reasoning, theory is a guide that may help us reach decisions. (Kant, for example, thought that his theory and decision procedure were implicitly known and acted on by the common good person. But he also thought that innocence could easily be corrupted, so it helped to have an explicit theory to use if we were subject to corruption and

self-deception.) Of course, analysis of principles lying behind decisions we are sure of may help us with *other* decisions we have difficulty making.

Decision procedures, general conceptions, principles, and general philosophical reasoning, then, are supposed to make a
difference in at least two ways: (1) by altering our decision about
how to act from what it would otherwise have been, (2) by providing
explicit justification to others, self-understanding, and guidance.
These two ways are interconnected. Having a justification may
make one surer of one's decision and firmer in action or, by pointing clearly to unfillable gaps in one's reasoning, make one more
modest in action and tolerant of those who disagree. Furthermore,
depending upon what identity conditions we have for decisions, we
may classify many more decisions as "different from what they
would otherwise have been" in virtue of philosophizing. For example, suppose someone would have voted for the MX bomber
before philosophical reflection (BP), and will vote for it after philosophical reflection (AP). But BP he was in favor of it as a way of
starting a war, AP he is in favor of it as a way of avoiding a war. To
say that philosophical reflection made no difference to what act he
performed conceals a lot.

The significance of the ability to give good justification for one's
decisions is made apparent by how uncomfortable one often feels in
the company of those who support the same actions one does, but
for what one considers bad reasons. Belief in the significance of
justification conflicts with a view, such as Stephen Toulmin's,[3] that
in applied ethics we can stop worrying about *why* we act, if we
essentially agree on how to act. Toulmin claims that there is widespread agreement on how to act, but differences in how to justify
our actions. Although one may disagree with the claim that there is
so much agreement on action (e.g., abortion), I am suggesting that
we should seek for agreement in justification as well.

Differences in theoretical justifications that do not show up in
different act recommendations still represent different understandings of why we think an act is wrong and so different views of
ourselves and our relations with other people. It is almost impossible for people not to try to provide themselves with some theo-

---

[3]"The Tyranny of Principles," *Hastings Center Report*, XI, 6 (December
1981): 31–39.

retical understanding of the decisions they make. But then, additionally, different theories or forms of justification that lead to the same conclusion in one case may well diverge on some other cases we will confront. We will then only be putting off having to examine our justifications in order to get agreement on decisions.

For example, we may think that letting someone die merely in order to inherit his money is as morally objectionable as killing someone in order to inherit his money. One theory to explain this is that killing per se is no different morally from letting die per se.[4] Another theory to explain the objectionableness of both behaviors is that not aiding is contrary to the duty of charity, and killing is contrary to the duty of justice (i.e., it violates a right).[5] The two theories may give different results in a case in which it is in someone's best interests to die, but he does not wish to die. The second theory (but not the first) may support the permissibility of not helping to keep such a person alive (since it is in his interest to die and therefore it is charitable to let him die), but prohibit killing him because it interferes with him against his wishes. The first theory, committed to the moral equivalence of killing and letting die per se, would seem to be committed to its being permissible to kill if it is permissible to let die.

Suppose supporters of the first theory decide about this second case directly, without using their theory, and in a fashion contrary to what their theory implies. Then the decisions of the supporters of theory 1 and theory 2 will again agree, but the supporters of theory 1 will have to revise their theory to avoid inner conflict. It is only if *all* decision data can be accommodated equally well by conflicting theories that we will not face the problem either of reaching different decisions or of having to revise theories to be consistent with decisions. And then of course we may still want to get agreement on theories just for the sake of shared self-understanding.

SOME NARROW OBJECTIONS TO THE MODEL

I now wish to consider some fairly narrow criticisms of this sketch of applied ethics. Indeed, some of these "critical" points merely em-

---

[4]Such a view is presented by James Rachels in "Active and Passive Euthanasia," *New England Journal of Medicine*, 292, 2 (Jan. 9, 1975): 78–80.

[5]Such a view is presented by Philippa Foot in "Euthanasia," *Philosophy and Public Affairs*, VI, 2 (Winter 1977).

phasize implications of the sketch itself. [(a), (b), . . . will refer to
the different views of the relation of theory to applications described
above.]

First,

the sketch implies that, before a philosopher works on a real-life
situation, that situation is recognized as involving a moral problem
to begin with. But one of the important roles of applied ethics is to
make individuals aware of moral issues, as well as answers, where
they had not seen any issue to begin with. This is one of the reasons
why it is important for ethicists to see a case firsthand, since descriptions of it given by someone who is not morally sensitive may
omit important information. (This is an argument in favor of an
"on-call" ethicist in some professional scenarios, rather than a review board that is not present at the scene of the problem and to
which professionals come with problems.) The possibility that data
crucial to establishing the presence of a moral issue or factor may be
omitted is a good reason for the philosopher not to rely solely on
descriptions provided by other professionals, but it is also a reason
for using the professional's case description, since he or she may see
meaning in a certain fact that the philosopher could not see.[6] The
possibility that an unnoticed problem based on a previously unrec-
ognized ethical factor can be present in a case also supports the
method represented by (e).

One problem with (c) is that it seems to assume that there is a
fixed set of factors that one must keep in mind, but it may be that
there is no such complete list, knowable in advance. This makes
description of a problem case a crucial and difficult matter, for one
could not easily tell (in selecting from a theoretically infinite set of
data) whether one had left out the data base for a morally significant factor.

---

[6]It is important to note that since philosophers are dependent on non-
philosophers for their knowledge of many factors in a case, their decision
about what is right to do is always hypothetical. For example, *if* the patient
is dangerous, then he can be detained, but the judgment of whether a
patient is dangerous may not be one a philosopher can make. (Although it
is probably true that philosophers should also evaluate via general philosophical reasoning the grounds for determining dangerousness which a
doctor uses.)

Some of the examples of failure to recognize moral problems which I have encountered in a medical academic setting I find quite striking.

One case raised for discussion in medical ethics involves a gynecologist who is asked by his colleague and friend to treat the latter's wife for the gonorrhea he gave her, without telling her what disease she has. (The husband contracted the gonorrhea while at a convention.) The gynecologist agrees, telling the patient that she has a recurrence of "that same old infection."

I asked the students whether their opinion of what should be done changed if the sex of the two doctors was changed from male to female, and the sex of the patient from female to male. One of the students thereupon accused me of being concerned with sexism and not with ethics. I explained that one of the techniques used in ethical discussion in order to make clear to ourselves what factors a decision was based on, was to change a factor and see whether the change made a difference to the decision. If it did, we could discuss whether the isolated factor (e.g., sex of the participants) *should* really affect our decision. Secondly, I suggested that the question of sexism *was* a moral issue, not merely a matter of group interest and power politics, and I tried to explain why. (The good aspect of the student's point was that he did associate ethics with more than group interest or power politics.)

I then discussed what the doctor told the patient, and suggested, in response to a student's view that a lie was a lie, that some lies might be worse than others. For example, the doctor's lie seemed to put "blame" on the woman's body, reinforcing the image of women's bodies as particularly subject to self-generated ills. If one tells a lie in a situation involving a group typically stereotyped and subject to feelings of inferiority (women, blacks, etc.), it would, I suggested, exhibit *moral* sensitivity to avoid telling an untruth that reinforced the stereotype, though it was just this sort of lie that might be more easily believed. Again, the students were surprised that this was a question of morality at all.

As another example of this procedure of isolating factors, I suggested creating a case in which a doctor is asked to conceal another doctor's having broken a nonmarital commitment to a patient; e.g., a doctor is asked to conceal the fact that a colleague broke a commitment to a patient not to transfuse him, when the transfusion resulted in the patient's current illness. The psychiatrist who attended the ethics class suggested that the two cases were radically different, since the second involved a broken commitment to a patient, whereas the original case involved *"only"* violating a commitment to one's wife. His point was that lying to one's wife was a far less serious matter than lying to one's patient, thereby raising another ethical issue.

Second,

the professional or public problems emphasized in the sketch offer too narrow a scope for applied ethics. Personal relations and feelings are subject to ethical analysis, and, even within a professional or public context, philosophers should feel free to discuss such issues as well. (We might refer to this as the *unlimited scope of ethics.*).

Third,

the emphasis in the sketch on arriving at decisions should be changed. There are several components to this objection, some of which connect with the justification given in the sketch itself for doing theory even when decisions do not, in an obvious sense at least, change.

Philosophers should try to bring "real-life" problems (and those who have them) *up* to the abstractions of philosophy, rather than just bring philosophy down to the level of the problems. That is, it should be an aim of an applied ethicist to get those whose initial interest in philosophical ethics comes from the help it can give them with their practical problems, to be concerned with very general concepts and theories of ethics in themselves, for at least two reasons.

First, the way in which a theory is applicable may be indirect— a general conception taken to heart, a change in one's world view, can eventually lead to different choices.

Indeed, it may well be that a concern with the more abstract can make some of the problems people think so important either disappear or seem less important. For example, the problem of how to reconcile certain strong personal desires with the claims of others, may disappear if one loses those strong personal desires through a change in one's deepest values or world view. Second, creative solutions to practical problems often come only after a period of detaching ourselves from them to consider more fundamental concepts. Third, emphasizing the discovery of solutions to problems conflicts with a detached interest that goes wherever an illuminating, but not obviously or immediately useful, aspect of a question leads one. Those who do applied ethics should be allowed to focus on *aspects* of problems, without feeling the need to provide a solution to them. Indeed, focusing on aspects of a problem may complicate matters and put off a decision rather than speed one up, but this is acceptable.

There is also a danger that we may misunderstand the import of the decision that theory may yield. That is, if it is believed that now, in contrast with the past, a decision is the product of specialists working with theories, we may come to believe that our decisions must really be the correct ones, and not brook much backtalk. But, of course, philosophers who do theory are constantly revising their theories, and so their own attitude to any applied-ethics solutions they offer is likely not to be dogmatic. They are likely to see the solutions less as final decisions than as stages in working things out. They see them as better, more informed, more insightful discussions of problems than occurred in the past, but do not necessarily place a guarantee on them as unchangeable. A philosopher should be able to think in this way; but a professional may mistakenly assume that there is a guarantee given—indeed assume that this was the point of having specialists with theories called in—and be impatient if there is none.

If philosophers who do applied ethics do not maintain such attitudes, in common with academic philosophers, they run the risk of being bad philosophers and becoming merely the bearers of simplified, falsely reassuring news from the theorists.

The emphasis in the sketch of Part I on decisions for problems that must be solved, directs our attention toward deciding how to act. But we should also apply ethics to situations in which we want to know what attitudes we should take, rather than what acts we should perform, and to the contemplation and analysis of acts and attitudes we already know are right, in order to understand what values they promote and why they are important. (This move away from solutions in the form of prescriptions for action is already present in that part of the sketch which emphasizes justification even when acts are agreed upon.)

Much of the work on *solving public problems* by providing prescriptions for *action* has employed liberal political philosophy, and so there is a tendency for liberal political philosophy—emphasizing rights and duties—to take over all of applied ethics, narrowing the range of acceptable ethical questions. It does this, in part, because it is thought that if someone has a right to do something, it would be wrong to interfere with his doing it, and if someone has a duty to do something, it must be done. Since applied ethics tends to be directed toward those who worry about how they should act and since rights and duties are thought to be the bottom line when it comes to acting or refraining from acting, these are of preeminent concern.

In the medical setting, the emphasis on *autonomy rights* of patients has led to the particular situation in which professionals exposed to philosophy have become convinced of a unique correct solution to a problem, yet are unable to enact it in practice. That is, they cannot apply at least a part of their applied ethics. For example, they may believe that someone in an irreversible coma is no longer a person and should be disconnected from life-support systems. But relatives may not agree, and want life support continued. It is likely that a "liberal" ethical theory will conclude that the relatives have a right to decide the matter (barring any living will of the patient's). If the professional and applied ethicist are concerned only with matters that bear on how to act, it may seem a waste of time even to discuss the issue of the status of the person in irreversible coma. No matter what one thinks, the applied-ethical solution *for action* is to let the relatives decide.

But rights-and-duties talk is only part of morality, and it is artificial for a philosopher not to consider whether it is *right* for someone to do what he has a right to do. It is certainly wrong to think, as some professionals exposed to philosophy do think, that, once we decide that someone has a right to act, no further judgment of his action is even possible. It is important to maintain a distinction between two types of respect for persons: respect for someone's rights, and respect for him in virtue of the sorts of things he does with his rights and the sorts of reasons he gives for what he does.

For example, if someone has a right to refuse to donate a bodily organ in aid, he may still exhibit a bad character by refusing. If a patient has a right to make use of any support network that is available to him, this should still leave us free to evaluate morally his willingness to use women friends as servants.

Further, not all such analyses are irrelevant for action. First, it should not be assumed that, if someone has a right to do something, this means we have no duty to or should not inform him of the ethical nature of what he is about to do. For example, it may be that we should require a woman who has a right to an abortion to hear a description of what it involves. If someone were about to give away an organ, we would require him to hear a description of what he was about to do to himself. Should we allow him to hear an ethical evaluation of what he is about to do if, within his rights, he refuses to give an organ? Especially if we think he is acting incorrectly, even if within his rights, we may feel obliged to talk to him.

Furthermore, it is recognized that rights are not absolute; they may correctly be infringed, overridden by other factors, and these factors may include welfare considerations, rather than merely stronger rights and duties.

Duties, like rights, are also not the last word in action. It seems that I sometimes may fail to do my duty in order to do what is clearly supererogatory. For example, I may be right to break a luncheon appointment in order to risk my life saving someone else's life. I may sometimes be right to lie in order to maximize utility, though it is not my duty to maximize utility. So, many considerations besides rights and duties can be relevant to action.[7]

Even when moral analysis that goes beyond rights and duties does not change action, the applied ethicist should feel free to point

---

[7]On permissibly infringing rights, see Judith Thomson, "Some Ruminations on Rights," *Arizona Law Review* (1977). On supererogation overriding duties, see my "Supererogation and Obligation," *Journal of Philosophy*, LXXXII, 3 (March 1985). It is important to point out that there are other, more suspect, ways in which the autonomy rights of a patient or relatives are combatted in medical settings. One approach remains very much within the fold of "liberal" ethics. The doctor asserts his/her autonomy rights. For example, if someone cannot personally afford to keep his comatose relative on life-support systems, the doctor may argue that the medical establishment has no duty to aid at great cost, and it can refuse to spend its money on causes it doesn't care for. Combining this view with a philosophically arrived-at conviction that there is no morally significant difference between refusing to plug someone into a life-support system and unplugging him from it, the doctor concludes that he can unplug the destitute

out all moral factors that are at stake in a case. Again, the important points are both that theoretical general ethics and applied ethics deal with issues other than rights and duties and that, in actual
settings in which applied ethics is applied, factors other than those
which can alter an action should be brought up. The emphasis on
factors relevant for action, to the exclusion of other forms of value
analysis, limits a philosopher's best handling of a case qua philosopher. It also limits the development of new capacities for evaluation
in the professional one addresses. The professional not only needs
to make better decisions, and better justify those decisions; he needs
to better understand all ethical aspects of situations he is in.

Essentially the question is whether the ethicist's aim is only to
help the professional solve ethical problems that arise in his specialty or also to try to ensure that general ethical awareness, which
should be present in all areas of life, is maintained by the professional when he practices his specialty. To do the latter we must
counteract the narrow conception of what an ethical issue is or what
a fit subject for philosophical discussion is, which many professionals have.

In summary, we should have a broad view of what an ethical
issue is, of which ethical factors bear on action, and of the significance of discussion not related to action.

BASIC OBJECTIONS

Basic attacks on applying ethical theory to particular problems in
the way the sketch describes take many forms. I will sketch several.

A. In teaching medical ethics, the first and most common resistance I have had to deal with among students is total subjectivism

---

comatose patient. The doctor may now find himself up against the law,
which does draw a distinction between not plugging in and unplugging.
(The theoretically correct ethical solution, considered independently of the
law, may be blocked in practice by the ethical view that, all things considered, it is right to obey the law.) At this point, I have heard a doctor with
exposure to philosophy, who considered the not plugging in/unplugging
distinction to be casuistic logic chopping, proceed to "chop" the following
(dubious) distinctions: (a) between unplugging a patient and stopping the
air supply to the machine, and, having stopped the air supply, (b) between
lying to relatives about stopping the air supply and telling them, truthfully,
only that the patient was not unplugged, and yet he died.

and their drive to deal with the most general skeptical questions of whether there are any ethical truths at all, at the level of theory *or* particular decisions. Combined with this is their desire to focus on cases *immediately* and *exclusively:* no moving down from theory to decisions, no moving up from decisions to development of systematic principles.

The best counter I have found is to emphasize that acquaintance with ethical theories and moral distinctions and concepts related to them will pay off both in helping us understand cases better and in showing exactly *what* sort of claim we are trying to defend the objectivity and truth of. Students begin by thinking that disagreement about cases *must* be based on irreconcilable, not discussable commitments to opposing basic principles. After discussion of theories and concepts they usually move toward the view that some basic principles are more reasonable than others and that many differences about cases are due to errors in one side's reasoning from the same principles rather than to differences in basic principles.

B. (1) The application of theory to cases is disputed on grounds of "realpolitik": we shouldn't do applied ethics because ethically correct solutions to problems are irrelevant to real life; i.e., it is not so much that theory cannot be applied to problems as that ethical solutions to problems cannot be applied. Kant, for one, thought that the supposed split between what it was theoretically right to do and what people could be expected actually to do did not exist.[8] He was aware that the so-called "practical man" thinks of the philosopher as an idealist whose views just will not work, but he insisted that he would take theory every time over so-called "realistic" policies.

Kant first makes this point in connection with motivation. His opponent argues that a distinction between acts done from duty and acts done for happiness may be theoretically (conceptually) correct, but in practice he cannot see that he ever does act simply from duty. Kant agrees that we may not be sure whether we completely succeed in acting from duty, but argues that, in fact, we know that we do deny ourselves some happinesses for the sake of acting correctly.

---

[8]My discussion of Kant on these issues is based on his essay "Theory and Practice," in *Kant's Political Writings,* Hans Reiss, ed. (Cambridge: Cambridge University Press, 1970).

Furthermore, as rational beings, we are indeed desirous of acting from a moral motive rather than in response to our self-interest. We are attracted to the more elevated conception of our will, and people's desire to do the right act is actually reduced if we give them motives other than moral ones.

To deny that we can act from duty and be motivated by an ideal of pure reason made practical is, in effect, to deny that people *ought* to do things, that they should even strive to be moral. To take this route, according to Kant, is to make us the wretchedest of all creatures, those who do not believe in their capacity to be free. Finally, for Kant the preeminent *practical* goal of our species is to be more morally perfect. So, to say that morality doesn't work in practice is, in a sense, to forget what goal we are trying to achieve in practice. Indeed, the attempt to bend morality, e.g., to be what Kant calls a "political moralist" rather than a "moral politician," will backfire, since it is contrary to this highest goal of our species.

Contemporary defenses of taking morality seriously in actual practice emphasize that situations in which we cannot justify our actions to others, in which others feel wronged, are inherently unstable. People are conscious of themselves as moral beings who deserve certain things, and solutions that ignore this are not practical.[9]

(2) Despite these defenses, it is important to note recent quasi-"realpolitik" attempts to deny that it is always reasonable to expect people to do the morally right thing. According to Bernard Williams,[10] if morality's demands (Kantian or utilitarian or Rawlsian) would make it impossible for a person to satisfy the projects that give him any desire to go on living, they cannot have a claim on that person, since he can always choose suicide. [This view would, of course, involve denying that our overriding project is to be moral. Furthermore, it also seems to leave the door open to all sorts of crimes committed against others for the sake of one's crucial projects. After all, suppose a person commits suicide rather than commit the murder needed in order to achieve the project that alone

---

[9]I have in mind Thomas Scanlon, "Contractualism and Utilitarianism," in Bernard Williams and Amartya Sen, eds., *Utilitarianism and Beyond* (Cambridge: Cambridge University Press, 1982).

[10]In "Persons, Character, and Morality," in his *Moral Luck* (Cambridge: Cambridge University Press, 1981).

would make his life worth living. Such a person is already letting morality—not to kill—rule his life.]

It is important to note, however, that many of these doubts about the application in practice of a theoretically correct moral solution, do not endorse any *simple* unwillingness to sacrifice personal self-interest for the sake of doing the right thing. Furthermore, in rejecting the demands of morality, these critics may be taking the view that morality's demands on the individual are extraordinarily high in general, and this may not be correct. Indeed, some have suggested that it is part of morality itself to see that demands made on people are not too great.[11]

(3) A particular sort of skepticism about the claims of morality may be peculiar to the medical context.

Philosophy and the sciences (at least on a traditional view of both) share some basic orientations, for example, a concern with truth and rational argument. There is also a mutual tendency to deromanticize problems, e.g., the doctor's tendency to think of permanently comatose patients as vegetables and some philosophers' attempts to establish self-consciousness as a minimal criterion for personhood. But ethicists and scientists—especially behavioral scientists and psychiatrists, under whose auspices many medical-ethics programs are run—may be at loggerheads in one very important respect: The behavioral scientist, in virtue of his professional views, may find it difficult to recognize the *autonomy* and *dominance* of ethics which many ethicists insist upon.

The 'autonomy of ethics' refers to the fact that ethics is not merely a branch of behavioral or biological science which describes the way people behave or the mores they live by. Ethics, like mathematics, physics, or psychology may be possible only because people are biological or psychological creatures of certain sorts, and we may even be able to give a genetic explanation of why someone develops the philosophical, psychological, or mathematical theory he does. (Though this might involve explaining why he is capable of recognizing the truth.) But we do not decide what ethical judgment is right or what proof is mathematically correct by considering the psychology or biology of the people who propose them. The content

[11]On these issues, see Thomas Nagel, *The View from Nowhere* (New York: Oxford University Press, 1985), and Samuel Scheffler, *The Rejection of Consequentialism* (Oxford: Oxford University Press, 1982).

of ethical judgments and mathematical proofs must be attended to and must be judged by the rational standards of the discipline. We cannot simply relate the content to biological or psychological causes and fail to judge its validity. Yet some psychologists would be willing to see ethics as a psychological phenomenon only (though they would not hesitate to attribute *validity* to *their* research on this matter; that is, they would not see their psychological theory as only a response to some psychological or biological cause).

Substituting biological or psychological accounts for reasoned value judgments is common. For example, in a discussion of Mill's theory of higher pleasures (e.g., intellectual achievement), the medical students and attending psychiatrist were quick to point out what possible neuronal or psychological mechanisms resulted in people's finding these things, rather than physical pleasures, satisfying. Somehow, this was supposed to put all sources of satisfaction on an equal footing, as if locating the biological or psychological mechanism for a state of mind made it unnecessary to decide which neuronal or psychological mechanisms, with their effects, it was better to have.

In other ways, behavioral scientists with whom ethicists must deal most closely in medical-ethical contexts have traditionally held professional views that attack the validity and possibility of ethical motivation. For example, they commonly adopt the (psychological egoist) view that people can be motivated only by the pursuit of their own happiness, that one does one's duty in order to avoid guilt, etc., denying the possibility of an independent motive simply to do the right thing because it is right. (Their rationale for these positions is often the same sort of confused conceptual argument examined in many introductory ethics texts, rather than any empirical theory.) They commonly see a situation in which someone does something morally wrong as one in which he behaves "antisocially," and suggest persuading him to act differently on the grounds that he *imprudently* courts social punishment. Or they may employ certain techniques of dubious ethical status, e.g., reverse psychology, which involves manipulation and deliberate pretense.

If they deny the autonomy of ethics, it is not hard to see why they might be suspicious of the *dominance* of ethics, i.e., the claim that activities (including their own) are ultimately subject to ethical restraint. (They would also be suspicious of the unlimited scope of ethics, i.e., the claim that every sort of behavior, feeling, or thought is subject to ethical evaluation.)

What is really going on here, perhaps, is a war for dominance between ethicists and behavioral scientists, with the scientist always ready with a genetic explanation of why the person is saying what he is saying, which makes no reference to the fact that what the person is saying is true, in contrast to the philosopher who takes the content and validity of what is said as of ultimate significance.

C. Those who are willing to agree there are true and false ethical decisions about cases and that the true ones should be carried out, may still attack the idea that theory either leads to or is derivable from such decisions.

There is an often expressed doubt about the possibility of deciding on a solution to a practical problem by using a theory involving a mechanical decision procedure [method (a)]. Supporters of methods (c) and (d) would probably take such a position. They claim there is no theory having the form of a routinized decision procedure which gives the correct result about what to do.

If there is no good routinized decision procedure, then that, of course, is an excellent reason not to try to derive solutions to practical problems from a routinized decision procedure. However, not all theories need be of this form. Those which are not [like (c), (d), and (e)] require sensitivity for noticing, weighing, and balancing factors, rather than mere mechanical skills. This is a reason, this time related to finding decisions, for emphasizing the attitudes discussed in section II above (under the third narrow criticism), for these attitudes are likely to increase such capacities for judgment.

One approach that has been taken to the question of whether utilitarianism is a true theory, however, bears on the use that could be made of any theory even if it were correct. It has been suggested that, if utilitarianism were correct, its goals would best be achieved if we did not believe that utilitarianism was correct and did not consciously apply it. If this point could be made of any correct moral theory, then knowledge of the theory would never be useful in practice, since we would be specifically barred from consciously using it and perhaps encouraged to use an incorrect theory as a heuristic device.

In connection with this, the greatest actual strain between doing theory, having good judgment, and acting well in particular practical situations, is likely to exist if the correct theory is radically different from the procedure it itself recommends we use in daily life to decide on problems. For example, suppose a "never lie" rule was justified because it maximized utility. Commitment to it might be strongest if the overall utilitarian justification for it were simply disbelieved. So the ability to do ethical theory well might weaken one's moral character, and the inability to do theory well might indicate a strong commitment to good moral judgment and action.

Therefore, it might be true that if a theory is incorrect we ought not use it, and, if it is correct, we still ought not to use it. What if we are not *sure* that it is correct? It may be that the correct theory has very bad consequences, worth suffering only if the theory is true, but not worth suffering so long as there is a chance the theory is wrong. (This assumes that bad consequences don't necessarily prove a theory false.) Libertarianism seems like such a theory. For example, if libertarianism were true, it might be right to let many people die rather than force some others to aid them. In the absence of a truly convincing proof of the theory, we might well decide not to use it in practical decision making. The cost of being wrong would be too great. So, if we are not sure that a theory with extreme consequences is correct, we may also avoid using it in practice.

However, not all theories necessarily have these problems. In particular, there may be no conflict between thinking about the true theory and deciding and acting in particular cases. This will be true especially of theories whose deepest reasons are not radically different from the factors pointed to in ordinary decision making. For example, if we are told not to lie, we will not feel alienated from a higher-level moral theory that accords to not lying intrinsic, non-derivative worth.

D. Stuart Hampshire suggests[12] that theory is irrelevant to moral decision making for essentially two reasons. Put briefly, these are: (1) There is no reason to believe that any theory takes account of all the morally relevant factors in a case, so we must look at the case and decide without deriving the decision from a theory. [This should eliminate approaches (a)–(d).] (2) We cannot derive theory from the cases, since at best we can give only incomplete explana-

---

[12]In "Morality and Pessimism," in S. Hampshire, ed. *Public and Private Morality*, (Cambridge: Cambridge University Press, 1978).

tions of why we have decided by pointing to salient factors. [This limits (e).] These salient factors alone would not have led us to decide as we do, but require many ill-defined contextual factors present in the particular case at hand in order to lead to a decision. They will, therefore, not help us in deciding another case.[13] For example, in one ethics case we may say that we decided as we did because we should not harm in order to aid, but in another case this factor might be overridden by other factors in the situation. Or we might point to the enormous gain in utility as the significant reason for deciding as we do in one case. Yet in another case the same gain in utility may be overshadowed by other factors, e.g., violations of rights.

Hampshire claims that it would not be surprising if most people could unconsciously and rapidly weigh factors correctly and yet not be able explicitly to give their reasons for deciding as they do. There are good evolutionary (survival) reasons for our being creatures who can make right decisions quickly and, he says, no good survival reasons for being able to give reasons. Further, the inability to give good reasons need not mean that one has not in fact decided for good reasons, and been rational.

In rebuttal of Hampshire, I believe the following points can be made. First, theories, concepts, or factors already in hand, as incomplete as they may be, can guide an examination of cases, even if they do not yield a decision. New factors noticed by examining cases can be introduced into an expanded theory. Second, it may be possible to go beyond salient features in working up from cases. Without claiming that we can find absolute nonoverridable principles, careful analysis can, for example, take us beyond such limited and excessively broad claims as "harming is never to be done in order to aid." We can examine cases, and get a more

---

[13]Arnold Isenberg emphasized a similar point in his account of giving reasons for critical decisions in art in "Critical Communication," in his *Aesthetics and the Theory of Criticism*, W. Callaghan *et al.*, eds. (Chicago: University of Chicago Press, 1973). When a critic points to the golden highlights in Rembrandt's "Nightwatch" and says that they are one reason why the painting is good, he is not saying that golden highlights in any painting improve it. It is the golden highlights of *this* painting that contribute to its being good, i.e., the very particular golden highlights they are, in the particular context in which they are. It is for this reason that pointing to salient features is not like providing general rules applicable in other contexts.

complete characterization of the correct principle concerning when we may and when we may not harm in order to aid.

I believe it is true that someone may hold a correct view and arrive at it rationally without being able, even post-decision, to explicitly defend his view. Furthermore, it would probably be wrong to act contrary to one's considered judgment about a case (i.e., when one decides in a calm frame of mind, looking at all the evidence, being on guard for partiality, etc.), simply because one cannot give an argument for one's position, even when someone else can present an argument leading to a different position. It may be that we can know that we *are* being rational in some way other than by constructing an argument for our position. It is only if one becomes convinced of one's opponent's arguments in such a way that one perceives the case in question differently, that one should change one's decision about it.

Holding fast to one's decision, even in the absence of good arguments of one's own, is especially to be recommended when one sees something wrong with one's opponent's reasoning. If one sees something peculiar about his arguments or attitude, one is not tempted by his views on the case; but if one is attracted by everything he says *except* his conclusion about the case, one may (rightly) begin to doubt one's own position, and feel obliged to look for reasons in support of it.

Hampshire's point, however, concerns the *general* separation of the ability to give explicit reasons: not only may there be occasions on which the right solution is arrived at for the right reason without the decider's being able explicitly to tell us the right reason, but this is *in general* likely to be true. As noted, Hampshire gives an evolutionary explanation for this ability to make rapid moral judgments, without explicit reasoning and without the capacity to give explicit justification.

Whether this explanation of rapid moral judgments is true is a matter for biology to decide, I suppose, but we cannot just assume that everything that would have survival value is provided by evolution or that moral judgment has such value. It must also become increasingly difficult for any innate judging ability to deal with complex problems that are the result of technology and social changes, changes that proceed more rapidly than biological evolution alone or combined with early acculturation. Further, the thesis that any moral judging *per se* programmed into us should be left untouched conflicts with the idea that morality goes beyond any biologically/culturally given dispositions and is subject to rational evaluation which may lead to changes in intuitive decisions. Presumably, Hampshire does not want to say that we must take just any natural impulse as the ultimate guide for evaluation.

Most importantly, his thesis seems to imply that everyone (uncorrupted by theory) would make equally good moral judgments (it being a matter of evolution/early acculturation that we can make moral judgments), just as we all speak a language pretty much the same way. But it seems clearly false that every (theory-innocent) person makes equally good moral judgments, let alone acts equally well. (Likewise, some of us also speak the language better than others.) (It is also worth noting that, if *evolution* were concerned to implant ethical judgments, one would expect such good judgments to lead, more uniformly than they in fact do, to good behavior. Would evolution be concerned with judgments and not with acts?)

Perhaps some people make better practical ethical judgments than others do because programmed responses are perverted by self-interest, or perhaps not everyone has evolved/been acculturated equally well. (I am here assuming that we could rationally evaluate the natural or culturally ingrained tendencies we have as either better or worse than those possessed by others, there being some standard outside the impulses we have by which to judge them.) But then it is possible that, although some judge well without explicit reasoning as an aid, others may need to have their attention directed to principles and general factors, or even to the particular facts of a case, in order to judge well.

Furthermore, the fact that some can make good judgments rapidly and without explicit reasoning, or lack the ability consciously to reconstruct reasoning, does not mean that this rapid solution was not made possible, at least sometimes, by prior explicit acquaintance with concepts and principles which then seep back to form the unconscious background of that person's thought. (The issues here are similar to those raised when we ask whether a writing workshop can help produce better writers, or whether one just has to be born with the talent to write. Many writers claim to have been helped by such workshops.[14]) Ideally, all instruction in general theories, concepts, and principles should come to be internalized, allowing for

---

[14]I owe this example to David Wasserman.

the rapid perception of the moral character of a situation. To think that learning general theories and concepts is merely learning new moral vocabulary is to aim very low, I think. Suppose there were a simple procedure for applying a general idea to particular situations, so that, if one knew that a situation had nonmoral property x, one would know it had moral property y, and, if it has property y, one should do act z. Our aim should still be to have someone *embody* the principle relating x, y, and z in himself, rather than apply it mechanically. Otherwise the person may know that the presence of y is bad and that action z is right, on authority, but never himself see that they are bad and right, respectively.

A comparable situation would arise in art if there were rules of taste. That is, a person could see that x was present and know according to a rule that this meant that a painting was dynamic and that this, in turn, meant the painting was good, and yet not *see* that the painting was either dynamic or good. He would have rules of taste but still lack taste. Similarly, his moral analogue would have rules of morality and could be moral insofar as he acted morally, but he couldn't himself see that an act was morally good or be motivated to act because he could see the moral character of the situation.

So there is no necessary conflict between judgment improving, at least sometimes, by acquaintance with general conceptions consciously brought to mind at some point, and quick "intuitive reasoning." Indeed, I offer as a psychological hypothesis that, when judgments are rapid, this may increase the subject's awareness of his reasons for deciding as he does and make him more likely to be directed by the judgment in action. Speed of judgment and consciousness of reasons may not pull apart, as Hampshire suggests; rather, they may move together. This may be because of a "motion picture" effect; i.e., if we look over things slowly we fail to see a pattern, but if we look over them more rapidly, with total attention, the pattern becomes obvious, and our will is more easily directed by it.

APPLYING APPLIED ETHICS

Suppose one has the correct theory to apply or even the solution to a problem in applied ethics. A few words should be said about some problems that arise in *actually* applying the theory or solution.

A. If one has in mind a set list of moral factors that will determine an outcome and for which one is searching in a situation, perceptiveness is necessary in order to know that the factors are present. For example, one may know that *if* someone is in pain, this counts toward helping him, but, if one is not sufficiently perceptive (or imaginative), one may not notice that someone is, in fact, in pain. Or one may know that the presence of a duty would be significant and yet fail to see that the case involves a duty. If one is not sure that one's list of factors is complete, general perceptiveness is even more crucial. The ability to do ethical theory does not necessarily imply this sort of perceptiveness to whether factors are present in an actual situation. So we might require a division of labor between a theorist and an applier.

Likewise, another division of labor might be called for in employing a theory in which many factors have to be balanced. The capacity to lay out such a theory does not ensure the ability to balance factors correctly, if there is no mechanical procedure for doing this. (Another division of labor might be called for in theory development, since someone might be sensitive to new morally relevant factors a theorist had not yet thought of, but only the theorist could reason adequately about them once his eyes had been opened.)

A division of labor would be especially good in cases in which someone's intuitive good judgment, moral imaginativeness, or most importantly, willingness to act in accord with good judgment, would be destroyed if he tried to work out explicitly what he was doing. (Like a writer trying to formulate the rules by which he works, the practical judgments and action of some may not profit at all from theory or reasoning. Likewise, someone who can reason about his decisions to some degree may be harmed or at least not helped by trying to develop a *grand* theory of how he reasons.) We should hesitate to diminish judgment and action just to improve justification and reasoned decision abilities. But, of course, no such conflict may arise.

A division of labor between actor and thinker might be called for, for another reason which Bernard Williams has discussed.[15] If the correct solution requires one to do something that is intrinsically wrong, Williams has suggested that it is good if we have great

---

[15]In "Politics and Moral Character" in *Moral Luck*.

difficulty in doing the right act or even have to delegate it to others. He thinks that, if we have decision makers who would be reluctant or unable to do certain things, they will be reluctant to decide in favor of such acts, which is as it should be. If someone who is capable of carrying out the act (and whom we assign to carry it out) were the decision maker, we might find such acts being recommended more often than is really necessary. So there may sometimes be a split between those who arrive at a theoretically correct solution to a real-life problem and those who actually apply that solution most effectively. (Alternatively, it might be suggested that no one should decide what must be done unless he would be willing to carry it out himself.)

B. One way of understanding the idea of a correct solution to a particular problem is that it takes into consideration the people who are being addressed in the situation, the limited funds, local prejudices, etc. and gives us the solution in the light of these factors. In science, when we say "it is the correct solution in theory, but not in practice," the theoretical solution is, in part, based on some counterfactual assumption, e.g., a perfect vacuum. But ethical theories need not have such counterfactual assumptions. They can consider all actual factors. This means that part of applied ethics just is the ethics of applying a proposed solution in practical situations. *Applied* applied ethics collapses into applied ethics.

Still, for reasons which I shall make clear, I believe that it is important to distinguish two levels in a decision process. The first level deals with what I would call the *ideal* theoretical solution to a problem. The first level tells us, via use of general ethical factors, what solution is ethically correct, independent of what distinctions those involved in carrying out the decision can grasp, independent of what the law actually says, independent of resources actually available, etc. The second level takes those factors into account.

It is important to take note of the two levels, because, if there is an ideal theoretical solution, a right direction in which to go, we may try to change the law, or find the resources, or work to increase people's ability to grasp distinctions. If there were no ideal solution we wouldn't have to bother about changing these things, since there would be no right direction in which to try to move people, the law, or the resources. If we accept the idea of two levels, we will need a theory of *applying applied ethics* which includes the ethics of reaching and applying decisions with people who have disagreed, in situations of resource scarcity, etc. This brings us to the next point.

C. Applying applied ethics can be dangerous. It often involves engaging in demanding moral arguments with people whose opinions differ, on subjects affecting them personally, deciding who is right and who is wrong, and acting on this. (Sometimes merely discussing certain applied subjects is enough to make one unpopular.) Since all aspects of life—including thoughts, feelings, personal relations—should be open to ethical evaluation, the issue of moralism may arise. In the past there would have been tolerance for different "value choices" or polite reticence, and things would have been left at that. Now we will not leave things at that, at least not so often. Special ethical issues arise, therefore, concerning when and how to engage in such reasoning and judging without humiliating or castigating people. Equally important issues arise concerning the protection of punishment. Fear of such punishment will of course have the effect of limiting the applied topics discussed. So, for example, if one could still jeopardize one's career by discussing certain aspects of sexism or social justice, the protections instituted for whistleblowers might be appropriate in the academic context.

If we were just dealing with developing the ethics of talking to people about sensitive matters, we would refer to this as doing applied ethics, straightforwardly. But, if we have already ethically examined the question of how someone should behave in a certain situation and want to think about the ethically right way to tell him what he should do or the ethically right way for him to respond to us when we tell him, we are likely to think of it as an ethical question about the application of applied ethics.

PART TWO

Specific Applications

11

Kant's Arguments in Support of the Maxim "Do What Is Right Though The World Should Perish"*

Sissela Bok

> *Fiat iustitia, pereat mundus*
> *Fiat iustitia, ruat coelum*

THE CHALLENGE

Do what is right though the world should perish; do what is right though the sky should fall: these ringing phrases have long been invoked by men and women claiming to act on principle even at the cost of livelihood, reputation, perhaps life itself. They offer the same guidance: let justice be done, refuse to lie or cheat or go against your moral principles, no matter how horrendous the consequences.

Individuals have relied on such guidelines as they underwent punishment or inflicted it upon others for the sake of what they thought to be just or sacred. Rulers such as Emperor Ferdinand I of the Holy Roman Empire have chosen the first as the motto best suited for guiding state affairs. Erasmus advocated the second in *The Christian Prince* as a stern alternative to the permissive advice of thinkers like Machiavelli.[1] And in "Perpetual Peace," Kant defended the first (as he would doubtless have defended the second) in the context of the world federation of liberal states that he held forth

---

*Also published in *Argumentation*, Vol. II, no. 1 (February 1988).

[1]See Martin Wight, "Western Values in International Relations," in Herbert Butterfield, *Diplomatic Investigations* (Cambridge, Mass.: Harvard University Press, 1966), p. 130; and Quentin Skinner, *The Foundations of Modern Political Thought* (Cambridge: Cambridge University Press, 1978), p. 250.

as the only sane alternative to ever more destructive warfare among nations.[2]

In this paper, I shall examine Kant's arguments in support of this maxim against the charges of moral fanaticism which he and all its holders know they invite. Do you really mean, John Stuart Mill or Henry Sidgwick might ask of Kant, that a person should do what is right even when this could endanger the fate of the entire world? Surely, they might argue, only a moral fanatic would insist on adhering to ordinary standards of "duty" at such a price. For Mill and Sidgwick and perhaps most others confronted with such a situation, the conclusion would be clear: nothing that could precipitate the end of the world could *be* right or just in the first place. Kant, on the other hand, maintained that doing what is right for the sake of duty is entirely different from acting only out of a concern for results. It would, therefore, matter to ask him how he stands with respect to the possibility of the most catastrophic and irreversible of results.

Kant exposes himself to such a challenge by taking a rigid position in favor of the priority of acting on duty not only in theory but with respect to a number of practical moral choices. In his article "On a Supposed Right to Lie from Altruistic Motives," he considered a familiar test case offered by the French thinker Benjamin Constant: Did Kant really mean that he would not even excuse lying to a murderer pursuing his friend, if he could thereby deflect the murderer from his path and save the friend's life? Kant answered that one should not lie even to save the life of an innocent victim who was also a close friend. To be truthful, he declared, is "a sacred and absolutely commanding decree of reason, limited by no expediency."[3] To breach that decree is to injure the system of communication among human beings and thus to endanger the very foundations of duty.

---

[2]Immanuel Kant, "Zum ewigen Frieden. Ein philosophisches Entwurf," 1795 (Leipzig: Felix Meiner, 1919), "Perpetual Peace: A Philosophical Sketch," in Hans Reiss, ed., *Kant's Political Writing* (Cambridge: Cambridge University Press, 1970), pp. 93–100. My quotations are from this translation, with some substitutions to come closer to the German meaning of certain words. Parenthetical page references in the text will be to this volume.

[3]"On a Supposed Right to Lie from Altruistic Motives," in Lewis White Beck, ed. and trans., *Critique of Practical Reason and Other Writings in Moral Philosophy* (Chicago: University of Chicago Press, 1949), p. 348.

But what if the challenge is pressed so as to question that very assumption with a choice that involves risking, precisely, the end of the whole world and thus of all communication? Would Kant carry his insistence on truthfulness so far as to rule out a lie even if it could prevent adversaries from bringing about the end of the world? Would he argue that it is wrong to lie to persons capable of such destruction just as much as to a murderer? Such is the challenge that the Latin motto could pose for Kant.

A caution is needed, however, before we turn to Kant's ingenious defense for the motto in an Appendix to his essay on "Perpetual Peace" (pp. 123-24). In his day, no one took such maxims literally: no one thought that the action of individuals—be they rulers or rebels or would-be saints—could actually ruin the world or bring down the sky. For, though many believed God capable of such action and though they might themselves sacrifice lives, perhaps scorch or pillage far and wide to carry out their aims, they had no reason to suppose that they could single-handedly bring about universal destruction. Nor did they imagine that governments or any other human institutions possessed such powers of devastation.

Since Hiroshima in 1945, however, the words about the sky falling and the world perishing through human action have taken on a more literal meaning. In the last part of this article I shall ask how this new meaning alters our perception of such maxims and might have altered Kant's. I shall suggest that the moral complexity that he denies in principle but appears to acknowledge in practice can help us to distinguish what is untenable from what remains indispensable in his views about the morality of war and peace.

KANT'S ARGUMENT

In his essay on "Perpetual Peace," Kant offers a scathing indictment of international politics—a realm that many, then as now, have thought outside the scope of moral philosophy—as a savage and lawless state (p. 105); and sets forth a blueprint for steps toward a lasting world peace. Seeing war as utterly evil, he nevertheless postulates a purpose for it: providence had intended war to become sufficiently horrible and economically draining so that mankind would be driven, in the end, to abolish it and to institute a system capable of resolving conflicts peacefully.

To speed this realization on the part of the public, Kant wants to demonstrate that it would be not only morally preferable but also politically advantageous for nations to act justly toward one another and to respect the rights of all citizens of all countries. Taking issue with the view, common since Machiavelli, of the realms of politics and morality as entirely distinct, he criticizes the dangerous short-sightedness of government leaders who imagine that politics can be insulated from or somehow prior to moral concerns.

Morality and politics can be brought to coincide in international affairs, Kant insists, in spite of all that skeptics in and out of government maintain. But no half-measures and compromises over human rights will suffice; such efforts would only lead to greater injustice and more brutal wars. Rather, politics "must bend the knee before right"; in return, politics may hope "to arrive, however slowly, at a stage of lasting brilliance" (p. 125).

Kant was not satisfied to argue for greater concordance between politics and morality than Machiavelli and his followers thought wise: he wanted to eliminate all possible escape clauses, even those of national security and of survival, invoked to legitimate deceit and violence between governments. It was in order to show that such exceptions are *never* either legitimate or necessary that Kant re-affirmed the Latin maxim *fiat iustitia, pereat mundus*—"Do what is right though the world should perish." He called the saying a "sound principle of right which blocks up all the devious paths predetermined by cunning or violence." Where the consequentialist response to the maxim might be phrased: "If it risks precipitating the end of the world it cannot be right," Kant's response will, in effect, be: "If it is right it cannot precipitate the end of the world."

1. Kant began his argument to this effect quite oddly. He changed the common translation of the Latin saying in the following way: "The proverbial saying *fiat iustitia, pereat mundus* (i.e. let justice reign, even if all the rogues in the world must perish) may sound somewhat inflated but is nonetheless true." Kant rendered "mundus"—a Latin word meaning "world," "universe," or "mankind"—as "all the rogues in the world." But the Latin says nothing about rogues.

What might explain this altered translation on the part of someone who had been schooled in Latin since childhood, who taught courses using Latin textbooks, and who sprinkled all his writings copiously with Latin terms? If it was not an error, was it a fabrication? More likely, Kant was indulging here in a practice he had used to good effect elsewhere: taking for granted that his readers were familiar with the maxim, he may have meant to give it added meaning. This was how he had interpreted a familiar motto from Horace—"sapere aude"—in his article "What Is Enlightenment?" Instead of mentioning the literal translation of the motto, "Dare to be wise," Kant gave it a new interpretation: "Have the courage to use your *own* understanding?"—one which resonated with the rejection, so central to Enlightenment thinking, of dogma and cant.[4]

Whatever the overtones he may have intended, however, his freewheeling interpretation of "Do what is right though the world should perish" becomes illegitimate as soon as he uses it to buttress the strict moral stance of the original Latin saying. With the help of such a translation, Kant has begun the task of setting up a straw man that he will in the end find it easy to demolish.

2. Kant's next steps take him further in that direction. He points out that the saying ought not to be taken as an invitation to pursue one's own rights with the utmost rigor. Instead, he argues that the maxim "should be seen as an obligation of those in power not to deny or detract from the rights of anyone out of disfavor or sympathy for others." He regards the maxim as stating an obligation to respect the rights of others rather than as a protection of one's own rights; and the obligation is one that binds primarily "those in power." Their respect for the rights of others, in turn (and this is where a further reinterpretation of the motto takes place)

> requires above all that the state should have an internal constitution organized in accordance with pure principles of right, and also that it unite with other neighboring or even distant states to arrive at a lawful settlement of their differences by forming something analogous to a universal state (p. 123).

We are now far from the common use of the motto as an exhortation to individuals to follow their consciences at all costs; far too, even if the motto is intended primarily for persons in power, from the advice that Erasmus and others meant the maxim to offer to rulers of *actual* states, however imperfect their constitutions, however mired their nations in conflict with others. Kant says that the motto requires justice within and between states. Does he mean that it is not applicable until such an ideal set of circumstances has been

---

[4] "What Is Enlightenment?," in Reiss, *Kant's Political Writing*, p. 54.

achieved? If so, he can hardly simply assert that the Latin saying is "true." By removing the debate from the existing predicament of actual individuals and governments, Kant fails to answer the problems that Machiavelli had posed about whether, for instance, a ruler should keep promises when others breach them at will or give a false impression of military strength in order to dissuade a neighboring dictator from resorting to violence.

3. Kant's next claim reaffirms the rigorous interpretation of this proposition: it means nothing other, he writes, than that political maxims

> must not be influenced by the prospect of any benefit or happiness which might accrue to a particular state if it followed them, that is by the end which it takes as the object of its will . . . ; they should be influenced only by the pure concept of rightful duty, i.e. by an obligation whose principle is given *a priori* by pure reason (pp. 123–124).

No prospects of benefits or happiness, and thus presumably not even that of the survival of the world, should influence the adoption of the maxims that rulers should observe. Maxims should be influenced, rather, "only by the pure concept of rightful duty." Taken by itself, this statement would appear to restate for rulers the strict moral law that Kant has often held with respect to all human beings. But, given the previous statement, the rulers to whom Kant's argument is addressed may be excused if they are not entirely sure whether he asks them to abide by the moral law at all times even when by so doing they risk great harm to their subjects and perhaps to the world, or only once the ideal circumstances of internal and external justice have eliminated such threats.

4. Having changed the translation of the Latin maxim and offered his own ideal requirements for the justice of which it speaks, Kant then reverts to the question of the world's perishing. He claims, quite rightly, that "the world will certainly not come to an end if there are fewer bad men." But though in its own right uncontroversial, this claim has next to nothing to do with the original Latin maxim. It seems, moreover, to slip the argument back to the actual world, not to the ideal system mentioned just before. Sidgwick or Mill would hardly accept such a claim as a sufficient answer to their challenge. Nor would those wondering whether to follow their consciences even at the risk of great disaster find such an interpretation helpful.

5. After claiming that the world will certainly not come to an end if there are fewer bad men, Kant goes on to present an argument which may be meant to dissolve any sense of responsibility for their demise. He introduces the notion of "moral evil," leaving readers to assume some connection between such evil and the "bad men" in the preceding sentence.

> Moral evil has by nature the inherent quality of being self-destructive and self-contradictory in its aims (especially in relations between persons of a like mind), so that it makes way for the moral principle of goodness, even if such progress is slow (p. 124).

Kant often states that moral evil is self-contradictory in the light of his Categorical Imperative; but that it is also self-destructive cannot be a statement of the same kind. He offers no proof here for what appears to be an empirical observation—one which has long antecedents in religious and philosophical debate and which is, at the very least, controversial. Nor does he make clear why, even if one were to assume that moral evil self-destructs over time, one should not take into account the evil that seems to spring up— either self-generated or brought about by corrupting or cruel circumstances. All that his readers know is that they have somehow been brought from thinking about the end of the entire world via a diminution in the number of bad men to a diffuse notion of self-destructive evil slowly making way for the moral principle of goodness.

Step by step throughout his argument concerning this maxim, Kant has wafted away one element after another of what seemed at first to be a powerful challenge to his moral absolutism and one that it would have been especially important to confront in the context of his article on "Perpetual Peace." He has altered the maxim altogether and in so doing succeeded in drawing all its teeth.

From the point of view of potential challengers of Kant's views, this argument attacks and defeats only a straw man. It does not suffice to justify either the Latin maxim or the ambiguous conclusion immediately following:

> Thus in objective or theoretical terms, there is no conflict whatsoever between morality and politics. In a *subjective* sense, however (i.e. in relation to the selfish disposition of man, which, since it is not based on maxims of reason, cannot however be called practice) this conflict

will and ought to remain active, since it serves as a whetstone of virtue (p. 124).

The reader is now led to understand that the conflict that Kant denied between politics and morality in theory or in practice still exists "in relation to the selfish disposition of man"—a disposition surely present in most circumstances of political and international relations. These are precisely the circumstances that government leaders would have cited in response to Kant's admonition that they seek righteousness in order to achieve the blessings of perpetual peace. Little wonder if they would remain as unconvinced by Kant's reasoning as Mill and other hypothetical challengers.

It is as if Kant simply retreated before this challenge, using every feint and shortcut at his disposal. Why should this be? I suggest that the challenge threatened not just the periphery of Kant's moral theory but two assumptions he regarded as central regarding the role of providence, and the impossibility of conflict between moral obligations.

The Role of Providence

For Kant to have explored the Latin maxim more fully would, first of all, have been to jeopardize an already unstable assumption which he saw as an indispensable foundation for his theory of political morality: that a divine Providence guides human progress. Kant assumed "a faith, for practical purposes, in a moral being who governs the world."[5] Sometimes he spoke of Nature as the embodiment of this supreme moral being; at other times he referred to Providence for the same purpose. Providence has so disposed the course of world events that justice between states will aid progress directly, whereas injustice will further it indirectly by providing warning examples to later generations, leading them to act more justly. Peace will end by issuing from human conflict itself. Like Marx in the following century, Kant aimed to speed the historical process by showing the needless suffering that results from ignoring it.

It is in his "Idea for a Universal History," that Kant develops most fully the theory of human history as progress toward peace

---

[5] "On the Common Saying: 'This May Be True in Theory, but It Does Not Apply in Practice'," in Reiss, *Kant's Political Writings,* p. 65.

and as the fulfillment of human capacities in accordance with Nature's intention.[6] Each individual's earthly existence is brief and flawed; but the human species may be capable of attaining a degree of rationality and harmony such that perpetual peace will in the end be ensured. Kant postulates history as a development through which man's moral destiny unfolds itself, directed by a Nature that knows how to employ human antagonism and evil to further the purposes of justice (pp. 46–47). Likewise in "Perpetual Peace," Kant argues that however lawlessly rulers and peoples act,

> enough of their kind will always survive to keep this process going without interruption into the most distant future, so that later generations may take them as a warning example. Providence is justified in disposing the course of world events in this way; for the moral principle in man is never extinguished, and reason . . . constantly increases with the continuous progress of culture, while the guilt attending violations of right increases proportionately (p. 124).

This bold assumption of purpose and lawfulness and progress enacted through history to benefit an immortal human species was nevertheless highly precarious. Kant acknowledged that human reason could neither prove nor disprove it; and he was acutely aware of the pettiness and mismanagement and cruelty in human affairs that seemed to contradict his assumption. In "Perpetual Peace" he stressed the depravity of human nature, "displayed without disguise" (p. 103) in the relations between states. And he warned that "a war of extermination, in which both parties and right itself might all be simultaneously annihilated, would allow perpetual peace only on the vast graveyard of the human race" (p. 96). This result could come about for Kant through mutual injustice, not through acting justly—but there is no doubt that he could envisage such a fate.

The very notion of states' gradually placing the world at risk of perishing was therefore, however foreign to eighteenth-century thinkers, far from inconceivable to someone with Kant's somber assessment of human nature. How, then, could he in the same ar-

---

[6]"Idea for a Universal History with a Cosmopolitan Purpose," in Reiss, *Kant's Political Writings,* pp. 41–53, esp. pp. 42, 52. See also Carl Joachim Friedrich, *Inevitable Peace* (Cambridge, Mass.: Harvard University Press, 1948), chs. 1–3; Wolfgang Schwarz, "Kant's Philosophy of Law and International Peace," *Philosophy and Phenomenological Research,* XXIII (1962): 71–80, at p. 74.

ticle talk on the one hand about enough of humankind always sur-
viving and the triumph of the idea of right, while on the other hand
warning of the annihilation of warring nations and of right itself on
the "vast graveyard of the human race"? If one looks at all his
writings on this subject, the answer seems to be that, although both
his religious background and the spirit of the Enlightenment led
Kant to have strong faith in the former, he could not entirely rule
out the latter; but that while he wanted to use the possibility of
catastrophe as a warning to spur improvement, he thought that to
take it too seriously would be to undermine any possible morality. If
man could not have as a goal that over the generations human
reason would approach its fullest potential,

> his natural capacities would necessarily appear by and large to be
> purposeless and wasted. In the latter case, all practical principles
> would have to be abandoned, and nature, whose wisdom we must take
> as axiomatic in judging all other situations, would incur the suspicion
> of indulging in childish play in the case of man alone ("Idea for a
> Universal History," p. 43).

Why should human beings regard their natural capacities as
"purposeless and wasted" unless they could believe in the achievement of full rationality in this world? The only reasons Kant offers
are psychological in nature: such beliefs offer grounds for hope concerning life on earth; without them, we would be reduced to hoping
for a rational aim for creation "only in some other world" (pp. 52–
53). Without assuming human progress, it would be impossible
both to believe in God and to know how "such a race of corrupt
beings" could have been created on earth.[7] But, apart from needing
the assumption about progress to sustain his faith, he offers no
reason why, in its absence, "all practical principles" (and thus morality) would have to be abandoned.

For someone entertaining beliefs so precarious, however widely
shared in his day and seemingly indispensable to moral theory, a
maxim requiring that one risk the perishing of the world for the
sake of justice is bound to be deeply troubling. By turning the
maxim inside out like a glove and making "Let justice reign though
the world should perish" seem to demonstrate that "if justice reigns

---

[7]See Keith Ward, *The Development of Kant's View of Ethics* (New York:
Oxford, 1972), for a discussion of the roots of this view in Kant's pietistic
upbringing and early metaphysical thinking.

the world won't perish," Kant guarded against more than a challenge to his absolutist moral theory; he also protected the world view that he saw as indispensable to *any* moral theory.

Still, moral theories have thrived before and after Kant without being founded on such a world view. And even thinkers sharing Kant's belief that the world is guided by divine Providence have rarely expressed the faith that this guidance would bring humanity close to harmony and perpetual peace in this life rather than in the next.[8] By now such faith is hard to muster. Few who have reflected upon the brutality of our own century have difficulty envisaging the heavens falling, the world perishing.

But though Kant might now recognize the genuine possibility of even the most extreme catastrophe and, therefore, be willing at least to question his optimistic assumption about the progress of mankind, he might still maintain his original stance on the Latin maxim. He might be reluctant to specify exceptions to his moral law, even at times of immense risk such as that assumed in the Latin maxim. For doing so risks opening up a rift in his theory with respect to the role of consequences and of responsibility in moral conflict.

Moral Conflict

Dealing seriously with the Latin maxim would have required Kant to consider challenges to his absolutist stance toward moral choice and thus to confront the possibility he had long denied—that there could be a conflict between moral duties. His method, he had insisted, could cope with all human choice in a unified manner. On the page in "Perpetual Peace" preceding his discussion of the Latin maxim, Kant had restated the Categorical Imperative in order to "ensure that practical philosophy is at one with itself," using the following formulation: " 'Act in such a way that you can wish your

---

[8]See e.g., John Wesley, Sermon on "Behold an Israelite Indeed, in Whom There Is No Guile," *Works,* vol. 7 (London: Wesleyan Conference Center Office, 1878). In *The Critique of Practical Reason,* Lewis White Beck, ed. & trans. (Indianapolis: Bobbs-Merrill, 1956), pp. 115–124, Kant postulated immortality in order that *individuals* might hope to achieve the rewards for virtue that he acknowledged were anything but assured on earth in anyone's life.

maxim to become a universal law (irrespective of what the end in view might be)' " (p. 115).

Philosophers and theologians have traditionally split in their recommendations for how to respond to cases where duties appear to conflict—so-called "cases of conscience." Those who allow for flexibility of certain kinds have the problem of countering the inevitable human tendency to abuse and to misinterpret exceptions to moral rules. Those others who, like Kant, allow for no flexibility whatsoever in principle have the problem of how to account for the felt conflict in cases of conscience and for the resulting departures from strict rules which seem warranted in practice.

Kant maintained that by invoking the Categorical Imperative in situations of moral choice—having to do, for instance, with whether or not to make a deceitful promise or whether or not to commit suicide—agents would find it easy to see that the right choice involved abstracting from prudential reasons. It is not that he counseled to ignore consequences; as John Rawls has pointed out, any theory that did not take consequences into account "would simply be irrational, crazy."[9] Rather, Kant advocated a concern for consequences through the Categorical Imperative itself: for, in thinking about whether or not one can wish one's maxim to become universal law, one has to ask what the world would be like if one's maxim became a universal law.

Everything changes when it is the world's perishing itself that is at stake. I suggest that no one could will the Latin maxim to become universal law, since the first person who adhered to it might destroy all further need for universal law. Willing the maxim to become universal law would therefore render it self-contradictory in Kant's sense of the word: once someone acts according to the maxim there might well be no human beings left for universal law to govern. The situation is analogous to that which he discusses in his *Foundations of the Metaphysics of Morals,* of making a false promise of repayment when one needs to borrow money but knows one will not be able to repay it. Kant holds that, if made into a universal law, a maxim endorsing such false promises "must necessarily con-

---

[9] *A Theory of Justice* (Cambridge, Mass.: Harvard University Press, 1971), p. 30.

tradict itself"; it would "make the promise itself and the end to be accomplished by it impossible."[10]

The same argument can be made for Kant's other formulations of the Categorical Imperative: "So act as to use humanity, both in your own person and in the person of every other, always at the same time as an end, never simply as a means"; and "So act as if you were always through your actions a law-making member in a universal Kingdom of Ends." No one with a concern for humanity could consistently will to risk eliminating humanity in the person of himself and every other or to risk the death of all members in a universal Kingdom of Ends for the sake of justice. To risk their collective death for the sake of following one's conscience would be, as Rawls said, "irrational, crazy." And to say that one did not intend such a catastrophe, but that one merely failed to stop other persons from bringing it about would be beside the point when the end of the world was at stake. For although it is true that we cannot be held responsible for most of the wrongs that others commit, the Latin maxim presents a case where we would have to take such responsibility seriously—perhaps to the point of deceiving, bribing, even killing an innocent person, in order that the world not perish.

To avoid self-contradiction, the Categorical Imperative would, therefore, have to rule against the Latin maxim on account of its cavalier attitude toward the survival of mankind. But the ruling would then produce a rift in the application of the Categorical Imperative. Most often the Imperative would ask us to disregard all unintended but foreseeable consequences, such as the death of innocent persons, whenever concern for such consequences conflicts with concern for acting according to duty. But, in the extreme case, we might have to go against even the strictest moral duty precisely because of the consequences. Acknowledging such a rift would pose a strong challenge to the unity and simplicity of Kant's moral theory.

Not only would there be a rift in situations of extreme risk; deciding what cases would go on either side of the rift would bring with it severe line-drawing problems. What level of risk of world calamity should precipitate a shift to the mode of resolution appro-

---

[10]*Foundations of the Metaphysics of Morals,* Lewis White Beck, trans. (Indianapolis: Bobbs-Merrill, 1959), p. 40.

priate to the catastrophic? High risks? Moderate ones? Any risk at
all? And what about the common circumstances today when some
see risks of ecological or nuclear catastrophe which others deny?
And risks from frequently opposite types of action? Thus some see
greater risk to humanity from the accumulation of nuclear weapons, while others are convinced that it is only by expanding our
nuclear arsenal that we have protection against a war that could lay
all of humanity waste. How is one to estimate the quality of their
judgment? Such distinctions, in turn, would require empirical
calculations—exactly what Kant wanted most to avoid—to determine at just what point something that is a stringent duty under
ordinary circumstances turns out to be *not* a duty after all.

To sum up my conclusions so far: Kant's explicit argument in
defense of the Latin motto is inadequate; his statements concerning
the intentions of Providence help explain but do not buttress this
argument; and his rejection of the possibility of a conflict of moral
principles even in extreme situations not only is counterintuitive
but produces self-contradictory responses to his own Categorical
Imperative.

Many have disagreed with Kant on this score. Thus Friedrich
Hegel rejected his rigid stance as too abstract, too distant from
moral choice as it is experienced by individuals and by governments. Neither welfare without right nor right without welfare constitute the good, he argued, insisting that *"fiat justitia* should not be
followed by *pereat mundus."*[11] Both welfare and right must be subordinated to the good as it is expressed in the world; even to consider
risking the end of the world for the sake of a narrow interpretation
of either reveals the folly of purely abstract philosophizing.

John Stuart Mill and consequentialists more generally have
taken issue with both Kant and Hegel, holding that specific comparisons of the welfare, pleasure, or happiness expected from alternative actions should determine moral choice. And even among
those who share Kant's deontological premises, some have argued
that one could retain his theory without agreeing with the practical
conclusions he draws from its application: employ the Categorical
Imperative in such a way as to have principled exceptions to prohi-

---

[11]T. M. Knox, ed. & trans., *Hegel's Philosophy of Right* (Oxford: Clarendon Press, 1942), p. 87.

bitions on such acts as suicide, lying, and promise-breaking in emergencies.[12]

From Kant's point of view, however, all such criticisms, whether coming from Hegel, Mill, or modern-day Kantians, would be ruled out as heteronomous as soon as they admitted deviations from his strict moral prohibitions. Formulating exceptions to moral rules, whether by consequentialists or deontologists, would be as undesirable as Hegel's subsuming the right under the diffuse notion of the good. Such approaches would not only raise problems of line drawing; they would also remove the element of self-evidence and of apodictic certainty which he saw as indispensable for moral choice and thus undermine it irretrievably.

In order to refute his opponents, Kant stressed the role of rigor and unconditional moral commands throughout his writings on ethics. But in "Perpetual Peace" he went further; crossing over to the terrain of his adversaries, he also attempted to persuade them by means of consequentialist arguments (p. 116). Kant never eschewed such arguments when he thought they could support what he had independently concluded was right; he only rejected appeals to consequences that went against what he took to be the moral law.

PRUDENTIAL ARGUMENT FOR ABSOLUTISM

Kant argued forcefully that a theory that acknowledged exceptions would, in addition to its inherent immorality, be undesirable on strictly prudential grounds: allowing for exceptions in principle would inevitably lead to abuse and misjudgment in practice. Exceptions would have to be judged according to expected consequences; yet doing so would require judgments far less certain than his own "rules of wisdom." Relaxing the standards would therefore lead to confusion and in turn to abuse; for "the evil principle within

---

[12]See, e.g., Alan Donagan, "Consistency in Rationalist Moral Systems," *Journal of Philosophy* LXXXI, 6 (June 1984): 291–309. And although Kant's *published* writings set forth the view of conflict that I have discussed, there are indications that, earlier in his career, before working out his moral theory, he may have taken a more flexible view. See the student notes from his lectures, sometimes erroneously referred to as written by him: *Lectures on Ethics,* Louis Infield, trans. (Indianapolis: Hackett, 1963), p. 227.

ourselves . . . is liable to exploit the weakness of human nature in order to justify any violation of justice" (p. 124). Once you allow deceit or violence the slightest legitimacy through incorporating them in certain exceptions to the moral law, you will confuse the moral perception of individuals and facilitate specious argumentation to expand the exceptions in order to gain greater leeway for abuses of all kinds. A strict stance in theory was more likely to block up "the devious paths predetermined by cunning or violence."

It is understandable that Kant should have wished to exclude exceptions from his theoretical account on such grounds—understandable that, given the inevitable slippage in practice, he should have thought it best to retain rigorism in principle. Such a position forces individuals to look for alternatives and to work out ingenious responses in order to avoid a breach of moral duty, rather than to reach instinctively for "cunning and violence" at the slightest provocation.

This is precisely how Kant, in his own life, approached the difficult practical moral choices that have led other thinkers to find the escape routes he deplored. It would be wrong to imagine that his strict principles limited him to robotlike moralizing without concern for the consequences to others. Rather, his effort was to restrict the apparent conflict in every legitimate way and to use all his ingenuity in so responding as not to breach moral principle. He defined what it was to lie, to break a promise, etc., in a careful manner and declared these acts prohibited by the moral law; but he stressed that not all that people loosely think of as lying or promise-breaking fits into those categories. He then explored difficult cases to find ways of acting that he could accept from a moral point of view without incurring the undesirable consequences that might flow from a simplistic pursuit of the moral path.

In practice, this meant that he could be subtle, ambiguous, and secretive if need be, so long as he knew his intentions were good and so long as he broke no strict moral rule. A few examples may illustrate his manner of proceeding. When, in 1794, King Frederick William II of Prussia asked Kant to stop writing on religious topics, he composed a submissive letter to the king; and, calling himself "your Majesty's loyal subject," he abjured further writings on religion. When the king died three years later, however, Kant resumed his writing, explaining that his letter, because of its wording, bound him only for the king's lifetime.[13]

And when Kant decided to fire his valet—a former Prussian soldier named Lampe, who had served him faithfully for many years, but who had grown slovenly and quarrelsome and taken to drink—he agonized for many days over how to write the necessary certificate of service. He could not bring himself to destroy Lampe's self-respect through a candid and thorough appraisal. Finally, according to a contemporary biographer and friend, Kant wrote, in ambiguous words that could easily, but need not, be interpreted as putting all blame on himself: "He has conducted himself faithfully, but no longer suitably for me, Kant."[14]

In argumentation, likewise, Kant used every subtlety of reasoning and all his ingenuity to temper the rigorism that his theories might otherwise seem to require. Consequently, as with his reasoning about the maxim concerning the world's perishing, he achieves results in practice that seem not to bind him to the severest conclusions one might otherwise draw from his moral theories.

The more one reads about Kant's life, the more one comes to suspect that, if he ever did chance to meet a murderer pursuing an intended victim, the murderer would be no match for *him*. Constrained though Kant might feel by his felt duty not to lie, he would do his best to save his friend in every other way. If forced to speak, he might well resort to so many intricate though truthful responses that the bewildered murderer would be hard put to interpret them correctly, leaving the friend plenty of time to escape.

Yet how could Kant, who championed against Aristotle and Aquinas and many others the sole need of a good will for moral choice, advocate such practical cleverness in the approach to the most serious moral conflicts? All individuals do not possess equal ingenuity and capacity to seek ways to abide by moral rules without allowing harm to be done. If Kant advises even the least imaginative to abide by the rules at all times, is he not rejecting caution in the face of great risk? Some people, adhering to his strictures, might unleash calamity; others could lose all bearings by going

---

[13]See *Religion within the Limits of Reason Alone*, Theodore M. Greene and Hoyt H. Hudson, trans. & intro. (New York: Harper & Row, 1960), Introduction, pp. xxxii–xxxvii, for a discussion of this episode.

[14]See L. E. Borowski, R. B. Jachman, A. C. Wasianski, *Immanuel Kant: Sein Leben in Darstellungen von Zeitgenossen*, Felix Gross, ed. (Darmstadt: Wissen-Schaftliche Buchgesellschaft, 1968), p. 261.

against Kant and their rigorist conscience in order, for instance, to save a life through lying: once having breached what they took to be the moral law, they might find it difficult to resist despair, self-reproach, and further breaches. Rigorists who turn into cynics are surely as familiar a sight in ethics or religion as in politics.

A second reason for not ruling out exceptions altogether is that even those who, like Kant himself, are ingenious in adhering to moral principle, might encounter a moral conflict leaving no leeway for ingenuity: one in which it is clear that they will precipitate a catastrophe unless they act against their principles. True, Kant might appeal, once again, to his theory of history. After all, he could argue if faced with such a dilemma, if he is right in his assumption concerning progress, then the worst won't happen since Providence does not intend it; and anything less than the worst will end by assisting the providential plan to bring about harmony on earth. But were he to invoke a theory of history that he himself acknowledges is unprovable, he would merely avoid confronting the question of what to do in cases of genuine and potentially catastrophic moral conflict.

Those less ingenious than Kant may encounter more occasions than he that call for exceptions to rigid moral prescriptions; but even he cannot rule them out. Nevertheless, his prudential objection to exceptions within his theory is more persuasive than those based on his faith in Providence and human progress or on the absolutist requirements of his moral system. Postulating exceptions regarding deceit and violence can indeed lead to confusion among people seeking guidance from moral principles, and allow abuses on the part of those who interpret the circumstances to suit their own purposes. But the very same prudential approach would point to similar risks from a rigid insistence on doing what is right at whatever cost to humanity; for the concept of what is "right" can itself confuse some and be misinterpreted by others to suit their purposes.

Although Kant's prudential cautioning is therefore persuasive against those whose standards would break down strong *prima facie* moral restraints, it does not suffice to rule out all exceptions, least of all those in which the end of the world is at stake. In such extreme circumstances his caution can be turned with equal ease upon his own theory. It is, therefore, preferable to follow Kant's own *practice* of taking the problems of acting unjustly seriously, without upholding his *principles* to the bitter end, nor counting on Providence to pull mankind out of the peril that might result from unreflecting obedience to moral rules.

We are left, when it comes to choices as extreme as those in the Latin motto, with a recognition of the inadequacy of an absolutist rejection of actions that one might regard as immoral and with an awareness that it may not always even be possible to draw clear lines between such choices and marginally different ones. This is the more uncomfortable if, in rejecting the apparent simplicity and clarity of Kantian absolutism, we nevertheless agree with Kant's cautioning against the apparent simplicity and clarity of routine appeals to weighing the consequences of alternative actions.

Still, most of us will never face a choice between doing what is right and precipitating the end of the world, any more than Kant or the rulers and public officials to whom he addressed his essay. For us, the Latin maxim can therefore retain the character of thought-experiment that it clearly had for Kant. But no such luxury of purely abstract argumentation is possible for today's government leaders. Some of them have already confronted such choices; others know that they may do so at a moment's notice.

JUSTICE AND INTERNATIONAL SURVIVAL

Since 1945, it is no longer inconceivable that the human pursuit of goals such as justice or revenge might unleash the actual falling of the sky or the perishing of the world. By now we can no longer only imagine such a fate; we watch the great powers relying on a threat of precisely such catastrophe in order to ward off attack. Today's government leaders cannot avoid weighing the risks to humanity from their policies, whether just or unjust. They may have to compare the risks of igniting large-scale war in refusing to deal with a terrorist group threatening nuclear blackmail with the risks of giving in to some of its demands; or to weigh whether or not to come to the assistance of allies under attack. The same is true of subordinates who may be in charge of firing nuclear missiles. They may have sworn oaths of allegiance and of obedience to orders that should bind them in any Kantian scheme to execute the orders of their superiors. Yet, if they regard as ill-advised an order to fire missiles from their submarine, their silo, or their bomber squadron, should they obey unblinkingly?

These risks illustrate the difficulty of opting either for a rigorist stance or for a more flexible one. With the stakes as high as they are now, it hardly seems wise to advocate that government officials in different nations, often with very different conceptions of what is right and just, simply act according to Kant's theoretical prescription. Some may harbor a Kantian confidence in Providence, others a fatalistic belief in the coming of Armageddon or some similar calamity; in either case, they may take risks with human survival in the name of justice that they would otherwise eschew.

But it seems equally unwise for officials to endorse what they acknowledge as immoral and unjust policies in the name of survival: to proceed uncritically on entirely pragmatic and self-serving principles, fashioning their own exceptions to the limited moral principles they may recognize in international affairs. The dangers against which Kant warned nations—of resorting to means so debilitating to international trust that they invite the perpetual peace of the graveyard—are all too evident.

By what standards, then, should government officials measure their actions? What might they learn from Kant's proposals, and where must they depart from them? If we accept the need for exceptions to moral principles in emergency conditions, it becomes necessary to take every precaution to avoid the dangers that Kant rightly stressed—of self-delusion, misunderstanding, lack of moral concern, shortsightedness, and ignorance on the part of government leaders and their advisers. These failures of moral perception often lead governments and individual officials to misinterpret and abuse any exceptions to moral prohibitions, however reasonable in the abstract; and, in the absence of firm guidelines, international conduct then risks sinking to the lowest common denominator as nations respond in kind to what they see as lapses and infractions on the part of others.

Awareness of such risks might lead policy-makers to formulate more specific exceptions to moral principles and the limited conditions under which they might be legitimate. But pressing for specificity opens the door to line-drawing calculations of a most distasteful kind: How serious must the risk be? How many lives must be at stake? What if only property is endangered?—the questions multiply. The alternative is to leave matters up to the best judgment of the officials faced with the choice—surely a cavalier attitude considering the variety of individuals who may have a hand in decisions affecting collective survival.

A compromise approach would call for setting forth clear-cut exceptions to moral rules, carefully limited and subjected to safeguards wherever possible in order to minimize confusion and abuse; but it would also explore ways to train the moral perception and judgment of public servants rather than to encourage them in hair-splitting about marginal and extreme cases. No one can know in advance all the circumstances of a particular crisis; even if they could, settling beforehand on one response or another might help precipitate a self-fulfilling prophecy of the most dangerous kind. Crises presenting choices that risk world catastrophe call, therefore, not so much for the correct theory as for decision-makers of wisdom, capable of broad and humane moral perception and of discriminating reasoning and choice.

But the fact remains: no one can be confident that all who are party to such choices will respond to them with anywhere near the requisite degree of judgment. To the extent that we find Kant's prudential misgivings about the fallibility and bias of human judgment persuasive, it matters, therefore, to reduce the chances of individuals' having to make choices in the first place that risk the perishing of the world. To this end, efforts to specify principles of international conduct and to train the judgment of public servants must be buttressed by steps to reduce the likelihood of crises severe enough to strain the principles intolerably and to undermine or bypass wise judgment.

Extreme cases strain all moral theories and all forms of human judgment. Whatever moral theory we may hold, it is therefore crucially important to reduce the chances that such cases will arise. John Rawls has written that, although there may be no alternative to giving up the priority of rules in more extreme and tangled cases, "we must try to postpone the day of reckoning as long as possible, and try to arrange society so that it never comes."[15] And, though philosophers disagree about just how much reckoning, how much

---

[15]*A Theory of Justice*, p. 303. See Robert Nozick, *Philosophical Explanations* (Cambridge, Mass.: Harvard University Press, 1981), pp. 494–98, for a discussion of possible combinations of teleological and deontological considerations.

evaluating, is necessary in the many extreme and difficult cases that unfortunately do arise for public servants, as for many others, I believe that they would all agree with Rawls about the need to stave off a day of reckoning—one that would pose just such a choice as that in the Latin motto.

Many efforts are currently under way to reduce the likelihood of acute nuclear emergencies through technological safeguards, crisis management, arms reduction, and negotiation. But too often they ignore the underlying distrust that prevents nations from entering upon international agreements to reduce the present level of danger and to reverse the policies of mutual deceit, threatened and actual violence, and betrayal which increase this distrust.[16] It is here that Kant's "Perpetual Peace" conveys his most forceful plea. It contains a series of proposals for how to arrange society so that a day of reckoning never comes.[17] The passion and urgency with which he wrote stem from a concern that unless the link between politics and morality is taken seriously and given practical political expression, it will not be possible to reverse the drift toward ever more destructive wars.

Kant insisted that the avoidance of a war of extermination will require nations fully to perceive that their own survival depends on that of all nations. War has now, as he predicted, become so terrible as to force nations either to give it up or perish. Giving it up requires perceiving the links between individual, domestic, and international morality. The question is whether the collective perspective on survival and on common humanity can be achieved before it is too late. If it can be achieved, Kant will even have turned out to be right in his optimistic prediction. Morality and prudence will have been brought to coincide—in order that the skies not fall, the world not perish.

---

[16]I discuss these moral constraints in my 1986 Joan and Erik Erikson Lectures on "Human Values and the Threat of War," forthcoming, Pantheon Books, as *A Strategy for Peace*, 1988; and in "Distrust, Secrecy, and the Arms Race," *Ethics*, 95 (Spring 1985): 412–727.

[17]See Michael W. Doyle, "Kant, Liberal Legacies, and Foreign Affairs," *Philosophy and Public Affairs*, XXII (Summer 1983): 205–35; and (Fall 1983): 321–353; John Bourke, "Kant's Doctrine of 'Perpetual Peace'," *Philosophy*, XVII (1942): 324–33; Otto H. von der Gablenz, *Kants politische Philosophie und die Weltpolitik unserer Tage* (Berlin: Colloquium Verlag, 1956).

12

The Moral Status of Intimacy

Jeffrey Blustein

In an essay of a few years back, Stephen Toulmin takes issue with
the traditional view that impartiality is a necessary feature of the
moral point of view and, in this way, attempts to make sense of
what he calls an "ethics of intimacy."[1] According to Toulmin, "absolute impartiality" requires "the imposition of uniformity or
equality on all relevant cases" (p. 34), but it is not always moral to
be absolutely impartial in this sense. On the contrary, acting morally is often a matter of "reasonableness or responsiveness in applying general rules to individual cases" (p. 34), equity rather than
impartiality, and this is particularly true as regards a person's dealings with his intimates. Here "discretion is all, and the relevance of
strict rules is minimal," whereas, among strangers, "respect for
rules is all, and the opportunities for discretion are few" (p. 35). I
believe, however, that Toulmin's analysis only scratches the surface
and that the notion of an ethics of intimacy can suggest something
more radical than this. Intimacy does not merely make exceptions
for particular persons, but involves valuing them as particular persons; and, if intimacy raises a special problem at all, it is whether
moral evaluation must always be a matter of applying objective and
impersonal rules to particular cases, even granting the need for
some flexibility in application.

An ethics of intimacy, as I shall argue, is not just another field
of applied ethics, like business ethics or biomedical ethics. Whereas

---

[1]"The Tyranny of Principles," *Hastings Center Report*, XI, 6 (December
1981): 31–39.

the latter uses various types of ethical theory developed in general normative ethics to resolve disagreements and dilemmas of public and professional life, the former contends that intimate relations (or some of them) have a moral significance that cannot be completely encompassed within the universalistic and impersonal perspectives of much traditional ethical theory. On this view, an ethics of intimacy is not a part of applied ethics in the usual sense, but an ethics that challenges the hegemony of the impartial point of view and circumscribes the role of impersonal principle in moral life. The problem-centered approach to practical ethics adopted by writers in applied ethics accepts the established categories of traditional ethical theory as starting points, but an ethics of intimacy requires a recasting of our familiar understanding of "the moral." Since intimate relations involve deep personal commitments that reverberate through the agent's perception of the substance and meaning of his or her life, the failure of the familiar justificatory approaches to account for the moral significance of intimacy is a defect in those approaches. In those areas of so-called "applied ethics" which concern the personal and private rather than the public and professional side of life, such as sexual ethics and family ethics, the values of an ethics of intimacy are particularly relevant, and the limitations of utilitarian and Kantian ethical theory are most apparent.

I

The first step in an investigation of an ethics of intimacy is to look more closely at the nature of intimacy and intimate relations. Some of their defining characteristics can be brought out by examining three species of nonintimates: strangers, role relations, and acquaintances.[2] *Strangers* (in Toulmin's article the term seems to stand for all types of nonintimates) engage in few reciprocal behaviors beyond merely responding to each other's general social existence when in each other's presence and displaying the minimal concern and respect due to persons as such. Strangers encounter one another as whole persons, but as instances of a general type, rather than as particular, irreplaceable individuals. *Role relations* act accord-

---

[2]For a typology of intimates and nonintimates, see Murray S. Davis, *Intimate Relations* (New York: Free Press, 1973), pp. xvii–xxv. See also Martin Fisher and George Stricker, eds., *Intimacy* (New York: Plenum Press, 1984).

ing to public systems of rules which specify certain forms of conduct as permissible or impermissible. Role players—like strangers—are intersubstitutable, and they engage in single-faceted, narrowly prescribed reciprocal behaviors between segments of themselves. If one occupant of a social position adds a "personal touch" to his relations with others, these are relations regarded as being friendly or friendlike, but the character of their relationship is determined primarily by the rules of the social practice in which they participate, not by their own private choices and personal preferences. (People in the so-called "helping professions" are expected, as part of their roles, to be warm, friendly, and caring. Nevertheless, their relationship with their clients remains substantially impersonal.) *Acquaintances,* sometimes called "casual acquaintances," are like strangers and unlike role relations in that, on at least some occasions, they encounter one another as whole rather than segmental persons. Acquaintances are also unlike both strangers and role relations in that on some occasions they encounter one another as particular, rather than replaceable, persons. Nevertheless, acquaintances, though their relationship is more personal than that of strangers and role occupants, are not intimates, because the encounters between acquaintances typically do not continue on a regular basis and because each acquaintance constructs a behavioral, psychological, and historical portrait of the other that consists only of elements falling somewhere in a middle range between the most salient and the trivial. Acquaintances do not trust each other enough to receive the salient elements and are not interested enough in each other to dwell on the minutiae of each other's lives. Also, acquaintances typically engage jointly only in activities in which they are oriented predominantly toward something outside their mutual interaction.

A fourth category, *enemies,* is sometimes considered a species of nonintimates, but I shall not regard it this way. Enemies may be oriented toward one another as whole particular persons. It is not merely certain isolated characteristics that each enemy dislikes or hates about the other, or the partial self that each projects through a particular role; they dislike or hate each other for these characteristics or because they are so closely identified with a particular role that to hate the role is to hate the person performing it.[3] A general,

---

[3] I am speaking here of personal enemies, not about political opponents and the like.

diffuse dislike or hatred of others is also to be distinguished from the focused destructive purposes of some enemies. Enemies can be more than acquaintances, and are certainly not always strangers to one another. Their contacts may be sustained, and their experience of and information about each other is not restricted to matters of middling importance.

As the example of enemies shows, intimacy between people may exist even when the people so related do not care about each other. Being intimate with another essentially has to do with the depth and detail of knowledge one has of the other's life, character, and desires, and with the degree to which one's happiness is contingent upon the fulfillment of the other's desires. Judged by these criteria, hate can be as intimate an emotion as love. Hostile intimacy involves desires for the frustrations rather than the fulfillment, of the desires of another person whom one knows well and deeply.

Despite the fact that intimacy is not exclusive to caring relationships, intimate hate relationships cannot very well be used to help make a case for an ethics of intimacy. We must turn for this to intimate relationships of love and friendship. ('Intimate relationship of love' is not redundant. Unrequited love is love in which the issue of intimacy does not yet arise.) The varieties of personal love include romantic love, parental love, and the love of friends. By *friends,* I mean persons in a continuing relationship characterized by extensive familiarity in which each wishes to do and, as far as he can, does what he thinks is good for the other as a whole person, out of disinterested concern for the particular person that the other is, and each knows this about the other.[4] Though love as we speak of it today is often contrasted with friendship, in part because of the sexual connotation of the former, all intimates (with the exception of intimate enemies) love each other in a broad sense of the term. It is advisable, too, to distinguish mutual intimate behaviors, which may or may not be expressive of love in this sense, from a relationship of intimacy in which such behaviors generally (but not on every occasion) express this. Lovers are sexually intimate with each

---

[4]In some respects, this resembles Aristotle's notion of *philia,* but there are crucial differences as well. Aristotle's "complete friendship" consists in loving another as a bearer of desired qualities rather than truly as an individual. This point is made by Gregory Vlastos, "The Individual as an Object of Love in Plato," in *Platonic Studies* (Princeton, N.J.: Princeton University Press, 1973), p. 33.

other—unlike friends, who need not be—but one can have sex and not be intimate at all and can even use sex as a way of avoiding intimacy. Further, though intimates act out of love for each other and acting out of love is not to be equated with acting for the sake of love, they develop a commitment to the relationship itself and seek to maintain its integrity against changes in residence, social circumstances, and other "external" factors.

Let us look more closely at certain features of intimate loving relations. First, loving intimates do not merely wish each other success in a certain occupation, nor do they help each other to realize their specific ends, indifferent to the impact such realization may have on the fulfillment of their other ends. Rather, what they wish and do for each other is what they believe will promote, or will not jeopardize, the other's happiness on the whole. Happiness in this sense involves the realization of one's ends, integrated into a unified scheme of conduct, and the sacrifice of one's less valuable ends for the sake of one's most important goals, when one cannot achieve them all at once. As my intimate, I will try to discourage you from engaging in pursuits which do not reflect your own value system and ordering of goals and which cannot be fruitfully combined with your other aims and interests in a unified whole. I may try to influence your choices and value judgments, but, if we are truly loving intimates, the ranking that you freely and rationally assign to different goals in your life as a whole is what determines for me what is good for you and what guides me in my efforts to promote and protect your good.

Secondly, loving intimate relations give substance to our deep conviction that individuals are not intersubstitutable. In a relationship of friendship, for example, each is committed to the good of his friend, not merely to the good of a person who happens to answer to the description of his friend's characteristics. The characteristics possessed by my friend might in fact be possessed by others, but love for a friend is distinct from regard for his virtues or admiration for his characteristics, and cannot be automatically transferred to another who embodies similar qualities. Even if someone should appear who instantiates my friend's properties, the logic of intimate concern is such that I am not required to extend my affection to cover both the original and the second embodiment of those features of my friend which I value. To suppose otherwise is to deny the historical dimension of love. Transference of love is not conceptually impossible, perhaps, but, given the fact that my friend and I have built up a history together and that it is virtually impossible to find someone else with whom I also share that history, interchangeability of loved ones is all but out of the question.[5] Our history together is important to me and is part of my reason for loving my friend. He is distinctive not in that he performs a job that no one else can perform or is better at something than anyone else, but in that there is no one else who can as a matter of fact exactly take his place for me. Others may help me to forget the loss of a valued friend, but there is a nontrivial sense in which no one else can actually be the friend to me that he was.

Thirdly, the reasons intimates give for helping or being with one another must contain uneliminable egocentric particulars; for I am intimate only with someone whom I have somehow come to think of as mine.[6] (This holds for enemies as well as loved ones.) To be lovingly intimate with someone is also to be particularly moved to care for him, and as Aristotle argues in *The Politics*,

> [T]here are two things which particularly move men to care for an object and to feel affection for that object. One of them is that the object should belong to yourself; the other is that you should like it.[7]

In contrast, if I am willing to replace the expression 'my friend' with a definite description in which the word 'my' does not appear, then I may genuinely care for this person, but not as intimates care for one another.

Reasons for helping a loved one who is in need or jeopardy are that he is a loved one or a person in need or jeopardy, and loved ones and persons in need or jeopardy should be helped, at least to some extent. But there is an element of particularistic care which comes into play in intimate relations, and even if I do see my relationship to my loved one in light of general categories, this is not all I do. I assist my friend because he is my friend, and this is not a

---

[5]Two kinds of irreplaceability might be distinguished here: metaphysical and empirical. The former is difficult to argue for without falling into excessive sentimentality about love. The latter and weaker claim is the only one I make here.

[6]'Mine' should not be understood here in a proprietary sense.

[7]Ernest Barker, trans. (Oxford: Oxford University Press, 1962), p. 1262b.

reason for me to help all persons (whether or not I have a relationship of friendship with them) similarly situated, nor is it a reason for others whose makeup and circumstances are similar to my own to help my friend. The reasons for action characteristic of intimate relations are not universalizable in these ways. On the other hand, if I claim that this person's being my friend is a reason for me to help him, then I must also be willing to say and believe that a person's being another's friend is a reason for that other to help him, and that another person's being my friend is a reason for me to help him as well. As participants in intimate loving relations, each of us has a reason of the same general type to help his own loved ones, not a reason to help loved ones in general. Nevertheless, when I help my friend, my action is also more than just an appropriate response to the fact that he falls under the general heading of 'friend.' My concern is direct and unmediated.

According to Thomas Nagel, intimate ties give an agent reasons to act in pursuit of ends that are his own personal ends. These he calls *agent-relative reasons of autonomy,* and they are to be "specified by reference to the agent for whom they provide reasons."[8] The observer of an intimate relationship, even of one in which he participates at other times, cannot from this perspective value the individuals involved as the individuals themselves do, and though he may recognize and understand the reasons they have for helping and being with one another, he cannot from that standpoint accept these reasons as his own. The reasons are subjective, and "in order to have and act on them one must occupy the perspective of a particular life and its aims" (p. 123). Further, in an intimate relationship, it is important to me how the benefits to my loved one are brought about. I do not just want my loved one to prosper; I want as far as possible to be the one to help him prosper. In contrast, the interests of strangers typically give one reasons to act in pursuit of ends which everyone ought to have and which are not particularly one's own. Everyone has a reason to want others not to be harmed or injured, and no one of us has a special reason to want strangers not to suffer unless he makes the protection of strangers his individ-

---

[8]"The Limits of Objectivity," in S. McMurrin, ed., *The Tanner Lectures on Human Values,* vol. I (Salt Lake City: University of Utah Press and Cambridge: Cambridge University Press, 1980), p. 119.

ual project, which he may or may not do.[9] What matters to us in the case of strangers is usually not so much that *I* prevent them from being harmed or injured, as that these preventive measures be taken and that their safety be secured, whether by my own efforts or by those of others.

There is certainly a sense in which intimate relationships generate personal reasons for action, but Nagel's characterization of these as reasons *of autonomy* is forced and misleading. We can readily agree that individual projects "acquire value only because of the interest we develop in them" (p. 122). But to similarly ground the value of loving attention to a particular other solely in the interest we take in him is to deny that the other's welfare has value in its own right, and this is not the attitude of persons who love. The initial concern involved in a love relationship may simply be something we want to show, but, once the love is in place, the relationship provides us with reasons for concern which are not conditional on our wanting to help.

II

Intimate love relationships involve the participants' recognition of each other as special, nonreplaceable individuals. If the reasons I have to care for my loved ones are to be shown to be *moral* reasons, and if the actions attendant upon this recognition are to be shown to have *moral* value, it is necessary to defend a richer notion of "the moral" than that found in either the utilitarian or the Kantian moral traditions, a conception that undercuts the usual distinction between "the moral" and "the personal."

As regards utilitarianism, it has frequently been pointed out that since this view holds that rightness consists in maximizing total aggregate satisfaction or utility, it is structurally indifferent to *who* experiences the utility, to who is the beneficiary of the maximizing. The standard of moral assessment counts the objects of each individual's preference, but not his own individual preferring, and abstracts utility from its subjects in requiring that the best overall state of affairs be achieved. Though the disinterested spectator of clas-

---

[9]Note, however, that I may have a particularly compelling reason not to want to be the *agent* of harm or injury to another, whether he be a stranger or a friend. This Nagel discusses under the heading of "deontological constraints" (*ibid.*, pp. 126ff).

sical utilitarian theory uses his powers of imagination and sympathy to identify with and experience the desires of others as if they were his own, he does so in order to "ascertain the intensity of these desires and assign them their appropriate weight in one system of desire."[10] Clearly, if it ultimately makes no difference to utilitarianism who the subjects are, it can ultimately make no difference to it that some of these subjects are my intimates and some are not. Our attachments to our loved ones are valued only as part of the general happiness, not in more direct and specific ways.

Kantian theory might seem to give some content to the notion that intimacy, as a way of relating to another person, has noninstrumental or personal moral value, because Kantianism is an agent-centered rather than outcome-centered morality. Kant speaks of persons as being ends in themselves having dignity and of dignity as having both "an unconditional and incomparable worth"—"unconditional" because whatever has dignity has value independent of any contingent needs or desires that it may satisfy, and "incomparable" because it is "exalted above all price" and "admits of no equivalent."[11] Unlike price, dignity "admits of no equivalent" because it cannot be quantified, and therefore it makes no sense to say that one amount of dignity can be legitimately exchanged for a greater amount of dignity elsewhere. The dignity in ten persons is not ten times the dignity in one, and the one is irreplaceable in the sense that his loss cannot be compensated for by the allegedly greater quantity of value in the ten which is brought about. However, the Kantian notion of irreplaceability of persons cannot give moral import to the notion of irreplaceability in intimate relations; for what has dignity for Kant is not the particular person him or herself, but the humanity *in* persons, and the ground of dignity is a property of the will of *every* rational being, the property of legislating to oneself universal laws without the sensuous motives of one's phenomenal self. As Max Scheler observes, the Kantian

> definition of the person as rational leads first to the consequence that every concretization of the idea of the person in a concrete person coincides at once with a depersonalization. For that which is here

[10]John Rawls, *A Theory of Justice* (Cambridge, Mass.: Harvard University Press, 1971), p. 27.

[11]*Foundations of the Metaphysics of Morals*, Lewis White Beck, trans. (New York: Macmillan, 1985), pp. 53–54.

called "person," namely, that "something" which is the subject of rational activity, must be attributed to concrete persons—indeed, to *all men*—in the same way and as something *identical* in all men. . . . Indeed, the concept of an "individual person" becomes, strictly speaking, a *contradictio in adjecto*.[12]

Persons are individuated by their particular empirical constitutions, but in Kant the empirical self has price, not dignity, and, from the point of view of reason, one empirical self can be replaced by another without any loss of value. Since intimate relations can be understood only as relations among empirical, embodied selves that admit of no equivalent, Kant cannot describe the acts expressive of intimate caring in moral terms.

We see then that both utilitarianism and Kantianism, as accounts of moral value, fail to take seriously the plurality and distinctness of persons and that they are unable to explain the moral significance of acts of intimacy except from some point of view external to the individuals involved in intimate relations. Though the utilitarian acknowledges that the patterns of motivation, feeling, and action characteristic of our intimate relations cannot be psychologically explained in terms of the pursuit of some impersonal good, he will insist that the moral significance of the special concern we show our loved ones is exhausted by its impersonal value.[13] If the utilitarian, using Richard Hare's "two-level approach," claims that the perspective of intimacy and the perspective of general utility involve different kinds of moral thinking,[14] we must be careful not to misunderstand him. The fact that the two perspectives differ with respect to emotional involvement would be taken by Hare not to

---

[12]*Formalism in Ethics and Non-formal Ethics of Values*, M. Frings and R. Funk, trans. (Evanston, Ill.: Northwestern University Press, 1973), pp. 371–72.

[13]As Robert Nozick claims, utilitarians who regard particularistic ties to individuals as derivatively justifiable, provided that the general interest is best advanced by an arrangement in which people act according to such ties, "misconstrue[s] the moral weight of particularistic ties." See *Philosophical Explanations* (Harvard University Press, 1981), pp. 456–57. Nozick also notes that "it is a worthwhile task . . . to investigate the nature of a more consistently particularistic theory—particularistic all the way down the line" (p. 457). This paper is engaged in such an investigation.

[14]See Hare, "Ethical Theory and Utilitarianism," in H. D. Lewis, ed., *Contemporary British Philosophy* (London: Allen & Unwin, 1976), pp. 122–23.

signify the presence of fundamentally different types of moral thinking, but only to show that moral decisions must ultimately be left up
to those who have no personal stake in the outcome of the decision.

Kantianism abstracts from the separateness of persons by focusing on the good will, which is not many, but one. Kant does regard
the injunction to love as one of the basic principles of ethics, and so
it might be thought that the love expressed in intimate relationships
does have moral significance for Kant after all, despite the fact that
the objects of this love are particular concrete persons rather than
persons in virtue of their humanity. This would, however, be a mistaken inference. Acts have moral value for Kant only if the motive
for performing them can be summoned up by the agent at will,
and, since love cannot be summoned up, but is something (as Kant
sees it) that we simply experience, acts done out of love cannot have
moral value. Kant in fact distinguishes between two kinds of love:
"practical love," which is love from duty, and "emotional love,"
which is love from inclination.[15] Anyone qualifies for the first kind of
love, and what one's own particular feelings are toward a friend or
loved one is neither here nor there. But to characterize the acts of
love performed in intimate relationships merely as acts of practical
love is to miss what is critical for identifying and appreciating these
acts. What intimates do is not merely bestow benefits upon each
other, for this description of their actions can apply as well to acts
that are not, properly speaking, acts of intimates at all. The good
we do our loved ones is not just something we could do as well for
others. Rather, it is often something that is very particular to the
emotional relationship we have with each other and to the particular
persons we are.

Some intimates (not the hostile kind) act out of emotional love
for each other, but this is not reducible to acting for the sake of
some end or set of ends. Intimates do often seek to help each other,
but *being* intimate is not as such a matter of seeking anything in
particular. What then is it for persons to be intimate? The answer, I
believe, is that persons are intimate with each other only when the
particular whole person that each is provides a general focus for the
goal-directed acts of the other. In intimate loving relations, this
general directedness or orientation is toward the individual value of

---

[15] *The Doctrine of Virtue,* Mary Gregor, trans. (New York: Harper &
Row, 1964), pp. 116–17.

an individual self, and it identifies the various acts performed on his behalf as acts of loving attention.

A description of intimacy should make a distinction between the individual person and the particular empirical qualities he possesses, without invoking, as Kant does, some general characteristic of persons lying beneath or standing above the accidental features of their empirical existence. Actions may manifest not only respect for some transcendental quality of a person, but also love for the individual person, who is more than the sum total of his qualities, which others might possess and which he might lose. By 'love for the individual person' I do not mean to suggest that love is a response to a prior valuation of an individual in his individuality. Love is not just a reaction to a value already perceived or appreciated. Rather it is in and through love that the distinctive value of an individual self is encountered and affirmed.

III

Now what is the connection between intimacy and the moral? Is the domain of personal relations a moral domain, and, if so, why? It is not entirely satisfying to argue that acts of particularistic care have as their object the good of other persons and that the good of others is a moral consideration. This is true, but we should consider whether it is possible to confer moral value on caring acts without sacrificing their distinctive character. A different account tries to do this by linking the moral point of view to commitment to an ideal of the person. The concept of a person is a moral concept or a concept the application of which is intimately linked with the application of moral concepts, but there is more than one way of conceiving of a person. An "ethics of intimacy" and an "ethics of strangers" can be distinguished not merely in terms of the relevance of strict rules to an understanding of our moral relations with others (which is how Toulmin differentiates them), but more fundamentally, in terms of the general conceptions of the person in which these moralities are grounded. These conceptions are genuinely different and are not just the same conception conjoined with different sets of factual beliefs. They need not be thought of as rival conceptions, however, for, though they may come into conflict with each other, they also work together to determine the shape of our lives by giving rise to distinct but complementary ideals of individual fulfillment.

From one standpoint, fulfillment is achieved through the pursuit of a rational plan of life under social conditions of mutual respect for the humanity in persons. From another, it is achieved through the establishment of relations of mutual affection which essentially involve individual, concrete persons.

Of course, in intimate love relations one's direct commitment is to a particular individual and not to an ideal of any kind, whether of a person or of something else, and we must be careful not to let this talk about different conceptions of the person mislead us into thinking otherwise. Indeed, I can be committed to an ideal of valuing an individual as an individual, in an abstract way, without being intimate with anyone at all. Commitment to this ideal becomes concrete in the case of those who actually take part in intimate relations.

Some might argue that an ethics of intimacy can be subsumed under an ethics of impartiality and impersonality. General rules admit of exceptions, and in certain circumstances we may make exceptions for our friends and loved ones and give them more attention than we give others. In this way, an ethics of intimacy might be viewed as part of, or covered by, a traditional notion of morality. But it is not clear from this account *why* the demand to be impartial between the interests of our loved ones and those of others is limited in its scope. Is strict impartiality a requirement that is waived merely as a concession to human nature? Or is particularistic attention to friends and loved ones itself essentially moral? If the latter, then impartial and impersonal ethics proves to be unable to give articulation to all aspects of morality. Different aspects of morality link up with different aspects or conceptions of the person: underlying some aspects is the generalized person, underlying others is the particular, concrete person. In saying this, however, I do not mean to suggest that there is something so distinctive about our loved ones that it cannot be found in others. The point is that, even if this is so, the distinctive value of the particular person with whom we have a particular relationship is the background condition of acts of love.

Desires in intimate relationships are personal in the sense that their objects essentially include first-person indexicals. The agent attaches value to its being *him* who does things to or for his intimate. At least some desires in intimate relationships are altruistic as well, that is, are specified by reference to the other's desires, and, therefore, each intimate finds his or her happiness in some ways contingent upon the fulfillment of the other's desires. As for love, it is, Scheler writes,

> the most personal of attitudes, but a thoroughly *objective* one none the less, in the sense that in it we are "objective" insofar as we free ourselves (in an unaccustomed fashion), from bondage to our own interests,[16]

that is, from the pursuit of ends desired only as a means to the advancement of our own self-regarding interests. Further, actions expressive of love can be said to exhibit or presuppose respect for persons, though there are radical differences between this and respect for persons in the usual moral contexts. When, in an intimate relation, persons are respected, their particular desires, moods, and tastes determine the form and shape of their relationship and the manner and timing of their interactions. This respect, in marked contrast to the sort that requires us to distance ourselves from our own desires and those of others, consists in responsiveness to another's idiosyncratic needs and wants, a responsiveness that itself varies according to the degree of closeness established by the participants in the intimate relationship. We need to know a great deal about the patterns of openness established by intimates before we can tell whether they are forcing their attentions on unwilling persons, and of course this is something it is wrong to do to anyone. But this observation should not be allowed to obscure the fact that the notions of respect for persons as such and respect for persons in intimate relations centrally employ different conceptions of the person. A full understanding of treating others as persons must not restrict itself to only one.

Respect for self, as a particular instance of respect for persons, also has its impersonal and personal forms. The impersonal form is respect for the humanity in one's own person, which consists in a willingness to acknowledge fully one's own basically equal moral status as defined by one's basic human rights. Self-respect in this sense is necessarily comparative; for the person who has it demonstrates in word and deed that he knows and cares about his position of equality in the moral community. Moreover, impersonal self-respect is a precondition of impersonal respect for others; for the

---

[16]*The Nature of Sympathy*, P. Heath, trans. (New Haven, Conn.: Yale University Press, 1954), p. 167.

person who disavows or denies his own moral rights is not in an adequate position to appreciate the rights of others. The personal form of self-respect can also be said to concern one's moral status, only now it is one's moral status as a particular individual rather than as a human being. Self-respect in this sense does not conceptually include comparisons with others; the person who has it does not just regard himself as being as good as anyone else or his interests as being as worthy of recognition as the next man's. Further, personal self-respect, like the impersonal mode, seems closely linked to the corresponding form of respect for others. The person who does not value his own distinctiveness, who does not have personal standards that he considers worth living up to or plans and goals that he considers worth pursuing just because they are part of his own particular life, is probably incapable of respecting others in the special way that friends and lovers respect one another and of engaging in intimate love relations.

Exactly how a person acquires this type of self-respect is difficult to say, but it is at least helpful if not necessary that he receive the sort of upbringing that nourishes his sense of his own specialness and in which he feels uniquely precious to those who care for him. Moreover, certain forms of social organization of child rearing are more supportive of personal self-respect than others. A society in which children do not experience the partiality and intimacy of family life because they are reared communally is not likely to be one in which persons place a high value on the sort of respect for self that depends on an awareness of the distinctiveness of one's life and character.[17]

It should be stressed that it is not my intention to force a choice between the personal and impersonal forms of respect for others and self. I argue instead for an integrated view of ourselves and others which includes both. On the one hand, recognition of the dignity and worth of the generalized other is certainly a necessary condition to define the moral standpoint, and impersonal self-respect is a primary human good of fundamental importance. One must not treat anyone, stranger or intimate alike, as a mere plaything, rather than as a person with needs and rights of his own.

---

[17]For more on the relationship between child-rearing structures and self-respect, see my book, *Parents and Children: The Ethics of the Family* (Oxford: Oxford University Press, 1982), part III, ch. one.

There is not, however, a further general duty to treat persons with the kind of respect intimates show one another, nor do we enter into intimate relations in order to have occasions for the discharging of a duty of personal respect. On the other hand, once in an intimate relationship, persons treat one another with a respect that strangers are not in a position to show.

The moral weight of intimate relations can be accounted for in terms of a concept of moral individuality no less valid than that involved in the relations moral persons more generally enter into. The preservation of a personal realm of intimate relations, as well as individual projects and commitments, can also be seen as helping to sustain and strengthen our commitment to impersonal morality. As Bernard Williams observes:

> Such things as deep attachments to other persons will express them-selves in the world in ways which cannot at the same time embody the impartial view . . . yet unless such things exist, there will not be enough substance or conviction in a man's life to compel his allegiance to life itself. Life has to have substance if anything is to have sense, including adherence to the impartial system.[18]

When I have an allegiance to life, I have somehow come to view it as mine; it is *my* life that I want to lead and to which I am devoted, not life in the abstract. Moreover, things have meaning for me only insofar as I identify my life with them, that is, only as parts or aspects of my life, the only life to which I am loyal. In particular, it is only within the context of my life—a life that is of value to me for reasons other than those which have led me to pursue specific goals and embrace specific ideals—that being moral matters to *me,* rather than just matters. Here intimate relations become important. For, if there were no private realm within which the impersonal and im-partial demands of morality cease to apply, if others were always to have a claim on our help, then for most of us our lives would not be our own. And, if this is so, then the demands for moral concern would turn out to be self-defeating.[19]

---

[18]"Persons, Character and Morality," in *The Identities of Persons,* Amelie Rorty, ed. (Berkeley: University of California Press, 1973), p. 215.

[19]Several people have offered helpful comments on earlier drafts of this paper. I particularly want to thank Raziel Abelson, Frances Myrna Kamm, Lowell Kleiman, and Virginia Held.

13

Applying Ethical Theory: Caveats from a Case Study

Roger Wertheimer

I

In a mature discipline theoretical and applied activities work a two-way street. The more purely theoretical dimension develops the system of the most basic concepts and lawlike generalizations distinctive to the discipline. The applied activity puts the resulting theories to work on situations covered by the generalizations, and feeds them insights and information that may force alterations of the theories.

Applied ethics is a revised edition of a venerable enterprise freshly named to declare a refreshed faith in the power of theoretical ethics to provide rational resolutions of serious practical perplexities. The hopes here remain premature. As things are, no ethical theory can be trusted in anything like the way that scores of theories in the physical, social, and formal sciences can. None can now boast the evidentiary backing that commands acceptance by reasonable people and commends their abandoning common sense in the face of the theory's conclusions or even justifies their letting themselves be led by it in times of uncertainty and indecision.

Whether any ethical theory could be competent to serve as a practical guide is often doubted, most often for bad reasons. My own doubts are directed more at the modes of ethical theorizing taught today than at all the imaginable but yet unimagined approaches. The ethical theorizing we have seen is, I think, too often too presumptuously prescriptive. Like classical epistemologists and philosophers of science, who laid down rules for acquiring knowledge, consulting only their own epistemological intuitions without first looking carefully at how people actually improved their understanding of the world, ethical theorists have issued ethical and metaethical pronouncements without sufficient respectful and unprejudiced study of how, in detail, people respond when actually confronted with morally serious problems.

Meanwhile, many ethical theorists humbly acknowledge the poor powers of their offspring and content themselves with claiming modestly that theoretical ethics at least supplies a store of analytical tools for sorting out issues and questions, refining our concepts and principles, and thereby rendering our deliberations more rational. That service, if well performed, is something to be proud of, but as things are, the quality of the contribution often does not merit the confidence with which it is offered.

I shall here review (all too briefly, I am afraid) some features of a topic—abortion—much treated in the short history of applied ethics. It is, I believe, a prime case in which reliance upon substantive, methodological, and metaethical concepts and principles developed and widely endorsed by ethical theorists is more hindering than helpful. One moral here is that we would be wise to put less faith in our theoretical presumptions and, instead, listen with less prejudice to untutored reasoning and allow theory to be challenged and informed thereby. Beyond that, the substance of the specific example may be of more interest than that moral.

II

The abortion debates present ethical theorists with a dilemma formed by a triad of facts:[1]

> F: The fact that some proposition is commonly believed is a good (but not conclusive) reason to presume it to be true.
>
> C: Common belief is committed to the moral principle S:
>
> S: The fact that something is a human being, one of our conspecifics, is itself a good reason for our refraining from harming it.

---

[1] See my "Philosophy on Humanity," in Robert L. Perkins, ed., *Abortion: Pro and Con* (Cambridge, Mass.: Schenkman, 1974): 107–128.

T: Currently respected ethical theories are committed to the principle B-S:

B-S: Biological properties in general and membership in the human species in particular are not in themselves morally relevant considerations.

Faced with this, a few theorists accept F, C, and thus S, and mistakenly deny T. Their justification of S (if any) usually derives from some currently respected ethical theory. This has some precedent, if not excuse, since more than one classical theorist has evidently seemed intent on justifying S. But their attempts manifestly fail since they really argue for the moral relevance of some psychological property (e.g., rationality, sentience) which is not always present in all human beings, let alone identical or essential to the biological property of being human.

Most theorists insist on T and deny S. Some of them concede C and deny F in general or claim that the presumption in favor of S is rebutted by their own expert moral intuitions or by T. Other theorists express commitment to F, but deny C. This latter position is a pretty illustration of a well-known principle that, to make sense of the words and deeds of others, we cannot but rely on our own conception of what makes sense, is rational, reasonable, and true, and thus we attribute to others principles and concepts as much like our own as we can. The consequences of these two positions are the same, and so too is their cause: an overweaning confidence in one's own convictions. Evidently these theorists are not seriously troubled by the possibility that what most people seem to believe could be correct and their own intuitions and theories flatly wrong.

The response, rarely displayed, that I recommend is to recognize the truth of T, F, C, and thus S, conclude that something must be wrong with our theoretical tradition, and then begin to develop ethical theory that accounts for the moral relevance of biological properties in general and of being human in particular. This task is formidable, yet seems feasible, and might well be rewarding. I will not pursue it here, though some suggestions may show through some of my remarks.

III

Most theorists deny S with little extended discussion of F, but many seem sympathetic to Michael Tooley's defense of their practice.

Tooley here addresses a restatement of F: "Other things being equal, what most people believe is likely to be true."

> What is one to say about a belief that, though shared by most people, is also rejected by most people who are knowledgeable about the subject area in question? Surely this is not a case where other things are equal. And in such a case where the views of most people are not shared by those who have been trained to think about the relevant issues, and who have spent considerable time doing so, is it not more likely that it is the majority that have mistaken beliefs? In view of the fact, then, that virtually all philosophers reject the Standard Belief (S), it is surely unjustified to view this as a situation where others things are equal, and hence as one in which one is justified in concluding that what most people believe is likely to be true.[2]

The general epistemic principle appealed to is sensible: Presume the opinion of a strong consensus of the experts is right, whatever most other people believe. Where we have clear criteria of knowledgeability, where genuine expertise is recognizable, the opinion of the uninitiated means little even if the experts are divided.

But is there such a thing as expert ethical opinion? If so, what "training" is necessary, sufficient, or conducive to developing expertise? Is it the kind of academic training typically undergone to attain a rank of instructor or professor of ethical theory? Ethical theorists are "knowledgeable" about ethical theories, but are they knowledgeable about what is right and wrong and how people should live? Are they more so than logicians, linguists, lawyers, historians, clergymen, social workers? How much more? (For most of these others do not reject S.) (I am ignoring the bit above about spending "considerable time" thinking about an issue, since my experience is that most theorists don't do that with S: they instantly dismiss it and never seriously consider it.)

IV

Put those questions aside for a moment and consider why the truth of F might be important for ethical theory (for note that Tooley's view denies it *any* importance there.)[3] A theory (ethical, scientific, or whatever) can be partially evaluated by internal considerations of

---

[2]*Abortion and Infanticide* (Oxford: Clarendon Press, 1983), p. 82.
[3]"Philosophy on Humanity," pp. 108–113.

consistency, comprehensiveness, simplicity, and the like. But, although theorists are specially adept at applying those criteria, internal considerations alone cannot determine the truth of a theory. To test the truth of a theory the judgments implied by its generalizations must be compared with the judgments from some external, independently credible source of judgment. Conjoining the generalizations with descriptions of situations covered by the generalizations entails judgments ("verdicts") about the situations. In science those verdicts are predictions (and retrodictions), and sense perception of the situations provides an independently credible source of judgments against which the empirically determinable verdicts can be checked. In ethics, the verdicts are to evaluate the situations and cannot be evaluated by them, so these verdicts are matched, not against sensory reports, but instead against moral intuitions. The source of such intuitive judgments is called "moral sense" (or "moral intuition"), by which is meant nothing more than that the judgment is made without use of the theory or its competitors.

Of course, the value of this kind of evaluation of a theory depends on the credibility or reliability of the independent source of judgment, be it perception or intuition. Such sources of judgment are inherently fallible; any of their judgments could be false. But insofar as they are genuine capacities for making judgments of the relevant kind, the judgments made do have some evidentiary value. How much evidentiary value a specific judgment has is determined by evaluating the condition of the judge's capacity in general and in the instant case by reference to a large, diverse, complex, and continually refinable set of criteria: Is the judge sane? sober? healthy? mature? experienced? careful? etc. Another criterion is the kind and degree of consensus on the judgment: How much agreement or disagreement is there among those whose judgments of the case is worth much?

v

Notice first that, even if the typical academic training of ethical theorists tended to refine and improve their moral intuitions, they would still have good reason to check their theories against the intuitions of the philosophically untutored, just because that very training renders their judgments suspect as not being truly independent of and uninfluenced by the operation of a theory, and that suspicion deepens along with the depth of the theoretical principle at issue.

Further, while their academic training improves general argumentative and analytical skills, those dialectical skills seem distinct and separable from the processes peculiar to making a moral judgment. Many, perhaps most, theorists would insist, on the basis of experience or metaethical theory, that although analysis and argument may be necessary for acquiring an adequate understanding of a factual situation, once the factual description of the situation is understood and agreed upon, the moral judgment about the situation is not rendered more reliable by training. Again, the training may improve the capacity to extrapolate from a collection of moral judgments and discern some unifying principle, but the judgments forming the collection are not rendered more reliable by the training.

If anything, the ethical theorist's habits of thought and feeling are likely to render his moral intuitions suspect and less reliable. The competitive, cold-blooded, or playful style of thought inculcated and practiced in current academic philosophy is generally regarded and treated as topic-neutral, as appropriate for investigation of substantive ethics as it is for studying symbolic logic, linguistic theory, or the pre-Socratics. That detached stance may well have some advantages in ethical theory, as elsewhere; some advantages may be shared by the similar attitudes of surgeons toward the unconscious hunks of meat they slice and sew upon. Still, it is suppositious metaethics to assume that that style has no risks or costs for the ethical theorist. Perhaps ideally a physical scientist's conception of an object is utterly unbiased by any concern for it, but that attitude appears more antithetical than appropriate to ethical judgment.

Perhaps ethical theorizing has some peculiar occupational hazards. Normally a proper moral judge confronts each new case impartially, is properly moved, swayed, outraged, and the rest as the evidence accumulates, and, at the end, favors one party over another. By contrast, as researcher and educator, the ethical theorist must regularly review and present the same cases over and over, and frequently has good methodological and pedagogical reasons for treating as an open question what normally he would have appropriately strong feelings about. He systematically stifles and bridles the natural attitudes of a competent moral judge. Those well-trained dispositions of detachment may themselves be reason enough for him to look carefully at the responses of those who consider cases from a more natural position.

The abortion controversy specially tests the propriety of a detached sensibility. Normally an equal and serious concern for the welfare of all parties affected by a dispute is a prerequisite for a fair evaluation of their competing claims. Yet with abortion the prime question is precisely what degree of concern is appropriate toward the fetus. Consider here that, presumably for good biological reasons, our sympathies are activated by the appearance of a human-like form. That fact figures prominently in the abortion controversy, not in a propositional format, but as fetuses in formaldehyde bottles and photos of little faces, little fingers, little feet.

"Proabortionists" rail against this practice, particularly when those pictures are thrust at prospective patients at abortion clinics. "It's so upsetting!" they complain. And of course it is and is supposed to be. But is it unfair or improper to inform adolescents and adults who frequently have only the blurriest, if any, ideas about what it is they are considering destroying? Is the information about what the thing looks like irrelevant to a well-informed decision to abort? And shouldn't that decision be well informed even if the decision maker would much prefer to be blissfully ignorant? (Can someone deny this while properly complaining about being called "proabortion" and insisting on the label "pro-choice"?) Or should we regard our natural sensibility as a prejudicial bias that we as "rational" agents had best overcome?

VI

The common conception of the abortion controversy is that the crucial question is, When does a human life begin? That fact is evidence of and explained by the truth of C, that people generally accept the principle S which recognizes being human as a property that provides a thing with a special moral status. Within the cloisters of ethical theory the question of hominization is sometimes discussed, sometimes insightfully, but more commonly it is curtly dismissed on the grounds that S is patently false, so whether the fetus is a human being is utterly irrelevant to the propriety of abortion and its legal prohibition.

To resolve moral questions about abortion (and other subjects), theorists have thus been led to seek some surrogate for S. But although the general problem of identifying reasonable principles comparable to S is a worthy theoretical pursuit (for, even if S is true, it cannot be the only principle of its kind), the enterprise is doomed to sterility when cut loose from any credible system of independent judgments against which a theory or principle could be tested. Then conceptual analysis can yield only empty semantic relations which link with substantive moral claims only via each theorist's own idiosyncratic moral intuitions. Expectably, the alternatives to S that theorists offer are all over the map, with no means of resolving their differences.

Further, even if some degree of "expert" consensus here were achievable, the relation of the results to the very real and pressing practical concerns of the public and policy makers would be quite remote. Consider, for example, the U.S. Senate bill S. 158, introduced in 1981, which would have Congress resolve that "human life shall be deemed to exist from conception." Legislators and legal theorists on both sides of the bill recognized that, if Congress were constitutionally empowered to and did pass S. 158, then governmental prohibition of abortion from conception to parturition would be constitutionally warranted and perhaps mandatory, and indeed abortion would perhaps then be barely if at all distinguishable from murder in our legal system—and that, if Congress could not or did not pass S. 158, then the only means of achieving its legal effect would be the proposed constitutional amendment with an equivalent content which was also before Congress. That complex fact about our legal system is a fact because here, as is generally the case, our legal system embodies and sanctions with the force of law the moral heritage of our culture. Within this context theorists are free to declare that the abortion problem is being "radically misconceived" and that our legal system should be radically reconceived so that S. 158 would not have the legal implications it presently has. In turn, policy makers and governmental authorities confronted by S. 158 and similar legislative and judicial issues are free to regard theoretical and applied ethics as paradigm ivory-tower pursuits. (The facts surrounding S. 158 are some fraction of the evidence for the truth of C.)

VII

Practical concerns aside, by dismissing S and declaring the question of when a human life begins a "biological" question that ethical theorists have no competence or concern to answer, theorists are perpetuating some sorry metaethical assumptions.

Though these theorists profess a wide diversity of metaethical views about the nature and relation of "facts" and "values," they seem to speak with one confident voice about the common conceptualization of the abortion problem. They say that S is a putative moral principle, that when human life begins is a "biological," a factual, empirical matter, and that, although someone can, implicitly or explicitly, use "human being" as a value term (e.g., to mean "a member of our species with a right to life") that usage unnecessarily combines two issues which are best left separate.

Merely labeling the claims and questions is not in itself incorrect. The implications of the labels are another matter. Consider: in many contexts classifying certain judgments as "analytic" (i.e., true solely in virtue of the meanings of the constituent terms, or something of that sort) and others as "synthetic" (i.e., roughly, judgments whose truth value is dependent on extralinguistic factors) can be a relatively harmless and somewhat helpful way of sorting out issues. Lately, however, philosophers have learned that the distinction is dubious, so relying on it to resolve a philosophical problem is perilous. The same is true of the fact-value distinction, and partly because it is intimately related to the analytic-synthetic distinction. Again, the labels "fact" and "value" can be applied, but, if we look at the abortion issue with a minimum of metaethical presumptions, we discover reasons for rethinking our conceptions of just what a fact is and what a value is.

The dating of hominization, the question of when a human life begins, is restatable as the question of whether and, if so, when a human fetus becomes a human being. This latter is manifestly a question of categorization and classification. Whether this entity (the fetus) belongs to the category of human beings is not itself a definitional or conceptual question, though it might naturally generate one. We would be asking the same sort of question if we were wondering whether to cage the creature before us while worrying whether it is a gorilla escaped from the zoo or some actor off the set of *The Planet of the Apes*. In the latter case no definitional or conceptual problem is presented, for our question is answered with some obvious empirical tests guided by uncontroversial classificational criteria.

By contrast, a salient feature of the hominization debates is that all the *relevant subsidiary* facts about reproduction, genetics, fetal development, and the like are (or are thought to be) available and uncontroversial: no further empirical tests are (or are thought to be) necessary. Thus, within the context of the public abortion debates where principle S holds sway, the issue of hominization seems to be something like what, in a law court, jurists would call a question of law rather than a question of fact. Before exploring this idea let us survey the surrounding territory.

VIII

Our current understanding of genetics, fetal development, and related matters is actually still primitive, but our vast areas of ignorance and uncertainty seem largely irrelevant to the dating of hominization. Not totally irrelevant, since determining the correct application of some proposed criteria (e.g., inception of a self) depends on yet unanswered questions. But presently we are still stuck with the prior question of which of many fundamentally different criteria to use, and for that question we have an expert consensus on the essential facts. We could be wrong about this. (I dream of seeing in the supermarket next week's *Star* headline: PEORIA ZYGOTE SELF-CONSCIOUS.) But suppositious worries about possible future discoveries need not distract us now, since our concern here is not to determine the dating of hominization, but rather to understand the attempts people have been making and their failure to form a consensus.

Ethical theorists regularly say or seem to assume that, since the concept of a human being is a "biological concept," the conflict over hominization has some unproblematic resolution. Consider the following quote:

> The concept of a Homo Sapiens is a biological one. If we want to know what it is for a thing to be a member of that species, we can find relatively determinate and uncontroversial criteria for answering this query.[4]

---

[4] Jay L. Garfield, "Introduction," in Garfield and Patricia Hennessey,

This writer does not say where these criteria are to be found, but presumably he is supposing, along with many of his colleagues, that these criteria are provided by what we call the empirical science of biology.

Now, to begin with, current science actually has no such criteria to offer. Taxonomical theorists have only recently begun to confront the daunting intellectual challenge of developing theoretically adequate criteria for individuating species and have yet to form a consensus on the major aspects of that problem. They have not even begun serious systematic work on the problem of individuating species members. Generally they now go about counting species members with the same conceptual equipment laymen use.

Amusingly, in response to attempts to legislate governmentally that a human life begins at conception, the membership of the National Academy of Sciences passed a resolution declaring that science could never provide a basis for a dating of hominization. It is likely that many scientists supported that resolution mainly from political motivations aided by confusions about the epistemology of science. (The resolution is not easily reconciled with the possibility of taxonomy's being a serious scientific discipline.) Of course, only a fraction of the supporters are themselves specialists in biology, but even the most eminent biologists are wont to spout silliness on this subject. Some, for example, suppose they offer insight by reminding us that human life is passed on from generation to generation without interruption and had its beginnings eons ago—which is true but irrelevant to the classification of an entity as a species member.[5]

Developing criteria of species membership is, let us assume, a proper task for taxonomical theory. What would or should result from properly pursuing that task is a matter wide open for speculation. Bear in mind here that the history of science shows again and again that what comes to be regarded as a properly "scientific" (let alone correct) hypothesis or procedure is not always generally recognized as such when first introduced. Despite the fact that this fact is

---

eds., *Abortions: Moral and Legal Perspectives* (Amherst: University of Massachusetts Press, 1984), p. 3.

[5]Daniel Wikler, "Concepts of Personhood," in Margery W. Shaw and A. Edward Doudera, eds., *Defining Human Life* (Ann Arbor, Mich.: AUOHA Press, 1983), pp. 15 ff.

well known, people (philosophers, scientists, and lay folk alike) keep succumbing to the temptation to suppose that we already know (in a rough and general way, they modestly disclaim) the sorts of procedures and products proper scientists will accept after exploring an area where gross ignorance now reigns, the rudiments of a serious theory lie in shadow, and no research has begun to uncover the inevitable unprecedented conceptual dilemmas lurking in the darkness.

I know of but one serious stab at treating the hominization problem in taxonomical terms,[6] and that was by a philosopher, not a respected taxonomist, and I have yet to find a biologist who finds his construction compelling. My own understanding of taxa and their contents is too skimpy for me to competently assess serious hypotheses here, but from the little I have learned of the mind-boggling diversity of life forms and life cycles, I am sure that here, at least as much as elsewhere in science, a large and complex variety of considerations must be weighed against one another when evaluating proposed criteria.

Presumably a major motivation will be the manageability of criteria in furthering scientific research. And that seems cause enough for ecologists and their colleagues to continue to use, as they have in the past, the criterion of birth for species with a life cycle like ours, since a population census is too damnably difficult if you have to count intrauterine individuals.

That consideration will likely be weighty, at least until we discover a convincing answer to the crucial question of what explanatory function the concept of a species member is to play in biological theory. The concept of a species is central to the complex of explanatory theories in biology, and the problem of developing criteria for individuating species derives its point and parameters from those explanatory structures. Though the members are ontologically more fundamental and prior to the species, that abstract metaphysical truth tells little about what, if any, role in explanations is served by a concept of species member, or by something close to it and contrasting with, for example, an assortment of stage sortals (e.g., pupa, larva).

---

[6]Lawrence C. Becker, "Human Being: The Boundaries of the Concept," *Philosophy and Public Affairs,* IV, 4 (Summer 1975).

Very likely, no usable unitary criterion for species membership will apply across all species. (Consider cases where the question is which things are colonies or clumps of conspecifics and which are conglomerative individuals. Consider the centrality of reproducibility to the concept of species, and relate it to essentially sterile individuals: Are worker bees really members or mere auxiliary parts of the "real" members?) Conceivably the criteria will vary with the order or genus or even the species. Conceivably in species in which culture is the key to survival the criteria should be defined by the cultures themselves or by the viable cultures. Some such possibility appears less implausible when we consider that, in its inherent quest for comprehensiveness, biology must integrate its conceptions with the findings not just of physics and chemistry, but ultimately of physical anthropology, geography, social history, urbanology, and the rest of the human sciences.

IX

But now, why suppose that taxonomical science is authoritative or even especially relevant to the dating of hominization? That hardly follows from the *biological* character of the concept of a human being. The quick way with the assumptions here is to note the absurdity of arguing that, since the concept of a tree is a biological concept and since, in fact, taxonomy has no use at all for any such category, there really are no trees, and questions such as How many trees stand in my back yard? are not legitimate empirical queries.

Classification of fauna and flora or phenomena in general would be wide open to a profusion of equally pretty schemata if (per impossible) the purpose of the schemata were solely for representing the world, describing it, reporting, announcing, asserting, recording, sorting, filing, and repeating truths. Schemata could be compared for consistency, comprehensiveness, simplicity, elegance, memorability, and manageability, but those considerations alone still leave an incalculable array of options. Classification must serve more determinative purposes if it is to have a more determinative evaluation.

If we have an interest in inferring truths beyond those implicit in the schema, if we have a need for systematic inferential relations beyond the logical relations implicit in any schema, if we wish to explain and predict phenomena or regulate and revise them, then our reasons for selecting some schema are much more selective. Yet explaining and understanding can themselves serve many purposes and take many forms. The classes used by carpenters and clinicians cut across the biologist's taxa; they do not correlate in any systematic way, but they do correspond just as much to contours *in rerum natura*, and they serve their purposes more powerfully than the biologist's taxa can.[7] The latter are free from particular practical purposes, unconstrained by special interests such as cooks and woodcutters have, so they can systematically connect a wider range of phenomena and provide a more unified comprehensive conception of things. That conception is superior, controlling, authoritative only for purely cognitive purposes, only when we act in the world with no interest other than enlarging and improving this kind of comprehension.

As rational agents acting in the world with a multitude of interests we would be crazy to constrain our understanding of the world by the categories of science. For one thing, the objects of an interest form a class that can and commonly does cut across all usable scientific categories. For another, we constantly create things and classes of things whose essential properties are functional, not natural. Many such categories may be understood and applied from the cognitively detached view of the world the scientist takes. But some cannot, for we have an interest not only in the world seen from a passionless point of view, but also in the world as we experience it, shaped and colored by our emotions and sensibility.

Moreover, as rational agents acting in the world, we use our categories not only to represent, understand, and explain the world, but also to regulate, rearrange, and reform it. In the practical realms science can contribute to but cannot control our understanding and application of categories. Our epistemic authority is a practical authority, which may be an institution exercising its legislative and judicial powers in accordance with the purposes of the institution. As the supreme institutional authority of a society, a state may determine the authoritative classifications of that society.

Our courts have now assumed the novel task of defining new biological kinds; for they have accepted the patentability not of hy-

---

[7]John Dupre, "Natural Kinds and Biological Taxa," *Philosophical Review*, xc, 1 (January 1981): 66–90.

brids, but of unprecedented life forms concocted by biochemists.[8] Every valid patent defines a class of objects, the profits from which the patent holder has claim to. Strip away the complexities, and the crucial questions of patent law—whether a patent is valid and whether an object (or profit from it) infringes the patent—are questions of categorization, of whether the patent class was contained in a prior patent class or contains the alleged infringing object. Taxonomical considerations may be pertinent to the new patents, but they are likely to play a minor role. Ultimately patent law and its classes, like law in general, will be evaluated by their service to the public interest, a great stew of competing interests in which purely cognitive and scientific concerns claim no priority.

The category of human being poses special problems for a state. The authority of any of a state's classifications derives its legitimacy from the propriety of the purposes it serves and its success in serving those purposes. We take for granted that the proper state purposes are defined in terms of serving the interests of persons and that our state is committed to recognizing every human being as a person. So the state cannot legitimately adopt some dating of hominization by any claim of serving the public interest without an independent determination of which beings are human beings. Any attempt by an institution or an individual to resolve the dating question on grounds of public policy or pragmatism inevitably begs the question.

x

So now, what interests or purposes does the category, human being, serve? And who is to determine its proper application? And how is he—or she or they or it—or we to do that?

"Human being" is, it seems, an all-purpose term, not subservient to any special interest, except perhaps a very general, pervasive, and obscure one: self-knowledge. Any discipline may add to or alter our understanding of the category, and a slew of special sciences are dedicated to doing that, but the concept is not the creature or under the control of any particular cognitive field.

The term is not indexical, like "I" or "we", but it refers to *our own* biological species, and that category is, like all our categories,

---

[8]*Diamond v. Chakrabarty,* 447 U.S. 303 (1980).

one of *our* categories, not some Martianese correspondent. As such, the category is our prime category of self-identification: a human being is what each of us most specifically is, biologically, physically, and metaphysically, and thus normally psychologically. And for that reason, due to that (our) nature, it is what each of those we most closely identify with most specifically is. Our biological being, sexual and social, creates special concerns and cognitive interests in our conspecifics. Our attentions and affections converge on our kind. Our needs, our sense of union and community, are naturally satisfied by ligaments of lineage. And our experience of the world, even the modern world, regularly teaches and reminds us that being human is what we most basically are. The category is central to our self-understanding, our self-concept, and self-ideal, and thus to our morality. Again, the term is not indexical, but it might yet be peculiar, for its application and extension might be constrained by our capacity for identification and affection.

Nowadays the term's application is uncontroversial, save in some special sets of cases, only one of which is of urgent concern. Taking out terata, any creature conceived and borne of human parents is a human being. That is virtually universally acknowledged of any being from neonate up to but short of neomort. Dissension erupts when we consider including or excluding the prenatally secluded. How should we determine the dating of hominization? A good place to begin is by looking carefully at how we *do* try to determine it.[9]

XI

Theorists aside, normally people do not persuade others or become persuaded of some dating by first formulating or referring to some *definition* of "human being" and then checking off the features of the fetus against the definition to see whether it satisfies the stated conditions. Normally people do not argue from or about any definition. What they do is look at the facts and respond to them, and their response is expressed in a judgment affirming or denying that the fetus at a certain stage is a human being. They may also subse-

---

[9]Cf. my "Understanding the Abortion Argument," *Philosophy and Public Affairs*, i, 1 (Fall 1971): 67–95.

quently look at the same facts or some others, or have some shoved in their faces by the world or their opponents, and then respond differently or the same. They may say that their judgment is the result of a "decision" or that they are "forced" to admit or concede the matter, or they may simply find themselves experiencing the fetus as a human being or not so experiencing it.

Arguments are offered. People point to various well-known facts to justify a dating. And normally the datings and arguments are comprehensible without supposing any shifts in the meaning or definition of "human being". Throughout, the term can be consistently rendered as "individual member of the biological species, Homo sapiens". The arguments may be said to assume or advocate differing criteria or conditions for species membership, and the application of a criterion does determine the application and extension of the term. However, the "choice" of a criterion is not dictated by strictly linguistic factors and does not alter what we mean to be saying of a thing when we apply the term to it. We all mean to mean the same, and we succeed as well here as we ever do. (The situation here is a prime example of the problems besetting the analytic-synthetic distinction.)

Some talk in this context *is* best described as involving shifting senses. A notorious example is the all too common sophism that an embryo is certainly human (not vulpine, canine, etc.) and certainly alive, a living being (not dead or inert), so it must be a human life, a living human being. The equivocation is evident, since the argument applies to any living cell of a human body. Also, commonly, pro-abortionists seem to concede that a fetus is a human being (usually when they seek to finesse the issue in hopes of focusing on other matters) when actually they think it is only a potential human being. Such liberals are notably less loose-lipped when they speak in our courts and legislative forums where our language is formalized and fixed to legal consequences.

Thus, although some factors may pull toward talk of people's having different definitions or senses of "human being", and although on some occasions ascriptions of idiolectical divergence are appropriate, generally it is more accurate and analytically useful to avoid such ascriptions. The fact is that people judge the dating differently. We should not say that they use the term in different senses, since that effectively precludes their genuinely disagreeing.

We *could* say that they have different concepts or conceptions of a human being or that they accept or employ different criteria for being a human being, but we probably *should not* say that, since that inevitably is understood as though it *explained* the disagreements when actually, at best, it only redescribes the fact of disagreement in judgment. Positing some ideational intermediary between people's beliefs about the subsidiary facts and their beliefs about the dating provides only a pseudoexplanation. If conflicts on the dating were due to factors that manifested themselves in other conflicts that are not simply consequences of the dating conflict (as a conflict over the propriety of abortion is), then it might be useful and accurate to speak of different concepts or criteria here. If, for example, affirmations and denials that members of another race are truly human beings (or inferior kinds of human beings) were generally correlated with certain datings of hominization, then we might have reason to talk of different underlying concepts or criteria here. That sort of thing might be present in some cases, but the available evidence indicates that this is not a general feature of the situation.

Certainly people have varying concepts of a biological species. Most minds remain relatively innocent of Darwinian theory and operate with some quasi-Aristotelian conception of a fixed immutable essence peculiar to each kind. Meanwhile, various candidate conceptions compete for acceptance among taxonomists. But the bearing of this on the conflicting datings seems dubious. After all, these conflicts are never about whether the fetus belongs to our species rather than some other species, subspecies, or sibling species.

Theorists do attempt to formulate, justify, and apply criteria here. Yet none of these processes need be operative in laymen for them to judge the issue competently. It is a hyperrationalistic delusion to think that laymen *must* be "applying some rule," at least unconsciously. Their conflicting judgments need not be due to applying different rules, because every rule is necessarily open to varying applications, and thus adding rules and rules for the application of rules cannot preclude the possibility of conflicting applications. The conflicting applications of the term 'human being' may have an explanation, but it need not involve differing ideational intermediaries.

The attempts by theorists to develop defensible criteria are not in principle misguided. Elsewhere they sometimes succeed in contributing to a reasoned consensus on a general principle. But their success is contingent upon various contextual factors (e.g., institutional powers and constraints) which are not operative in this instance. Moreover, their endeavor is parasitic upon the pretheoretical judgment making, and the plausibility of any proposed criterion derives from its consonance with those pretheoretical judgments. But in this instance every serious proposal is equally good at catching the whole class of consensual judgments from birth on, and then seeks to show some coherence in a region where the dissensus is very wide and very strong. The efforts of theorists may be worth making and may produce various useful results in the process, but nothing guarantees them a real chance of success: there need not be a compelling justification of some criterion awaiting discovery. And there is reason to think there is none.

XII

Again, people select some date, some event (conception, birth, viability, etc.) and often cite some facts to explain their selection. But often they can say little about which items or aspects of the situation caught their eye. That may be due to lack of skills of reflection and articulation (which need not at all impugn their judgment) or to a sense that the matter is so obvious that there is nothing worth adding to what is immediately apparent. Such silence should be taken very seriously here.

Given the facts, all the popular datings have an obvious appeal. They make some sense, and not just to those who accept the datings. We can, if we allow ourselves, see the attractions of the datings we reject. We may feel moved, but not very far, though perhaps we might be more so if we were not concerned (as we properly are) about the practical consequences of the dating. Yet, when we try to formulate a compelling argument for any dating, we quickly discover that we really do not have much to say and that what we do say is all too easily rebutted.

Yet it is hardly that "anything goes" here. There really are not very many serious candidates (not if we exclude the far-fetched proposals which fascinate only a theorist or two). It is important for appreciating the depth of the cognitive dimension here to recognize that many possible datings have little natural appeal—including some that at one time did, but, given what we now know, no longer do. Quickening is the clearest case. We can readily understand why it once made sense (and was indeed *the* standard for centuries) and why it is never taken seriously now.

Consider the birth date. Its cross-cultural popularity is impressive and utterly unsurprising. It seems completely natural, yet it may be the hardest to articulate any respectable rationale for. Since the newborn is undoubtedly a human being, the reasoning is directed at explaining the denial of that title to the babe before birth. At first glance the differences seem obvious and enormous, yet when we try to describe them it all dribbles away into the sand. When we consider incubated premature infants, the morphological and histological structures and capacities seem no longer relevant. The newborn's independence of the mother seems significant until we try to specify it, for the neonate is utterly dependent in so many vital ways. It soon seems that we are excluding the secluded simply for being sequestered, and that can seem to make no sense at all.

By contrast, although to many it seems plain zany to consider a zygote one of the folks, the argument for that conclusion is disturbingly elegant, simple, and direct, so much so that it can seem sheer sophistry, quite unconvincing. Yet there it is: the same spatiotemporal-causal-organic continuity linking an adult with an infant goes back as far as the zygote and stops there. The unblinkable biological and metaphysical fact is that the individual human organism begins back then. (Or a few days thereafter, since apparently the possibility of twinning is determined by post-conception events and, since the zygote cannot be identical with both of two distinct individuals and apparently is no more identifiable with one than the other, it cannot be identified with either; so the inception of each twin occurs at segmentation, and, arguably, so does the inception of any individual even when no twin appears.) But, having noted the fact of continuity of organism, the antiabortionist has nothing much to add to overcome the natural reluctance to regard the early mass of undifferentiated cells as a being no different from you and me. Yet, those who balk at the conclusion as an insult to common sense have not found much to say beyond that the cell mass seems too undeveloped, too different from what we have in mind when we think of a human being.

XIII

Here it is worth interjecting an example of how the kind of thinking peculiar to philosophical theorists can make a genuine contribution to common thought. Notably, it is not the application of any theory, but rather of the type of thinking practiced and developed in the process of developing and evaluating theories.

People generally agree on the application of the term 'human being' in most post-natal cases, and also in some instructive imaginable cases. It seems coherent to imagine (though its realization is remote) removing a human being's brain (and perhaps some other requisite sections of her nervous system) and transplanting it in the body of another in such a manner that her mind, her personality, character, memory, beliefs, and desires remain largely unaltered from the pretransplant time. And it seems that, confronted with this hypothetical situation, people find it natural to say that her former body becomes a corpse, that the human organism dies, but that she, the human being, continues to exist and live embodied in another organism.[10]

This need not mean that "human being" does not express a biological concept: for one thing, it seems that we would individuate the same way with a transplanted brain of an ape or a dog or any creature with much of a mind to move. It may mean that our concept of the biological has unsuspected contours and comes apart in curious ways. Perhaps what we call "biological science" is best conceived as concerned with biological organisms and not per se with the organically embodied experiencing subjects who can be objects of our "personalized" attitudes. (Though we may fear any kind of threatening thing, what calls forth our feelings of sympathy, affection, anger, and the like must, it seems, be conceived in some personal or anthropomorphic manner.)

The import of this Gedanken experiment for the issue of hominization is its providing some substance to a distinction needed by proabortionists. For it permits (but does not require) a reasoned resistance to the central antiabortionist argument that identifies the entity at the time of conception (implantation, or segmentation) with the individual at every subsequent stage it attains. That the life

---

[10]Cf. Mark Johnston, "Human Beings," *Journal of Philosophy*, LXXXIV, 2 (February 1987): 59–83.

of the individual organism begins back then seems as certain as any bit of biology. Yet since we elsewhere display a conceptual distinction between the organism and the human being, we are not being arbitrary if we refuse to concede that the life of a human being necessarily begins coincident with that of the organism. Actually, extending that Gedanken experiment suggests a contrary conclusion. For, so it seems, if we consider a case of transplanting a neonate brain, we get the same result as with an adult. But our intuition becomes decreasingly confident as we consider transplanting the decreasingly developed brain and nervous system of a fifth-, fourth-, third-, and second-month fetus. And the first-month cell mass (and much of the second-) is too undifferentiated for the supposition to have any sense.

All this makes the case for the first-month, and perhaps first-trimester, hominization less compelling, but not necessarily incorrect. Then too, this dialectical sword is double-edged, for all this also makes the case against hominization increasingly less compelling as time goes on, indeed rather tenuous (but not untenable) from perhaps as early as midterm on. Perhaps this form of argument will come to seem more compelling when we know more about the development of the cortex and its connections with what we would be willing to or forced to consider a self, something, someone who calls out our sympathies and calls upon our capacity for identification.

XIV

The power of such considerations may be substantial, but should not be overstated. It is doubtful they can be decisive. For note now a curious feature frequently found in the common-sense debates. The considerations people offer in favor of a dating are not normally moral or value claims. People point to factual matters and seem to treat the dating as a factual matter. The arguments do not pretend or aspire to show that the events of the favored date involve the acquisition of some morally relevant property, some attribute (power, process, or whatever) which in itself would justify moral or legal discrimination. The reasons are reasons for classifying the entity as a human being, and the moral and legal consequences flow from affirming or denying that classification, not from the reasons for the classification itself.

This is not always so, or not always obviously so, but the main exceptions are arguments concocted by ethical theorists. Theorists sometimes argue directly for some dating by arguing for the moral relevance of some property acquired at the time; often their datings are selected explicitly on that basis. (Sometimes this aspect is ambiguous, since the dating fixes on a feature that might plausibly be thought to be itself of moral significance or, independent of its moral significance, to be a conceptually appropriate mark of membership in our species: e.g., the inception of consciousness.) But this is rarely found in pretheoretical thought.

The curious part of the public debates is that what people commonly use as reasons for *rejecting* some dating are manifestly moral considerations. The antiabortionist denies the reasonableness of the proabortionist datings by insisting that the differential properties lacked by the fetus (just) prior to the date of birth (viability, brain activity, or whatever) are not morally relevant differences at all or anyway not sufficiently significant differences to warrant the profound difference in moral and legal consequences. Conversely, the pro-choice proponent denies the reasonableness of the pro-life datings by insisting that the properties possessed by the fetus at conception (segmentation, motility, etc.) are not morally relevant properties at all or anyway not sufficiently significant to warrant the profound moral and legal consequences that flow from that dating. The proabortionist may also turn the antiabortionist's form of the argument against him to produce a reductio ad absurdum: what is lacked by the entity just before your dating of conception is not morally significant enough to deny it those moral and legal protections, so you will have to protect sperms and eggs as well. So too, the pro-life proponent turns the proabortionist ploy against him and presents the threat of a slippery slope: the properties possessed before birth are not enough for you, and the properties added by birth are not morally significant enough to begin providing the protection, so you will have to permit infanticide, and then. . . .

Such arguments can be persuasive, though each side has ways of blunting the objections directed against it. In any case, theorists aside, people do not rebut such objections by denying the propriety of that kind of moral argumentation. They do not claim, as presumably a biological taxonomist would, that a property's lack of (sufficient) moral significance is totally irrelevant to its being a necessary or sufficient condition for membership in a biological category. So an ethical theorist who sees this is likely to admit that, if such moral argumentation is allowed, then the taxonomist's efforts cannot themselves resolve the dating dispute.

The theorist is also likely to go a step further and complain that, if this is the situation, the controversy can't be kosher. He may say: "You are confused and deluded if you think that any answer you get with this kind of procedure could be some kind of objective empirical fact. Your term "human being" is not really the name of a biological species, but rather of some moral category. It's like "person" or "property" or "saint" (in some of their uses). By "human being" you evidently mean something like "member of our moral community." It's a category defined by some set of moral principles, and such principles don't define objective categories (though, of course, given some set of principles, it may be an objective fact that some entity satisfies its specification.)" But this theorist's response misdescribes the situation.

xv

The term "human being" does appear in moral principles like S. The importance of the term and of its application and its extension derives from that. Its application is debated against the background of such principles, but they do not define its intension or extension. S does require for *its* application that a human being be able to be harmed, but even a single cell is harmable.

The conflicting datings are not due to conflicting moral principles or differing conceptions of what properties are morally significant. Appearances and opponents' allegations notwithstanding, pro-choice advocates do not suppose that being in or ex utero is itself a morally relevant factor. So too, contrary to antiracist rhetoric of the last few hundred years, there is precious little evidence that racists have thought that skin pigmentation is in itself a morally sufficient reason for discrimination. White racists have thought, and quite rightly, that skin color normally evidences and is explained by membership in a particular race. It is the membership in another race—a kind differing from his kin, a kind he thinks inferior to his kin—that the racist focuses on. And, although it may not be obvious how or why that might be morally relevant, it is not such an obviously absurd idea, for, if it were, there would be no motive for the persistent misattribution of the racist's beliefs about skin color.

For animals as visually oriented as we are, skin color is no doubt a psychologically powerful fact which may well explain some aspects of racist attitudes, but the racist need not regard it as a good reason for his attitudes. So too, the fact that the fetus is hidden out of sight could hardly leave us unaffected, but those who date hominization at birth are not committed to crazy conceptions about the value of visibility.

XVI

It is also wrong to apply the label "value term" to "human being" if you have in mind any of the usual paradigms. Though "human being", like "man", does have an honorific usage, that is not the use involved here. We do praise someone for being a *real* human being, a Mensch, someone who is kind to those of his kind, just as we praise someone for being a man, manly, brave, courageous, and true. But no one is contesting whether to commend an embryo; no one is asserting or denying some virtue in fetuses.

That should be obvious, but we might be confused here since the whole abortion issue is commonly and confusingly said to be about the *value* of fetal life as compared with the value of things it might conflict with, such as the health or well-being of the mother. This talk of value rather than category invites us to model the abortion question on a question such as whether to destroy a sapling tree that threatens to obstruct the path leading from your home out into the world at large. If the sapling is your property (and assuming it impractical to transplant it elsewhere) then your question is whether you and your family value the joys of its beauty and the pleasures of caring for it and the comforts it may provide more than you value your convenience and safety. However, if the sapling belongs to your neighbor, you have no right to decide its fate on the basis of its value to you. In the abortion issue what is contested is not per se the value of the "property," but rather whose property it is: Is the fetus your neighbor whose tree of life you are cutting down?

People do speak of a human being's having a special inherent value, a value that inheres in simply being a human being. This value is unlike the value of a virtue or an artwork or a workhorse or anything else. The *conception* of value operating here is radically unlike our conception of value operating elsewhere, more radically different than people recognize. The conception is indeed of questionable coherence (and talk of this value is largely confined to modern, propter-Kantian culture). This value provides no reason for possessing or producing the things possessing this value: the world does not become a better world just by an increase in the number of human beings in it. We talk as though this value explained and justified principles like S, as though our reason for refraining from harming a human being derived from his having this value, whereas actually the attribution of value is a consequence of the rationality and categorical character of moral choices, not a precondition of them. The propriety of sacrificing one person to save the life of many in some cases and the impropriety of doing so in other cases cannot be explained on any coherent calculus of value. At any rate, a fetus acquires this value only by becoming a human being, and whether it has become one is not discoverable by checking for its possession of this value; so we cannot settle the abortion issue by any direct assessment of the value of fetal life.

XVII

I suspect that theorists misconceive the hominization debate partly because they regard the truth of the moral principle S and the truth of any dating of hominization as two separate and distinct issues which should and can be investigated in isolation from each other. They want us first to set out criteria for the term "human being" appearing in S and then do a fetal examination to see if and when it matches up.

Well, we do have criteria for that term, and generally they do just fine, but after the fetal inspection folks come to different conclusions. At this point theorists seem to be telling us that we need to reconvene the moral legislature and enact more specific principles to resolve the conflict. But that is a philosopher's fantasy: there is no such thing as enacting or adopting moral principles and no ur-position we can betake ourselves to. We find ourselves in the world regarding certain things as reasons for doing (saying, believing, wanting) other things, and among those reasons are means for improving our understanding of the world and of our reasons, and for sometimes refining, sometimes revising, sometimes rejecting them. But we don't enact, adopt, or choose our reasons.

We are not and cannot be moral legislators. At best we are competent moral judges for whom S is a given, a fixed point of our common moral-law heritage around which we deliberate the dating of hominization. Our task of classifying the fetus is adjudicatory, not an exercise in taxonomy taken on out of curiosity. Our task of classifying cannot be pried loose from practical consequences of inherently profound importance, and we would be derelict in our duty if we let ourselves be forgetful of that fact.

The correctness of our classifying and the correctness of our interpretation of the principle are not two separate questions. And, since we properly assume that the principle is valid moral law, we are bound to insist that its interpretation and application be judged by considerations of justice. Is it fair to exclude an individual from protection by this principle when it does not differ in morally significant ways from those included? Is it fair to include an individual and, thereby, heavily burden those who are certainly included, when it lacks any morally significant features? Those questions are properly and inescapably part of the classificational considerations in this case.

Does this mean that "human being" is a value term or the name of a moral category? Or does it mean that some facts in our world are framed and formed by moral principles or incomprehensible apart from our morality?[11]

---

[11]The development and refinement of this essay owes much to the charity and patience of the editors of this anthology, for which I thank them.

14
Ethics, Feminism, and Abortion
Milton Fisk

INTRODUCTION

A great source of confusion and mystification in moral philosophy in the United States today is the implicit and explicit use of the liberal theory of human nature as bedrock. This theory is associated with a view of individual rights which lies in the background of many concrete moral discussions. The course of events sometimes ignores the liberal theory, as is evident from the great movements of our time. People see their grievances as shared grievances, thus prompting them to act in solidarity with those whose roles are similar to their own.

Little motivation comes from within philosophy for philosophers to abandon points of view that can no longer serve a practical purpose. Such motivation can come only from identification with a movement outside philosophy. Philosophy can then perhaps provide a model that adds coherence to the moral patterns developing in such a movement.[1] And with that added coherence, partisans of the movement can have lifted from them the suspicion that somewhere the intellectuals of the day have justified a higher morality than that of their movement.

---

[1]Antonio Gramsci, "The Study of Philosophy," in *The Modern Prince and Other Writings,* L. Marks, trans. (New York: International Publishers, 1957), p. 63. Such interpretive models do not always come from within the movements that make use of them. After rightly criticizing Engels' subordination of the women's movement to the class movement, feminists have been able to employ Engels' idea that capitalism opens up the possibility of

To illustrate this conception of the relation of philosophy to morality, I choose the example of the feminist movement. If we are to
deal coherently with the ethical questions arising within feminism
and about feminism, a social conception of human nature needs to
replace the liberal theory of the individual. Liberal theory at* *mpts
to deal with these questions as though there were no such thing as a
feminist movement. This leads to treating formulations such as,
"Do women have rights to their own bodies as property?" and
"Does the fetus have the full range of rights of a person?" as starting places, rather than as problems arising where the points of
struggle of a group have first been identified.

Arguing that a change in the model of the individual is needed
here is, I think, a philosophical project. It is rarely the role of the
philosopher to tell a movement what it wants or what is right for it.
But, when enemies of the movement tell it that what it wants is
forbidden fruit, it is important that the movement have a response.
A movement is, after all, about the business of winning partisans,
and silence in the face of criticism will not pull people off the fence.
The opposition would like to monopolize all the models with which
legitimate discourse can operate. The availability of alternative
models is the task of the philosophy of any movement.

ORGANIZING AGAINST OPPRESSION

Liberal theory has little tolerance toward organizing for special interests. This can be seen by examining how it views conflict and
conflict resolution.

Given a multitude of independently defined centers of action
whose actual social roles are accidental in relation to what they
are—the conflicts that occur will be rooted in squabbles among
individuals. Lust, greed, ambition, and pride will set individuals on
collision courses with one another. The mechanism needed to prevent such collisions can be a third party who, without prior alle-

---

women's liberation by eliminating the patriarchal family as the unit of
production, even though in other ways it is a major obstacle to women's
liberation. And, after rightly criticizing Freud's sexism, feminists have
been able to employ his conceptions of the Oedipus and Electra complexes
to forward their understanding of male control today. On both points, see
Juliet Mitchell, *Psychoanalysis and Feminism* (New York: Pantheon, 1974).

giance to either side, has good enough sense to intervene before maximum damage is done.[2] Since such collisions are widespread and since reasonable third parties cannot be expected simply to volunteer their services, the state is formed as an overarching third party.

The state in liberal theory is, then, a neutral force protecting rights wherever they might be threatened. The sheer variety of the invasions of rights rules out the usefulness of a partisan force. After all, no organization could rightfully be dedicated to protecting the rights of women alone, for there are plenty of cases in which men's rights are invaded by women. If women set up a partisan force to protect their rights, men would form a counter organization. We would end with something more than individual squabbles between men and women; there would now be group warfare between organizations of men and organizations of women.[3] If men do seem on the whole to be more in the wrong than women, this is no reason for bypassing the state with special-interest organizations. The state was designed to limit wrongdoing without taking the side of the most frequently wronged. After all, it is not a question of who is most often wrong but of how to stop the individual squabbles. Philosophers can, it is supposed, be of help in listing the rights that individuals have. In this way the state is informed about when it should intervene to protect rights. Those rights are antecedent to the squabbles in which they are infringed.

Moreover, by taking individuals to be independently defined centers of action, liberal theory makes the whole enterprise of independent organization against oppression suspect. In the first place, the very idea of social oppression is suspect. To the ears of the

---

[2]John Rawls, *A Theory of Justice* (Cambridge, Mass.: Harvard University Press, 1971), pp. 240, 268, 336.

[3]Pluralism did, to be sure, get grafted onto liberal theory; see John Dewey, *Reconstruction in Philosophy* (Boston: Beacon Press, 1957), pp. 203–4. But there is no inherent reason for the groups recognized by pluralist theory to do battle with one another. When they do have squabbles, they submit to the adjudication of the state, the neutral power set above them. By contrast, movements against oppression do not characteristically submit to such a discipline. There will, though, be wings of most movements that push in the direction of putting pressure on the state rather than of developing a more independent form of organization.

liberal theorist it suggests the implausible idea of a relatively permanent and systematic conspiracy of the members of one group
against those of another. This implausibility follows from treating
the individual as an independently defined center of action. In contrast, if individuals are social in nature, oppression need not be said
to involve a conspiracy. It becomes thoroughly plausible within the
framework of group opposition.

In the second place, the very idea of threatening to redress
grievances through independent group action is seen as an unwar-
ranted attack on the social bond.[4] It short-circuits the process of
petitioning the state to redress grievances. The social bond depends
on the recognition of the sovereignty of the state in the handling of
disputes. If there is no satisfaction from the state, then civil disobedience is allowable. But, generally, civil disobedience implies an
acceptance of the state as sovereign even when it is fallible, slow,
and insensitive in providing redress.

Independent organization against oppression is a challenge to
this sovereignty. Independent organizations not only do not subordinate their decisions to oppressing groups but do not subordinate
them to state organizations. They need not project the overthrow of
the state, but at least they posit a dual center of political initiative
and of social and economic power.

A neutral state enveloping atomized individuals and their
squabbles is too simple a model for a society where people are organizing themselves both against oppression and for oppression. Adding to the model the liberal right to form factions fails to provide the
needed complexity. The liberal right to form political factions
amounts to no more than the right to contest control of the state
from within the established mechanisms of change of office and
representation. The Republican challenge to the Democrats in the
U.S. or the Communist challenge to the Christian Democrats in
Italy is legitimated by this right to factions. But a black movement

---

[4]John Locke, *The Second Treatise of Government*, ch. III, "Of the State of
War," #21: "Had there been any such court, and superior jurisdiction on
earth, to determine the right between Jephthah and the Ammonites, they
had never come to a state of war; but we see he was forced to appeal to
heaven . . . and then prosecuting and relying on his appeal, he leads out
his army to battle."

and a feminist movement are not legitimated by this liberal right. Still, many influential members of these movements, as well as many influential people with no sympathy for these movements, have done all in their power to bring these movements within the established mechanisms, where they would be legitimated by the liberal right to factionalize.

THE RIGHT TO ORGANIZE AGAINST SEXUAL OPPRESSION

The right to organize for any purpose is to be considered in light of the interests of a group. It is not derivative from the rights of individuals in a state of nature. But it is not a right that conflicts with what people in the group are. They are what they are as members of this group, and its interests are among the interests its members have. There are lots of problems about how wide and how narrow groups of the sort relevant to morality can be. Instead of dealing with those problems, it is best here to concentrate on the main lines of the difference with liberal theory.

Suppose the grievances that women have with individual men are treated as local squabbles, instead of as part of a pattern of grievances. A man's beating his wife would then be merely an instance of the schema "Person x beats person y." His beating her is treated as just another beating. The wife might, from this perspective, just as well have beaten the man, had she been as angry and had she thought to grab the poker in order to stun him first. And so it seems that one should not take the side of one gender in these squabbles, but only attempt to prevent them or prevent them from going to dangerous extremes.

We think we know why such interpretations are inadequate. For it seems clear that many men believe that society gives them control over their wives. They exercise this control in many matters without any sanction from society. And, if they cannot control their wives to their satisfaction, who is to tell them that they cannot subdue them by violence? The society may interfere at this point, but the ambivalence of the interference reflects the wide recognition that a man has control over his wife. Thus the wife did not grab the poker to stun him and then beat him senseless. Since she did not have control over him, her anger expressed itself rather in hysterical shouting or sobbing.

Shelters for abused women exist not because women are merely an identifiable segment of all those in the population who get beaten, but because abused women are victims of efforts to enforce male control. The organization of those shelters is an organization against aspects of male control, insofar as shelters allow women and their children to escape male control when it is enforced with violence.

This will serve as an illustration of the kind of thing I am driving at when I say that liberal theory has trouble seeing beyond local squabbles. To say that wife beating reflects social oppression is to cease to view the man and his wife as independently defined centers of action. One must see them both as actors within a system of male control. Many men become members of the dominant group in that system, and many women become members of the dominated group in that system. Actors so defined can do more than engage in local squabbles; their conflicts need to be understood as part of a pattern of conflicts. These actors are only acting out who they are in the system of male control when they attempt to organize either as oppressors or as the oppressed. In so doing, they join with those like them to struggle against the counterforce of the other group. The asocial individuals of liberal theory are not distinguished by such conflicting roles, and thus they would be organizing against their own kind if they did more than organize a neutral state as a power outside themselves.

The idea that the state is neutral seems plausible when it is counterposed to individuals and their isolated squabbles. But once we have said that the society includes a system of domination within which one group is decidedly dominant, the neutral state looks less plausible. Relative to the power of the neutral state, individuals are supposed to be equal. Yet the forces supporting male control are not in general equal before the state to those against it. The state itself acts in a patriarchal fashion. The welfare state relates to its recipients as fathers do to their children and dependents. And, without continuing pressure from women, the state does little to shake entrenched standards of male control. The lack of neutrality is to be found counterfactually in what would remain in the absence of a determined struggle.[5] So, with the abandonment of the liberal

---

[5] Nicos Poulantzas, *Classes in Contemporary Capitalism*, D. Fernbach, trans. (London: Verso, 1978), p. 161.

model of individual and conflict, the liberal model of the state crumbles.

This analysis clears the obstacles placed by liberal theory in the way of a right to organize independently against male control. Since the state leans toward perpetuating social oppression, independent organization to overcome oppression—through a challenge to the state's role as resolver of conflicts—is thoroughly warranted. Not relying on the state breaks no social bond that was not already broken.

The acid test for any kind of organizing, such as the setting up of shelters, is whether it contributes to the interests of the oppressed group. The characteristic thing about *an oppressed group* is that its members get what is required to satisfy their basic needs only by accepting conditions which are imposed by another group and which impede the realization of other aspects of what those in the oppressed group are. Workers get their livelihood only if they accept the necessity of producing a surplus for the owners. Women can get companionship in the family, a livelihood in the workplace, and benefits from the state only if they accept the decisions of men and the secondary social and economic status that results from this. To make claim to what they get without accepting the imposed conditions is rebellion and an assertion of the right to liberation.

Once people only half perceive the possibility of obtaining what they need without paying the price of conditions imposed by another group, they will begin, however tentatively, to organize against their oppression. This may be self-destructive in the absence of a clear vision of the path. But, once rage has been combined with a conception of where it is possible to take the struggle without disastrous defeats, an internal morality begins to take shape within the movement of the oppressed itself. And one of the first clear precepts of such a morality is that there is a right to organize independently against oppression.

Who is obliged to recognize this right? How is it frequently denied? On what does the right rest? If, as I contend, the right rests on the interests of the group or, equivalently, on what those in the group are, then its validity does not depend on its confirmation by other groups, unless of course their interests are tied up with the interests of the given oppressed group. It is, for example, necessary for the men in the working class to recognize the right of women to organize against male control. Without this recognition the solidarity needed for overcoming exploitation will be impossible.[6] The struggle to overcome sexism is, then, part of the class struggle. It is not a problem at the edge of the class struggle, to be dealt with at some later time when male workers find it convenient.

The right-wing movement of the 1980s in the United States wishes to deny women the right to organize against their oppression. It sees its interests as tied to continuing male domination. It then violates no right and hence misses no obligation in rejecting independent organization by women. Attributing such an obligation to the right wing would have no practical effect anyway. This movement senses that social control is effective only under conditions of stability, yet to allow liberation in one area would lead to its spilling over in another. It wants a stable system of "growth"— growth through reproduction in the family, exploitation in the workplace, and rolling back communism in the world. Domination over workers, women, minorities, and other states is, then, a seamless system. To say that the right wing is wrong in failing to grant a right to independent organization by the oppressed is merely to say that *from the point of view of the oppressed* there should not be any oppressors.[7]

The anti-feminist "right to life" movement is not an instance of independent organization against oppression. It is neither against women's oppression nor independent. It is clearly subordinate to male-dominated groups of the right-wing movement.[8] The American feminist movement is itself divided between currents favoring independent organization and others tending to fold the move-

---

[6]Compare the analogous thesis about the right of oppressed nations to organize in V. I. Lenin, "The Right of Nations to Self-determination," *Collected Works* (Moscow: Progress Publishers, 1964), vol. 20, pp. 395–454.

[7]What is of practical significance is the reluctance of much of the left really to believe that women have the right to organize independently of men and of the institutions men have dominated. It is of practical significance since there are ways of demonstrating that this reluctance is plainly counter to the best interests of the groups the left takes itself to be representing. See my "Feminism, Socialism, and Historical Materialism," *Praxis International,* II (1982): 117–40.

[8]Deirdre English, "The War against Choice," *Mother Jones* (February/March, 1981): 16–32.

ment into mainstream politics. Among basically independent
movements—the Polish Solidarity movement, the Palestine liberation movement, the Salvadorean liberation movement—it is usually
possible to find both currents.

THE RIGHT TO CHOOSE

The issue of abortion becomes public through struggle. The rise of
the women's movement in the 1960s brought it to the fore, and now
the right-wing backlash keeps it there. Even liberal theorists have
taken to writing about the problem in these periods, though they
write about it as an eternal question. The connection between feminism and abortion is, though, not accidental; for a woman's right to
choose is counterposed to the male's right to make choices for her.

If our model switches from persons as independently defined
centers of action to persons as in important ways group-defined
centers of action, then what had been thought of as rights based on
the universal feature of being a person become rights based on
being a person in a certain group. The effect of making this switch
is frequently canceled by harmonistic assumptions about groups.
On the one hand, it is admitted that the model of a person in liberal
theory is an abstraction, but, on the other hand, it is claimed to be
a useful abstraction, since individuals of the major groups of a society have complementary rather than conflicting interests.

These harmonistic assumptions are of a piece with the liberal
theory of the neutral state. They limit inevitable conflicts to local
affairs, whereas social conflicts are to be resolved by conversation
between groups. It is not claimed that at any given time there is
harmony, but it is proposed, for example, by Jürgen Habermas[9] and
Richard Rorty,[10] that conversation can be pursued between the parties till it is evident that the further we go in dialogue the more the
motives for a fight are alleviated. This is traditionally the tactic

---

[9]"On Systematically Distorted Communication," *Inquiry*, XIII (1970):
205–218; "Toward a Theory of Communicative Competence," *ibid.*,
360–75.

[10]"Pragmatism, Relativism, and Irrationalism," Presidential Address,
Eastern Division American Philosophical Association, December 1979,
part III; reprinted in Rorty's *The Consequences of Pragmatism* (Minneapolis:
University of Minnesota Press, 1983).

of the party that holds all the cards. But occasionally it is the expression of the naiveté of the weaker party, as when in 1979 the National Organization of Women sought to reason with the right-to-lifers over the issue of attacking abortion clinics.

Is there a way of choosing between the practice of the harmonizers and that of those who fight against oppression? Presumably some moral principle will enable us to make this choice if the choice is not arbitrary. It is indeed not arbitrary, but there is no moral principle for the job that stands above groups. Those in an oppressed group will have a morality, more or less articulate, that condemns deals with the oppressor which compromise the goal of liberation. Movements against the oppressor will come and go against the background of an implicit understanding that some way out of the system of oppression must be used.[11] The existence of such a morality is a factional threat, but it is not a bit less legitimate for that. A philosophical model merely puts this legitimacy on a footing that makes sense to the practitioner of the morality of the oppressed.

The morality of the harmonizers also has a historical basis, however much it would like to claim a timeless pedigree. It is the morality of the cultural, political, religious, economic, and educational institutions dedicated to ensuring that the dominant social order is not destabilized. The existence of such a morality is a threat to factional movements. Through its institutional dissemination it exists, alongside the morality of the oppressed, in the oppressed themselves. Ultimately it is a morality that serves the interests of oppressing groups, since its universalistic form serves to limit protest from oppressed groups to issues affecting a "common good."

A moral philosophy linked with the cause of the oppressed has, then, a relativist thrust. When a universalist culture puts itself forward as a higher culture, a philosophy of the oppressed needs to point out that the place of harmonizing universalist ideas is itself a historical place. It needs to reiterate that this place is found alongside other historical places and has a validity that is local despite its universalist form. This relativist thrust gains some plausibility if we look at the way in which institutions supposedly representing universalist interests treat abortion.

---

[11]Simone de Beauvoir, *The Second Sex,* H. M. Parshley, trans. (New York: Vintage, 1974), p. 546.

According to *Genesis* women are deservedly an oppressed group. The weakness of Eve was the source of patriarchy, since God gave husbands the right to rule over their wives because of Eve's eating of the forbidden fruit. Henceforth the lot of woman would be to have her childbirths multiplied and made sorrowful. The rights of God's children were then decided by Him in typical patriarchal fashion.

The U.S. Supreme Court has consistently seen the protection of potential life as a legitimate concern of the various states. Its interpretation of what this concern implies has changed. In *Roe v. Wade* in 1973, the Court ruled that abortion was a constitutional right, but it gave the states the right to regulate or prescribe third-trimester abortions, in view of their interest in potential life. A woman's medical need was, though, allowed precedence over the state's interest in potential life in the second trimester. And no restrictions were placed on abortions in the first trimester. But, in 1977, the Court ruled that individual states could refuse to fund nontherapeutic abortions. And, in 1980, in *Harris v. McRae*, the Court upheld the Hyde Amendment, passed in Congress in 1976; federal funds could be used for abortions only in cases of rape, incest, and danger to the mother's life. This left it open to the states to withdraw matching funds in all but these cases. The argument was that the states' interests in protecting potential life was more important than equal protection of the right to choose as between rich and poor women. The rights of women are decided here by a male-controlled court to be limited by male-controlled states.

But, if women's oppression is not the price of original sin, if women are not children of the courts, if, in short, women's rights are not to be defined by male-dominated institutions, and if universalism cannot function except as a vehicle for men so long as men are the oppressors, then there is no obstacle in the way of seeing women as having a right to fight in a manner consistent with their liberation. The right to choose on reproductive matters is central in this fight. So long as the interests of states, the dictates of the Church, certification by doctors, or obedience to a husband is allowed to override the interests of women in the choices of reproduction, there is cooperation with the structures of male dominance.

In the United States in the nineteenth century, it was the efforts of doctors to expand their control to reproductive matters that was

behind the antiabortion movement.[12] Midwives had regularly performed abortions; medical practice had to be snatched away from
them. With 73 percent of American Catholics thinking that abortion should be legal in all or at least some circumstances in 1977,
the National Conference of Catholic Bishops thought it necessary to
involve the Church in lobbying for a "Human Life Amendment" to
the U.S. Constitution and to make the Church the major institutional and financial force behind local and national right-to-life
committees. The amendment was introduced into both houses of
Congress in January 1981, but so far has gone nowhere.

The right to choose on reproductive matters is incorrectly represented by its critics as a matter of selfish individualism. With this
it has little to do. It is a matter of women who identify themselves as
members of an oppressed gender saying that, whether they choose
in individual cases to have an abortion or not, unless they are allowed to make this choice they will be denied other choices that are
crucial to their liberation. To let Justice Potter Stewart, who wrote
the Court's position in *Harris v. McRae,* or Pope John Paul II, who
spoke against abortion during his American trip, decide about
abortion is to let men determine the outcome of efforts for child care
and for women's gaining equal status in the church.

It is not just that these things are linked. Reproductive choices
are where it all starts: they determine the capitalist's next-
generation labor force, the bishop's next-generation flock, the husband's heir and pride, and the state's new taxpayers. Naturally, the
thinking male supremacist is not going to agree to the idea that
mere women should be handed this key to the future of the ever-so-
painstakingly constructed man's world. It is difficult to see, then,
how a feminist movement could consistently neglect the fight for the
right to choose in all reproductive matters.

In sum, women have the right to choose an abortion. This right
is based on several things. At the concrete level, it is based on the

---

[12] *Women under Attack: Abortion, Sterilization Abuse, and Reproductive Freedom,*
Committee for Abortion Rights and against Sterilization Abuse, PO Box
124, Cathedral Station, New York, N.Y., 10025, 1979, Chapter III. In-
credibly, the right-to-life ideologue John T. Noonan, Jr., in *A Private Choice*
(New York: Free Press, 1979), p. 52, takes Dr. Horatio R. Stoner's 1859
AMA statement against "snuffing out life in the making" at face value.

key role the right to choose has among other rights women are struggling for. At a more general level, it is based on the way the morality of an oppressed group is formed by the goal of liberation for that group. That group takes precedence as regards morality over others—the church, the state, the medical profession, the nation. Such a precedence looks like a step backward from the standpoint of a universalist culture. For it accords privileges to particular interests over the universal interests of some qualified elite or of humanity itself. Here is precisely where the battle over philosophical models occurs.

The liberal version of universalist culture holds out for a uniformity in human nature which makes any kind of particularism in morality rest on what is contingent and accidental in people. This model of human nature leads to a call for a mechanism for adjusting conflict that treats all parties to the conflict as equals. One such mechanism is the neutral state; another is dialogue.

In contrast, the group model of human nature presented here considers some failures of universality to be based on what people truly are rather than on what is accidental to them. From the perspective of this model, the morality of a group fighting oppression can be valid, not because it might be universal, but because it properly interprets the interests of that group in winning liberation. This model is useful for purposes of understanding the liberal theory in its various forms. It sees liberal theory as useful to those who have some stake in making oppression only an accidental fact about those who are oppressed. The needs of the oppressed can then wait until the neutral state or dialogue becomes effective in satisfying them.

THE RIGHT TO LIFE

One approach to the problem of abortion is to treat the matter, as we have just done, from a group perspective. From the perspective of women as a group seeking liberation, the fetus may have no right to life. But let us return for the moment to treating the problem of abortion in the absence of any consideration of groups. Appeal will be made directly to the rights of persons. All persons will then have rights which women in their struggle must respect. In particular, if the fetus is a person, he or she has rights that cannot be subordinated to the liberation of women. We shall find that, upon application of this nongroup view, difficulties emerge which lead us back to the group model.

A right in one person is usually thought to imply support from other persons. Otherwise a right is no more than a permission to do something. With a right to life the fetus has a call upon others to support his or her life. In particular, the fetus has a call upon the mother to the use of her body until he or she becomes independently viable. One of the fuzzy facts about a right is, though, that, even with widespread recognition of the right, there is unclarity about *how much* others must sacrifice in order to provide the called-for support.

Judith Jarvis Thompson has dramatized the issue of the degree of sacrifice with her hypothetical plugged-in violinist whose life depends on his blood being run through someone else's kidneys. How much support does the violinist's right to life demand? Must someone spend the rest of his/her life plugged in to the violinist to support his life? Thompson and both her critics and supporters have intuitions to offer in profusion, but they have no systematic way of answering the question about the degree of sacrifice.[13] It won't do here to counterpose a presumptive right of the mother to the use of her own body. This only adds another right to the list, and adding it doesn't tell us how it is to be weighed against the fetus's right to life.

If we limit considerations to individuals taken by themselves, there seems to be no basis for saying what the degree of support for a right should be. Should the degree of support I give be such that it does not inconvenience me? Should it be such that it is compatible with my life plan? My convenience seems a lame excuse for avoiding the sacrifices required to protect the rights of others. And an individual whose life plan could be defined without relation to any group would, at least from a naturalist view of ethics, fail to fall within the domain of the moral. A duty to support the rights of others would not apply to such a being.

On the group model for human nature and morality, the way sacrifices to protect rights would affect groups becomes relevant.[14] A right exists when to deny it would be incompatible with the interests characteristic of the group relative to which there is the right. And

---

[13]"A Defense of Abortion," *Philosophy and Public Affairs*, 1 (1971): 47–66.

[14]See my *Ethics and Society* (New York: N.Y.U. Press, 1980), p. 203.

it must be supported when not doing so would go against those interests. But there are limits to the degree of support, limits to be defined in terms of these group interests. When giving support calls for sacrifices that would be a greater setback to the group than would result from giving no support, we have reached those limits.

Of course, there must be some way to identify interests characteristic of a group. This will be no easy job for any group, owing in large part to group overlappings and to the ideology promoted by official institutions. Women will be divided by class, by religion, by race, and by politics. There will be no consensus on feminist issues among women, just as there is no consensus within the working class on class issues. Despite the overlappings, women from all groups have participated in movements that have recognized the oppression of women. Those movements—the women's rights and suffrage movement of the late nineteenth and the early twentieth centuries and the liberation movement beginning in the 1960s—overcame some of the divisions through struggle around concrete issues. In those struggles a wide sense of the need to eliminate sexual oppression caught hold and for a time did not lose its grip, even after the struggles subsided and backlash eroded commitment.

It is in the context of struggles focusing on sources of oppression that consciousness of interests develops. Struggles that do not focus on sources of oppression but pit women allied with their oppressors against other women will not have the same potential for revealing group interests. The interests characteristic of a group are to be decided not abstractly but in conjunction with struggle against oppression. The moral philosopher must look to these struggles, rather than to moral intuitions acquired in isolation from those struggles, in attempting to decide what sacrifices have to be made to protect rights.

There are limits to the degree of sacrifice that must be made for the fetus's right to life. What those limits are will depend on the group relative to which those limits are to be determined. When that group is the female gender, those limits are determined on the basis of the goal of overthrowing male control. If what is sacrificed by a general policy of supporting the fetus's right to life is the ability of women to carry on an effective struggle against male control, then they have gone beyond what is required. Going beyond what is required to support the fetus will lead many women to accept the responsibilities of motherhood in a society in which men still refuse an equal share in child rearing, will lead many women to accept the financial responsibility for child rearing when they cannot afford adequate medical care, housing, and child care, and will lead many women to accept the traditional family simply because the single mother finds it difficult to survive on the low-paying jobs open to her.

Childbearing in the circumstances many women find themselves in today thus puts women in a position that strengthens the power of men over them. If this is the case for a large number of women, as it surely is, then it will tend to strengthen male control as an overall institution. Thus it is in the interests of women generally, insofar as they are opposed to male control, to support the right of women to choose whether they will carry a fetus to term or not. This does not mean that the right choice will be made in every case, but that women have the right to decide how far to go in supporting the life of the fetus on the basis of their interests as women.

This argument still holds in the case of the viable fetus. Medical technology has pushed the point of viability to earlier and earlier stages of pregnancy. So the right to abortion becomes more and more restricted if only the nonviable fetus may be aborted. Yet the argument above disallows such a restriction. Whether the fetus could survive a premature delivery or not leaves unchanged the fact that, under circumstances faced by many women today, childbearing strengthens the power of men over them. Putting up the neonate for adoption does not solve this problem. For male control is maintained by women's being forced to deliver a viable fetus and to undergo the wrenching experience of giving it away. Is this compulsion still illegitimate if the viable fetus has a right to life? This question takes us back to the issue of the limits on sacrifices for protecting rights. Those sacrifices need not be made if they set back the struggle against male control.[15]

I turn now to another issue about sacrifices for rights. Some liberal philosophers have claimed that the sacrifices to be made for the life of the fetus are to be greater when the mother is responsible for the pregnancy. The sorts of matters thought to reduce this responsibility are the condom's breaking or intercourse while under

---

[15]Mary Anne Warren, "On the Moral and Legal Status of Abortion" and "Postscript on Infanticide," in J. P. Sterba, ed., *Morality in Practice* (Belmont, Calif.: Wadsworth, 1984), p. 153.

the influence of alcohol. Joel Feinberg helpfully lists a spectrum of responsibility, beginning with rape and ending with a joint decision to have a child.[16] But, like other moral concepts, the concept of responsibility cannot be treated apart from groups.[17]

Those forces in society which want to reinforce the male-dominated family, which want women to constitute a cheap labor force, and which do not want to take responsibility for making child rearing less a burden for women find it convenient to say that, except in cases of physical coercion, the woman is responsible for her pregnancy and thus should go through with it. Their sense of the meaning of responsibility derives from the realization that they would be threatened with the realization of many of the ideals of women's liberation if the woman did not take responsibility for her pregnancy. They do not hold consistently to this sense of responsibility on all occasions. Individual men will urge abortions on their girl friends when they want to avoid financial responsibility for the offspring of short-term relationships. But some of the same men would be outraged if their wives unilaterally decided to abort their potential heirs.

From the perspective of the struggle against male control, responsibility looks quite different. From this perspective there is a variety of ways in which the woman's responsibility for the dependent unborn person is reduced. It must be recognized that the mother alone cannot always meet the needs of the fetus and the neonate. The surrounding society must provide some support. When the mother herself is needy, the society can provide pregnancy care, decent conditions for childbirth, and a promise of adequate conditions for child rearing. In addition, the surrounding society must avoid restricting the woman's freedom. Wanting the child before the pregnancy should not result from an ideology that makes motherhood the chief role of the woman. Equally, the pregnancy should not be the result of social circumstances that make companionship with children born out of wedlock preferable to the domination of male partners. All these things affect the degree of responsibility of the mother for the dependent fetus. When the soci-

---

[16]"Abortion," in T. Regan, ed., *Matters of Life and Death* (New York: Random House, 1980), pp. 212–13.

[17]See my *Ethics and Society,* pp. 194–96.

ety fails to take its share of the responsibility and when it constrains the woman to seek motherhood, she can rightly refuse to take full responsibility for the fetus's life.

Saying that the woman is responsible for the life of the fetus she has got through voluntary sex is, then, a form of guilt-tripping. If the society can exist only through being reproduced and if it promotes its existence with the cult of motherhood, then it shares responsibility with the mother for the life of the fetus. A male-dominated society will still tell the woman she has full responsibility for seeing that the fetus is carried to term. For the woman, the only way to avoid taking most of the responsibility is, in many cases, to have an abortion. Representative Hyde, whose amendment cutting off federal funds for most abortions was supported by the Supreme Court, has supported bills to cut the Food Stamp Program and to cut back decent public housing.[18] His view would have to be that pregnancies resulting from voluntary sex impose no responsibility on society, but considerable responsibility on the woman. The interesting thing is that liberal philosophers fall right in with this atomized view of responsibility because they do not take the point of view of women as a group in determining responsibility to the fetus. Liberal theory was not designed to support factional causes, and it is no wonder that it has such limited success when used on women's issues.

CONCLUSION

Philosophy as I have spoken of it here is not speculative in the sense that nothing is ever done with it. Yet it is not practical in the sense that it would be merely the application of good sense to thinking about knotty problems. It stands in the middle as interpretive. It involves the proposal of a model about human nature that might itself be put to speculative uses, but is in fact used to interpret writing and action that has come from the women's movement. Using the model to interpret that writing and action involves show-

---

[18]*Women under Attack*, chapter V. In response to this type of argument, Noonan contrives the following sophism: "The liberty [to abort] is oppressive to the poor. Its existence has led to depriving the pregnant poor of assistance for their independent unborn children" (*A Private Choice*, p. 190).

ing how their parts fall into place when looked at in terms of the model.

Women are asking for something that pertains to them as women; specifically they are asking for the ability to determine their lives as producers of new life. A model of human nature as determined by groups and, derivatively, a model of morality as relative to groups would seem to be helpful in this context. It provides a unity that the liberal theory of human nature cannot provide for the women's movement. That movement is not about civil rights, at which the liberal theory is moderately good. It is not just about human rights because part of it is about the right to organize against the sectors of humanity defending male-supremacist institutions and part of it is about women as the reproducers of life.

What the relations between men and women might be as male control sinks to extinction is a matter of speculation until the struggle develops further. But as far as the present stage of the struggle is concerned, it is being suggested here that it would be fruitful for the women's movement to recognize the limitations of interpreting itself in terms of liberal theory and the advantages of interpreting itself in terms of the group model of human nature. The continuity of the movement and the development of its perspective depends on the presence of some unifying model at this general level. Otherwise the movement is condemned after lulls to bring itself to life again by piecing together random new bits from the history of oppression in the absence of any foundation. The critique of old models like the liberal one will have to be redone, and momentum will build up without a clear direction.

15

Ideal Taxation*

Lawrence C. Becker

Vain is the word of a philosopher which does not heal any suffering of man. For just as there is no profit in medicine if it does not expel the diseases of the body, so there is no profit in philosophy either, if it does not expel the suffering of the mind.

Epicurus, *Fragments*

People ask me, if I were on a desert island, what one cosmetic would I take. My usual answer is a blusher—although, if I were on a desert island, I'd be tan.

Cheryl Tiegs, *Parade Magazine*

Moral philosophy is in constant danger of sliding into absurdity. If it rejects the epigraph from Epicurus, it runs the risk of being a mere pastime—more closely related to chess than to medicine. If it accepts that epigraph, it risks an overweening ambition—which hopes for too tight a connection between theory and practice, for example, or which wants philosophers to be kings. Philosophy must

---

*This paper was drafted over ten years ago and put into its present form in 1982. I still stand by its eccentric results, but if I were to rewrite the paper today I would—in addition to taking account of recent legislative developments—replace much of its syncretistic theoretical argument with an account of why the moral requirement of reciprocity supports these conclusions about taxation.

For discussion and bibliographical help, I owe thanks to Thomas Edwards, Richard Epstein, Mary Houska, and the participants in Rice University's 1978 conference on justice, equality, and the distribution of wealth.

be more like medicine than like chess, else its self-estimate and somber tones for the last 2500 years have been pretentious absurdities. But it must also be more like basic science than like medicine, else its claim to be distinct from ordinary deliberation is false. (When philosophers forget the distinctly theoretical nature of their enterprise—and still try to give professional advice—the result is usually something like the second epigraph.)

Moral philosophy can do better than that. Without application it is pointless, and without theory it is powerless; so it must have both. The best theory accommodates itself to the requirements of practice; the best practice accommodates itself to the requirements of theory.

This essay explores the requirements of theory for practice. I take some principles on which competing moral theories agree and apply those principles to a topic moral philosophers usually ignore. The results are somewhat surprising and adequately illustrate, I hope, the legitimacy of this form of applied ethics.

TAX THEORY: GENERAL REMARKS

Since the late nineteenth century, political philosophers have left most of the details of tax theory to economists, lawyers, and politicians. Philosophers of a libertarian or anarchist bent have continued to address themselves to the general justifiability of taxation and, along with others, to the question of what sorts of tax-supported public programs can be justified. But discussions of equally fundamental topics, such as the forms and limits of taxation, have all but disappeared from philosophic literature.[1]

---

[1]There are, for example, only three indexed references to taxation in the *Philosopher's Index* since 1967. There is no indexed reference to taxation or to the theory of public finance in *The Encyclopedia of Philosophy* (New York: Collier-Macmillan, 1967). In part this is due to the Balkanization of academic fields. In a perfectly good sense of the term, anyone who writes on the theory of public finance is a philosopher. Similarly, political essayists often make sustained philosophical arguments on these matters. But, in terms of "professional" philosophy, my point remains true. An example: at its December 1979 meetings the American Philosophical Association offered a symposium on taxation; the main paper was by an economist.

This neglect has been a serious mistake. Experts in public finance proceed unchallenged with a highly contestable assumption: that "equity" is simply one element in the list of desiderata for an ideal tax.[2] (The other elements in the standard list are administrative efficiency, adequacy of the tax base, and neutrality or nonneutrality of economic impact.) Technical discussion of ideal taxation simply assumes the legitimacy of taxation *per se* and then asks what sort of tax would be ideal. Equity naturally appears as one of the elements of the ideal. (After all, who would claim that an *inequitable* tax was ideal?) The problem is that, when equity is regarded as *only one* of the characteristics of an ideal tax, it looks as though it could justifiably be compromised on behalf of any of the others—compromised to get the best overall mix. Thus it is that we find staunch defenders of progressive taxation who admit that sales taxes are regressive, but are willing to vote for them because they are so easy to collect.

I conclude here that such trade-offs are wrong. I argue that both of the equity principles in the theory of public finance (proportioning tax burdens to ability to pay and to benefits received) are actually indispensable conditions of the moral justification of taxation *per se*. If this is so, then equity cannot be compromised on behalf (say) of efficiency. To do so is simply to construct an efficient but unjustifiable tax. If I am correct, this has startling consequences for tax theory.

In brief, those consequences are as follows. First, contrary to what is implicit in some current accounts, the benefit and ability-to-pay principles (the two equity principles) do not stand in opposition to each other. Second, the equity principles are necessary conditions for justifiable taxation, whereas the other standard elements of the ideal tax are mere desiderata. (This much is the burden of the argument in section II.) Finally, on the basis of the results of section II, I argue in section III that only an individual-expenditure tax is clearly justifiable. Sales taxes, property taxes,

---

[2]For example, one of the standard texts in public finance does this: R. A. Musgrave and P. B. Musgrave, *Public Finance in Theory and Practice*, 2nd ed. (New York: McGraw Hill, 1976), pp. 210–11; hereafter, Musgrave and Musgrave. Richard Posner does the same in *Economic Analysis of Law*, 2nd ed. (Boston: Little Brown, 1977), pp. 371–72.

corporate-expenditure or income taxes, and *ad valorem* taxes are in principle *un*justifiable.

It should be noted that user taxes (such as the tax on gasoline) present special problems and that the choice of the expenditure tax over the income tax is a very close call. But if the argument of the paper is sound, the consequences (in moral theory) for tax policy are sweeping nonetheless.

My conclusion in favor of the expenditure tax is not novel, of course, even among recent writers. (Nicholas Kaldor believed in part of it.[3]) But in the current intellectual climate it is certainly eccentric—and on its face naive. The fact that it appears so is entirely due, I think, to neglect of some important considerations in the justification of taxation *per se*.

Definitions and Method

I shall treat the problem of justifying taxation *per se* as a special case of the problem of justifying nonvoluntary social obligations. By an *obligation* I shall mean a normative requirement on conduct, rather than merely a value or an ideal for it. By a *social* obligation I shall mean an obligation designed to benefit all the members of the group that generates it. Membership obligations, the duties of citizenship, and familial obligations are good examples. By a *nonvoluntary* obligation I mean simply an obligation imposed without regard to whether the bearer wants or has consented to it.

There are, of course, cases in which people want to pay or explicitly contract to pay taxes. These voluntary tax obligations present different and interesting justificatory problems of their own. But to confine the discussion of ideal taxation to those cases is to confine oneself far too narrowly. The problem of nonvoluntary obligations is the more difficult problem and, with respect to taxation, by far the more important. Most taxes are collected without regard to people's desire to pay or explicit agreement to pay.

I shall not, however, tackle the entire problem of nonvoluntary obligation. I want to show only that the principles of equitable taxation are necessary components of any plausible strategy for justifying such obligations. By *plausible strategies* I mean utilitarian,

---

[3]Nicholas Kaldor, *An Expenditure Tax* (London: Allen & Unwin, 1955); hereafter, Kaldor.

contractarian, and natural-rights theories. I leave aside collectivist, natural-order, divine-order, and divine-right approaches. (If these other theories work at all, I am confident they will generate the same equitable principles. I simply do not think they show much promise of working—at least in terms of current standards of philosophical rigor. That is why I do not consider them here.)

A final word about method. An essay like this cannot do much to resolve the conflict between competing moral theories. As it happens, I do not believe that the conflict *can* be resolved; I believe that each of the major types of theory is necessarily incomplete and that we should spend at least as much theoretical effort on finding ways to coordinate the theories as we do on elaborating new versions of each one. But that is another story. The fact is that competing ethical theories agree on many principles for conduct. What I shall do here is describe one such area of agreement and show its consequences for tax theory. It will not be a case of shoring up one bad argument with others. It will rather be a case of showing that, whatever our final judgment may be on the relative merits of these theories, the consequences for tax theory (at least the consequences discussed here) will be unchanged.

NECESSARY CONDITIONS FOR JUST TAXATION

Moral theories converge at two points relevant to tax policy: (a) they impose obligations only on those competent to carry them out, and (b) they try to provide compensatory benefits scaled to the sacrifices imposed on obligation bearers. These two convergence points define requirements, rather than mere desiderata, for nonvoluntary obligations—and these are joint requirements rather than substitutable alternatives. With respect to tax theory, they yield the principles called *ability to pay* and *benefits received,* respectively.

Fair warning: The thesis that the ability-to-pay and benefit principles are *joint* requirements is just as important and just as controversial as the thesis that they are requirements rather than desiderata. The two principles have often been treated as competing alternatives—alternatives that support radically different choices in tax policy. (The benefit principle, for example, favors user taxes; the ability-to-pay principle is associated with the graduated income tax.) I cannot, however, find any basis in moral theory for thinking that the two principles are competing alternatives.

Utilitarian Theory and Nonvoluntary Obligation

The controlling concern of utility theory is aggregate welfare. Every act, every social policy or practice must ultimately meet the test of being the best choice available for maximizing welfare. Obligations are no exception. Whether *any* are justifiable, and if so which, must be answered in the same way that all other moral questions are answered—by considering the consequences. Obligations must produce a net balance of favorable consequences for aggregate welfare.

The question is, Can they do so? Can it ever maximize welfare to obligate people to do things that they never consented to do or wanted to do? I shall assume here that the answer is Yes—that is, that some acceptable version of utilitarianism will justify some nonvoluntary obligations (such as the obligation not to commit murder). What I will argue is only that, in order to meet the test of utility, any nonvoluntary obligation must also satisfy two subsidiary (necessary) conditions—called the *possibility rule* and the *compensation rule,* respectively.

The Possibility Rule

In most cases it clearly makes no sense, in terms of utility, to impose obligations on people which are impossible for those people to fulfill. Obligate me to fly to the moon if you like, but it will do no good. Such obligations, when beyond one's power to fulfill, are unjustifiable. Some utility will be lost in the process of imposing the obligations and will not be recovered by getting benefits from the successful performance of the obligations, so there will be a net loss of aggregate welfare. Satisfaction of the possibility rule, then—the rule that people are never obligated to do the impossible—seems a necessary condition of any workable utilitarian theory of obligation.

The only apparent difficulty with the rule is raised by the issue of indirect benefits. Granted that we will not get "direct" benefits from imposing impossible obligations, are there not times when we realize indirect benefits? Strict-liability rules, for example, may have utility either as loss-distribution arrangements (e.g., as in no-fault accident insurance) or as general deterrents. If vendors, for example, know that selling liquor to minors will be punished no matter how innocent the circumstances, they are likely to be much more careful about all their sales. And that indirectly realized benefit may be worth the cost. Further, setting impossible tasks for ourselves or others may be instructive or useful in developing our abilities. (Think of an athlete setting an impossible goal.) If so, they too might be worth the cost. Such cases appear to violate the possibility rule.

They do not, however. Strict-liability rules have utility, after all, only where it is possible for people either to absorb the cost of violations or to eliminate their exposure to the risk of liability. Consider: in loss-distribution cases, there can be no utilitarian advantage in imposing costs on people who cannot pay. And in general deterrence cases, there is no point in imposing strict liability unless people in general can take steps to reduce their exposure to risk. (That is the indirect benefit one seeks in imposing such obligations.) So although it may not be possible, at a given level of risk, to fulfill such an obligation, it must be possible to avoid that level of risk. Strict-liability rules therefore meet the test of possibility. Similarly, I submit that imposing impossible tasks as a way of teaching or achieving (indirectly) other goals has utility only in very special circumstances. I can think of cases in which impossible *goals* or *standards* can be productive, and even cases (though this begins to strain the imagination) in which impossible *voluntary* obligations might have utility. But the usefulness of imposing impossible *non*voluntary *social* obligations seems extremely remote. Certainly taxation would not be such a case. Requiring more from people than they can possibly pay simply leads to failure to collect, evasion, or rebellion. Simple failure to collect is not cost-effective. And though evasion and rebellion might have utility in moving a social order toward justice, they cannot be anything more than temporary expedients. A well-ordered society would have no need of them.

As an ingredient in the utilitarian theory of nonvoluntary obligations, then, the possibility rule seems secure. I shall argue later in this section that the possibility rule can be extended to yield one of the standard principles of equitable taxation: ability to pay.

The Compensation Rule

The other principle of equitable taxation (the benefit principle) comes out of another aspect of utilitarian theory—one I shall call the *compensation rule*. Maximization of social utility is the theory's controlling principle. But it is individuals, not abstract entities called "societies," whose welfare is ultimately at stake. Improvements in social welfare serve no useful purpose unless they result in improvements in individual welfare. The question is, therefore, one of distribution: To whom are the benefits of one's sacrifice to go? The answer from utilitarian theory is unequivocal: Other things equal, they must go to everyone, oneself included. Each person counts for one and only one. With respect to one's own interests, there is no reason (in terms of maximizing *social* utility) to distribute one's own goods to others, unless doing so adds to social welfare. In some cases, the principle of utility will require self-sacrifice. But it is clear that whenever I can improve my own welfare (while still doing the best I can for everyone else's) I should clearly do so. Any other course would by definition fail to maximize social welfare. Failing that, my object must be to preserve as much of my own welfare as possible.

Translated into the context of constructing a theory of nonvoluntary obligations, the moral is obvious: Utilitarians must adopt whatever versions of the needed obligations best improve (or failing that, best preserve) the welfare of the obligation bearers. Concern about compensatory benefits is therefore a necessary ingredient in any utilitarian theory of obligations. Faced with two otherwise equally good options, one of which compensates the obligation bearer and the other of which does not, utility necessarily favors the former. Further, it favors alternatives that *scale* benefits to sacrifices. Benefits that exceed the sacrifice are best; benefits commensurate to sacrifice are second best; benefits proportional to sacrifice are next in line. But in any case the scaling of benefits directly to sacrifice is necessary whenever we have the chance to do so within the frame of the controlling concern for maximizing aggregate utility.

Requirements, Not Desiderata

With respect to tax theory, the thing to notice here is that utilitarian theory treats these two rules very differently than it treats matters of efficiency, collectability, and neutrality of economic impact. These latter factors (elements in the standard list of desiderata for an ideal tax) are matters of degree which, at the extremes, are also requirements. (A tax that "costs" more than it yields is prohibited by utilitarian theory.) But these factors are *also* second-level issues. Once the necessary conditions for justifiability have been met, the theory will want to *maximize* the efficiency, collectability, and desired economic impact of the tax system. And one may well trade off a little efficiency to get more of a desired economic impact (e.g., stimulation of a certain industry). But the question of maximizing these things does not even arise if the tax is not minimally justifiable— that is, if it does not meet all the *necessary* conditions of justifiability. The possibility rule and the compensation rule are among the necessary conditions. Their satisfaction cannot be sacrificed to get second-level benefits.

Contractarian Obligations

In social-contract theory, justifiable obligations are obligations to which people actually agree to be bound ("actual" contract theory) or to which people *would* agree, if asked ("hypothetical" contract theory). It is reasonable to believe that both varieties incorporate the possibility and compensation rules as necessary conditions of justifiable nonvoluntary obligations.

Actual Contracts

It is notoriously difficult to construct a satisfactory account of justice by reference to actual contracts. And it is implausible to suppose that any large-scale society ever has or ever could manage to organize itself according to such a theory. But suppose for the moment that it is possible. Suppose, that is, that some society either has achieved or can achieve the following:

1. It has found an effective, nonarbitrary, and noncircular method for determining who will be parties to the contract. (Children? The senile?)
2. It has obtained unanimous consent from the parties on a set of procedural rules for creating and enforcing obligations—e.g., rules for creating a constitution, etc. (The agreement at this stage must be unanimous. Just as a private contract is not binding—as a mutual agreement—unless there is agreement among all the parties, so too for the social contract. Majority rule is a procedural device—without moral force in the contract unless agreed to by all.)
3. It has solved the problem of binding new arrivals, *contractually*, to those procedural rules. That is, it has found a fair and workable way to deal with children coming of age and immigrants—people who were not parties to the original agreements.

The question then is, Would such a society adopt the possibility and compensation rules as necessary conditions of nonvoluntary social obligations? I know of no way to answer that question empirically, because I know of no large-scale socirty that has organized itself along these lines. But if the evidence from small communities can be extrapolated safely (which I doubt) the answer is Yes. Such communities certainly do not enforce impossible nonvoluntary *social* obligations on members, and they go to some lengths to insist that the obligations they do impose benefit everyone—the obligation bearers included.[4] But extrapolation from such evidence is little better than free speculation.

Hypothetical Contracts

The alternative is no more comfortable. It is to construct an account (in terms of some assumptions about human nature) of what sort of contract actual people *would* agree to if they had the chance. This might be called *actual-agent* contract theory. Here everything turns on the psychological assumptions used. If sadism/masochism is assumed to be strong, the possibility rule might be ignored. If altruism is assumed to be strong, the compensation rule would not be necessary. But I shall assume that something closer to the broad outlines of a Hobbesian view of human nature is correct— specifically, that human beings are basically egoistic, but with an important and limited amount of altruism. I take it that those assumptions have been confirmed by behavioral science. And I think it is clear that, on those assumptions, the adoption of the possibility and compensation rules—as necessary conditions of nonvoluntary obligations—is highly probable.

Similarly for versions of social-contract theory that deal with hypothetical rather than actual agents—versions that ask what agreements "rational" people would make under conditions of free

----

[4]It is, after all, implicit in the very idea of small "communities within communities" that they are better for their members than life-as-usual in the wider world. So even in purely "nonprescriptive" communities (where the only obligation, in principle, is noncoercive behavior) all the members are meant to benefit. See, for example, Michael Fellman, *The Unbounded Frame: Freedom and Community in Nineteenth Century American Utopianism* (Westport, Conn.: Greenwood Press, 1973).

and fair choice. Again using plausible assumptions about the egoism and altruism of human beings, the reasoning leading to the adoption of the two principles is straightforward, as follows.

The Possibility Rule.

Obligations impose liability. What rational ground could there be for agreeing to such liability (for oneself) in cases where the conduct in question is impossible to perform? Strict liability rules might be agreed to, but, as in utilitarian theory, only on the condition that one has some control over exposure to risk or the ability to absorb the sanctions for failure. So, in either case, the agreement to a strict-liability rule is not an agreement to an impossible obligation. Likewise for impossible tasks imposed as a means to other goals. One might well want to try such a task voluntarily, but would one agree to a rule that allowed others to impose such tasks against one's will? I suggest there is no reason to think so. Everything points to the conclusion that hypothetical contract theory would adopt the possibility rule as a necessary condition for all nonvoluntary obligations.

The Compensation Rule.

The same is true for the compensation rule. Rational contractors are by definition agents who want something for themselves from the bargains they strike. They must (to make the theory work) achieve unanimous agreement. Perhaps none (but certainly not all) would agree to a disadvantageous sacrifice. Returns in excess of sacrifice would be best; commensurate benefits would be second best; proportionate benefits would be next. But, in any case, the principle of scaling benefits directly to sacrifice is required to get consent from rational contractors.

Rights Theory

Theories of justice based on natural rights yield the same results even more directly. If X has a natural right to life, then others have nonvoluntary obligations to refrain from murdering X. So the existence of some nonvoluntary obligations is built into the theory from the outset. (Whether paying taxes can be among them will be considered in the next section.) The question here is merely whether natural-rights theory requires that such obligations meet the possibility and compensation rules. I think it must. The reciprocal nature of rights and obligations builds the benefit rule into the very structure of rights theory. The return to me for my fulfillment of obligations is my right against others for the same conduct toward me. And the possibility rule is likewise built in. Any deontic theory (a theory that makes duties and rights fundamental) will argue, just as Kant did, that "ought implies can" is a *formal* principle that limits the imposition of duties.[5]

Equitable Taxation

I hope I have said enough to establish that the possibility and benefit rules are necessary ingredients—requirements—in the justification of nonvoluntary obligations *per se*. (At least this is so with respect to the three justificatory strategies I have discussed.) What remains in this section is to show how these requirements translate into requirements on taxation—specifically, how they become the so-called "principles of equitable taxation": scaling taxes in accord with ability to pay and in accord with benefits received by the taxpayer.

The Benefit Principle

"Benefits scaled to sacrifice" is a rule embedded in all three justificatory strategies, and it needs no translation to become the benefit principle of equitable taxation. Only two things need emphasis. One is that this principle, as it comes out of moral theory, does not state a mere desideratum—something that can be compromised (say) to get an increase in administrative efficiency. It states a precondition of all justifiable nonvoluntary tax obligations. In Rawlsian jargon, this condition is lexically prior to the desiderata of efficiency, adequacy of the tax base, collectability, and desired economic impact. The importance of this point—about both the benefit and ability-to-pay principles—is hard to overstate. The fact

---

[5]In fact, since the "ought implies can" thesis is usually taken to be a purely definitional matter, this will be a formal principle of any sort of theory where the notion of moral blameworthiness is considered cogent.

that justifiable taxes must conform to these requirements rules out many sorts of taxation at the outset.

The other point to be emphasized is that the benefit principle provides a ground for exempting (from the relevant obligations) those who are unjustifiably excluded from social benefits and for imposing more heavily on those who reap higher than average benefits. A tax *rate*, as opposed to a simple tax, is an analytic consequence.

Ability to Pay

The possibility rule presents a bit more difficulty. It is apparently an all-or-nothing affair, whereas the ability-to-pay principle is scalar. My contention is, however, that scaling obligations to the level of an agent's abilities is simply a necessary extension of the possibility rule. People who are able to fulfill an obligation may nonetheless be so disadvantaged with respect to it that fulfilling it would consume an inordinate amount of their time or energy or resources. (An inordinate amount, for example, compared to what an "average" person would have to use.) We may properly think of such cases as analogous to impossibility—on the ground that increasing difficulty approaches impossibility as a limit. Somewhere along the path toward impossibility we typically draw a line that says "If it is this difficult, we do not have the obligation." This is no more than a recognition of the fact that whether or not a person "can" fulfill an obligation is often tied to the presence of and ability to fulfill other, equally important obligations. For example, suppose that fulfilling obligation X is so difficult for me that doing so would mean that I then would have no resources with which to fulfill three other obligations, each of equal importance to X. Yet if I were released from X, I could easily fulfill the other three. The justifiability of releasing me from X is clear.

The ability principle is double-edged, however. Increased ease of performance removes an obstacle to increases in obligations. It does not, by itself, *justify* an increase; it simply removes an obstacle. But the consequence for taxation is this: tax obligations go down as ability to pay diminishes; they *may*, if otherwise justified, go up as ability increases.

But is this scalar principle required by the justificatory strategies? I think so. We have seen that the benefit principle is required, and the "level of ability" principle is necessary to permit coherent use of the benefit principle. The argument goes this way: consider a case in which it costs me more and more (in time, energy, or other sacrifices) to fulfill my obligations as I age. (Suppose my tax obligations go up after I retire on a fixed income.) Now suppose that the benefits I receive from performing these obligations are inelastic. (There is only so much national defense one can "consume"; yet reducing it is also out of the question.) How can we keep benefits scaled to sacrifice in such a case? Clearly, the only way to do it is by reducing obligations—by scaling sacrifices to ability to pay. Thus the level-of-ability principle is not merely desirable. It is required to render the theory of nonvoluntary tax obligations coherent.

Joint Requirements

One final thing: the justification of nonvoluntary tax obligations requires *both* the ability and benefit principles. As principles of equitable taxation, then, they are neither competitors nor substitutable alternatives. Justifiable nonvoluntary taxation must satisfy both requirements.

IDEAL TAXATION

We are now ready to consider the question of the ideal form of taxation. In a sense the term 'ideal' is misleading. I shall instead be concerned with what sort(s) of taxes can be justified *at all* (as nonvoluntary social obligations). As I said at the outset, my contention will be that only a comprehensive individual expenditure tax passes muster.

Taxation Is Not Theft

The first thing to dispose of is the libertarian slogan that "taxation is theft." Such a view is plausible only if one makes one or both of two assumptions: first, that voluntary agreements provide the only rigorous and clear justification for social obligations—a view that casts a very dark shadow on all nonvoluntary obligations from the outset (taxes included); and, second, that property can be acquired unencumbered by social obligations. Neither assumption is justified. I have already said enough about nonvoluntary obligations to indicate plausible justifications for them. And I have argued else-where[6] that no sound general justification of private property can yield an immunity from social obligations with respect to the property. I shall not repeat the property arguments in detail here, but a brief summary is in order, stating the case explicitly in terms of taxation.

It should be intuitively clear that a utilitarian theory of property cannot support a general immunity from taxation. No doubt, con-fiscatory taxation would discourage people from acquisition enough to damage social welfare. But history makes it plain that taxes *per se* will not do so. As a result, even if considerations of utility mandate an extensive system of private property (as I think they do), they do not yield the conclusion that taxation cannot be justified.

Similarly for the libertarian's favorite property argument—the labor theory. As nineteenth-century critics of Locke made abundantly clear, the only way (in Locke's version of the argument) that my labor alone can give me debt-free ownership of anything is for it to meet the following two conditions. The first is that the labor I do must be beyond what I am morally required to do for others. Otherwise, the labor—and hence its products—would be "owed" to those others. The second condition is that my acquisition of things must not constitute a "loss" to others. The quickest way to see the necessity for this is to paraphrase Proudhon's outraged response to Locke: Why should I pay—in the form of respecting your property rights—for labor I did not ask you to perform?[7] The only satisfactory answer (within the framework of the labor theory) is Mill's: Well, you shouldn't have to pay me, that's true. But when it is "no payment" at all—when my having the thing constitutes no loss for you—then why shouldn't I have property in the things I produce with my labor?[8]

Under these two conditions then, Locke's labor theory is sound. But the second condition—the no-loss requirement—is *very* strin-

---

[6]*Property Rights: Philosophic Foundations* (London: Routledge & Kegan Paul, 1977).

[7]Pierre Joseph Proudhon, *What Is Property?* [published in 1867] (New York: Howard Fertig, 1966), p. 84.

[8]J. S. Mill, *Principles of Political Economy,* in *The Collected Works of John Stuart Mill,* vol. II (London: Routledge & Kegan Paul, 1965), book II, ch. II, 6 (p. 230).

gent indeed whenever goods are scarce. The first condition makes prior satisfaction of moral obligations to others a necessary prerequisite of property acquisition. In other words, the argument leaves open the issue of whether or not there are social obligations that limit one's right to property.

The only other sound version of the labor theory which I can construct fares no better. It holds that, if my labor produces benefits for others (as well as for myself), then sometimes the granting of property rights is an appropriate (i.e., deserved) reward for me. But this principle is obviously double-edged. Far from establishing immunity from taxation, it creates a justification for it whenever my labor *damages* others (e.g., by being a nuisance or by depleting scarce resources).

The final argument for property—the argument from political liberty—also fails to block the justification of taxation. This argument proceeds on the assumption that people need to and want to acquire things and that, to make a general prohibition on acquisition actually effective, we would have to abridge political liberties to which people are entitled, morally. It should be obvious that this argument is too weak to prohibit taxation *per se*. Some taxation—indeed, quite a lot of it—is perfectly compatible with extensive systems of political liberty.

In short, the libertarian's sweeping attack on taxation fails. Voluntary agreements are not the only sources of obligations; there are some nonvoluntary obligations as well. And property theory provides no justification for general immunity from taxation. So the way is clear for the justification of a nonvoluntary obligation to pay taxes.

Tax Obligations

In fact, the justification of a general nonvoluntary obligation to pay taxes is not very difficult. The tricky questions are, What kinds of taxes? and How much? I leave those questions aside for the moment. Here I simply want to outline the obvious rationale for tax obligations *per se*.

The starting point is that we are born into citizenship in a state in which the government does all sorts of things for which it needs tax revenue and in which very few of the citizens favor the abolition of all such governmental activity. As a result, the inevitability of taxation is plain, and (in principle) has general support from the populace. The obligation to pay taxes is in fact imposed, and not opposed by any group powerful enough to change matters. That is the nonvoluntary part.

The justification for such obligations—when they are imposed on people who do not consent to them or whose "consent" is compromised by the lack of available alternatives—is a straightforward application of the strategies outlined in section II. Whether one talks only about the ideal—that is, the way government ought to be arranged, given what we know of human nature—or whether one starts with what exists and asks how it should be changed, all the available strategies support taxation in principle. Utility supports it, for there are some essential public goods that rational self-maximizers will not voluntarily cooperate to produce, even though they want them and recognize their necessity. (I have in mind, here, the usual sort of n-person Prisoner's Dilemma analysis of public-goods problems.[9]) Contractarianism supports it, even if the state is to be restricted to a night-watchman role. And rights theory supports it—at least to the extent that taxes are required to enforce rights.

What Kind(s) of Taxes Can Be Justified?

As I remarked at the outset of this paper, standard discussions of the forms of taxation make "equity" (meaning the benefit and ability principles) simply one element in a list of desiderata for an ideal tax. As the preceding arguments have shown, however, the principles of "equitable taxation" control the very justifiability of (nonvoluntary) tax obligations *per se*. The possibility, benefit, and ability principles are not things one can play off against administrative efficiency (or whatever) in the process of constructing justifiable taxes. Nonvoluntary tax obligations that do not satisfy these principles cannot be justified at all.

It turns out that many forms of taxation can be ruled out on these grounds alone. The desiderata of an ideal tax apply only to the remaining possibilities.

---

[9]See, for example, Mancur Olsen, *The Logic of Collective Action* (Cambridge, Mass.: Harvard University Press, 1965).

Personal versus Ad Rem and Indirect Taxation

For example, all taxes are paid ultimately by individuals—that is, by "natural" persons as opposed to corporations or other entities. Individuals are said to be taxed "personally" when taxes are levied *directly* on their incomes, expenditures, or wealth. Taxes levied on corporations are paid *indirectly* by individuals—passed on to them either in increased prices or in reduced earnings from wages, salaries, and dividends or in reduced wealth (e.g., in the value of capital investments). Similarly, taxes levied on "things"—so called "*ad rem*" taxes such as the retail sales tax, property taxes, and value-added taxes—are paid by individuals either directly or indirectly.

Indirect and *ad rem* taxes are by definition not proportioned to the individual's ability to pay. They are therefore not justifiable as parts of a system of nonvoluntary tax obligations. The point can be made without an elaborate argument. Retail sales taxes—as we know them—are obviously not scaled to ability to pay. No one considers how much income or wealth individuals have in order to determine the amount they must pay. Similarly for use taxes. Even if they are scaled to benefits received, as the gasoline tax is supposed to be, they are not scaled to ability to pay. And the use of *both* principles is necessary for the justification of a nonvoluntary tax obligation. Property taxes—as distinguished from taxes on personal wealth—are also *ad rem* in character. They are by definition not scaled to ability and in practice not scaled to benefits either. The same is true of all the taxes corporations pass on to people. Whether the burden falls out in the form of higher prices or in lowered income or wealth, the nature of the tax prevents the requisite scaling.

The conclusion is thus inescapable: to be justifiable, a nonvoluntary tax obligation must be scaled to benefits and ability, and the only taxes that can be so scaled are "personal" taxes levied directly on individual expenditure, income, and wealth.

Objections.

It might be objected that this conclusion is both naive and unworkable. It is naive (it might be said) for two reasons. First, it ignores the autonomous nature of corporations—the fact that they have "lives of their own" which give practical significance to the legal fiction of the corporation as a "person." Thus surely corporations can be taxed in ways that are not passed on to individuals (e.g., taxes on net profits or on retained earnings). And, even if that were not so, surely they must be taxed to prevent vast and permanent concentrations of economic power.

Second, the objection continues, the conclusion is naive because it ignores the necessity for governmental controls (in the form of tax policy) in areas crucial to a healthy economy—and perhaps even to our survival. If we must slow corporate growth or consumption of fossil fuels, then we must be able to tax these things.

The third source of naiveté concerns the market system. If it is morally justifiable to let free markets fix the price of goods, then people must pay prices—even for survival goods—which are not scaled to their ability to pay. How does that differ from obligating them to pay use taxes or sales taxes? There is an inconsistency here.

And, finally, it might be said that the elimination of all indirect and *ad rem* taxation is just unworkable. Governments need vast revenues; indirect and *ad rem* taxes are already in place as important sources of revenue, and people would just not tolerate the replacement of these customary and mostly hidden taxes with a dramatic increase in direct taxes on income, expenditure, or wealth.

Reply.

These are important objections, but not cogent ones. I shall take them in order. First, whatever autonomy corporations have, it is not the case that they can pay taxes without passing them on. Taxes on profits or retained earnings *must* show up in the pocketbooks of investors and employees—either in the form of reduced dividends and earnings or in the form of the reduced value of their capital assets.[10] They are thus passed on to individuals, and not in ways that can be scaled to ability to pay.

Second, on the matter of preventing concentrations of economic power and controlling the economy generally, I remind readers that these objections depend on the confusion—mentioned earlier—which treats the benefits and ability principles as simply elements in

---

[10]For a review of the incidents of taxes on business, see R. A. Musgrave, *The Theory of Public Finance* (New York: McGraw Hill, 1959) ch. 13; hereafter, Musgrave.

the list of desiderata for an ideal tax. They are instead part of the justification of nonvoluntary tax obligations *per se*. The very conditions that make a tax justifiable cannot be sacrificed to make the tax a more powerful instrument of social control. When that happens, one just gets a powerful but unjustifiable tax. Further, tax policy is not the only means of control at the government's disposal. Direct regulation is often possible. And, finally, of course, individual income, expenditure, and wealth taxes provide significant tools for controlling the economy and accumulations of wealth.

As for an inconsistency with the market pricing of goods, so much the worse for market pricing. I take it that just this sort of objection to the market system (i.e., about some people's inability to pay market prices) lies behind the various social programs that provide a safety net or pricing "offsets" for the disadvantaged. These programs are supported by tax revenues. How ironic it is to collect those revenues—designed to improve ability to pay—with forms of taxation that are *not* scaled to ability to pay! But the crucial flaw in this objection is that, through welfare programs, market pricing in principle permits (indirect) scaling for ability to pay. *Ad rem* taxation does not.

I therefore do not think that the proposal to disallow indirect and *ad rem* taxes is naive. And, on the matter of its workability, I can only say that a government forced to perpetuate injustice through deception cannot be a very good government. If people are unwilling to pay *directly* taxes that they are now paying *indirectly*, there seems to me to be a presumption in favor of the conclusion that the government is at fault—either for not educating its citizens or for not producing benefits commensurate with the taxes it assesses. Until that issue is resolved, I am not willing to concede the point about unworkability. How fast the needed changes can be made is an empirical question. But that they *ought* to be made is clear, and that they *can* be made by a decent government and a reasonably well-informed public is something I choose to believe until I see evidence to the contrary.

Objection.

It might also be objected, however, that at least some direct or *ad rem* taxation is as harmless in practice as it is objectionable in principle. Sales taxes on $90,000 yachts, after all, though not in theory scaled to ability to pay, are so scaled as a practical matter, since only the very rich will pay them. Similarly, it has been argued recently that existing property taxes, which in principle have a regressive character, in practice do not have the character (or at least, not enough to worry about.[11] Thus it might be said that there is no need for sweeping aside indirect and *ad rem* taxes just because they cannot *in principle* be proportioned to ability to pay. If as a matter of fact (as in sales taxes on high-priced luxuries) they are in general paid only by those who can "afford" them, then they are permissible.

Reply.
My reply to this objection has two parts. First, taxes whose legitimacy is purely fortuitous are likely to run into serious justificatory trouble as social and economic conditions change. Henry Simons, for example, thought that the gasoline tax was perfectly legitimate because people who could afford the luxury of driving could afford the taxes.[12] And, writing in the late 1930s, he was probably right about the "overall" impact of the tax. But times have changed. What was once a luxury is now a near necessity. Yet the tax remains. It is much better, it seems to me, to impose a tax that is justifiable in principle than to be constantly testing the impact of other taxes to see whether or not they remain fortuitously justified.

Second, it should be noted that what is true "in general," or in the aggregate, is not necessarily true of every case. To say that, overall, property taxes are not terribly regressive in their impact is not to deny that they are *quite* regressive for many individuals. Similarly for taxes on the most extraordinary luxuries. One can easily imagine cases in which relatively poor people need such goods and for whom an *ad rem* tax would have quite a different impact from what it has on the typical buyers of such goods. I think, for example, of the need a small entrepreneur might have for a yacht or the need a blind person might have for otherwise luxurious audio equipment.

---

[11]See the publication from the Brookings Institute: Henry J. Aaron, *Who Pays the Property Tax? A New View* (1975).

[12]*Personal Income Taxation* (Chicago: University of Chicago Press, 1938), p. 38.

Objection.

Now it might be thought that the *aggregate* of consequences is precisely what concerns utilitarians. A utilitarian, so the argument goes, would be willing to put up with occasional damage to a few individuals if, overall, the tax at stake was not regressive in its impact. Consequently, it appears that utilitarian theory might justify some indirect and *ad rem* taxes even if contractarian and rights theory would not.

Reply.

That sort of reasoning has a superficial plausibility, but it will not withstand scrutiny. To begin with, the first question for the utilitarian here is the same as for other theorists: the justifiability of imposing nonvoluntary tax obligations across the whole class of citizens. And I have argued that, no matter whether one is concerned about aggregate welfare or about individual rights, a rule imposing nonvoluntary tax obligations can be justified only if the obligations are scaled to ability to pay and to benefits received. The question is whether, given the way things actually work out with respect to aggregate welfare, the utilitarian rule can ignore these principles.

The answer is No. Taxes that do not conform to those principles will always harm some people, and, unless their refusal to pay would decrease aggregate welfare (which is unlikely), it is not justifiable to force them to pay. Indeed, on utilitarian grounds they ought *not* to pay. Yet sorting out these people in the collection process (for indirect and *ad rem* taxes) would be administratively inefficient at best. So we are back where we began—with the unjustifiability of taxes that cannot, in principle, be scaled to the individual's ability to pay and to benefits received.

My conclusion, therefore, remains that all indirect or *ad rem* taxes are unjustifiable. That leaves only taxes on individual income, expenditure, and wealth as possibilities. And, since income and expenditure taxes are mutually exclusive options (because to have them both would be inefficient at best),[13] the next steps in the argu-

---

[13]It should be noted, however, that economists generally think that an expenditure tax would have to be phased in gradually and carefully. So for a time it would coexist with the income tax. The only attempts of which I am aware to change from the income to the expenditure tax were in India (1957–

ment are, first, to decide which of the two is best and, then, to decide whether to tax wealth as well.

Income versus Expenditure Taxes

Taxes on the flow of wealth to and from individuals may in principle be of two sorts, as mentioned: taxes on accretions to a person's wealth (i.e., income taxes), and taxes on the "spending" or "consumption" of wealth (i.e., expenditure taxes). Wealth is defined in static terms—as one's "stock" of goods or one's exchange-value "position." All these indices of "taxable capacity" are to be measured in money terms.

The I-Tax.

The income tax is a familiar device; so I shall defer discussion of it for the moment—except to remark that a major difficulty with it has always been finding and applying the proper definition of 'income'. Cash income is not a particular problem, whether it comes in the form of wages, salaries, interest, dividends, gifts, bequests, or even in the form of "realized" capital gains—that is, the gains people get when they actually sell something for a higher price than they paid for it. There may be arguments about whether all these sorts of income should be taxed at the same rate—whether, for example, capital gains should be taxed at a lower rate than wages. But there is no serious dispute over whether any of these accretions to a person's wealth is "really" income.

The situation is a bit more confusing, however, with respect to income "in kind" (such as fringe benefits), unrealized capital gains (that is, accretions to the value of property one holds but does not sell), and "imputed income" (such as whatever cash value one can assign to leisure, the perquisites of a job, and so on). But more of that later.

---

66) and Ceylon (1959–63). The two taxes coexisted there for a time, but the expenditure tax never gained a significant foothold and was eventually abandoned. For an overview of the practical problems of expenditure taxes, see Richard E. Slitor, "Administrative Aspects of Expenditure Taxation," in Richard A. Musgrave, ed., *Broad-based Taxes* (Baltimore: Johns Hopkins University Press, 1973), pp. 227–263.

The E-Tax.

The expenditure tax is less familiar than the income tax, but the general idea is simple. The expenditure tax is levied on *persons* (in this case, on human individuals) in much the same way an income tax is. The only difference is that one reports (and is taxed on) spending rather than income. Spending, moreover, is not merely income minus savings. It also includes "dis-savings"—that is, spending *from* savings or capital. So, under an expenditure tax, if I am spending not only the $10,000 a year that I earn, but also $10,000 a year from the family fortune, I would be taxed on the total of $20,000 a year. It should be noted that an E-tax is, therefore, sharply distinct from retail sales taxes and various indirect taxes placed on the things we buy. Unlike them, it can be scaled to ability to pay.

The expenditure tax has been thought superior to the income tax—on equity grounds—by a long line of distinguished writers.[14] Until recently, however, it had also been thought—by those same writers—to present insuperable administrative difficulties. Those difficulties have now been solved (Kaldor, pp. 12–13). So what remains is the question of equity—which in this essay becomes the question of which of the two forms of taxation can best be scaled in accord with the benefit and ability principles. In addition, there are some technical issues concerning the economic impact of both income and expenditure taxes, but they are of secondary importance.

Ability to Pay: The E-Tax.

Most of the argument over equity, here, concerns which of the two taxes is the better way of getting at "taxable capacity"—that is, which can best be scaled to an individual's ability to pay. Proponents of the expenditure tax have pointed to several flaws in existing income-tax laws. For one thing, at present, the money that low- and middle-income people save is often taxed no differently than the income they spend—or the income spent from a great fortune. It does not seem fair that the part of my income I have to put aside for

---

[14]Kaldor, *An Expenditure Tax,* p. 11, lists Hobbes, Mill, Alfred Marshall, and A. C. Pigou, among others.

emergencies and retirement should be treated in just the same way as the income I can spend—or in the same way as the income the wealthy derive from their fortunes, *all* of which is spendable (since they already have a stockpile for emergencies).

Further, at present, capital gains are either not taxed at all (for example, when holdings appreciate in value but those gains are not cashed in—not "realized" by selling the holdings) or taxed at a more favorable rate than other income. And "dis-savings"—or spending from capital—are not taxed either. Thus someone with a large fortune can spend from those parts of it which show no capital gains, pay no income tax at all, and (counting the unrealized gains on the rest) be no worse off than before. Or perhaps be better off. All of this favors the wealthy by ignoring important aspects of their "spending power" or "ability to pay."

In addition, Mill and a long list of others have argued that an income tax that does not exempt savings actually taxes savings twice—first by taxing the income from which they are derived and then by taxing what they yield (i.e., interest). In contrast, the same money, if spent rather than saved, would be taxed only once (by the income tax) since the goods it yields would not themselves be taxed.[15]

Ability to Pay: The I-Tax.
Proponents of the income tax, on the other hand, have argued that all its supposed flaws as a measure of ability to pay can be remedied by a suitably revised definition of 'income'.[16] Savings for retirement can be exempted if desired; realized capital gains can be treated as ordinary income; unrealized capital gains can be reached through taxing, as income, gifts and bequests; and, if necessary, interest on savings can be exempted.

Furthermore, most important kinds of "imputed income" (such as is received "in kind" through perquisites and fringe benefits) can in principle be reached by the income tax every bit as well as by the expenditure tax. [On the other hand, it is not clear to me how any

---

[15]See Mill, *Principles of Political Economy,* book V, ch. II, 4, and works referred to by Kaldor, p. 80.

· [16]Musgrave and Musgrave, pp. 220-1 and 243.

income tax could reach the spending (in effect) of unrealized capital gains through dis-savings.]

Finally, everyone is agreed that regressive, proportional, and progressive tax rates, income (or expenditure) averaging, time payment of taxes, and indexing to the inflation rate can be managed easily under either sort of tax. Similarly, complex structures of exemptions and deductions are possible under each.

In short, on the matter of ability to pay, arguments for income rather than expenditure, or the other way around, seem indecisive. Most writers think an income tax, suitably defined, has the edge; but their reason for thinking so—apart from the comfort they take in the number of people who agree with them (see Musgrave, p. 163)—is not very clear. A few writers continue to press for the expenditure tax, admitting that the balance of arguments on the ability-to-pay issue is "delicately poised (Kaldor, pp. 52-3). But, again, I do not have confidence that the case can be decided on this ground.

The Benefit Principle.
The justification of tax obligations, however, requires that taxes be scaled in accord with the benefit principle as well as the ability-to-pay principle. Here the expenditure tax seems to me to have a decided edge—and this is not usually denied by defenders of the income tax (Musgrave, pp. 163-64).

The argument is straightforward, and can be traced at least as far back as Hobbes.[17] It holds that it is fairer to tax people on what they "take out of the common pool of resources" (as represented by their spending) than on what they put into it (as represented by their income). In terms of the present essay, the point is that what one "takes out" are, by definition, benefits of the sort that justify nonvoluntary obligations. What one "puts in" are the benefits reaped by others. And taxes must be proportioned to people's effective demand for benefits—not to their effective provision of benefits to others. Such demands—insofar as they are for consumer goods and services, public or private—are directly measured by expenditures. Income is at best only an indirect measure here. Thus it may

---

[17]Kaldor finds it in *Leviathan*, ch. XXX.

be said that one's spending level is a more appropriate index to the benefits received from a society than is one's income level.

Still, the decisiveness of the case should not be exaggerated. Income is not always unreasonable as an index to benefits received. And the notion that spending is "taking" benefits whereas getting income is "putting them in" can be a misleading metaphor. After all, getting income often involves activities that deplete resources, create the need for public services, and so forth.

The Preferability of an E-Tax.

But the conclusion must be, I think, that, in terms of the purely conceptual elements in the justification, the expenditure tax has a slight overall edge. Since it is only slight, the final choice may be influenced, I suppose, by the answers to various empirical questions. For example: What would the impact of each type of tax be on savings? On the incentive to work? On inflation? On the administrative efficiency of tax collection? On the stability of tax revenues? The expenditure tax would obviously stimulate savings. But is that good? It would be more difficult to collect (through withholding schemes), but is that bad? It is probably a less predictable source of revenue than income, but is that a serious problem? The conventional wisdom favors the income tax in all of this. But, in an overheated economy, which is fast depleting its nonrenewable resources, there is much to be said for the other side.

In addition, Nicholas Kaldor makes a final technical argument which again tips the balance decidedly toward the expenditure tax. He reminds us that the argument for the income tax (as a measure of ability to pay) depends on adopting a comprehensive definition of income—one which includes *both* realized and unrealized capital gains, for example, and both actual and (some kinds of) imputed income. Now the expenditure tax must reach these things too, but it has one great advantage: taxpayers themselves, in deciding how much to spend, automatically do the computations (so difficult to do "from the outside") of the actual value of unrealized and imputed income. Kaldor's argument is worth quoting:

> Once actual spending is taken as the criterion [of taxable capacity] all the problems created by the non-comparability of work-incomes and property-incomes, of temporary and permanent sources of wealth, of genuine and fictitious capital gains resolve themselves; they are all

brought into equivalence in the measure in which they support the actual standards of living. . . .

Accruals from the various sources cannot be reduced to a common unit of spending power [taxable capacity?] on any objective criteria. But each individual performs this operation for himself when, in the light of all his present circumstances and future prospects, he decides on the scale of his personal living expenses. Thus a tax based on actual spending rates each individual's spending capacity according to the yardstick which he applies to himself. . . .

[I]f capital gains are taxed to the extent that they are actually spent, there is no need to inquire how far they are fictitious; it is left to the individual recipient of these gains to sort these things out for himself, in deciding how far he is justified in treating them as spendable gains.[18]

If Kaldor is right about this, the case for the expenditure tax is significantly improved. I think, all things considered, that this is decisive—at least at the level of political philosophy.

Taxes on Wealth

I turn now to the final possibility for justifiable tax obligations— namely, taxes on an individual's stock of goods, or wealth. These taxes, as long as they are levied on persons rather than things—i.e., on net or gross worth rather than on pieces of property—can also be scaled according to the benefit and ability principles.

Efficiency and Equity.

The argument for a wealth tax is rather thin, however. Assuming that we have a suitably comprehensive income or expenditure tax— which reaches capital gains, imputed income, gifts, bequests, and so forth—we will already have had an opportunity to tax wealth when it is acquired or expended. Further, a wealth tax will not be needed for revenue—since it is reasonable to assume that either income or expenditure alone will be an adequate tax base. So wealth taxes would not be needed for what is presently a large part of their rationale—as a supplement to other individual taxes, both to remedy inequitable loopholes and to add needed revenue.

---

[18]*An Expenditure Tax,* pp. 47–8. (The three excerpts are not in the order in which Kaldor presents them.)

But what about the economic efficiency of a mixed system (wealth plus either noncomprehensive income or expenditure taxation) versus a "pure" system of either I or E taxes alone? Here the standard texts on public finance come to two conclusions: wealth taxes alone do not make sense in a modern industrial society; and there is no particular *economic* advantage to a mixed system.[19]

The Ideal of Equality.
So the crux of the matter is really something altogether different: the use of wealth taxes to help realize the ideal of equality. For it might be thought that, without wealth taxes, even if we have confiscatory gift and death taxes and steeply progressive income or expenditure taxes, we might not be able to prevent individuals from accumulating large fortunes. Further, the break-up of existing fortunes would be hampered. If great inequalities of wealth are not justifiable, then wealth taxes may be necessary. Or so the argument goes.

I do not find this argument persuasive, largely because I think that all justifiable progress toward the ideal of equality can be achieved through a properly defined income or expenditure tax. But it is worth going over the arguments against inequality of wealth to see why this is so.

Wealth and Control of Organizations.
The social consequences of wealth as opposed to income or expenditure—that is, of static stocks of valuables as opposed to the movements of them—mostly have to do with a certain sort of economic power: the power to create or eliminate jobs, to hire and fire workers, to raise or lower workers' incomes, and the power to decide what will be produced.[20] In other words, the economic power associated with wealth is typically mediated through organizations and consists in having control of them. Having such control con-

---

[19]Lester C. Thurow, for example, who does argue for a mixed system, does so on grounds of distributive justice—and on the assumption that unrealized capital gains would not otherwise be reached. See his *The Impact of Taxes on the American Economy* (New York: Praeger, 1971), ch. 7.

[20]Kaldor, pp. 99–100. My argument here was suggested by Kaldor's remarks.

tributes to our well-being to the extent that it gives us control of our lives. It may also increase self-esteem.

The difficulty here for moral philosophy is that the exercise of such economic power often involves manipulating other people to their detriment. But it is evident that taxes designed to limit such power will merely shift the locus of it away from the possession of wealth and toward the possession of status in the organization. After all, managerial power will not evaporate, and, from the point of view of the people being manipulated, the consequences are the same whether that power is vested in plutocrats, salaried managers, civil servants, or workers' councils. At bottom, then, the issue is essentially how we want to control the allocation of managerial power. If we want it controlled politically, wealth taxation is irrelevant. Instead, the enterprises must be put under political management, and, since the wealthy can gain inequitable control of politics only by using their wealth—by *moving* their holdings—the appropriate tax remedies are income or expenditure taxes.

Wealth and Direct Control of Individuals.

People can also be manipulated directly, of course, in ways unmediated by organizations. But unmediated control—such as paying people to do one's bidding—necessarily involves the *movement* of valuables. Merely threatening to benefit or harm others is not sufficient to control them if they know the threat cannot be carried out. Carrying out the threat—in any way that taxation can frustrate— requires the movement, or "flow," of wealth. And such flows can in principle be reached by flow taxes: income or expenditure taxes. To the extent that an individual's exploitation of others can be controlled by taxation, therefore, it is controllable through properly designed income or expenditure taxes.

Objection.

Now I suppose it might be objected that it is easier to conceal transactions than it is to conceal great wealth. Thus it would be possible for the wealthy to fail to report those exploitative transactions which they did not want taxed. A wealth tax, on the other hand, would go directly to the sources of exploitative power.

Reply.
But that objection is self-defeating. If great wealth cannot be concealed, then neither can transactions, for they must show up in audits. So again, whatever power wealth taxation has as a means of social control can be exercised through flow taxes as well.

Objection.
As a last-ditch maneuver, it might be argued that certain spendthrifts would still be exempt. Suppose my wealth was acquired before the imposition of a properly defined income or expenditure tax, and I use my wealth to exploit others without any attempt to restore what has been used. Without a tax directly on my wealth, would I not then be immune from tax control of my exploitative activities?

Reply.
The answer is: Not necessarily. The spendthrift example is too far-fetched to be taken very seriously. But even so, an expenditure tax could control this directly and immediately. An income tax could not, and that is, perhaps, one more thing to be said in favor of the expenditure tax. But, in any case, such a situation could last only until the wealth was either used up or transferred or transmitted at death. I do not think it poses a serious problem.

I therefore see no justification for adding a tax on individual wealth to a properly designed income or expenditure tax. To the extent that a properly designed "flow tax" is politically or administratively impossible to achieve, of course, wealth taxes may be a needed supplement. But, in principle, they are not needed, no matter how egalitarian one's purposes.

16

The Reality of Human Wickedness

Mary Midgley

A bizarre feature of the relation between ethical theory and practice in this century has been the virtual outlawing from theory of the notion of wickedness. This is taken for granted in educated moral discussion today in a number of forms, centrally perhaps as the principle that we ought not to make moral judgments. The adjective 'judgmental' has been invented to describe culprits who are guilty of this offense and conveys fairly strong disapproval. The reasons for this move are obvious in the mistakes of earlier epochs; it has arisen as a correction to certain misplaced and excessive tendencies to blame and punish. But it has been generalized in a way which makes it a real distraction today. Its oddity appears, of course, in the paradox that it is itself a moral judgment, and apparently a very general one. Judgers are *blamed,* often quite severely. Closer inspection of the principle shows some other oddities. The ban on judging does not usually seem to extend to favorable judgments; we are allowed to praise people. Nor does it commonly extend to the rich and powerful; we are allowed to blame political figures of whose acts we disapprove. The ban lies, of course, particularly heavily on blaming the poor, the helpless, and the misguided; so we might be tempted to take it simply as a ban on *wrong* moral judgments, since there are special reasons for not blaming people for what they could not help. But it is viewed as something more general than this. Its application has, however, further discrepancies. It is applied much more strongly to blaming others, and especially others of whom we know little, than to blaming ourselves. This does seem unavoidable. If we could never judge our own actual or contemplated conduct to be wrong, we could not direct it at all, and could certainly not criticize it as being (for instance) too judgmental. It sometimes seems, too, that the ban is directed rather against intrusive expression of opinions than against merely having them, since everybody secretly recognizes that opinion formation is something we cannot help.

Does this ban on judging people, then, amount to anything more than the sensible, but not startling, advice that we should avoid shooting off our mouths too readily about other people's faults, especially when we don't know what we are talking about? It has certainly been taken to mean much more than this. And it has been treated in its extended form as a serious practical principle, not just as a piece of empty rhetoric. It has guided people's conduct widely in such fields as social work and psychotherapy, and also in their personal relations. In this wide use it has been seen as a general veto on moral judgments, made necessary by skeptical reasoning. This reasoning has been of various kinds, but in the public consciousness they have largely merged into something more extreme than any one set of them would really have justified. In official moral philosophy, the skepticism was very drastic indeed, though it was not supposed to affect practice. We were told not just that our information was insufficient for moral judgment, but that the whole field was one to which thought did not apply. We were still allowed to pin the name 'moral judgment' on our attitudes, but were told that these attitudes were only personal quirks or idiosyncrasies. In the social sciences, the emphasis was rather on our ignorance. Much stress was laid on the differences between cultures, between subcultures, and also between individuals. Skill in extracting from these differences relativistic or subjectivist arguments which seemed to invalidate the moral judgments of unsophisticated people—especially their unfavorable judgments—seemed to be the central mark of intellectual training. In the fascination of this pursuit, the possibility that some other judgments might be valid was not usually denied, but it was amazingly neglected. The conditions that would allow validity were not explored.

The upshot of all this was a loss of the whole dimension of evil from the scene of official moral theory. Since in real life everybody, or at least every adult, is aware of moral evil as a very serious element to be reckoned with, this produced an unreality which we need to attend to, and I shall try to attack it here. This paper is about the problem of evil, but not quite in the traditional sense, since I see it as our problem, not God's. Commonly, it is treated as a problem about why God allows evil. The inquiry then takes the form of a law court, in which Man, appearing as both judge and accuser, arraigns God and convicts him of mismanaging his responsibilities. We then get a strange drama, in which two robed and wigged figures apparently sit opposite each other exchanging accusations. But this story seems to me unhelpful, and I shall not add to it. If God is not there, the drama cannot arise. If he is there, he is surely something bigger and more mysterious than a corrupt or stupid official. Either way, we still need to worry about a different and more pressing matter, namely the *immediate* source of evil—not physical evil, but moral evil or sin—in human affairs. To blame God for making us capable of wickedness is beside the point. Since we are capable of it, what we need is to understand it. We should not be put off from trying to do this by the fact that Christian thinkers have sometimes been overobsessed with sin and have given confused accounts of it. The phenomenon itself remains very important in spite of all the mistakes that are made about it. People often do treat each other abominably. They sometimes treat themselves abominably too. They constantly cause avoidable suffering. How are we to view this habit?

There is at present a strong tendency for decent people, especially in the social sciences, to hold that wickedness has no internal cause in human nature—that it is purely the result of outside pressures which could be removed. Now, obviously, there are powerful outside causes. There are physical pains, diseases, shortages, and dangers—everything that counts as "natural evil." There are also cultural factors, bad example, and bad teaching. But these cultural causes do not solve our problem, because we must still ask, How did the bad cultures start? How do they spread? and Why do they resist counterconditioning? If people are merely channels, out of what tap does the wickedness flow?

The difficulty about this concentration on external causes is its silence about the way in which people *respond* to these pressures. Frost may bring on frostbite, but only in creatures with a suitable circulatory system. Like frostbite, resentment, envy, avarice, cruelty, meanness, and hatred are in themselves complex conditions. Outside events may indeed bring them on, but, like other malfunctions, they would not develop if we were not prone to them.

Simpler, nonsocial creatures are not capable of these responses and do not show them; neither do some defective humans. Emotionally, we are capable of these vices, because we are capable of states opposite to them, namely the virtues, and these virtues would be unreal if they did not have an opposite alternative. The vices are the defects of our qualities. Our nature provides for both. If it did not, we should not be free.

These sinister psychological states involve a whole range of much wider natural motives, whose very existence recent liberal theorists have, in the name of decency, denied—aggression, territoriality, possessiveness, competitiveness. All are wide, having good as well as bad aspects. All are (more or less) concerned with power. The importance of power in human motivation used to be recognized as a commonplace. Hobbes, Nietzsche, Adler, and others have suggested that it was in fact the central human motive. (This suggestion is of course wildly oversimple, but it is not just silly.) All these power-related motives are important in the lives of other social animals and appear there in behavior which is, on the face of it, strikingly like much human behavior. If we accept the view that we evolved from very similar creatures, it is natural to take these parallels seriously—to conclude, as we certainly would in the case of any other creatures we were studying, that there is a real underlying similarity. The physiology of our glands and nervous system, too, is close enough to that of other primates to lead to their being constantly used as experimental subjects for investigations of it. Common tradition has never hesitated to treat such dangerous motives as natural, and has often been content to call them "animal instincts." The burden of argument lies on those who today reject this obvious way of thinking, not on those who accept it.

They have two main reasons for rejecting it. Both reasons are moral rather than theoretical. Both are in themselves extremely serious; but they are not actually relevant to this issue. They are the fear of fatalism and the fear of power worship. Fatalism appears to loom because people feel that, if we accept these motives as natural at all, we shall be committed to accepting wicked conduct as inevitable, and power-worship appears to follow because what seems inevitable may command approval. This alarming way of thinking is confused. It is quite wrong to conceive of a wide and complex motive like aggression on the model of a simple drainpipe, a channel down which energy flows ineluctably to a single outcome—murder.

No motive has that simple form. Aggression and fear, sex and curiosity and ambition, are all extremely versatile, containing many possibilities and contributing to many activities. And the relation of motives to value is still more subtle. We do not need to approve of everything we are capable of desiring. It probably *is* true in a sense that whatever people actually want has *some* value for them, that all wanted things contain a good. But there are so many such goods and so much possibility of varying arrangements among them that this cannot commit us to accepting anything as an overall good, just because it is in some way wanted. The relations among these many goods must correspond to the relations among the needs of conscious beings, and conflicts can be resolved only in the light of a priority system among these. What we really need, if we are to understand them, is a full analysis of the complexities of motivation.

This analysis, however, would be complicated. And people tend to feel that what we have here is an entirely simple issue. As they see it, the whole notion of natural aggression is merely an unspeakable abomination, a hypothesis that must not even be considered. This is a strangely one-sided view. What actually, are the moral consequences of admitting that motives like aggression and dominance have internal, natural causes as well as outside causes? Morally, the balance sheet between these alternatives seems to be one between confidence and honesty, between hope and self-knowledge. To deny inside causes of wickedness does offer us a high opinion of our essential selves and of the human race. It thereby increases our confidence for reform. By denouncing sin as something alien to us, it outlaws the fatalistic acceptance of wicked behavior. It deals with the manifest confusion of the old phrase 'original sin' very simply, by pointing out that actual sin must by definition be deliberate, and that nothing deliberate can be part of our original constitution. But it says nothing about what may be called the "raw materials" of sin—natural impulses which are indeed not sinful in themselves, but which will lead to sin unless we are conscious and critical of them. By ignoring these, it may make sin itself vanish entirely, and leave only "inconvenient conduct." This is no gain, because it leaves a large and important slice of the phenomenon unexplained and unconsidered. The difference between sin and accidental damage is actually very important. On the other side of the account, if we accept inside causes of wickedness, this move also offers an important moral gain, namely honesty. On the face of it, there *are* sources of evil within us, since we are capable of quite complicated and varied reactions to temptation. It seems very important to admit and understand them, both for the practical purpose of controlling them and for the sake of our self-knowledge, our wholeness, our integrity. As Carl Jung has pointed out, every solid object has its shadow side. To deny one's shadow is to lose solidity, to become something of a phantom. Self-deception may give us confidence, but it threatens our wholeness.

Now of course this balance sheet, though I have tried to restrict it to moral considerations, cannot be complete without some decisions about the facts, because both sides invoke them. Honesty will not tell us to accept dangerous natural motives unless those motives are present. But, equally, the hope of eliminating aggression by cultural means is not valuable unless it is justified. *False* hope, based on mistaken factual judgments, is no use to anyone. The facts do not justify either extreme conclusion. Obviously they do show that we are free beings, capable of virtue. So far they support hope. But they also—to me equally obviously—show that our natures do contain certain genuine, chronic dangers. Honesty as well as prudence demands that we attend very seriously to these.

To examine these dangers effectively, we need to use a set of concepts which are notoriously slippery—for a start, freedom, choice, necessity, motivation, determinism, and personal identity. Our first job, therefore, should be philosophical: to analyze the difficulties about these and get them clear. The issue is *not* simple; these conceptual problems cannot be bypassed. The controversy, however, has usually gone on without much attention to this work, and is treated as a straight factual dispute. It is often assumed that only two possible conclusions need to be considered, both very extreme—namely, that evil is entirely social, alien to us, and removable, or that it is internal, inevitable, and quite outside our control. Facts are then collected in support of these two conclusions. This is never difficult. On such very general issues, there are always many interpretative theories which can be combined with the data if one does not mind using a few epicycles. Both sides, given their different approaches and a free hand for selection, can accumulate plenty of supportive facts, and, given the vulnerability of all complex investigation to doubts of some kind, each can continue to throw suspicion on the other's.

But this is a game we do not want to play. Both half-truths are obviously inadequate. The position is simply more complicated than this. Moreover, the dispute is clearly not just theoretical. Like most questions about the psychology of motives, it is also conceptual and moral. It is a search for the presuppositions we can best live with and for the best ways of using them in our lives. As with political theory, psychological inquiry here just provides data for this. Of course we must get the facts right. But we want more than that. We want a workable understanding of motive, which can be used. The motives we are talking about are not just those of distant peoples whom we want to excuse or of experimental subjects. They are our own and those of the people we must directly deal with. In this context, how could we get on if we thought of bad motives merely as the result of external social pressures? In our own case, the effect would presumably be to make us excuse ourselves. The odious motives that consume you and me may well be motives that our society inculcates and encourages. If society were the only possible source of our conduct, we would have no escape from them, and therefore a complete excuse. Moreover, if we are being consumed by odious motives that our society does not approve of, something very odd is happening. We shall have to assume that the society is, unconsciously, at war with itself. The individual agent vanishes from the scene altogether along with his or her wickedness. Each person becomes just a locus of conflicting social forces. In one's own case, this makes no sense at all. In other people's it may be a trifle clearer, but it is still fearfully inadequate. It looks convincing only because the background of natural alternatives is always secretly taken for granted.

When we ask why someone acted as he or she did, we are not only asking what the culture demanded. We also want to know why—in terms of general human needs—that culture made those demands; what did they mean? And we also want to know how he or she—the individual, Cromwell, Napoleon, General Dyer, Mary Tudor, Catherine de Medici—responded to those requirements. To do this, we have to understand something about the emotional and intellectual constitution normal to human beings, in order to grasp how the particular individual varied from it. Neither constitution nor culture *forced* each of them to act in a particular way. Both, equally, disposed and enabled them to do so. To understand the act, we need to understand both.

The extraordinary thing about this dispute is that those who deny internal causes for fear of fatalism do not fear fatalism over social causes. Neither social nor constitutional causes are actually *fates*, but, if one was, the other would be too. Free will is at least as hard to reconcile with outside causation of conduct as with that from inside, and, if anything, more so. When change takes place, people act outside their existing social roles. Their most usual reason for doing this is dissatisfaction with the way those roles suit their nature and the natures of those around them. In developing that dissatisfaction they act not like billiard balls hit by cues, but exactly as they would in making any other change in their lives—by reflectively altering their thoughts and attitudes to accord with the new insight. Any serious social change must alter not just external arrangements, but people's attitudes as well. Here real emotional obstacles arise, and it is of the first importance to understand them. To give an example less alarming than aggression: sheer force of habit is a potent obstacle to all reform. Everybody finds change difficult. This subservience to habit is a product not of culture, but of our animal nature. It is what makes culture possible. It is a condition of the way our nervous system works. We share it with an immense range of creatures, from flatworms onwards, and it is a central structural feature of our lives. But this by no means commits us to being fatalistic about it. We are perfectly capable of resisting it on occasion, of discriminating among available habits, and of deliberately using it to form new ones. Habit is not our doom unless we choose to make it so, because it is not our only motive. The same thing is true of other motives that are potentially sinister. In general, motives are not tyrannous and irresistible fates. They are merely patterns which make explanation and prediction possible. And, because there are many such patterns, prediction is always incomplete. By our own efforts—which are a real causal factor as much as any other—we can use existing predictions to alter the expected outcome. We can do this—we constantly do do it—by working on our system of motives quite as much as by working on the economic system. Fatalism is the belief that human efforts cannot have any effect, that they make no difference to the course of events. It is demonstrably false, and as false of the scene within us as of that outside.

The problem about fatalism, however, leads into the deeper problem about power worship. Does accepting a motive as real commit one to approving of it? Now it seems clear that, for any general motive, we do recognize a corresponding good that it aims at, but we also recognize that particular forms of it may be bad—indeed very bad—because they conflict with other, more central goods. Somebody in the throes of a conflict, however, has not sorted this problem out yet. Let us consider briefly how temptation works. A town councillor, say, is attracted by the idea of accepting a bribe to keep his mouth shut. Now to be attracted at all is to have an experience that is within one's own emotional repertoire. It is not just to be pushed from outside. What is outside one's own nature will not catch on as a temptation at all. This does. But it is contrary to his normal personality and to the principles on which he runs his life.

What happens next is complicated, and demands for its description a dramatic form, the splitting of the choosing individual into distinct personae. (This is where personal identity comes in.) Is the noxious wish a part of the self, or an intruder? It is possible to view the tempting wish as something quite alien, to think of it as like a demonic possession. This is done both by those who treat such wishes as merely parts of their culture and by those who blame their bodies for them, dissociating the self from the body, as well as by those who keep exorcists in business. Tempting motives can simply be disowned. The disadvantage of this policy, however, is that it divides the self dishonestly, generating bad faith and endangering sanity. The tempted person needs instead to acknowledge the wish as his own—as part of him—and then to go on to ask *what* part, to relate it to the rest of his system of purposes. This twofold move seems necessary for a realistic notion of a being capable of choice. Such a creature cannot be a pure, abstract will. It must have some internal complexity; it must contain its conflicts within it. If its choice is not to be just a hollow form, both its alternatives must genuinely attract it. In the traditional, God-centered discussions of evil, our need to be free has of course been brought forward as an "excuse" for God's having created us capable of sin. At present, we are not concerned to weigh the force of this excuse for God, but just to grasp the implications of our actual freedom. I am suggesting that one such implication is that we have genuinely conflicting natural motives. People find this morally intolerable because they understand it as meaning that we have some major natural motives which are merely and entirely bad, which exist, as it were, merely to be rejected. This would certainly be strange. We don't expect that either God or evolution will provide such valueless motives. But the real position is rather that all our important motives are wide, and contain a full range of alternatives. Our town councillor, for instance, only wanted to prosper, but there are many ways of doing so. Love, for instance, has many forms, from the meanest forms of possessiveness to the most admirable forms of outgoing. Aggression is the spring of heroism as well as of cruelty. And so forth.

Let us consider for a moment the parallel case of fear. Is fear innate? Fear is a useful parallel to aggression for several reasons. (1) Fear too unquestionably produces sin. Sheer cowardice, even without any other faults, can produce one of the most worthless lives imaginable. And, by inhibiting all helpful action, it can also immensely harm others. (2) As is well known, fear is "natural" in the sense of having plain, substantial physiological causes. The nervous and glandular changes it involves are very marked. They can easily be studied and are in general much the same for human beings as for other comparable species. So is much of the outward behavior that fear produces. But nobody thinks that we are doomed to uncontrollable cowardice, still less that we must positively praise it. In the first place, the physical system for fear is no isolated machine, but is just a small part of our whole emotional system. Even on a simple mechanistic way of thinking, it no more needs to prevail than a brake needs to in a car. What, however, about value? Does our capacity for fear commit us to praising and honoring it, or can we despise it? Is fear good or bad? No one, probably, will be tempted to give a simple answer to this question. In general, no doubt, security is a good. But, plainly, there are some things that ought to be feared and others that ought not. Somebody entirely without fear, like Wagner's Siegfried, would be almost as incapable of managing life as somebody who could not feel pain. And someone who does not fear hurting others is a psychopath. Fear of a special kind enters into respect, which is an absolutely necessary kind of response for the recognition of any kind of value ("The fear of the Lord. . ."). Rashness is, in general, as real a fault as cowardice. In short, if somebody presses the crude question whether fear is a good or a bad thing, we can only give Aristotle's kind of answer—a kind that may look evasive, but is absolutely necessary for crude questions. Fear is all right in moderation. There should be neither too much nor too little of it. And this moderate level is not just an arithmetical mean, halfway between extreme rashness and extreme cowardice. It involves fearing the *right* things, not the wrong ones, and fearing them as much as, not more than, their nature calls for. It involves understanding what are suitable objects for fear, and what kind of fear is suitable for them. And so forth.

This kind of answer is in fact much more substantial and less evasive than it looks. It would be evasive if it did not suggest a context for deciding on "the right level." But it does. It refers us to the context of a whole life and sends us for the details to investigate how the various parts of that life are lived and fit together (including, of course, the culture). It rightly refuses to judge the weight to be given to one element in the priority system of the whole without considering the shape. It tells us to reject as inadequate any simple moral rule about fear, such as the rule, that "nobody ought ever to run away in battle" or that "anyone is a fool who risks his skin for an ideal." Certainly there are problems about how to evaluate total ways of life, problems which we must take seriously. They are the sort of problems that we must study if we want to judge the simple moral rules and also if we want to understand the whole relation between motives and values. To indicate them is not to evade them; they must be considered separately. If we are to get guidance about values from our nature, it will have to be from that nature taken as a whole, not from the occurrence of a single motive.

There is, however, a sharper positive point here. Reference to moderation excludes any ideal that calls either for the unlimited development of any natural motive or for the complete extinction of it. But there are ideals that do seem to do this, such as the unconditional exalting of love. Is love something you cannot have too much of? and is fear or anger something that ought to be entirely eliminated? These remote questions arise when we think about Utopias, about the directions in which we want society to move. It is natural, at a glance, to view fear as an evil and to suppose that we should simply try to get rid of it. This thought was expressed in the term 'freedom from fear'—one of the Four Freedoms declared as ideals at the end of the last war. The same seems true of pain. Yet people born without the capacity to feel pain do not live long or happily. Pain and fear, equally, are indications of something *wrong* and are necessary responses to it. So is anger. Maybe nothing will go wrong in Utopia, but will nothing be about to go wrong? Clearly, people there will still need to *fear doing wrong* and to fear disaster to others.

Even physiologically, a fear-free existence is scarcely conceivable. Children's play involves the constant, subtle use of fear to heighten the tensions; it seems designed as an inoculation for an essential aspect of human experience. Adults, too, naturally want excitement; it seems essential to a healthy life. Without real danger, people get bored. They gamble; they fall into depressions; they go mountain climbing; they pick quarrels. Morally, as I have suggested, total security would impoverish life drastically. *Brave New World* illustrates this, but of course it does not complete the project of abolishing fear. If that were done, the virtue of courage would vanish altogether. As C. S. Lewis pointed out, it would take a great part of the other virtues with it—

> Courage is not simply *one* of the virtues, but the form of every virtue at the testing point, which means at the point of highest reality. A chastity or honesty or mercy which yields to danger will be chaste or honest or merciful only on conditions. Pilate was merciful till it became risky. (*Screwtape Letters* [London: Geoffrey Bles, 1942], xxix, p. 148.)

All this may seem rather remote, since we don't have the choice of introducing such a Utopia. My point, however, is that we don't. Attempts to legislate for Utopia are irrelevant distractions. We are not going to run out of evils, nor do we need to expect to in order to undertake social change. A belief in the total perfectibility of man is not a necessary piece of equipment for undertaking change. The kind of science-fiction speculation which deals in such fancies is harmful, because it distorts our approach to problems that actually do lie before us. This distortion becomes important when we turn to the more worrying case of aggression. Ought we to try to make it possible to live without anger? ("Freedom from anger" . . . ?) Psychologists have suggested that it is possible, but the snags are tremendous. At the simple, primitive end of the spectrum, we see that anger and attack, both real and simulated, play a most important part in the lives of very small children. Real disputes, properly expressed and resolved, seem essential for their emotional unfolding. They learn to control their anger, to understand it, and to reason themselves out of it. But they also need to learn that anger can sometimes be justified, to learn the difference between justified and unjustified anger, and to accept that justified anger in others is the proper consequence of bad conduct. What they learn is not to eliminate anger and attack from their lives, but to use these things rightly. And in adults, right up to the level of saints and heroes, this is a necessary skill. It is worth noticing here that the physiological system for anger is closely related to that for fear. Both are based on adrenalin, and the whole complex of reactions is called the "fight-or-flight syndrome." One motive can hardly be allowed as part of the human condition without the other. The whole concern appears as an organ to be used, not as a malfunction. This no more commits us to *misusing* it than our possessing feet commits us to kicking people.

The proper function of anger, then, is to resist bad conduct. This is why it seems plausible to say that we ought to aim at a world in which anger is unnecessary. In a way, so we should. We should move *in that direction*. But the ideal is so remote that the thought of it is elusive and obscure. It has always proved impossible to describe heaven or to fill out the idea of it imaginatively, without sounding merely boring. Certainly we do have glimpses of heaven, but they are fitful. No doubt they play their part in moving us. But what chiefly rouses us to any serious struggle is our horror at the evils in the world. And to these, intelligent anger is the only entirely proper response. Someone who never felt anger on hearing of certain kinds of personal or political action and never attacked anything would be not an exceptionally charitable person, but a callous and unimaginative one. Charity, in such circumstances, may be a proper secondary development later; it cannot be the right primary response. We cannot bypass anger. So it is just as well that aggression is innate in us.

I have been comparing aggression with fear in order to correct the crude notion that it works on the drainpipe model, that it is a simple, brute motive with only one possible outcome: murder. Fear is obviously not like that. Fear is not just a simple tendency to run away. It can be expressed in an endless number of ways. Fear varies its form, not just according to circumstances, but according to our thinking. As we change our views on the *kind* of danger that threatens, we change both our feelings and our actions. When it is not so strong as to paralyze thought, fear provokes and involves a great deal of thinking, because dangers must be understood. So fear is perfectly compatible with discrimination and, therefore, with freedom. The same is true of anger.

Actually, the simple drainpipe model does not work well for any important motive except hunger. Hunger is exceptional in being virtually the only motive that has only one possible outcome. Hunger can be satisfied only by eating. But for ambition or curiosity, spite or compassion, vindictiveness or a love of adventure, no such restriction holds. It does not hold for sex either, though people often think that Sigmund Freud said so. Freud made many mistakes, but not that one. He defined lovemaking, in fact, as whatever gives anyone an orgasm, and he went to some trouble to point out how diverse such things were, how versatile and various sexual feeling can be. People criticize him for his use of hydraulic models—flows of libido, floods, diversions, and blockages—and of course much of this criticism is justified. But the trouble about hydraulic talk is not that it uses water imagery. That use is often justified. It is that it uses it crudely. And Freud is not always crude.

By the time he has finished his explanations of sex, the hydraulic model does not look at all like a drainpipe, but much more like a variegated garden, watered indeed from a single source and obeying the physical laws of conservation, but certainly not thereby reduced to monotony. Freud by no means accepts sex as a standard product, which is always OK. Some sex is OK, some is not. Freud's aim was to help us distinguish. Since he wanted to trace the normal, healthy course of sexual development, he was very often concerned to point out which forms of sexual activity were *not* OK—which, in the particular circumstances, were regressive, infantile, destructive, diseased. Freud's fault was not that of simplifying sex, for he diversified it amazingly. His fault was that of not taking other motives seriously and, therefore, not pointing out their complexities as well. Recognizing the complexity of all motives is the key to freedom.

All our main motives then—as well as aggression—have to be understood as highly versatile—as gardens rather than as drainpipes. The names of all do the same kind of explanatory job. An action, in itself insignificant, begins to have a meaning when it is seen as flowing from fear or ambition, spite, kindness, curiosity, or parental affection. This is possible only because we know these to be wide and complex motives. We need to trace out a particular branch of them with which the act can be intelligibly connected. This interpretative principle is the same for human actions as for animal actions and requires, as a background condition, the normal workings of the nervous system. But that is no bar to freedom, because acting from a motive is not a compulsive affair, like being knocked off a cliff or moved by a nervous spasm. It is acting for a reason. When several motives are present, conflict arises, and this, in human beings, is where free deliberation comes in. Had the motives not been present in the first place, freedom could not have been present either. And culture alone could never supply a motive, though it does, of course, supply the detailed items proposed for choice, and shapes the terms in which the choice is seen.

To conclude: in this paper I have tried to break the isolation that often obscures the topic of aggression. I have suggested that we should look at it in the context of other motives that commonly lead to the phenomenon known as "wickedness." It is not possible to understand these motives from external causes alone. We have to consider, too, the natural tendencies in ourselves on which these causes work. To admit such tendencies may be alarming, but it is not disastrous. They are what we ought to expect in free beings, since free choice requires real alternatives. Alarming motives like aggression present a special puzzle only if they are seen, on the drainpipe model, as simple reflexes, capable of leading only to bad outcomes. And they are not at all like this. They are wide and flexible, with good uses as well as bad. And, as a whole, they always have a positive function. It is true that, if we were living in Utopia, the function of aggression and related motives would become much less important, though it is not clear that even there it would vanish entirely. Utopian existence would change the function of many other motives as well. In any case, we do not live in Utopia. As things are, the right approach to our natural aggressive motivation seems to be much the same as that required for other sources of energy. We need to understand it, not to be intoxicated by it, to appreciate its dangers, to study its proper use, to channel it where it is needed, and to learn to control it. All this is made much easier if, for a start, we cease to deny its existence. But, for a great part of this century, social scientists have largely labored under the impression that they needed to deny its existence, in order to defend freedom and to make virtue possible. Moral philosophers meanwhile, as well as often sharing this conviction, have added to it, by way of belt and braces, the strange ruling that facts had no bearing on values. This meant that, even if any disagreeable psychological facts should unfortunately be established, they could still have no relevance to morals. Thus a cordon of obligatory skepticism has been established, roping off a great area of human motivation from disciplined examination—an area without which choice, and especially bad choice, becomes quite incomprehensible. Since bad human choice is one of the most dangerous forces loose in the world today, this is not a trivial misfortune. Both the intellectual fashions just mentioned are certainly now on the wane, and the case, which I have argued here, for considering a realistic psychology of motive— a psychology that makes wickedness intelligible—as acceptable and harmless to freedom, will fortunately not sound so strange as it would have done a couple of decades back. But it still needs a great deal of work and attention. Theory that has once got loose from practice and become accustomed to floating in an empyrean of its own, takes some time to get back into relation with the world, particularly when the facts to which it is recalled seem upsetting to human pride. I have tried to suggest ways in which this upset can be seen as useful and even reassuring. But whether this helps or not, one way or another, we shall surely have to bring the issue back to real life.

Contributors

ANNETTE BAIER is a professor of philosophy at the University of Pittsburgh. She has previously taught at Carnegie-Mellon University, The University of Sydney, The University of Auckland, and The University of Aberdeen. She studied at The University of Otago and Oxford University. She has published many articles in the philosophy of mind, ethics, and the history of philosophy, some of which are collected in her recent book, *Postures of the Mind* (Minneapolis: University of Minnesota Press, 1985; England: Methuen Press, 1986). She is also working on a book about David Hume.

LAWRENCE C. BECKER is Professor of Philosophy at Hollins College, Virginia, where he has taught since 1965. He is the author of *On Justifying Moral Judgments* (1973), *Property Rights: Philosophic Foundations* (1977) and *Reciprocity* (1986) and coeditor of *Property: Cases, Concepts, Critiques* (1984). He is currently an associate editor of the journal *Ethics*.

JEFFREY BLUSTEIN is Associate Professor of Philosophy at Mercy College, Dobbs Ferry, New York. He is the author of *Parents and Children: The Ethics of the Family* (Oxford University Press, 1982), and has published numerous articles in ethics and social philosophy. He is currently at work on a book about caring, integrity, and intimacy.

SISSELA BOK teaches philosophy at Brandeis University. She is the author of *Lying: Moral Choice in Public and Private Life*, *Secrets: On the Ethics of Concealment and Revelation*, and, most recently, *A Strategy for Peace*.

MILTON FISK teaches philosophy at Indiana University—Bloomington. His writings include work on metaphysics (*Nature and Necessity*, 1973), ethics (*Ethics and Society*, 1980), and politics (*The State and Justice*, in manuscript). In addition, he is active in union work and in a number of social movements.

RICHARD M. HARE is Graduate Research Professor of Philosophy at the University of Florida at Gainesville, and White's Professor of Moral Philosophy Emeritus at the University of Oxford. He is the author of *The Language of Morals* (1952), *Freedom and Reason* (1963), and *Moral Thinking* (1981).

DALE JAMIESON is Associate Professor of Philosophy and Associate of The Center for Values and Social Policy at the University of Colorado, Boulder. He has worked in various areas of practical ethics including Environmental Ethics, Biomedical Ethics, Science and Technology Policy, and Art Policy. His interests also include Moral, Social, and Political Theory.

FRANCES MYRNA KAMM is Associate Professor of Philosophy at New York University. She specializes in ethics, social and political philosophy, and has taught these at N.Y.U. Medical and Law Schools as well. She has published articles on applied and theoretical ethics and is completing a book, *Morality/Mortality*, to be published by Oxford University Press.

RUTH MACKLIN, Ph.D., is Professor of Bioethics at the Albert Einstein College of Medicine, Bronx, New York. Her most recent book is *Mortal Choices: Bioethics in Today's World*, published by Pantheon. She has authored or edited six other volumes and contributed over ninety articles to scholarly and professional journals in philosophy, law, ethics, and medicine. She is a Fellow of the Hastings Center, and has served as a consultant to federal, state, and local agencies.

MARY MIDGLEY, born Mary Scrutton, 1919, received a 1st class degree in Greats (Classics and Philosophy) at Oxford in 1942. She worked during the war as a civil servant, secretary, and teacher, then became a philosophy lecturer at the University of Newcastle on Tyne until 1980. She developed a strong interest in biology and evolution. She is the author of *Beast and Man, Heart and Mind, Women's Choices; Philosophical Problems Facing Feminism* (with Judith Hughes), *Animals and Why They Matter, Wickedness* and *Evolution as a Religion.*

JAN NARVESON, B.A. (Chicago), Ph.D. (Harvard), is Professor of Philosophy at the University of Waterloo in Ontario, Canada. He is the author of many papers in philosophical periodicals and anthologies, mainly on ethical theory and practice, and of *Morality and Utility, An Examination of Libertarianism* (in press), and the editor of *Moral Issues.* He is also on the editorial boards of *Ethics, Social Philosophy and Policy,* and several other journals.

JAMES W. NICKEL is Professor of Philosophy at the University of Colorado, Boulder, where he served as Director of the Center for Values and Social Policy from 1982–88. Nickel is the author of *Making Sense of Human Rights* (University of California Press, 1987).

ONORA O'NEILL teaches Philosophy at the University of Essex in England. Her recent work has concentrated on Kantian ethics, on problems of Human Rights, and on difficulties in the enterprise of Applied Ethics. These themes are brought together in her recent book, *Faces of Hunger: An Essay on Poverty, Justice, and Development* (1986).

JAMES RACHELS is University Professor at the University of Alabama at Birmingham. He is the author of *The Elements of Moral Philosophy* (1986) and *The End of Life: Euthanasia and Morality* (1986).

PETER SINGER is Director of the Centre for Human Bioethics at Monash University, Victoria, Australia. He has also taught at University College, Oxford, New York University, La Trobe University, the University of Colorado at Boulder, and the University of California at Irvine. He has written extensively in ethics and bioethics. His books include *Animal Liberation, Practical Ethics, The Expanding*

Circle, Making Babies (with Deane Wells) and *Should the Baby Live?* (with Helga Kuhse).

ROGER WERTHEIMER: Erstwhile deputy sheriff, psychotherapist and academician turned entrepreneur, he has lately been designing and marketing orthopedic academic seating. The author of *The Significance of Sense* and numerous articles in theoretical ethics and diverse fields of applied ethics, he is now at work on a book about abortion and kindred issues.

ECHEANCE   DATE DUE

JAN 3 1 1991

JAN 1 5 1993

APR 2 7 1997

UNIVERSITY OF SUDBURY
UNIVERSITE DE SUDBURY

UNIV. OF/DE SUDBURY

3 0007 00293361 1